E A R T H

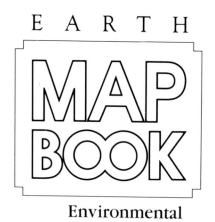

Environmental
Atlas

Interarts, Ltd

EARTH **MAP**BOOK
Environmental Atlas

Published in the United States of America by
Interarts Ltd
15 Mount Auburn Street, Cambridge, Massachusetts 02138 USA
Tel: 617-354-4655   Fax: 617-354-1476

Copyright © 1994 Liber Kartor AB (Map Service), Stockholm, Sweden
Produced by Liber Kartor AB and
Maps International AB, Stockholm, Sweden
International Marketing rights by Maps International AB
Skeppsbron 26, S-11130 Stockholm, Sweden
Telefax 46-824-7838

Environmental maps designed, compiled, edited and drawn by the
cartographers, geographers, technicians and artists at:

Liber Kartor AB, Stockholm, Sweden
Maps International AB, Stockholm, Sweden
Interarts Ltd, Cambridge, Massachusetts USA

Design Counsel: Turnbull and Company
Cambridge, Massachusetts USA

ISBN #1-879856-32-8

Printed in Slovenia

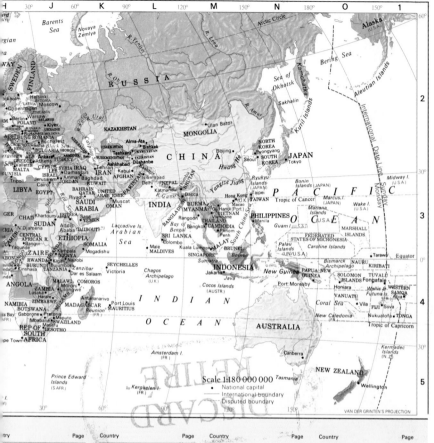

Country	Page	Country	Page	Country	Page	Country	Page
...try	21	Peru	72,73	Sri Lanka	36	United States	62,66,67
...ania	50	Philippines	39	Sudan	52,56	Uruguay	76
...ius	58	Poland	17	Surinam	73	Uzbekistan	30-31
...	68	Portugal	20	Swaziland	59	Vanuatu	46
...va	22	Qatar	24	Sweden	18	Vatican State	21
...o	21	Republic of Ireland	16	Switzerland	21	Venezuela	72
...alia	32,34	Republic of South Africa	58	Syria	24	Vietnam	37
...co	50	Romania	22	Tajikistan	31	Western Samoa	46
...mbique	59	Rwanda	56	Taiwan	35	Yemen	53
...r	37	Saint Kitts and Nevis	69	Tanzania	56	Zaire	56
...ia	58	Saint Lucia	69	Thailand	37	Zambia	58
...	46	Saint Vincent	69	The Bahamas	69	Zimbabwe	58
...lands	36	San Marino	21	The Gambia	50		
...	16	São Tome and Principe	55	Togo	54		
...ealand	45	Saudi Arabia	24,53	Tonga	46		
...gua	68	Senegal	50	Trinidad and Tobago	69		
...	51	Seychelles	57	Tunisia	51		
...a	55	Sierra Leone	54	Turkey	23		
...Korea	35	Singapore	38	Turkmenistan	30-31		
...y	18	Slovakia	17	Tuvalu	46		
...an	53	Slovenia	21	Uganda	56		
...n	31	Soloman Islands	45	Ukraine	26		
...na	69	Somalia	57	United Arab Emirates	24		
...New Guinea	44	South Korea	38	United Kingdom and			
...uay	76	Spain	40	Northern Ireland	16		

THE CONCISE WORLD

READER INFORMATION

Reader information	6	**Legend**	7

THE WORLD

The World, environment	8–9	**The World, Time Zones**	12–13
The World, political	10–11		

EUROPE

Europe, environment, flags   14–15

British Isles and Central Europe   16–17
Belgium, Czechoslovakia, Germany, Luxembourg, Netherlands, Poland

Northern Europe   18–19
Belarus, Denmark, Estonia, Finland, Iceland, Latvia, Lithuania, Norway, Sweden

Southwest Europe   20–21
Austria, Croatia, France, Italy, Liechtenstein, Portugal, Switzerland, Slovenia, Spain

The Balkans   22–23
Albania, Armenia, Bosnia-Herzegovina, Bulgaria, Cyprus, Georgia, Greece, Hungary, Makedonia, Moldavia, Romania, Turkey, Yugoslavia

The Middle East   24–25
Bahrain, Iran, Irak, Israel, Jordan, Kuwait, Lebanon, Qatar, Syria, United Arab Emirates

Western Russia and Ukraina   26–27
Belarus, Kazakhstan

ASIA

Asia, environment, flags   28–29

South West Asia   30–31
Afghanistan, Azerbajan, Iran, Kazakhstan, Kirgizia, Pakistan, Tadzhikistan, Turkmenistan, Uzbekistan

North East Asia   32–33
Mongolia

China and Japan   34–35
Mongolia, North-Korea, South-Korea, Taiwan

India and South East Asia   36–37
Bangladesh, Bhutan, Burma, Cambodja, Laos, Nepal, Sri Lanka, Thailand, Vietnam

The East Indies   38–39
Brunei, Indonesia, Malaysia, Philippines

AUSTRALIA

Australasia, environment, flags	40–41	**New Guinea and New Zealand**	44–45
Australia	42–43	**Oceania**	46–47
		Melanesia, Micronesia, Polynesia	

AFRICA

Africa, environment, flags   48–49

Northwest Africa   50–51
Algeria, Libya, Morocco,
Mauritania, Niger, Tunisia

The Nile Valley and Arabia   52–53
Bahrain, Egypt, Iraq, Israel, Jordan,
Kuwait, Lebanon, Oman, Qatar,
Saudi-Arabia, Sudan, Syria
United Arab Emirates, Yemen

West Africa   54–55
Benin, Burkina Faso, Cameroon, Chad,
Congo, Eqvatorial-Guinea, Gabon, Ghana,

Guinea, Guinea-Bissau, Ivory Coast,
Liberia, Mali, Niger, Nigeria, São Tomé
and Principe, Senegal, Sierra Leone,
The Gambia, Togo

East Africa   56–57
Burundi, Central African Republic,
Djibouti, Eritrea, Ethiopia, Kenya, Rwanda,
Somalia, Sudan, Tanzania, Uganda, Zaire

Southern Africa   58–59
Angola, Botswana, Comores, Lesotho,
Madagascar, Malawi, Mauritius,
Mozambique, Namibia, South Africa,
Swaziland, Zambia, Zimbabwe

NORTH AMERICA

**North America,
environment, flags**   60–61

Alaska and Western Canada   62–63
incl. Aleutian Islands

Eastern Canada   64–65

The United States   66–67
incl. Mexico

**Central America and
the West Indies**   68–69
Belize, Costa Rica, Cuba, El Salvador,
Guatemala, Honduras, Mexico, Nicaragua
and The Caribbean Archipelago

SOUTH AMERICA

**South America,
environment, flags**   70–71

South America, northern part   72–73
Brazil, Colombia, Ecuador, Guyana,
Panama, Peru, Surinam, Venezuela

South America, central part   74–75
Bolivia, Brazil, Chile, Peru

South America, southern part   76–77
Argentina, Bolivia, Brazil, Chile,
Paraguay, Uruguay

POLAR REGIONS

The Arctic, environment   78

The Antarctica, environment   79

STATISTICS

The World   80–81
Europe   82–91
Asia   92–101
Australia   102–105

Africa   106–116
North America   116–120
South America   120–125

INDEX

Index   127–

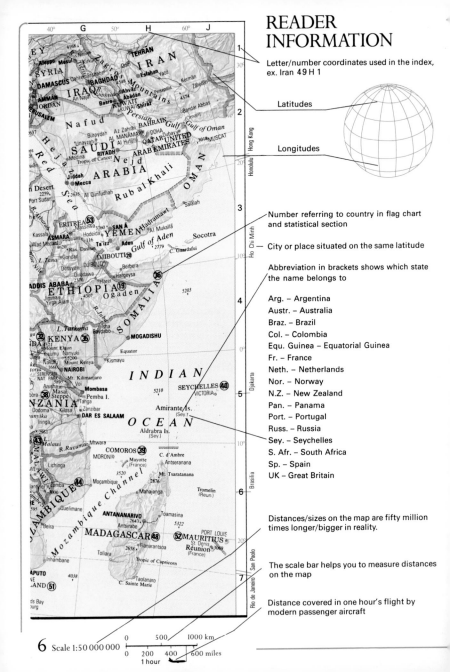

READER INFORMATION

Letter/number coordinates used in the index, ex. Iran 49 H 1

Latitudes

Longitudes

Number referring to country in flag chart and statistical section

— City or place situated on the same latitude

Abbreviation in brackets shows which state the name belongs to

Arg. – Argentina
Austr. – Australia
Braz. – Brazil
Col. – Colombia
Equ. Guinea – Equatorial Guinea
Fr. – France
Neth. – Netherlands
Nor. – Norway
N.Z. – New Zealand
Pan. – Panama
Port. – Portugal
Russ. – Russia
Sey. – Seychelles
S. Afr. – South Africa
Sp. – Spain
UK – Great Britain

Distances/sizes on the map are fifty million times longer/bigger in reality.

The scale bar helps you to measure distances on the map

Distance covered in one hour's flight by modern passenger aircraft

6 Scale 1:50 000 000

0   500   1000 km

0   200   400   600 miles
1 hour

Symbols   Scale 1:10 000 000, 1:20 000 000

⚑**Bombay**	More than 5 000 000 inhabitants	——	Major road	' ₄₈₀₇	Height above sea-level in metres
☙**Milano**	1 000 000-5 000 000 inhabitants	——	Other road	'₃₀₆₈	Depth in metres
▣**Zürich**	250 000-1 000 000 inhabitants	----	Road under construction	⬭	National park
●**Dijon**	100 000-250 000 inhabitants	——	Railway	⚊ Niniveh	Ruin
∘ **Dover**	25 000-100 000 inhabitants	----	Railway under construction	⚌	Pass
∘ Torquay	Less than 25 000 inhabitants	....	Train ferry	KAINJI DAM	Dam
∘ Tachiumet	Small sites	▪▪▪▪	National boundary		Wadi
WIEN	National capital	▪ ▪ ▪	Disputed national boundary		Canal
<u>**Atlanta**</u>	State capital	——	State boundary		Waterfalls
		- - - -	Disputed state boundary		Reef
		◠◠◠	Undefined boundary in the sea		

Symbols   Scale 1:30 000 000 1:50 000 000 1:54 000 000 1:60 000 000 1:75 000 000

☙**Shanghai**	More than 5 000 000 inhabitants	——	Major road	' ₈₈₄₈	Height above sea-level in metres
▣**Barcelona**	1 000 000-5 000 000 inhabitants	——	Railway	'₁₁₀₃₄	Depth in metres
●**Venice**	250 000-1 000 000 inhabitants	----	Railway under construction	2645	Thickness of ice cap
∘ Aberdeen	50 000-250 000 inhabitants			⚊ Thebes	Ruin
∘ Beida	Less than 50 000 inhabitants	▪▪▪▪	National boundary	⊃⟋	Dam
		▪ ▪ ▪	Disputed national boundary		Wadi
∘ Mawson	Scientific station	——	State boundary		Canal
CAIRO	National capital	- - - -	Disputed state boundary		Waterfalls
		◠◠◠	Undefined boundary in the sea		Reef

Colour Key

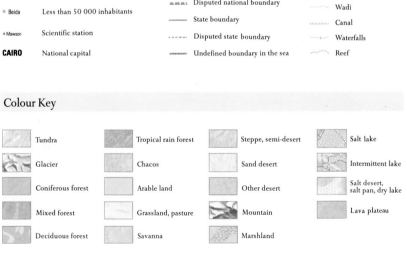

Tundra	Tropical rain forest	Steppe, semi-desert	Salt lake
Glacier	Chacos	Sand desert	Intermittent lake
Coniferous forest	Arable land	Other desert	Salt desert, salt pan, dry lake
Mixed forest	Grassland, pasture	Mountain	Lava plateau
Deciduous forest	Savanna	Marshland	

7

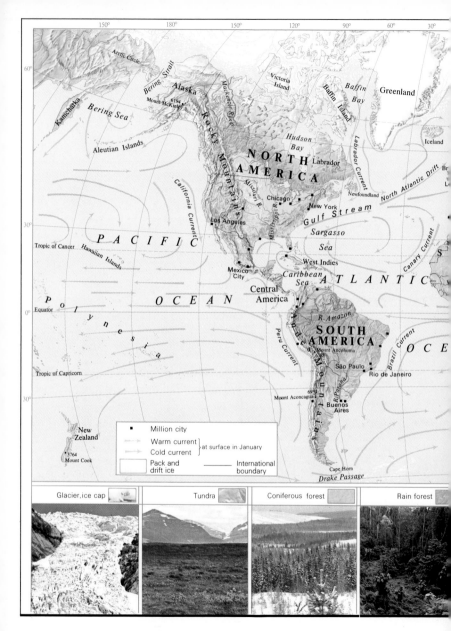

Million city

Warm current
Cold current } at surface in January

Pack and
drift ice — International boundary

Glacier, ice cap

Tundra

Coniferous forest

Rain forest

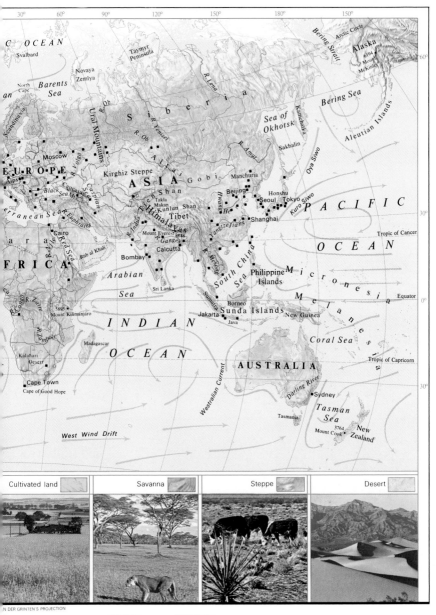

ARCTIC OCEAN

Svalbard

North Cape

Scandinavia

EUROPE

Alps

Moscow

Black Sea

Caucasus Mts.

Caspian Sea

Mediterranean Sea

Cairo

Red Sea

AFRICA

R. Congo

R. Zaire

Mount Kilimanjaro

Kalahari Desert

Cape Town
Cape of Good Hope

Barents Sea

Novaya Zemlya

Ural Mountains

R. Ob

R. Volga

Kirghiz Steppe

Tien Shan

Takla Makan

Kunlun Shan

R. Indus

Mount Everest

Ganges

Bombay

Calcutta

Arabian Sea

Sri Lanka

INDIAN OCEAN

Madagascar

Taymyr Peninsula

R. Lena

S i b e r i a

R. Yenisei

R. Ob

Altai

A S I A

Gobi

Tibet

Himalayas

Yangtze Jiang

R. Mekong

Sumatra

Jakarta

Java

Sunda Islands

Borneo

South China Sea

Bering Strait

Arctic Circle

Alaska

6194 Mount McKinley

Sea of Okhotsk

Kamchatka

Sakhalin

Manchuria

Beijing

He

Shanghai

Honshu

Seoul

Tokyo

Oya Siwo

Kuro Siwo

Bering Sea

Aleutian Islands

P A C I F I C

O C E A N

Tropic of Cancer

Philippine Islands

M i c r o n e s i a

New Guinea

M e l a n e s i a

Equator

Coral Sea

AUSTRALIA

Tropic of Capricorn

Darling River

Sydney

Tasman Sea

Tasmania

Westralian Current

West Wind Drift

3764 Mount Cook

New Zealand

Cultivated land	Savanna	Steppe	Desert

(photographs of Cultivated land, Savanna, Steppe, Desert)

VAN DER GRINTEN'S PROJECTION

Scale 1:180 000 000
at the equator

0 400 800 km
30°
60°
200 600 1000 km

0 200 600 miles
30°
60°
100 300 500 miles

9

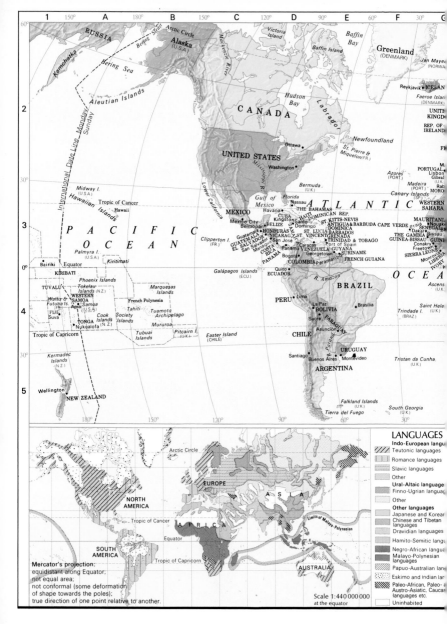

THE WORLD

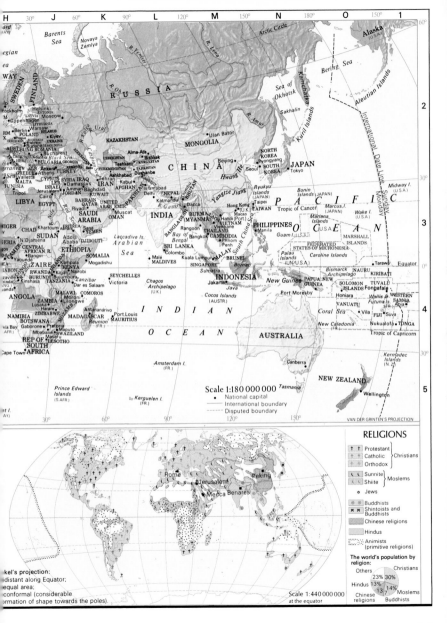

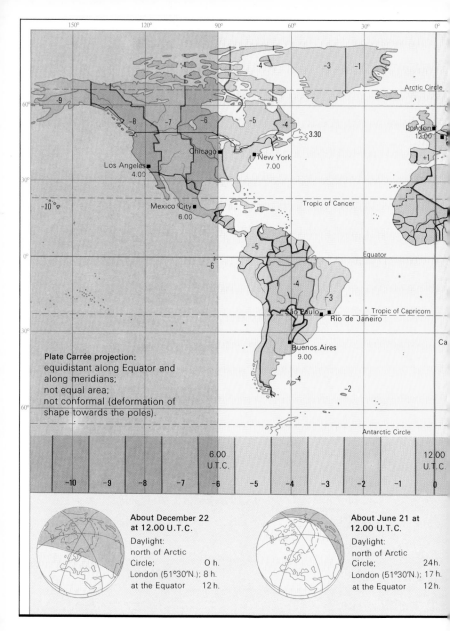

Plate Carrée projection:
equidistant along Equator and
along meridians;
not equal area;
not conformal (deformation of
shape towards the poles).

6.00
U.T.C.

12.00
U.T.C.

| -10 | -9 | -8 | -7 | -6 | -5 | -4 | -3 | -2 | -1 | 0 |

**About December 22
at 12.00 U.T.C.**

Daylight:
north of Arctic
Circle;   0 h.
London (51°30′N.); 8 h.
at the Equator   12 h.

**About June 21 at
12.00 U.T.C.**

Daylight:
north of Arctic
Circle;   24 h.
London (51°30′N.); 17 h.
at the Equator   12 h.

12   TIME ZONES

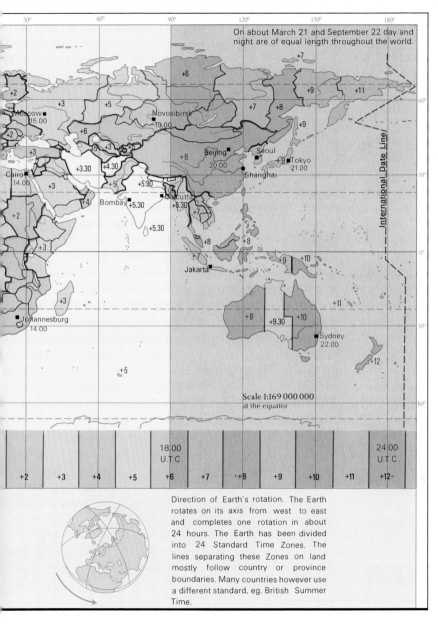

On about March 21 and September 22 day and night are of equal length throughout the world.

+7

+6

+9

+11

+2

+3

+5

+7

+8

Moscow
15.00

Novosibirsk
19.00

+9

+2

+6

Seoul

+9 Tokyo
21.00

+3

+5

+3

+8

Beijing
20.00

+3

+3.30

+4.30

Shanghai

Cairo
14.00

+5

+5.30

+3

Calcutta

+4

Bombay
+5.30

+6.30

+2

+7

+5.30

+8

+8

+3

+7

+9

+10

Jakarta

+3

+11

+8

+9.30

+10

Johannesburg
14.00

Sydney
22.00

+5

+12

International Date Line

Scale 1:169 000 000
at the equator

| +2 | +3 | +4 | +5 | +6 | +7 | +8 | +9 | +10 | +11 | +12− |

18.00
U.T.C.

24.00
U.T.C.

Direction of Earth's rotation. The Earth
rotates on its axis from west to east
and completes one rotation in about
24 hours. The Earth has been divided
into 24 Standard Time Zones. The
lines separating these Zones on land
mostly follow country or province
boundaries. Many countries however use
a different standard, eg. British Summer
Time.

13

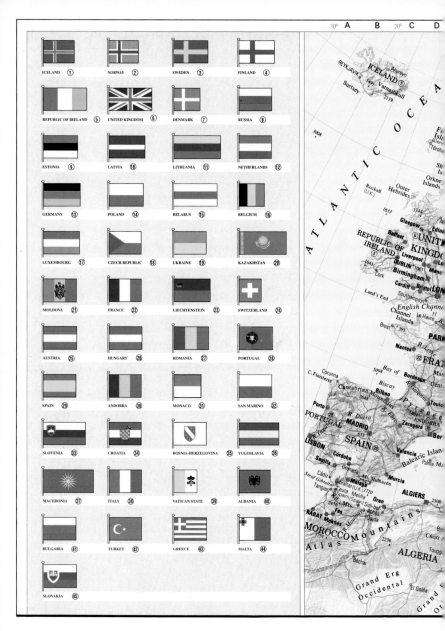

ICELAND ①	NORWAY ②	SWEDEN ③	FINLAND ④
REPUBLIC OF IRELAND ⑤	UNITED KINGDOM ⑥	DENMARK ⑦	RUSSIA ⑧
ESTONIA ⑨	LATVIA ⑩	LITHUANIA ⑪	NETHERLANDS ⑫
GERMANY ⑬	POLAND ⑭	BELARUS ⑮	BELGIUM ⑯
LUXEMBOURG ⑰	CZECH REPUBLIC ⑱	UKRAINE ⑲	KAZAKHSTAN ⑳
MOLDOVA ㉑	FRANCE ㉒	LIECHTENSTEIN ㉓	SWITZERLAND ㉔
AUSTRIA ㉕	HUNGARY ㉖	ROMANIA ㉗	PORTUGAL ㉘
SPAIN ㉙	ANDORRA ㉚	MONACO ㉛	SAN MARINO ㉜
SLOVENIA ㉝	CROATIA ㉞	BOSNIA-HERZEGOVINA ㉟	YUGOSLAVIA ㊱
MACEDONIA ㊲	ITALY ㊳	VATICAN STATE ㊴	ALBANIA ㊵
BULGARIA ㊶	TURKEY ㊷	GREECE ㊸	MALTA ㊹
SLOVAKIA ㊺			

Scale 1:10 000 000

| 0 | 100 | 200 | 300 | 400 | 500 km |

| 0 | 100 | 200 | 300 miles |

1/2 hour

17

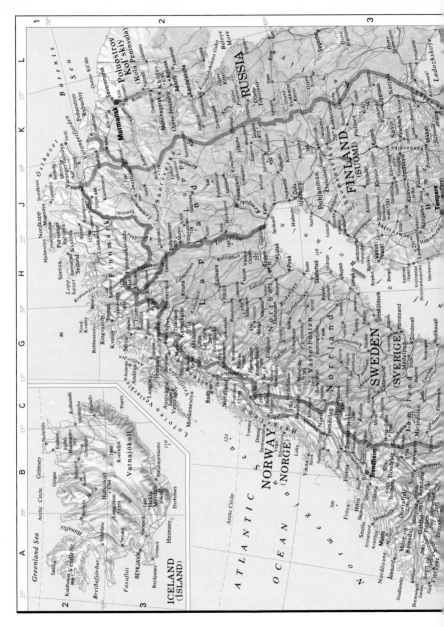

Scale 1:10 000 000

19

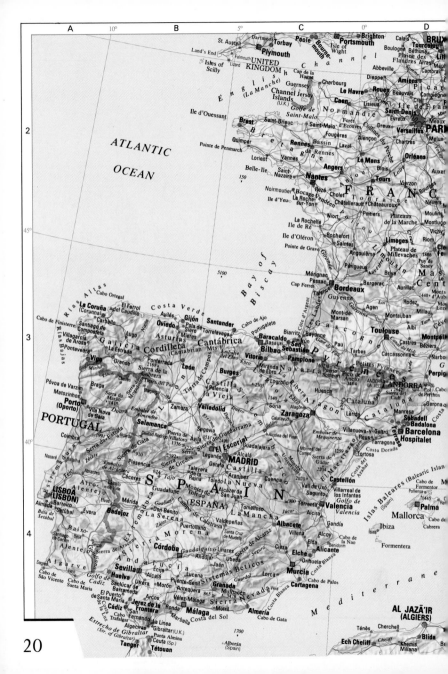

ATLANTIC

OCEAN

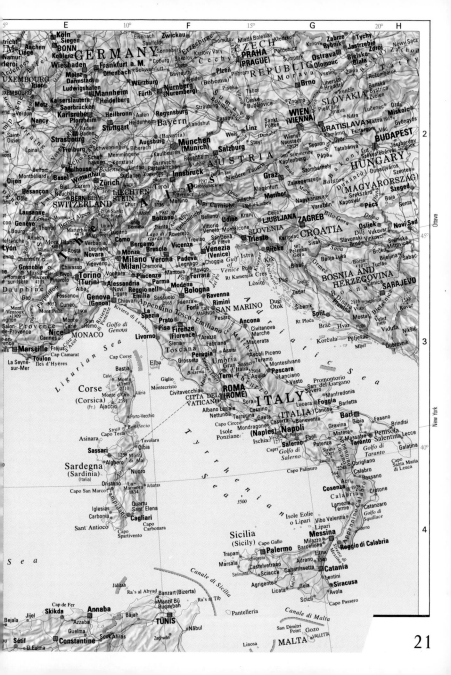

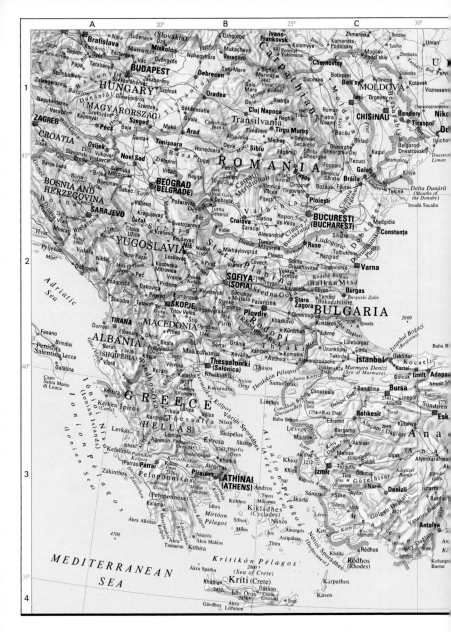

22   THE BALKANS

1 foot = 0,30 m
1 meter = 3,28 feet

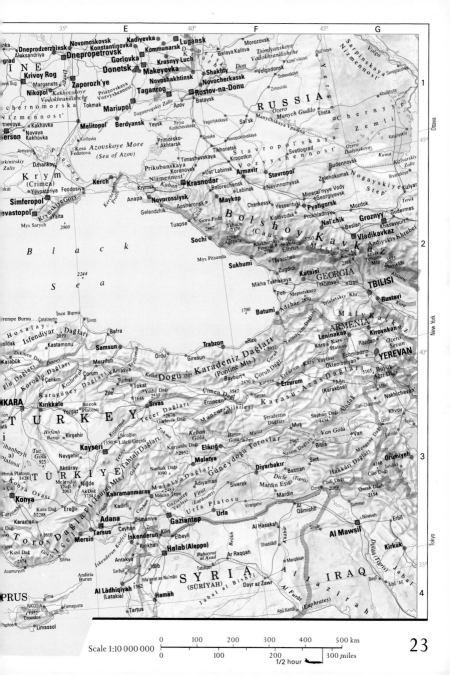

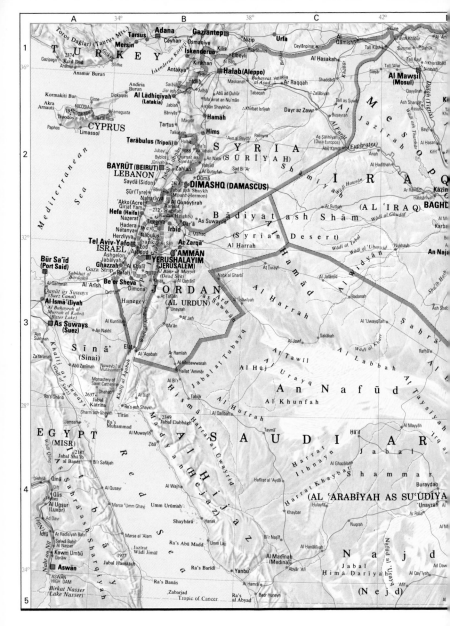

24   THE MIDDLE EAST

1 foot = 0,30 m
1 meter = 3,28 feet

Scale 1:10 000 0

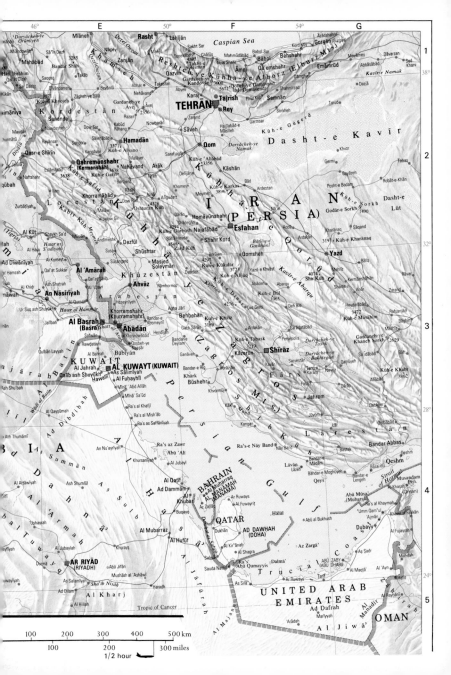

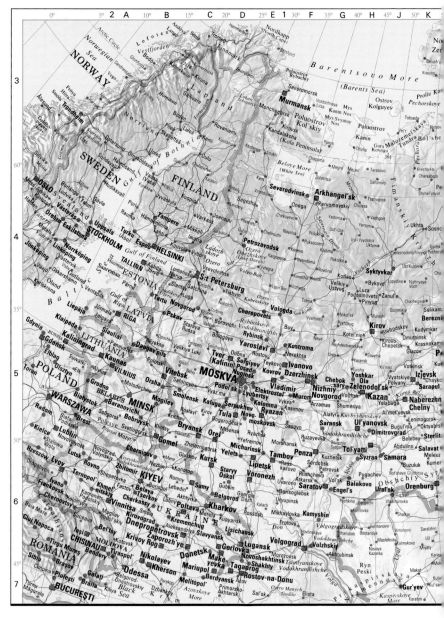

WESTERN RUSSIA AND UKRAINE

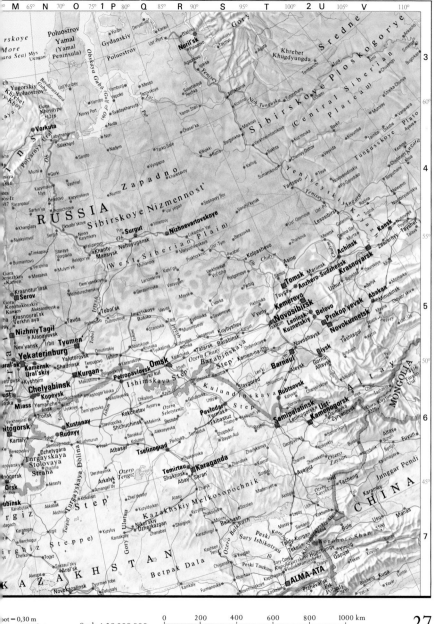

Top coordinate labels: M 65° N 70° O 75° 1P 80° Q 85° R 90° S 95° T 100° 2U 105° V 110°

Right side latitude labels: 3, 60°, 4, 55°, 5, 50°, 6, 45°, 7

Major regions and labels:
RUSSIA, KAZAKHSTAN, MONGOLIA, CHINA

Zapadno Sibirskoye Nizmennost' (West Siberian Plain), Sredne Sibirskoye Ploskogor'ye (Central Siberian Plateau), Tungusskoye Plato

Ishimskaya Step', Barabinskaya Step', Kulundinskaya Step', Kazakhskiy Melkosopochnik, Turgayskaya Stolovaya Strana, Turgayskaya Dolina, Turgay Step' (Turgay Steppe), Kirgiz Step' (Kirgiz Steppe), Betpak Dala, Sary Ishikotrau, Peski Taukum, Jungar Pendi, Altay, Gorno Altaysk, Horoho Shan

Cities and towns (selection):
Noril'sk, Vorkuta, Surgut, Nizhnevartovskoye, Khanty-Mansiysk, Nefteyugansk, Serov, Krasnotur'insk, Nizhniy Tagil, Yekaterinburg, Kamensk Ural'skiy, Chelyabinsk, Kopeysk, Miass, Tyumen, Kurgan, Petropavlovsk, Omsk, Tobol'sk, Tomsk, Anzhero-Sudzhensk, Kemerovo, Novosibirsk, Belovo, Prokop'yevsk, Novokuznetsk, Leninsk-Kuznetskiy, Achinsk, Krasnoyarsk, Abakan, Minusinsk, Kansk, Tayshet, Zelenyy, Biysk, Barnaul, Rubtsovsk, Semipalatinsk, Ust'-Kamenogorsk, Pavlodar, Ekibastuz, Kustanay, Rudnyy, Tselinograd, Atbasar, Temirtau, Karaganda, Shakhtinsk, Dzhezkazgan, Balkhash, ALMA-ATA, Novokazalinsk, Orsk

Rivers and water bodies:
Ob', Irtysh, Ishim, Tobol, Yenisey, Angara, Ozero Chany, Ozero Tengiz, Ozero Balkhash, Ozero Zaysan, Ozero Seletyteniz

Bottom scale and notes:

oot = 0,30 m
meter = 3,28 feet

Scale 1:20 000 000

0   200   400   600   800   1000 km
0   200   400   600 miles
1 hour

27

RUSSIA ①
KAZAKHSTAN ②
GEORGIA ③
ARMENIA ④

AZERBAIJAN ⑤
TURKEY ⑥
CYPRUS ⑦
LEBANON ⑧

SYRIA ⑨
ISRAEL ⑩
JORDAN ⑪
IRAQ ⑫

KUWAIT ⑬
IRAN ⑭
TURKMENISTAN ⑮
UZBEKISTAN ⑯

KYRGYZTAN ⑰
TAJIKISTAN ⑱
MONGOLIA ⑲
JAPAN ⑳

NORTH KOREA ㉑
SOUTH KOREA ㉒
SAUDI ARABIA ㉓
BAHRAIN ㉔

QATAR ㉕
UNITED ARAB EMIRATES ㉖
AFGHANISTAN ㉗
PAKISTAN ㉘

CHINA ㉙
NEPAL ㉚
BHUTAN ㉛
BANGLADESH ㉜

BURMA (MYANMAR) ㉝
TAIWAN ㉞
YEMEN ㉟
OMAN ㊱

INDIA ㊲
LAOS ㊳
THAILAND ㊴
VIETNAM ㊵

CAMBODIA ㊶
PHILIPPINES ㊷
BRUNEI ㊸
SRI LANKA ㊹

MALDIVES ㊺
MALAYSIA ㊻
SINGAPORE ㊼
INDONESIA ㊽

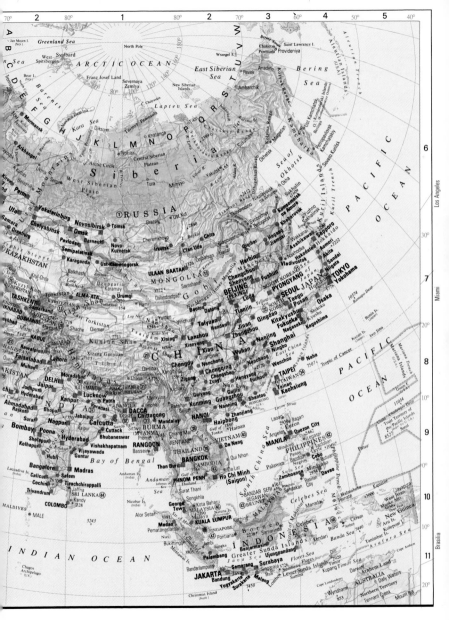

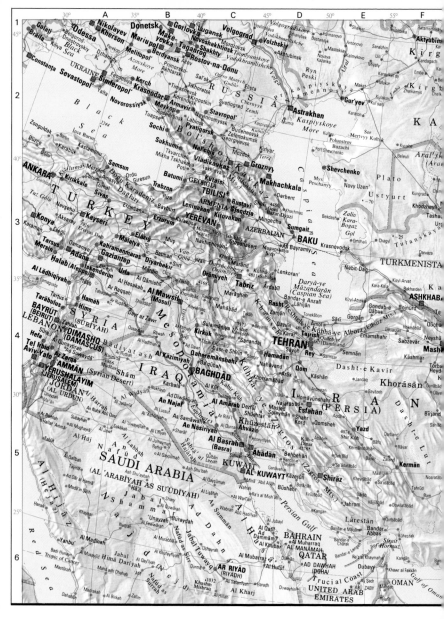

30 SOUTH WEST ASIA

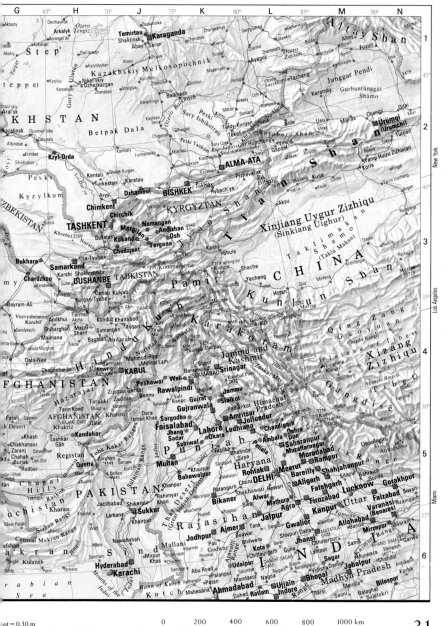

Scale 1:20 000 000

ot = 0,30 m
eter = 3,28 feet

| 0 | 200 | 400 | 600 | 800 | 1000 km |

| 0 | 200 | 400 | 600 miles |

1 hour

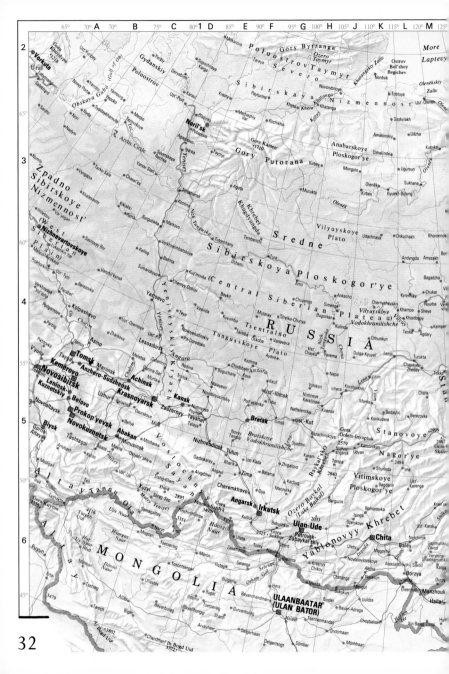

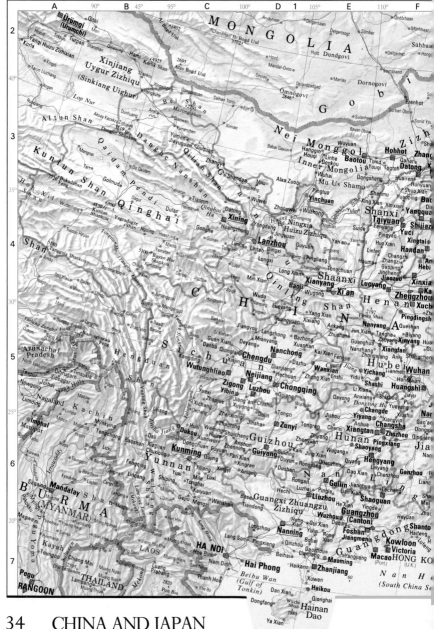

34 CHINA AND JAPAN

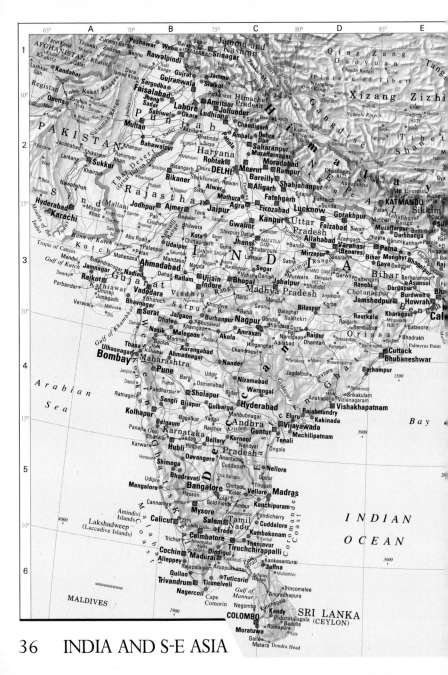

A
B
C
D
100°
105°
110°
115°
1
2
3
4
5
10°
5°
0°
5°
10°
BURMA
(MYANMAR)
Tavoy
Nakhon Pathom
Thon Buri
BANGKOK
Rat Buri
Samut Songkhram
Samut Prakan
Chon Buri
Phet Buri
Battambang
Sisophon
Tabeng
ANGKOR
Mekong
Stung Treng
Pleiku
Hoai Nhon
Phu My
Qui Nhon
CAMBODIA
Tonle Sap
Kompong Chhnang
Kompong Thom
Sambor
Ban Me Thuot
VIETNAM
Sattahip
Trat
1813
Phnom Aural
Mergui
Mergui
Archipelago
Kui Nua
Snoul
Nha Trang
Da Lat
Cam Ranh
PHNOM PENH
Kompong Cham
Chon Thanh
Di Linh
Bokpyin
Thap Sakae
Takeo
Ca Na
Gulf of Thailand
Kompong Som
Kampot
Long Xuyen
Sa Dec
Ho Chi Minh (Saigon)
Vung Tau
Andaman Sea
Isthmus of Kra
Chumphon
Rach Gia
My Tho
Ko Phangan
Phu Vinh
Khanh Hung
Mouths of the Mekong
Vinh Loi
Surat Thani
Takua Pa
THAILAND
Nakhon Si Thammarat
Mui Bai Bung
Nam Can
Thung Song
Ko Phuket
Phuket
Trang
Kantang
Songkhla
South
China Sea
Balabac
Hat Yai
Yala
Butang Group
Kangar
Kota Baharu
Langkon
Alor Setar
G. Kin
4101
Kota Kinabalu
Saba
Banda Aceh
George Town
Kuala Terengganu
Beaufort
BRUNEI
Taiping
Gunung Tahan
2189
MALAYSIA
BANDAR SERI BEGAWAN
Peureulak
G. Abong Abong
2985
Ipoh
Kampar
G. Batu Puteh
2130
Miri
2371
Gunung Mulu
G. Leuser
Binjai
Telok Anson
Kuantan
Kepulauan Natuna
Seumanyam
3381
Medan
Tebingtinggi
Strait of Malacca
Bintulu
Tambalan
Kelang
KUALA LUMPUR
Pematangsiantar
P. Simeulue
Tanjungbalai
Seremban
Kepulauan Anambas
Matu
Sibu
Sarawak
2012
Hose Mountains
Peg. Muller
Iran
2988
Tarutung
Melaka
Muar
Keluang
Tanjung Api
Rantauprapat
Saratok
Sibolga
Padangsidempuan
Johor Baharu
SINGAPORE
Kuching
Simanggang
Mauralasar
Pulau Nias
Pulau Padang
Pulau Bintan
Pemangkat
Kalimantan
2145
G. Sorikmerapi
Pekanbaru
Kepulauan Riau
Monterado
Semitau
1744
Mandor
(Borneo)
Equator
S. Kampar
Kepulauan Lingga
Sintang
S. Kutai
Bukittinggi
Payakumbuh
Pontianak
Padangpanjang
1758
2278
Gunung Saran
Peg Schwaner
Muara Teweh
Selat Mentawai
Sumatera
Padang
Telukbatang
Tanjung Samak
Sungai Barito
Gunung Kerinci
3805
Batang Hari
Jambi
(Telanaipura)
Nangatayap
Pulau Siberut
Bangko
Pulau Bangka
Selat Karimata
Palangkaraya
Kepulauan Mentawai
Pangkalpinang
Kendawangan
Sukaraja
Amuntai
2933
Bukit Masurai
Sampit
G Besar
Kandangan
1892
Palembang
Pulau Belitung
Banjarmasin
Tebingtinggi
Muaraenim
Pegunungan Barisan
Teluk Kumai
Pulau Laut
Bengkulu
3159
G. Dempo
Tanjung Jabung
Tanjung Selatan
INDONESIA
Kotabumi
Laut Jawa
(Java Sea)
Bandar Lampung
Pulau Enggano
Kotaagung
Serang
JAKARTA
Tangerang
Indramayu
Cirebon
Tegal
Pekalongan
Kepulauan Kangean
Rangkasbitung
Bogor
Cianjur
Kudus
Rembang
Pulau Madura
Pamekasan
INDIAN
Sukabumi
Bandung
Magelang
Semarang
Kediri
Surabaya
Laut Bali
Tasikmalaya
Surakarta
Madiun
Bondowoso
Singaraja
Lombok
Cilacap
Yogyakarta
Tulungagung
Malang
Bali
Jawa
(Java)
Banyuwangi
Denpasar
Praya
OCEAN
Christmas Island
(Austr.)

Main map labels

Olongapo
MANILA
Quezon City
Lipa
Batangas
Lubang Islands
Calapan
Mindoro
Sibuyan
Mindoro Strait
Polillo Islands
Daet
Catanduanes
Naga
Boac
Legaspi
Virac
Sorsogon

Masbate
Sea
Calbayog
Samar
Roxas
Visayan
Catbalogan
Sea
Panay
Tacloban
Cuyo Islands
Iloilo
Cadiz
San Carlos
Leyte
Ormoc
Bacolod
Cebu
Dinagat
Negros
Cebu
Bohol
Stargao
Taytay
Dumaguete
Bohol Sea
Surigao
Puerto Princesa

PHILIPPINES

Philippine Trench

Cagayan de Oro
Butuan
Oroquieta
Gingoog
Dipolog
Malaybalay
Ozamiz
Iligan
Marawi
Pagadian
Mindanáo
Cotabato
Kalaong
Caraga

Zamboanga
Moro Gulf
Basilan City
Davao
Basilan
Jolo
General Santos
Tawitawi Group
Tinaca Point

Sulu Sea

Sulu Archipelago

Pulau Karakelong
Kepulauan Talaud

Laut Sulawesi
(Celebes Sea)

Kepulauan Sangihe

Pulau Morotai

Minnahassa Peninsula
Manado
Tondano
G. Malino
Gorontalo
Boroko
Bumbulan
Kompot
Kepulauan Togian
Teluk Tomini

Pulau Morotai

Oba
Halmahera
Jailolo
Buli
Bukit Sulat

Laut
Halmahera

Pulau Waigeo
Equator

Wosi

Mega
Sorong
P. Salawati
Gunung Kwoka
3000
Warbumi
New Guinea
Pulau Biak

Sulawesi
(Celebes)
Lokikalaki
Lemoro
Poso
Kolonodale
Kepulauan Banggai
Pulau Taliabu
Pulau Mangole
Kepulauan Sula
Fluk
Pulau Misool
Cendrawasih
Pulau Yapen
Teluk Cendrawasih
Serui
Waren
Sarmi
Teba
Irian Jaya

Palopo
Pulau Labengke
Wawotobi
Kendari

Maluku

Pinu
Wahin
Namlea
Gunung Binaiya
3055
Masohi
Angar
Arandai
Bomberai
Selassi
Babo
Murana
Hamuku
Karufa
Pegunungan Maoke
5030
Puncak Jaya

N E S I A

Watampone
Pulau Butung
Mutia
Baubau
Kepulauan Tukangbesi

P. Buru
Seram
Ambon

Laut Seram

Umari
Agats
Atsy

Kepulauan Kai
P. Kai Besar
Pulau Wokam
Kepulauan Aru
Kobroor
Pulau Trangan

Laut Banda
(Banda Sea)

Mapi

Barangbarang
Pulau Selayar

Kepulauan
Pulau Wetar

Tenggara

Laut Flores
(Flores Sea)
Flores

Larantuka
P. Lomblen
P. Alor
Lospalos
Baucau
Viqueque
Kepulauan Leti

Kepulauan Babar
Pulau Selaru
Kepulauan Tanimbar
Pulau Yamdena

Laut Arafura
(Arafura Sea)
Pulau Jos
Sodarso
Tanjung Vals
Okaba

Sumba
Ende
Waingapu
Atambua
Gunung Mutis
Timor
Kupang

Sawu Laut

Laut Timor
(Timor Sea)

Baing
Pulau Roti

AUSTRALIA

Cape Van Diemen
Cape Croker
Croker Island
Cape Wessel

Bathurst Island
Melville Island
Van Diemen Gulf
Buckingham Bay

Inset map (upper right)

Balintang Channel

Laoag
Cape Engaño
Vigan
Juguegarao
Ilagan
Mount Pulog
2842
Cordillera Central
PHILIPPINES

Lingayen
Baguio
Tarlac
Cabanatuan
Angeles
Olongapo
MANILA
Lubang Islands
Quezon City
Lipa
Polillo Islands
Daet
Batangas
Calapan
Boac
Legaspi
Naga
Catanduanes
Virac
Mindoro
Sibuyan
Sorsogon

P A C I F I C
O C E A N

Palau Islands

Scale

ot = 0,30 m
eter = 3,28 feet

Scale 1:20 000 000

0   200   400   600   800   1000 km

0   200   400   600 miles

1 hour

39

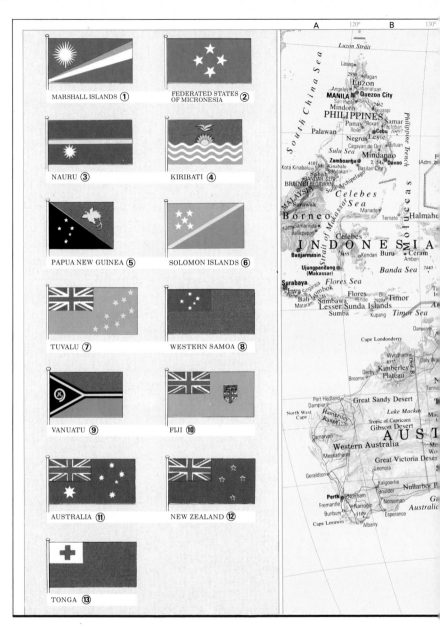

MARSHALL ISLANDS ①

FEDERATED STATES OF MICRONESIA ②

NAURU ③

KIRIBATI ④

PAPUA NEW GUINEA ⑤

SOLOMON ISLANDS ⑥

TUVALU ⑦

WESTERN SAMOA ⑧

VANUATU ⑨

FIJI ⑩

AUSTRALIA ⑪

NEW ZEALAND ⑫

TONGA ⑬

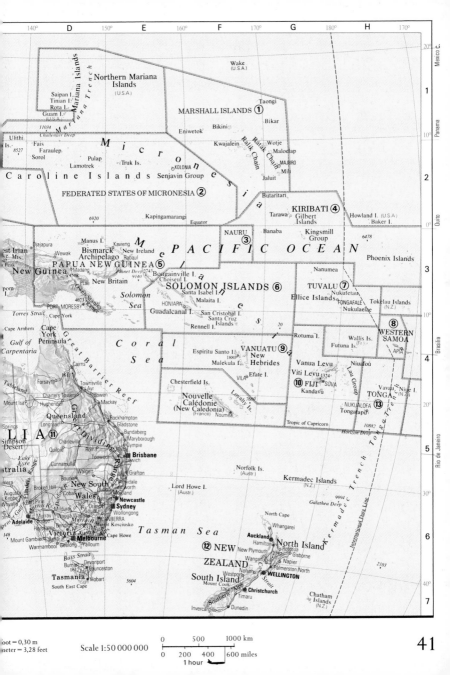

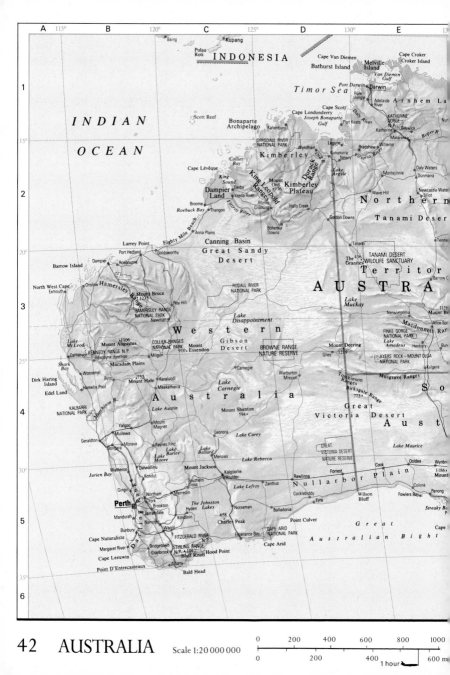

42 AUSTRALIA Scale 1:20 000 000

1 foot = 0,30 m
1 meter = 3,28 feet

43

44   NEW GUINEA AND NEW ZEALAND

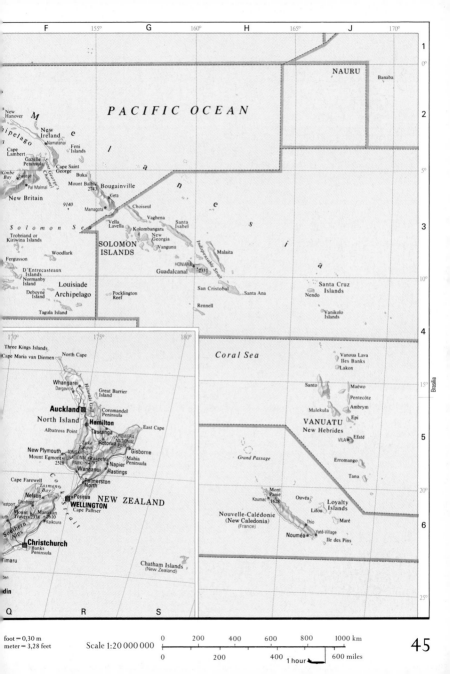

PACIFIC OCEAN

NAURU
Banaba

M e l a n e s i a

New Hanover
New Ireland
Namatanai
Feni Islands
Cape Lambert
Gazelle Peninsula
Kimbe Bay
Kokopo
Pal Malmal
New Britain
Cape Saint George
Buka
Mount Balbi 2743
Bougainville
Kieta
9140
Mamagota

Choiseul
Vaghena
Santa Isabel
Vella Lavella
Kolombangara
New Georgia
Vangunu
Vanguna

SOLOMON ISLANDS
Solomon Sea
Trobriand or Kiriwina Islands
Woodlark
Fergusson
D'Entrecasteaux Islands
Normanby Island
Louisiade Archipelago
Deboyne Island
Tagula Island
Pocklington Reef

Malaita
Indispensable Strait
HONIARA 2331
Guadalcanal
San Cristobal
Santa Ana
Nendo
Rennell

Santa Cruz Islands
Vanikolo Islands

Coral Sea

Vanoua Lava
Iles Banks
Lakon
Santo
Maéwo
Pentecôte
Malekula
Ambrym
Epi
VANUATU
New Hebrides
VILA
Efaté

Three Kings Islands
Cape Maria van Diemen
North Cape

Whangarei
Dargaville
Great Barrier Island
Auckland
North Island
Hamilton
Coromandel Peninsula
Albatross Point
Tauranga
UREWERA NATIONAL PARK
East Cape
New Plymouth
Lake Taupo
Rotorua
Gisborne
Mount Egmont
TONGARIRO NATIONAL PARK
Ruapehu 2518
Napier
Mahia Peninsula
Wanganui
Hastings
Cape Farewell
Palmerston North
Tasman Bay
Nelson
Porirua
WELLINGTON
NEW ZEALAND
Cook Strait
Cape Palliser
Westport
Glenhope
Mount Travers 2338
Manakau 2610
Kaikoura
Southern Alps
Christchurch
Banks Peninsula
Timaru
Grand Passage

Erromango
Tana

Mont Panié 1628
Koumac
Ouvéa
Loyalty Islands
Lifou
Nouvelle-Calédonie (New Caledonia) (France)
Thio
Maré
Nouméa
Yaté-Village
Ile des Pins

Chatham Islands (New Zealand)

Dunedin

Brasília

foot = 0,30 m
meter = 3,28 feet

Scale 1:20 000 000

0   200   400   600   800   1000 km

0   200   400   1 hour   600 miles

45

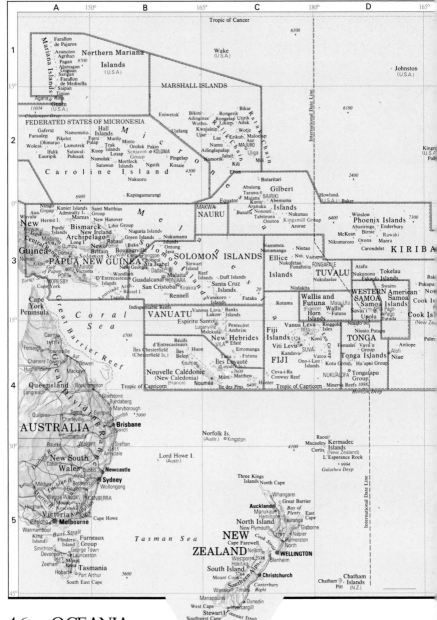

46 OCEANIA

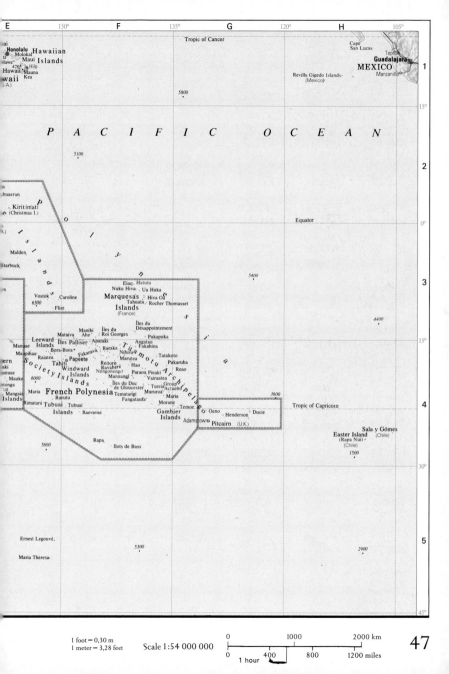

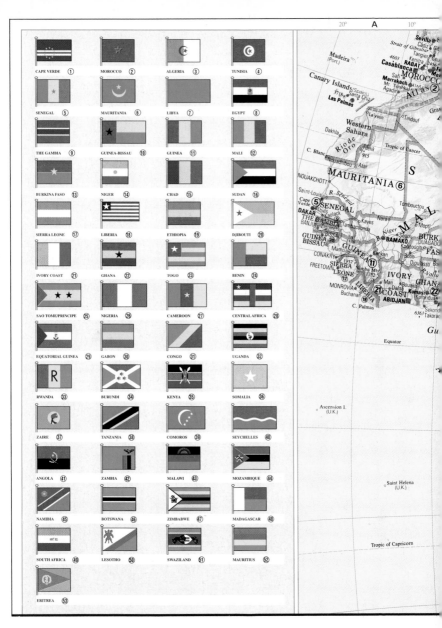

CAPE VERDE ①
MOROCCO ②
ALGERIA ③
TUNISIA ④
SENEGAL ⑤
MAURITANIA ⑥
LIBYA ⑦
EGYPT ⑧
THE GAMBIA ⑨
GUINEA-BISSAU ⑩
GUINEA ⑪
MALI ⑫
BURKINA FASO ⑬
NIGER ⑭
CHAD ⑮
SUDAN ⑯
SIERRA LEONE ⑰
LIBERIA ⑱
ETHIOPIA ⑲
DJIBOUTI ⑳
IVORY COAST ㉑
GHANA ㉒
TOGO ㉓
BENIN ㉔
SAO TOME/PRINCIPE ㉕
NIGERIA ㉖
CAMEROON ㉗
CENTRAL AFRICA ㉘
EQUATORIAL GUINEA ㉙
GABON ㉚
CONGO ㉛
UGANDA ㉜
RWANDA ㉝
BURUNDI ㉞
KENYA ㉟
SOMALIA ㊱
ZAIRE ㊲
TANZANIA ㊳
COMOROS ㊴
SEYCHELLES ㊵
ANGOLA ㊶
ZAMBIA ㊷
MALAWI ㊸
MOZAMBIQUE ㊹
NAMIBIA ㊺
BOTSWANA ㊻
ZIMBABWE ㊼
MADAGASCAR ㊽
SOUTH AFRICA ㊾
LESOTHO ㊿
SWAZILAND 51
MAURITIUS 52
ERITREA 53

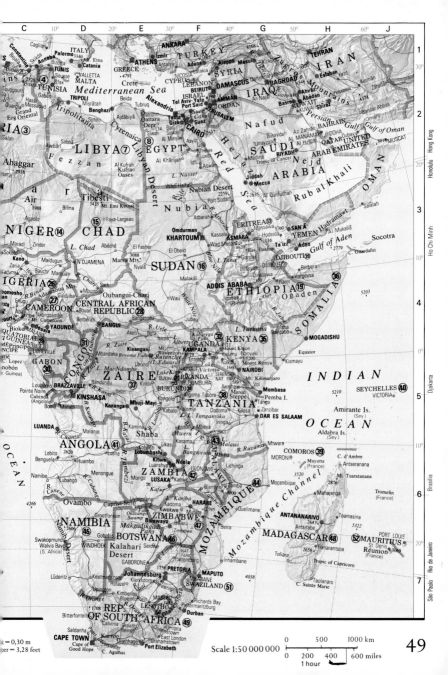

Scale 1:50 000 000

| 0 | 500 | 1000 km |

| 0 | 200 | 400 | 600 miles |

1 hour

49

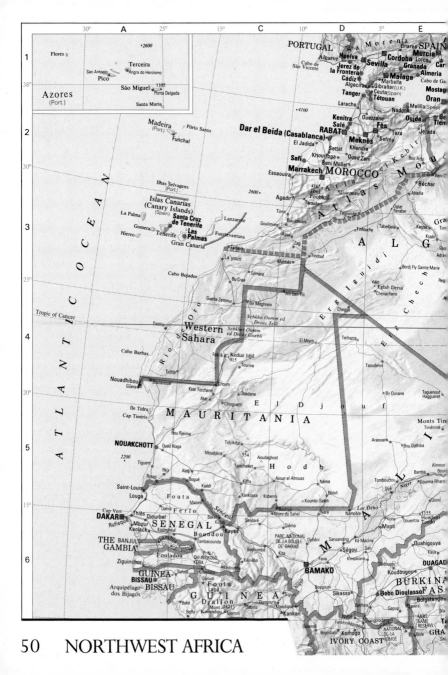

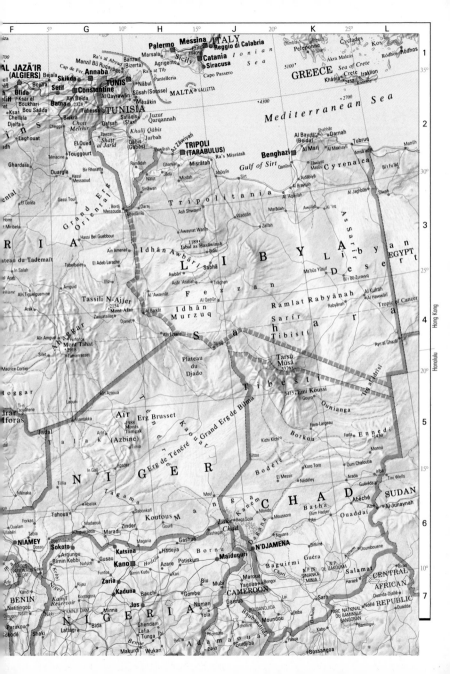

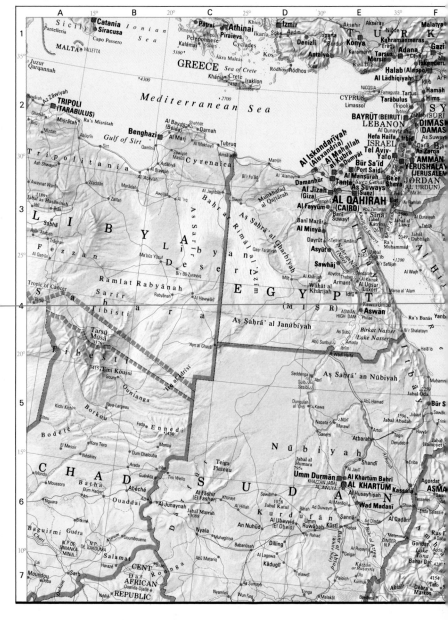

THE NILE VALLEY AND ARABIA

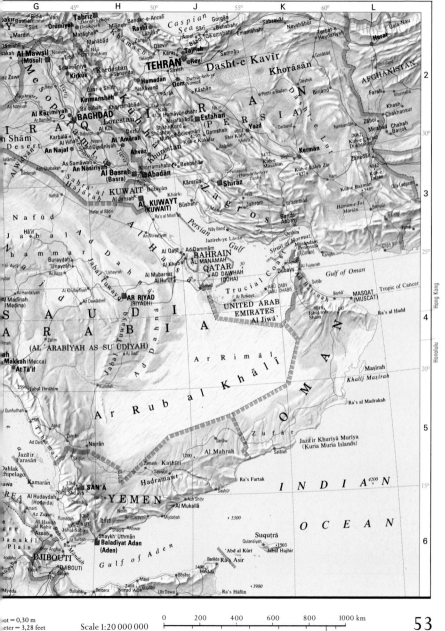

Batman Bitlis Van
Muş Bandar-e Anzalī Gorgān Sabzevār Qala Nau
Siirt Orūmīyeh Marāgheh Rasht Lāhījān Caspian Sea Sārī Qā'emshahr Emāmshahr Neyshābūr Torbat-e Heydarīyeh Herāt
Mardīn Tabrīz Daryācheh Orūmīyeh Qazvīn Amol Bābol Shīndand
Al Mawṣil (Mosul) Nīneveh Erbil Takāb Karaj TEHRĀN Semnān AFGHANISTAN Farāh
Sulaymānīyah Hājī Ibrāhīm Zanjān Rey Dasht-e Kavīr Khorāsān Khash Chakhānsūr
Kirkūk Kordestān Sanandaj Sāveh Qom Gonābād Deyhūk Khāsh Barjok
Qaṣr-e Shīrīn Nahāvand Hamadān Kāshān Namak Birjand Nehbandān Mīrābād Chahah
Al Kāẓimīyah Kermānshāhī Borūjerd Arāk Najafābād Esṭahān Yazd Darband Kūh-e Chehel Dokhtarān
BAGHDAD Lorestān Khorramābād Golpāyegān Eqlīd Shahr Kord Shūshtar Masjed Soleymān Qomshen Kūh-e Kūkalar Mehrīz Bīrjand 2062 Zābol
Babylon Ad Dīwānīyah Dezfūl Ahvāz Khūzestān Persepolis Daryācheh-ye Tashk Sīr Kūh Kūh-e Bāzmān Kūh-e Taftān
Karbalā' Al Hillah Al Kūt Shūshtar Behbehān Shīrāz Bam Zāhedān
An Najaf An Nāṣirīyah Al 'Amārah Ābādān Kāzerūn Jahrom Kermān Dāsh
As Samāwah Al Baṣrah (Basra) Khorramshahr Bandar Abbās
Rafḥā' KUWAIT Būbīyan Kharḡ Nāy Band Strait of Hormuz Qeshm
Ḥafar al Bāṭin Al Jahrah KUWAIT (KUWAIT) Būshehr Jazīreh-ye Lāvān Musandam Peninsula (Oman)
Ra's al Mish'āb Persian Gulf Dubayy Gulf of Oman
Ar Ruwais Ad Dammām Al Qaṭīf BAHRAIN AL MANAMAH QATAR AD DAWḤAH (DOHA) Ṣawḥ Sūḥār Barkā MASQAṬ (MUSCAT) Tropic of Cancer Ra's al Ḥadd
AR RIYĀḌ (RIYADH) Al Khubar Al Mubarraz Al Hufūf ABŪ ẒABY (ABU DHABI) 'Ibrī Jabal ash Shām Ra's al Madrakah
SAUDI ARABIA UNITED ARAB EMIRATES Al Jīwā' OMAN
Al 'Arabīyah as Su'ūdīyah Ad Dahnā' Ar Rimāl Maṣīrah Khalīj Maṣīrah
Ar Rub al Khālī Jazā'ir Khurīyā Murīyā (Kuria Muria Islands) Zufār Ṣalālah
Najrān Al Mahrah Ra's Fartak INDIAN
Hadramawt Al Mukallā Suquṭrā 'Abd al Kūrī OCEAN
SAN'A YEMEN Baladīyat Adan (Aden) Ra's 'Asīr
DJIBOUTI Gulf of Aden Boosaaso Ra's Hāfūn

Scale 1:20 000 000

0   200   400   600   800   1000 km
0   200   400   600 miles
1 hour

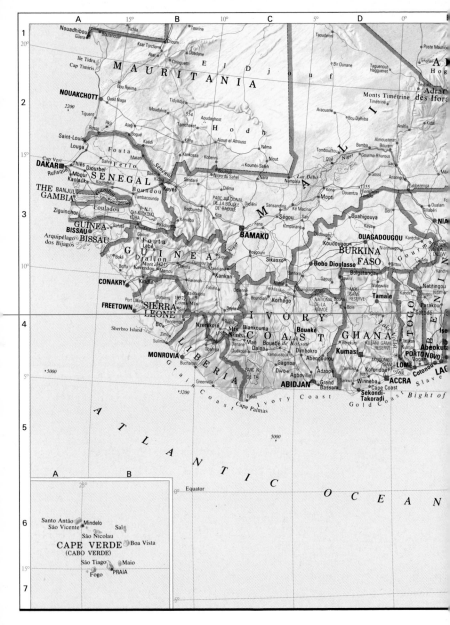

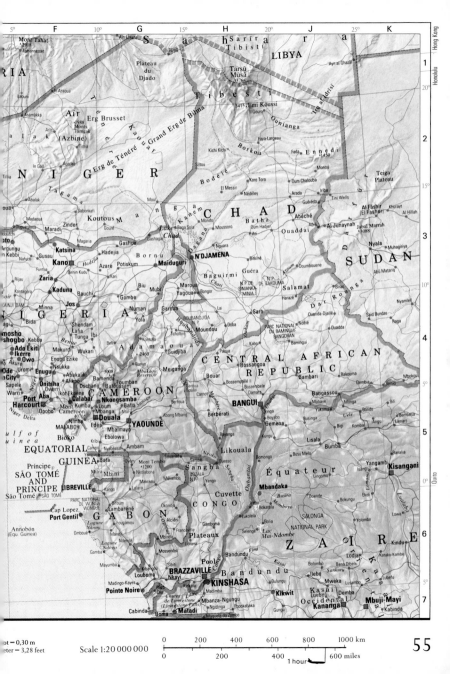

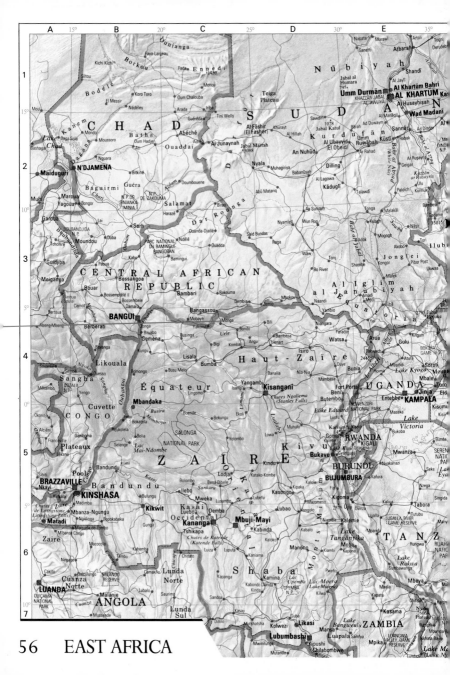

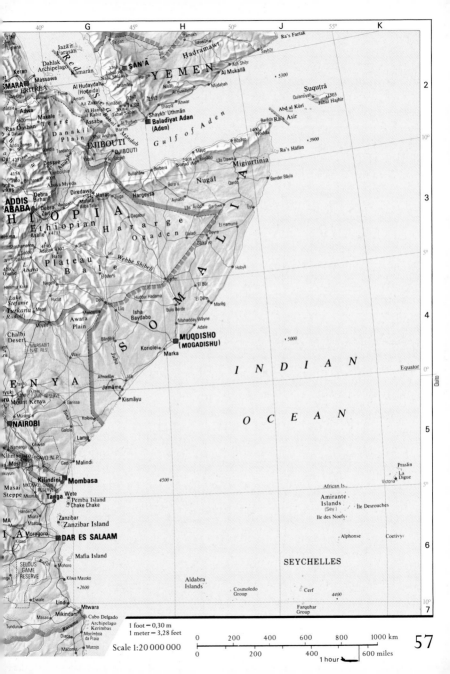

40° G 45° H 50° J 55° K

Jazā'ir
Farasān   Zamakh   Sayḥūt   Ra's Fartak
Dahlak   Sa'dah   Ḥadramawt
Keren Archipelago Kamarān   Ḥuraydah   Sayḥūt
Massawa   'SAN'Ā   Adh Shiḥr   Ra's Fartak
SMARA   ERITREA   Niṣāb Al Mukallā   2
Adwa   Al Ḥudaydah Midahah •5300
          (Hodeida)
          Az Zuqur   Shaqrā Anwar   Suqutrā
Ras Dashan   Al Hanish Ta'izz 3000 Qulansiyah •1503
al Dabat   al Kabir Jabal Sabir Shaykh 'Uthmān Jabal Hajhir
Tegre   Assab   Baladiyat Adan   Abd al Kūrī   Ra's 'Asir
Danakil   (Aden)   Barim   Bara0 1400
ADDIS Plain DJIBOUTI   Gulf of Aden Boosaaso Hodda 10°
ABABA DJIBOUTI   Mayd   Ra's Ḥāfūn
        'Aliˉ Sabˉih Surud Ad Engago •3900
THIOPIA   Berbera Bura'o Migiurtinia
Debra Diredawa Harar Jinga Las Anod Gardwe' Bender Bȧyla 3
Birhan Mulata Asba Tafari Dagabur 'Aynabo
Aselle Hararge Galadi   El Hamurre
    Ogaden Goyra Garoe
  Plateau Webbe Shibeli   Hobyā
  Bale   El Mero Harfer
Lake Hudat Mega Huddur Hadama El Bur
Stefanie Moyale Luq Isha Mahadday Wёyne El Dёre Marёg 4
(Rudolf) Awara Baydabo Adale •5000
Chalbi Plain Bārdera MUQDISHO
Desert   Koriolei (MOGADISHU)
MARSABIT Wajir Marka
ENYA   Afmadow Jilib   INDIAN Equator 0°
iyuki Mount Kenya Jamāme
NAIROBI Garissa   Kismāyu   OCEAN
  Kolbieo Lamu   5
Kilimanjaro Galole
Moshi TSAVO N.P.   Praslin
  Voi Malindi •4500   African Is La
Masai Kilindini Mombasa   Victoria Digue 5°
Steppe Tanga Wete   Amirante
  Pemba Island   Islands Ile Desrouches
  Chake Chake   (Sey)
Zanzibar Island   Ile des Noefs
DAR ES SALAAM   Alphonse Coetivy 6
Mafia Island
SELOUS   SEYCHELLES
GAME
RESERVE Kilwa Masoko
Lindi •2600 Aldabra Cosmoledo Cerf
Mikindani Islands Group •4400
Mtwara   Farquhar 10°
Cabo Delgado   Group 7
Archipelago

1 foot = 0,30 m
1 meter = 3,28 feet
          0   200   400   600   800   1000 km
Scale 1:20 000 000
          0   200   400   600 miles
          1 hour

57

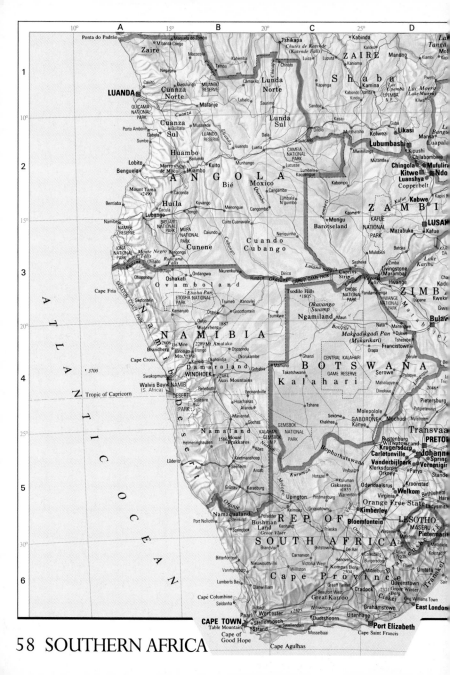

58 SOUTHERN AFRICA

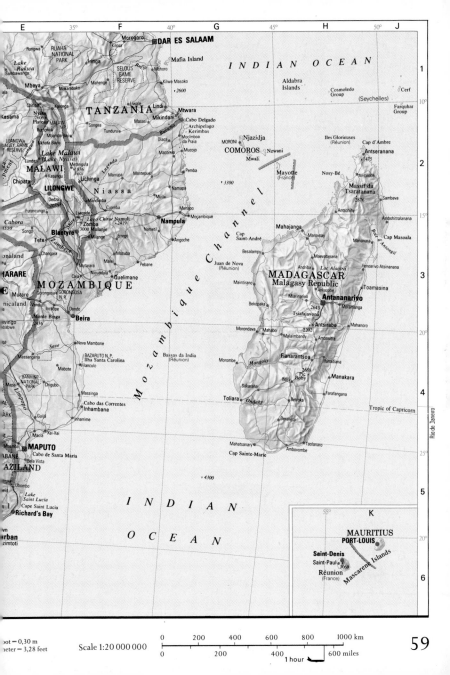

INDIAN OCEAN

Rungwa
RUAHA
NATIONAL
PARK
Kilosa
Morogoro
DAR ES SALAAM
Lake
Rukwa
Sumbawanga
Iringa
Mbeya
Mahenge
Mafia Island
Makambako
SELOUS
GAME
RESERVE
Mohoro
Kasama
Njombe
2600
Aldabra
Islands
Cosmoledo
Group
Cerf
(Seychelles)
Liwale
Kilwa Masoko
Kaputa
Nyika
Plateau
MALAWI
Mbamba Bay
Songea
TANZANIA
Lindi
Mtwara
Masasi
Mikindani
Tunduru
Cabo Delgado
Archipelago
Kerimbas
Farquhar
Group
LUANGWA
VALLEY GAME
RESERVE
Lichinga
Lake Malawi
(Lake Nyasa)
MALAWI
Chipata
Metangula
Kasungu
LILONGWE
Niassa
Mandimba
Marrupa
Montepuez
Mocímboa
da Praia
Diaca
Macomia
MORONI
Njazidja
COMOROS
Nzwani
Mwali
Iles Glorieuses
(Réunion)
Cap d'Ambre
Antseranana
Nyika
2606
Dedza
Namapa
Pemba
Mayotte
(France)
Nosy-Bé
Ambilobe
1475
Massif du
Tsaratanana
2876
Furancungo
Mandimba
Cuamba
Namapa
Moçambique
Sambava
Antsohihy
Cabora
1530
Songo
Tete
Zomba
Blantyre
Mulanje
Errego
3000
Lago Chiuta
Namuli
2419
Nametil
Nampula
Angoche
3300
Mahajanga
Cap
Saint-André
Morovoay
Amboabitralanana
Cap Masoala
Baie d'Antongil
MADAGASCAR
HARARE
Changara
Caia
Nicuadala
Mutarara
Malei
Quelimane
Pebane
Besalampy
Juan de Nova
(Réunion)
Maintirano
Andriba
Lac Alaotra
MADAGASCAR
Malagasy Republic
Antananarivo
Fenoarivo Atsinanana
Toamasina
Mutare
Gorongosa
GORONGOSA
N.P.
Dondo
Beira
Bekopaka
Miarinarivo
2643
Tsiafajavona
Antsirabe
Manoro
Mahanoro
MOZAMBIQUE
Monte Binga
2436
Nova Mambone
Save
BAZARUTO N.P.
Ilha Santa Carolina
Vilanculo
Bassas da India
(Réunion)
Morondava
Mahabo
2202
Malaimbandy
Ambositra
Morombe
Mangoky
Fianarantsoa
Ifanadiana
Manakara
Massangena
Mabote
Massinga
Inharrime
Maputo
Cabo das Correntes
Inhambane
Morombe
Toliara
Onilahy
Sakaraha
Ihosy
2643
Pic
Boby
Betroka
Farafangana
Tropic of Capricorn
Massingir
Guijá
Chigubo
Guijá
Bela Vista
Xai-Xai
MAPUTO
Cabo de Santa Maria
Mahatsanary
Betroka
Berakéta
Ambovombe
Taolanaro
Cap Sainte-Marie
INDIAN
Lake
Saint Lucia
Cape Saint Lucia
Richard's Bay
OCEAN
4300

MAURITIUS
PORT-LOUIS
Saint-Denis
Saint-Paul
Réunion
(France)
Mascarene Islands

55°
K

oot = 0,30 m
meter = 3,28 feet
Scale 1:20 000 000

0   200   400   600   800   1000 km

0   200   400   600 miles

1 hour

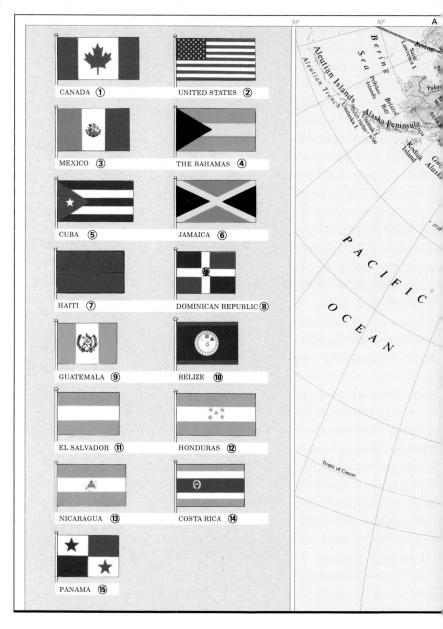

CANADA ①   UNITED STATES ②

MEXICO ③   THE BAHAMAS ④

CUBA ⑤   JAMAICA ⑥

HAITI ⑦   DOMINICAN REPUBLIC ⑧

GUATEMALA ⑨   BELIZE ⑩

EL SALVADOR ⑪   HONDURAS ⑫

NICARAGUA ⑬   COSTA RICA ⑭

PANAMA ⑮

Bering Sea

Aleutian Islands

Aleutian Trench

Saint Lawrence I.

Bering

Pribilov Islands

Bristol Bay

Dutch Harbor Unalaska I. 6700

Alaska Peninsula

Yuko

Kodiak Island

Gu Alask

PACIFIC OCEAN

3716

Tropic of Cancer

50°   60°   A

60   **NORTH AMERICA**

1 foot = 0,30 m
1 meter = 3,28 feet

Scale 1:50 000 00

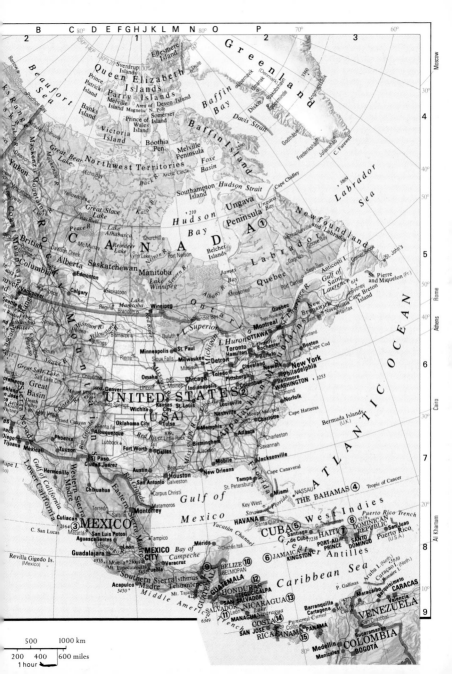

62 ALASKA AND WESTERN CANADA

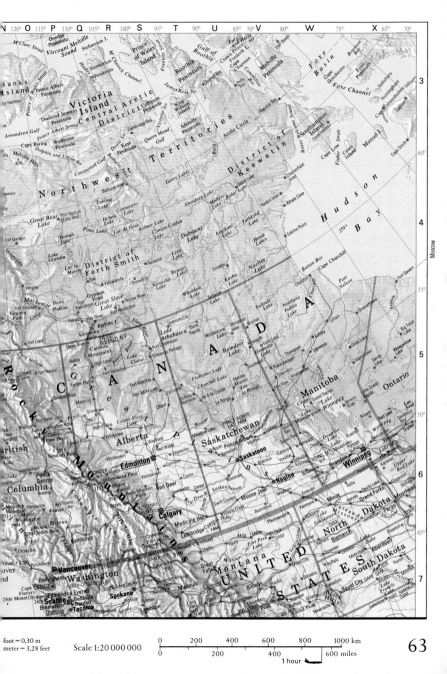

foot = 0,30 m
meter = 3,28 feet

Scale 1:20 000 000

| 0 | 200 | 400 | 600 | 800 | 1000 km |

| 0 | 200 | 400 | 600 miles |

1 hour

63

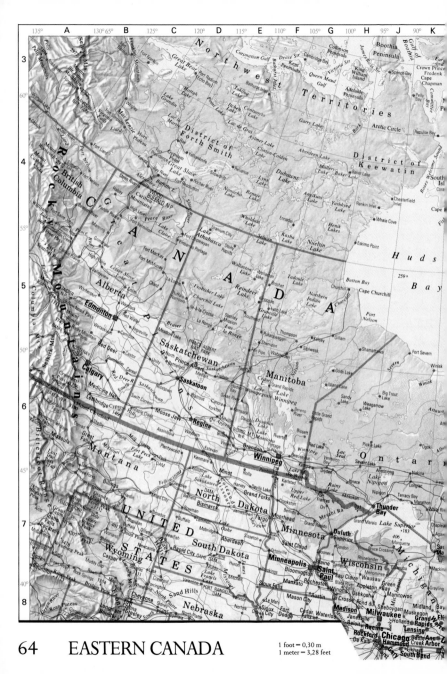

1 foot = 0,30 m
1 meter = 3,28 feet

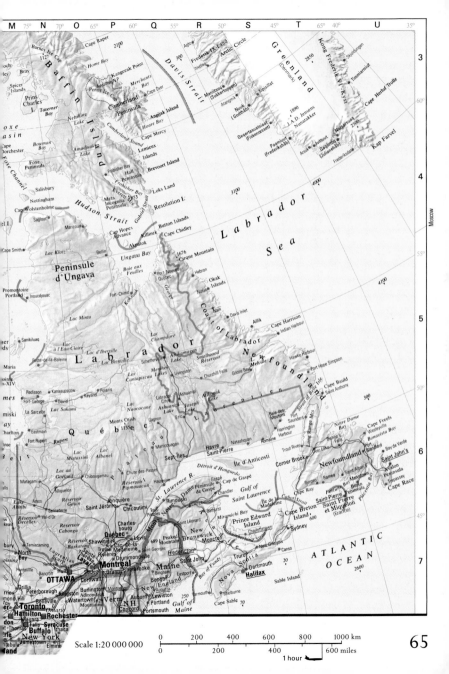

Scale 1:20 000 000

| 0 | 200 | 400 | 600 | 800 | 1000 km |

| 0 | 200 | 400 | 600 miles |

1 hour

65

THE UNITED STATES

1 foot = 0,30 m
1 meter = 3,28 feet

Scale 1:20 000 0

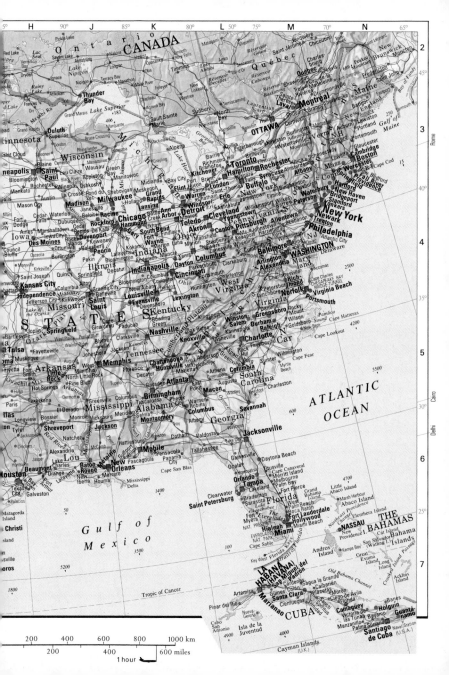

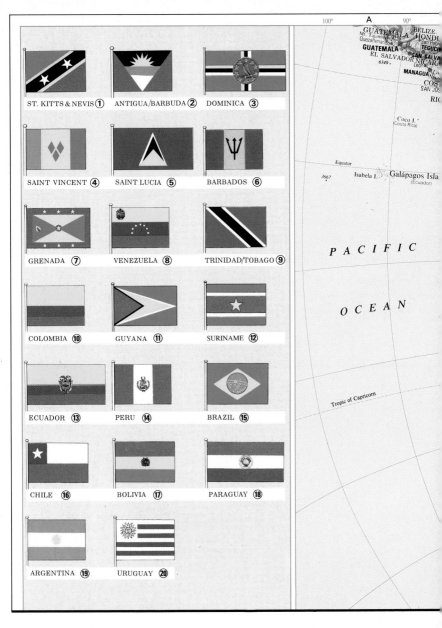

ST. KITTS & NEVIS ① ANTIGUA/BARBUDA ② DOMINICA ③

SAINT VINCENT ④ SAINT LUCIA ⑤ BARBADOS ⑥

GRENADA ⑦ VENEZUELA ⑧ TRINIDAD/TOBAGO ⑨

COLOMBIA ⑩ GUYANA ⑪ SURINAME ⑫

ECUADOR ⑬ PERU ⑭ BRAZIL ⑮

CHILE ⑯ BOLIVIA ⑰ PARAGUAY ⑱

ARGENTINA ⑲ URUGUAY ⑳

100° **A** 90°

GUATEMALA BELIZE
Mt. Tajumulco HONDU
Quezaltenango San Pedro
GUATEMALA TEGUCIG
EL SALVADOR NICARA
6349 Leon
MANAGUA La
COS
SAN JOS
RIC

Coco I.
(Costa Rica)

Equator
3667 Isabela I. Galápagos Isla
(Ecuador)

PACIFIC

OCEAN

Tropic of Capricorn

1 foot = 0,30 m
1 meter = 3,28 feet

Scale 1:50 000 0

South America

JAMAICA

Caribbean Sea

Puerto Rico (U.S.A.) ①

ST. KITTS NEVIS ④

ANTIGUA AND BARBUDA ②

Guadeloupe (France)

Pointe-à-Pitre

DOMINICA ③

Lesser Antilles

MARTINIQUE ⑤

Fort-de-France

ST. LUCIA ⑥

Aruba I. Curaçao I. ST. VINCENT ⑦

BRIDGETOWN

BARBADOS ⑧

ATLANTIC

P. Gallinas
Barranquilla
Santa Marta
Cartagena
Maracaibo

GRENADA ⑥

Colón Coro

PANAMÁ

TRINIDAD AND TOBAGO ⑨

PORT OF SPAIN

Valencia
Barcelona
Ciudad Guayana
Cumaná

CARACAS ⑦

Medellín
Bucaramanga

San Cristóbal

VENEZUELA ⑧

Orinoco R.
Ciudad Bolívar

OCEAN

Manizales
Ibagué 2610

BOGOTÁ

Angel Falls 2244

GEORGETOWN

PARAMARIBO

COLOMBIA ⑩

Mt. Roraima

SURINAME ⑫

French Guiana

Cayenne

Boa Vista
Roraima

Mt. Cotopaxi

GUYANA ⑪

ADOR ⑬

Guayaquil

Equator

Macapá

Amapá

St. Peter and St. Paul Rocks (Braz.)

5450

Fernando de Noronha I. (Braz.)

Negro R.

Marajó

Fonte Boa

Manaus

Belém

São Luís

Santarém

PERU ⑭

Leticia

Amazon R.

Amazonas

Parnaíba

Fortaleza

Iquitos

Selva s

Juruá R.

Purus R.

Madeira R.

Pará

Maranhão

Teresina

Ceará

Mossoró

Rio Grande do Norte

C. São Roque

Natal

Acre

Porto Velho

BRAZIL

Tapajós R.

Xingu R.

Tocantins R.

Caatingas Piauí

Paraíba

João Pessoa

Campina Grande

Pernambuco

Recife ⑮

LIMA

Callao

Rio Branco

Guajará Mirim

Rondônia

Mato Grosso

Juàzeiro

Garanhuns

Maceió

Lake Titicaca

LA PAZ

BOLIVIA ⑰

Cochabamba

SUCRE

Santa Cruz

Goiás

Barreiras

São Francisco R.

Bahia

Feira

Aracaju

Alagoinhas

Salvador

Ilhéus

Itabuna

Campos

Distrito Federal

Goiânia

BRASÍLIA

Anápolis

Uberlândia

Brazilian

Minas Gerais

Teófilo Otoni

Governador Valadares

Vitória

Mato Grosso do Sul

Belo Horizonte

Highlands

Espírito Santo

Vitória

PARA-GUAY ⑱

Presidente Prudente

São José

São Paulo

Campinas

Juiz de Fora

Campos

Niterói

Rio de Janeiro

ASUNCIÓN

Iguaçu Falls

Formosa

Paraná

Londrina

CHILE ⑯

Curitiba

Santos

Tropic of Capricorn

Trindade I. (Braz.)

Martin Vaz Is. (Braz.)

Resistencia

Corrientes

Posadas

Santa Catarina

Joinville

Florianópolis

Tucumán

Rio Grande do Sul

Passo Fundo

4995

Santa Fe

Rosario

Porto Alegre

L. dos Patos

Córdoba

Mendoza

Pelotas

URUGUAY ⑳

Lake Mirim

SANTIAGO

Valparaíso

BUENOS AIRES ⑲

MONTEVIDEO

Juan Fernández Islands (Chile)

ARGENTINA

La Plata

Río de la Plata

Mar del Plata

Pampa

ATLANTIC

5303

Bahía Blanca

Neuquén

Valdivia
Osorno

Gulf of San Matías

Puerto Montt
Chiloé I.

2652

OCEAN

Rawson

Gulf of San Jorge

Cerro San Valentín
Puerto Aisén

Comodoro Rivadavia

Puerto Deseado

6212

Falkland Islands (U.K.)

Río Gallegos
Strait of Magellan

Stanley

South Georgia (U.K.)

2913

Tierra del Fuego

Ushuaia 3359

Cape Horn

S BIPOLAR PROJECTION

500   1000 km

200   400   600 miles

1 hour

71

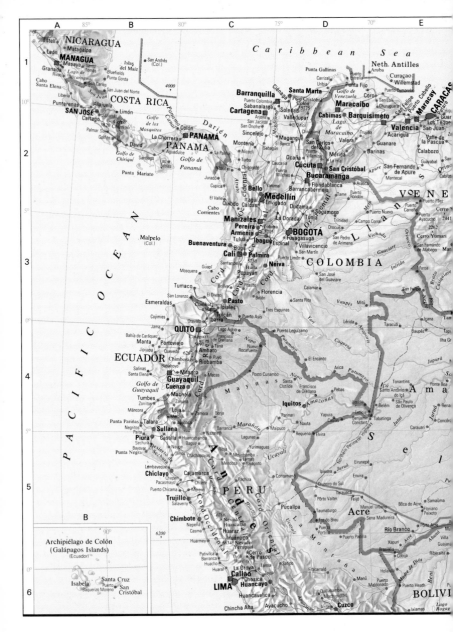

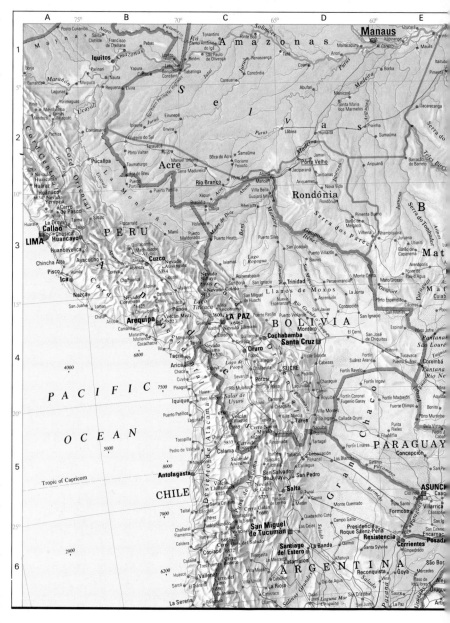

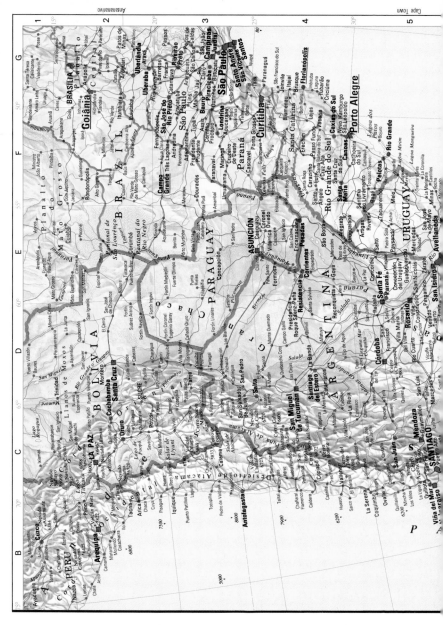

SOUTH AMERICA, SOUTH

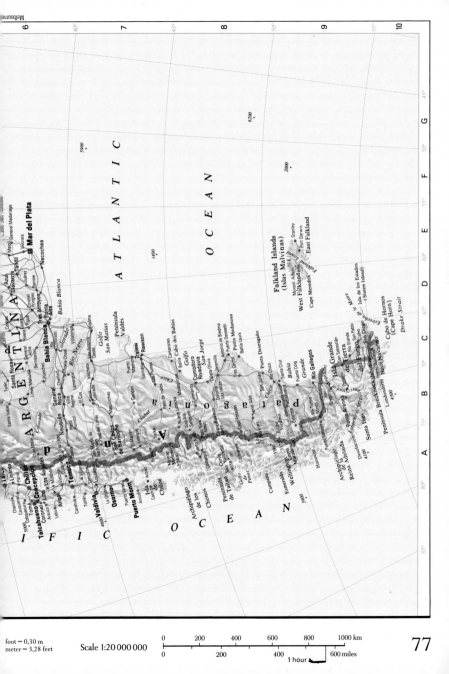

foot = 0,30 m
meter = 3,28 feet

Scale 1:20 000 000

| 0 | 200 | 400 | 600 | 800 | 1000 km |

| 0 | 200 | 400 | 600 miles |

1 hour

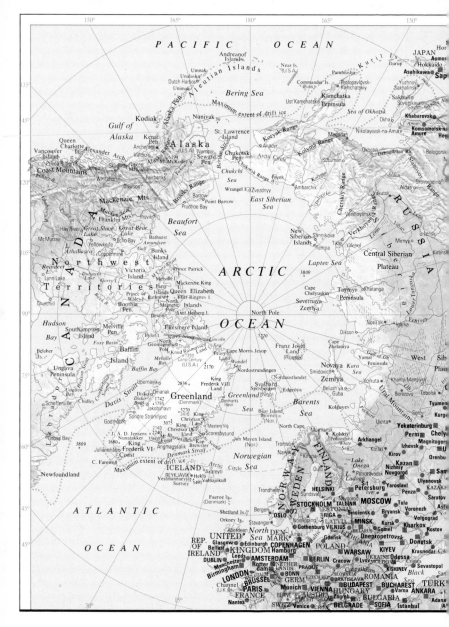

78 THE ARCTIC

1 foot = 0,30 m
1 meter = 3,28 feet

Scale 1:60 000 0

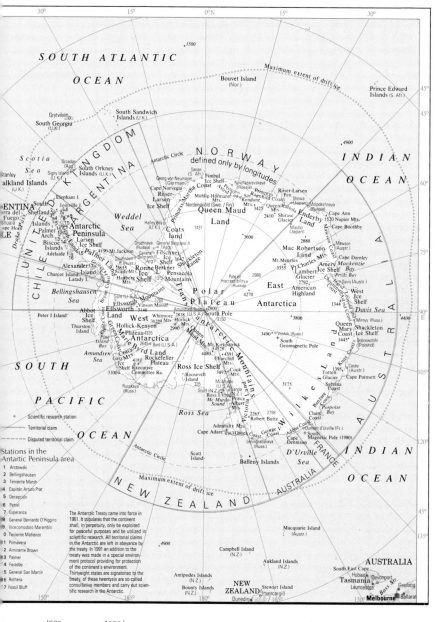

SOUTH ATLANTIC OCEAN

,1500

Maximum extent of drift ice

Bouvet Island (Nor.)

Prince Edward Islands (S. Afr.)

45°

45°

Grytviken
South Georgia (U.K.)

South Sandwich Islands (U.K.)

,4900

INDIAN OCEAN

60°

Scotia Sea

Orcadas (Arg.)
Signy Island (U.K.)
South Orkney Islands (U.K.)

Antarctic Circle

Sanae (S. Afr.)

Fimbul Ice Shelf

Novolazarevskaya (Russia)

Cape Ann
1820 Napier Mts.
Cape Boothby

Stanley
Falkland Islands (U.K.)

N O R W A Y
defined only by longitudes

Georg von Neumayer (Germany)
Cape Norvegia

Princess Martha Coast
Prinsesse Astrid Coast
Ragnhild Coast

Molodezhnaya (Russia)

60°

Tierra del Fuego
Cape Horn

Elephant I.
South Shetland Islands
Joinville I.

Riiser-
Larsen
Ice Shelf

Nordenskiöld (Swe. / Fin)

Shirase
Glacier

Mizuho (Japan)

Riiser-Larsen Pen.

Syowa (Japan)

Lützow-Holm Bay

Enderby
Land

ENTINA
CHILE

ARGENTINA

UNITED KINGDOM

Weddell Sea

Queen Maud

1431

Land

,3600

2880

2410

,3355

Mawson (Austr.)

Mac Robertson Land

Cape Darnley
Amery Mackenzie
Ice Shelf Prydz Bay

75°

Palmer
Arch.
Biscoe Islands
Adelaide I.

Antarctic Peninsula

Larsen
Ice Shelf

4190 Mt. Jackson
Druzhnaya (Russia)

Halley Bay (U.K.)

Coats
land

Druzhnaya II (Russia)
General Belgrano II (Arg.)

Filchner
Ice Shelf

Berkner
I.

Pensacola
Mts.

2988

Mt. Menzies
Prince Charles Mts.
3555
Lambert
Glacier
2792

Davis (Austr.)

**East
Highland**

West
Ice
Shelf

75°

Charcot Island
Latady I.

Alexander I.

Ronne
Ice Shelf

Hauberg
Shelf

Shackleton
Range
1372

Pole of
Inaccessibility
(Russia)

American

1344

Davis Sea

Bellingshausen Sea

Sole (U.S.A.)
Ellsworth
Mts.
Vinson Massif
,5140

1760

Gamburtsev
Mountains

Polar

4270

Antarctica

90° E

Peter I Island

Abbot
Ice
Shelf

Thurston
Island

Hollick-Kenyon
Plateau 4335

2818
Whitmore
Mts.
10244 Mts.
Horlick
Mts.
2990

Plateau

3150

,3800

4400

Ellsworth
Land

West

South Pole

Queen
Maud Mts.

,3490 Vostok (Russia)
South
Geomagnetic Pole

Mirny (Russ.)

Queen
Mary
Coast
1445

Shackleton
Ice Shelf

2645 Byrd (U.S.A.)

Marie Byrd Land

Antarctica

Rockefeller
Plateau

Executive
Committee Ra.

31004

4391

4480

Mt. Kirkpatrick
4528
Churchill
Mts.

Cook Mts.
3493

3175

Dobrowolski
(Poland)

1395
Casey (Austr.)
Totten
Glacier
Sabrina
Coast
Cape Poinsett

Amundsen Sea

Roosevelt
I.

4181

Ross Ice Shelf

Mt. McMurdo
Ross (U.S.A.)
Vanda

3265
2798
Robert Butte

Banzare
Coast

Porpoise
Bay

Claire
Coast

SOUTH

Russkaya (Russ.)

Scott (N.Z.) U.S.A.)
McMurdo
Sound
Mc Murdo
Prince
Albert
Mts.

1143 Oates
Coast

George V
Land

Adélie Coast
Dumont d'Urville (Fr.)

South
Magnetic Pole (1980)

120°

PACIFIC

Ross Sea

Cape Dennison

105°

OCEAN

○ Scientific research station

— Territorial claim

··· Disputed territorial claim

**Stations in the
Antarctic Peninsula area**

1 Arctowski
2 Bellingshausen
3 Teniente Marsh
4 Capitán Arturo Prat
5 Decepción
6 Petrel
7 Esperanza
8 General Bernardo O'Higgins
9 Vicecomodoro Marambio
0 Teniente Matienzo
11 Primavera
12 Almirante Brown
13 Palmer
14 Faraday
15 General San Martín
16 Rothera
17 Fossil Bluff

Cape Adare
Leningradskaya (Russ.)

AUSTRALIA

Balleny Islands

D'Urville Sea

INDIAN

Scott
Island

Antarctic Circle

OCEAN

45°

Maximum extent of drift ice

N E W   Z E A L A N D

FRANCE

AUSTRALIA

120°

135°

The Antarctic Treaty came into force in 1961. It stipulates that the continent shall, in perpetuity, only be exploited for peaceful purposes and be utilized in scientific research. All territorial claims in the Antarctic are left in abeyance by the treaty. In 1991 an addition to the treaty was made in a special environment protocol providing for protection of the continent's environment. Thirtyeight states are signatories to the treaty, of these twentysix are so-called consultative members and carry out scientific research in the Antarctic.

,4900

Macquarie Island (Austr.)

135°

Campbell Island (N.Z.)

Aukland Islands (N.Z.)

AUSTRALIA

South East Cape
Hobart
Devonport
Tasmania
Launceston

Antipodes Islands (N.Z.)

**NEW
ZEALAND**
Dunedin

Bounty Islands (N.Z.)

Stewart Island
Invercargill

Bass Str.

Geelong
Ballarat
Melbourne

150°

165°

180°

165°

150°

1000		2000 km

| 1 hour | 500 | 1000 miles |

ANTARCTICA 79

THE WORLD'S longest, greatest, highest, largest

Area: 150,000,000 km² (57,500,000 mi²)
(Land: 26%, Water: 71%, Ice: 3%)
Population: 4,912,600,000

Greenland

Mount McKinley •

NORTH AMERICA

Great Brit

Missouri   Lake Superior

Mississippi

Milwaukee Depth •

Amazon

SOUTH AMERICA

Lago Titicaca

Cerro Aconcagua •

Grande de Tierra
del Fuego

World's Longest Rivers
1. Nile (Africa) 6.690 km (4,160 miles)
2. Amazon (South America) 6.570 km (4,080 miles)
3. Mississippi-Missouri (North America) 6.020 km (3,740 miles)
4. Yangtze (Asia) 5.980 km (3,720 miles)
5. Yenisey (Asia) 5.870 km (3,650 miles)

Greatest Depth in each ocean
Arctic: North Polar Basin 5.500 m (18,040 ft.)
Atlantic: Milwaukee Depth (Puerto Rico Trench) 9.219 m (30,238 ft.)
Indian: Java Trench 7.450 m (24,436 ft.)
Pacific: Challenger Deep (Mariana Trench) 11.034 m (36,192 ft.)

Highest Mountain in each continent
Africa: Kilimanjaro 5.895 m (19,340 ft.)
Antarctica: Vinson Massif 5.140 m (16,863 ft.)
Asia: Mt. Everest 8.848 m (29,028 ft.)
Europe: Mont Blanc 4.810 m (15,771 ft.)
North America: Mount McKinley 6.194 m (20,321 ft.)
Oceania: Puncak Jaya 5.030 m (16,502 ft.)
South America: Cerro Aconcagua 6.959 m (22,831 ft.)

Largest Island in each continent
Africa: Madagascar 587.000 km² (227,000 sq.mi.)
Antarctica: Alexander 1 43.200 km² (16,700 sq.mi.)
Asia: Borneo 737.000 km² (285,000 sq.mi.)
Europe: Great Britain 219.000 km² (84,400 sq.mi.)
North America: Greenland 2.131.000 km² (823,000 sq.mi.)
Oceania: New Guinea 790.000 km² (305,000 sq.mi.)
South America: Grande de Tierra 48.000 km² (18,700 sq.mi.)
del Fuego

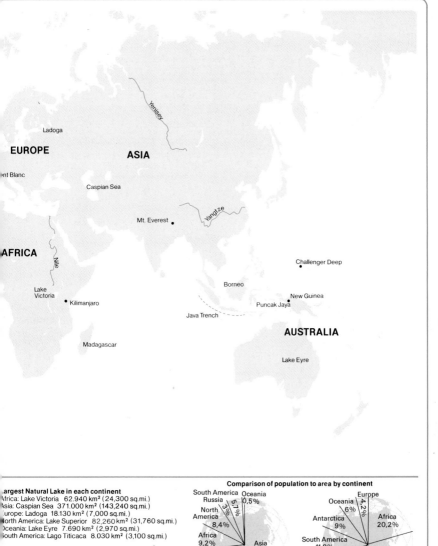

EUROPE

ASIA

Ladoga

Yenisey

Mont Blanc

Caspian Sea

Mt. Everest

Yangtze

AFRICA

Nile

Challenger Deep

Borneo

New Guinea

Lake
Victoria

Kilimanjaro

Puncak Jaya

Java Trench

AUSTRALIA

Madagascar

Lake Eyre

Largest Natural Lake in each continent
Africa: Lake Victoria 62.940 km² (24,300 sq.mi.)
Asia: Caspian Sea 371.000 km² (143,240 sq.mi.)
Europe: Ladoga 18.130 km² (7,000 sq.mi.)
North America: Lake Superior 82.260 km² (31,760 sq.mi.)
Oceania: Lake Eyre 7.690 km² (2,970 sq.mi.)
South America: Lago Titicaca 8.030 km² (3,100 sq.mi.)

Comparison of population to area by continent

South America
Russia
North
America
Africa
8,4%
9,2%
Europe
14,6%
Oceania
0,5%
5,7%
3%
Asia
58,6%

Population

Europe
4,2%
Oceania
6%
Antarctica
9%
Africa
20,2%
South America
11,8%
Asia
23,1%
Russia
8,8%
North
America
16,9%

Area

EUROPE

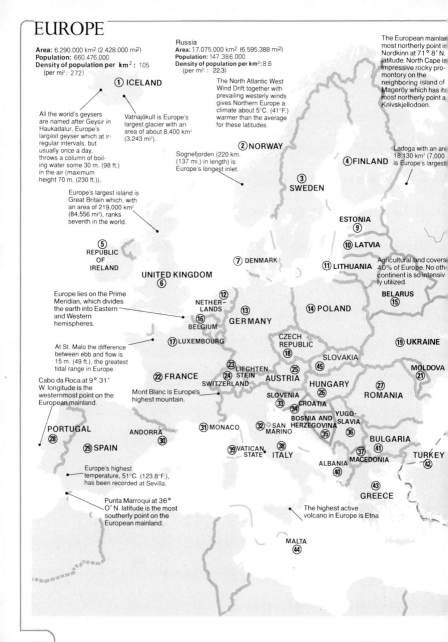

Area: 6.290.000 km² (2.428.000 mi²)
Population: 660.476.000
Density of population per km²: 105
(per mi²: 272)

Russia
Area: 17.075.000 km² (6.595.388 mi²)
Population: 147.386.000
Density of population per km²: 8.6
(per mi²: 22.3)

The European mainland's most northerly point is Nordkinn at 71° 8' N. latitude. North Cape is an impressive rocky promontory on the neighboring island of Mageröy which has its most northerly point at Knivskjellodaen.

① **ICELAND**

All the world's geysers are named after Geysir in Haukadalur, Europe's largest geyser which at irregular intervals, but usually once a day, throws a column of boiling water some 30 m. (98 ft.) in the air (maximum height 70 m. (230 ft.)).

Vatnajökull is Europe's largest glacier with an area of about 8,400 km² (3,243 mi²).

The North Atlantic West Wind Drift together with prevailing westerly winds gives Northern Europe a climate about 5°C. (41°F.) warmer than the average for these latitudes.

② **NORWAY**

Sognefjorden (220 km. (137 mi.) in length) is Europe's longest inlet.

④ **FINLAND**

Ladoga with an area 18.130 km² (7,000 is Europe's largest

③ **SWEDEN**

Europe's largest island is Great Britain which, with an area of 219,000 km² (84,556 mi²), ranks seventh in the world.

ESTONIA ⑨

⑩ **LATVIA**

⑤ **REPUBLIC OF IRELAND**

⑦ **DENMARK**

⑪ **LITHUANIA**

Agricultural land covers 40% of Europe. No other continent is so intensively utilized.

UNITED KINGDOM ⑥

BELARUS ⑮

Europe lies on the Prime Meridian, which divides the earth into Eastern and Western hemispheres.

⑫ **NETHER-LANDS**

⑬

⑭ **POLAND**

⑯ **BELGIUM**

GERMANY

At St. Malo the difference between ebb and flow is 15 m. (49 ft.), the greatest tidal range in Europe.

⑰ **LUXEMBOURG**

CZECH REPUBLIC ⑱

⑲ **UKRAINE**

Cabo da Roca at 9° 31' W. longitude is the westernmost point on the European mainland.

⑳ **FRANCE**

㉓ **LIECHTENSTEIN**
㉔ **SWITZERLAND**

SLOVAKIA

MOLDOVA ㉑

㉕ **AUSTRIA**

㊺

HUNGARY ㉖

㉗ **ROMANIA**

Mont Blanc is Europe's highest mountain.

SLOVENIA ㉝

CROATIA ㉞

PORTUGAL ㉘

ANDORRA ㉚

㉛ **MONACO**

㉜ **SAN MARINO**

BOSNIA AND HERZEGOVINA

YUGO-SLAVIA

㉟

㊱

BULGARIA ㊶

㉙ **SPAIN**

㊳ **VATICAN STATE**

㊳ **ITALY**

ALBANIA ㊵

㊲ **MACEDONIA**

TURKEY ㊷

Europe's highest temperature, 51°C. (123.8°F.), has been recorded at Sevilla.

Punta Marroqui at 36° O' N. latitude is the most southerly point on the European mainland.

The highest active volcano in Europe is Etna

㊸ **GREECE**

MALTA ㊹

82

⑧
RUSSIA

Volga is 3,690 km.
[9]2 mi.) long, Europe's
[long]est river. It also has
[the] greatest rate of flow.

⑳
KAZAKHSTAN

[A] traditional boun-
[dary] between Europe
[and] Asia divides both
[Turk]ey, Russia and
[Kaz]akhstan into an
[Euro]pean and an Asian
[part.]

[Alon]g this line Europe
[exte]nds to about 60° E.
[long]itude in the Ural
[Mou]ntains.

㊵	ALBANIA	③	SWEDEN
㉚	ANDORRA	㉔	SWITZERLAND
㉕	AUSTRIA	㊷	TURKEY
⑮	BELARUS	⑲	UKRAINE
⑯	BELGIUM	⑥	UNITED KINGDOM
㉟	BOSNIA AND HERZEGOVINA	㊴	VATICAN STATE
㊶	BULGARIA	㊱	YUGOSLAVIA
㉞	CROATIA		
⑱	CZECH REPUBLIC		
⑦	DENMARK		
⑨	ESTONIA		
④	FINLAND		
㉒	FRANCE		
⑬	GERMANY		
㊸	GREECE		
㉖	HUNGARY		
①	ICELAND		
㊳	ITALY		
⑳	KAZAKHSTAN		
⑩	LATVIA		
㉓	LIECHTENSTEIN		
⑪	LITHUANIA		
⑰	LUXEMBOURG		
㊲	MACEDONIA		
㊹	MALTA		
㉑	MOLDOVA		
㉛	MONACO		
⑫	NETHERLANDS		
②	NORWAY		
⑭	POLAND		
㉘	PORTUGAL		
⑤	REPUBLIC OF IRELAND		
㉗	ROMANIA		
⑧	RUSSIA		
㉜	SAN MARINO		
㊺	SLOVAKIA		
㉝	SLOVENIA		
㉙	SPAIN		

① ICELAND

L´ydveldid Ísland
(Republic of Island)

Area: 103.000 km^2 (39.786 mi^2)
Population: 247.357
Population growth per annum: 1,1%
Life expectancy at birth: Males 73 years, females 79 years
Literacy: 99,9%
Capital with population: Reykjavík 87.300
Other important cities with population: Akureyri 13.856
Language: Icelandic
Religion: Protestant
Currency: Króna = 100 aurar

The island of the Norse sagas. Iceland´s "althingi" claims to be the World´s oldest parliament, enacting laws since 930. The Icelanders kept the old Norse myths and sagas alive by oral tradition until Snorri Sturluson collected them in his epic Edda. A sight to be seen was the original Geysir but Iceland has many more geyers. Independent 930, 17 Jun 1944.

② NORWAY

Kongeriket Norge
(Kingdom of Norway)

Area: 386.957 km^2 (149.469 mi^2)
(including Svalbard and Jan Mayen)
Population: 4.198.300
Population growth per annum: 0,5%
Life expectancy at birth: Males 72 år, females 78 år
Literacy: 99 %
Capital with population: Oslo 453.730
Other important cities with population: Bergen 209.831, Trondheim 135.524
Language: Norwegian
Religion: Protestant
Currency: Norwegian Krone = 100 øre

Norway, proclaimed "the land of the Midnight sun" might rather be called the Land of Fjords. These spectacular inlets between vertical mountain walls dissect Norway, and have made the Norwegians a people who sail and fish. The Sognefjorden is 220 km(137 mi.) long – Europe´s longest bay. Independent 1905.

③ SWEDEN

Konungariket Sverige
(Kingdom of Sweden)

Area: 449.964 km^2 (173,806 mi^2)
Population: 8.458.880
Population growth per annum: 0,5 %
Life expectancy at birth: Males 72 years, females 79 years
Capital with population: Stockholm 669.485, (Greater Stockholm 1.471.242)
Other important cities with population: Göteborg 430.763, Malmö 231.575
Language: Swedish
Religion: Protestant
Currency: Swedish krona = 100 öre

The metallurgical industry that gave the World " Swedish steel" has traditions that reach beyond the Viking Age. The world´s oldest company, Stora, chartered in 1280, is still working the mine of Falun, that produced the copper that once made Sweden a great power.

④ FINLAND

Suomen Tasavalta - Republiken Finland
(Republic of Finland)

Area: 338.145 km^2 (130.614 mi^2)
Population: 4.938.602
Population growth per annum: 0,3%
Life expectancy at birth: Males 69 years, females 77 years
Literacy: 99%
Capital with population: Helsinki (Helsingfors) 490.034
Other important cities with population: Tampere (Tammerfors) 170.533, Turku (Åbo) 164.569
Language: Finnish, swedish
Religion: Protestant
Currency: Markka (mark) = 100 penniä (penni)

The "land of a thousand lakes" (actually almost a hundred thousand) has also become known as "the land that pays its debts" – by repaying not only U.S. loans but also a huge war indemnity to the Soviet Union after World War II. Exporting high quality manufactured goods to East and West has brought prosperity to the Finns. Independent 6 Dec 1917.

⑤ REPUBLIC OF IRELAND

Poblacht na L'Éireann
(Éire)

Area: 70.283 km^2 (27.148 mi^2)
Population: 3.538.000
Population growth per annum: -0,1%
Life expectancy at birth: Males 70 years, females 75 years
Literacy: 98%
Capital with population: Dublin 920.956
Other important cities with population: Cork 173.694, Limerick 76.557
Language: Irish, english
Religion: Roman catholic
Currency: Irish pund (punt Eirennach) = 100 pence

"The Emerald Isle" is perhaps most famous for its people – for boisterous bards, for poets and playwrights and Irish Eyes – but also for Irish coffee, whiskey and Guinness beer. Ireland justly prides itself also on the Book of Kells – and maybe more reluctantly for the Blarney Stone, kissed by many. Independent 1916, 1922.

⑥ UNITED KINGDOM

United Kingdom of Great Britain
and Northern Ireland

Area: 244.103 km^2 (94.289 mi^2)
Population: 56.930.200
Population growth per annum: 0,3%
Life expectancy at birth: Males 70 years, females 76 years
Literacy: 99%
Capital with population: London 6.770.400, (London City 4.700)
Other important cities with population: Birmingham 998.200, Glasgow 715.600, Leeds 709.000
Language: English, scottish, welsh
Religion: Protestant, roman catholic
Currency: British pound = 100 new pence

Britannia ruled the waves for over three hundred years, and finally gracefully resigned from the role of "peacekeeper" after the Pax Britannica had been broken by two world wars. The sun may have set over the Empire, but it still shines on the Union Jack in many places all over the world.

⑦ DENMARK

Kongeriget Danmark
(Kingdom of Denmark)

Area: 43.075 km^2 (16.638 mi^2)
Population: 5.129.254
Population growth per annum: 0,1%
Life expectancy at birth: Males 72 years, females 78 years
Literacy: 99%
Capital with population: København 468.704
(Great Copenhagen1.400.000)
Other important cities with population: Aarhus 258.028,
Odense 174.016
Language: Danish
Religion: Protestant
Currency: Danish krone = 100 øre

*Danish kings have ruled not only all of Scandinavia but also
England. Today no other country has larger overseas
territories. They include the world's largest island, Greenland.
Friendly Denmark now serves as an important link between
the Nordic countries and the rest of Europe, especially the
E.E.C*

⑧ RUSSIA

Rossijskaja Federatsija. Rossija

Area: 17.075.000 km^2 (6.595.388 mi^2)
Population: 147.400.000
Population growth per annum: –
Life expectancy at birth: –
Literacy: 99%
Capital with population: Moscow 8.970.000
Other important cities with population: S:t Petersburg
5.020.000, Nizjnij Novgorod 1.440.000,
Yekaterinburg (Sverdlovsk) 1.370.000
Language: Russian
Religion: Orthodox
Currency: Rubel = 100 kopek

*Russia alone is almost a continent, with over 10% of the
World's land area, in size equal to South America; the largest
nation of all. Close to 75% of the area is Asiatic (Siberia) but
95% of the population lives west of the Ural Mountains. The
now lost colonial empire of Czars and commissars lasted only
a century, an episode in the millennia of Asiatic History.*

⑨ ESTONIA

Eesti Vabariik
(Republic of Estonia)

Area: 45.100 km^2 (17.048 mi^2)
Population: 1.573.000
Population growth per annum: –
Life expectancy at birth: Males 67 years, females 75 years
Literacy: 99%
Capital with population: Tallinn 503.000
Other important cities with population: Tartu 120.000,
Narva 82.000, Kohtla-Järve 78.000
Language: Estonian, russian
Religion: Protestant, orthodox
Currency: Kruun (Krona) = 100 öre

*The unique, humane freedom fighters of Estonia fought with
Estonian songs as their only weapons – and wone back their
freedom when also the Russians themselves threw off the yoke
of communism. Hundreds of thousands used to come to the
regular Song Festivales of Tallinn to manifest their national
identity. Independent 1918, 20 Aug 1991.*

⑩ LATVIA

Latvijas Republika
(Republic of Latvia)

Area: 63.700 km^2 (24.588 mi^2)
Population: 2.681.000
Population growth per annum: –
Life expectancy at birth: Males 66 years, females 75 years
Literacy: 99%
Capital with population: Riga 915.000
Other important cities with population: Daugavpils
127.000, Liepaja 114.000, Jelgava 74.000
Language: Latvian, russian
Religion: Protestant, roman catholic, orthodox
Currency: (Latvian rubel) Lats = 100 santim

*The peace loving people of Latvia have never been noted for
wars or forays against neighbours– but instead too often as
victims. Before 1991 Latvia enjoyed only a short period of true
independence between the two World Wars, as one of the
newly established "rand states" supposed to reduce tensions in
Eastern Europe . Independent 1918, 21 Aug 1991.*

⑪ LITHUANIA

Lietuvos Respublika
(Republic of Lithuania)

Area: 65.200 km^2 (25.167 mi^2)
Population: 3.690.000
Population growth per annum: –
Life expectancy at birth: Males 67 years, females 76 years
Literacy: 99%
Capital with population: Vilnius 582.000
Other important cities with population: Kaunas 430.000,
Klaipeda 210.000, Siauliai 150.000
Language: Lithuanian
Religion: Roman catholic
Currency: (Lithuanian rubel), Litas = 100 centas

*The once mighty Lithuanian kingdom suffered the same fate as
Poland and became just another part of Empire of the Czars of
Russia. The freedom of the Lithuanians was restored after
World War One – but again lost in Hitler's and Stalin's scramble
for territories – that finally led to World War Two.
Independent 1918, 11 Mar 1990.*

⑫ NETHERLANDS

Koninkrijk der Nederlanden
(Kingdom of the Netherlands)

Area: 41.863 km^2 (16.170 mi^2)
Population: 14.757.848
Population growth per annum: 0,7%
Life expectancy at birth: Males 72 years, females 78 years
Literacy: 99%
Capital with population: Amsterdam 691.738
Other important cities with population: Rotterdam
574.299, 's-Gravenhage (Haag) 444.313
Language: Dutch
Religion: Roman catholic (38%), protestant (30%)
Currency: Guilder = 100 cens

*More than one third of the country lies below sea level. Some
Dutch say that 'God created the world, exept the Netherlands,
which we had to create ourselves'. This task was begun in the
15th century, when they learned to reclaim their slowly sinking
land from the encroaching sea. Independent 19 Apr 1839.*

⑬ GERMANY

Bundesrepublik Deutschland
(Federal republic of Germany)

Area: 357.039 km^2 (137.817 mi^2)
Population: 77.947.335
Population growth per annum: -0,1%
Life expectancy at birth: Males 71 years, females 77 years
Literacy: 99%
Capital with population: Berlin 3.300.600, Bonn
Other important cities with population: Hamburg
1.593.600, München 1.188.800, Köln 927.500
Language: German
Religion: Protestant (43%), roman catholic (36%)
Currency: Deutsche mark (DM) = 100 pfennige

*Like the mythical Phoenix, Germany has miraculously sprung
from the pyre of total defeat and destruction since 1945, united
again in 1990 with Berlin as capital (but with Bonn as seat of
most of the ministries). The division in two separate states was
caused by and did not last longer than the rivalry of the
victorious powers after World War Two.*

⑭ POLAND

Rzeczpospolita Polska
(Republic of Poland)

Area: 312.683 km^2 (120.779 mi^2)
Population: 37.764.000
Population growth per annum: 0,3%
Life expectancy at birth: Males 67 years, females 75 years
Literacy: 99%
Capital with population: Warszawa 1.671.400
Other important cities with population: Lódz 844.900,
Kraków 744.900
Language: Polish
Religion: Roman catholic
Currency: Zloty = 100 groszy

*Time and again conquering armies have swept over Poland
and divided the spoils, but Polish people never gave up. After
World War Two the U.S.S.R pushed the land and people west-
wards over former German land, annexing 1/3 of prewar
Poland in the east. Independent 966, 10 Nov 1918.*

⑮ BELARUS

Respublika Belarus
(Republic of Belarus)

Area: 207.600 km^2 (80.100 mi^2)
Population: 10.200.000
Population growth per annum: –
Life expectancy at birth: –
Literacy: –
Capital with population: Mensk (Minsk) 1.600.000
Other important cities with population: Gomel 500.000
Language: White Russian
Religion: Orthodox, roman catholic
Currency: Rubel = 100 kopek

*The name byelo meaning white is interpreted as "free" – a
name from the days the mongols became masters of the other
Russian principalities. Stalin gave Belarus together with Russia
and the Ukraine status as one of the founding members of the
UN – but in reality the country joined the family of free nations
first in 1991.Decl. of Independent 25 Aug 1991.*

⑯ BELGIUM

Royaume de Belgique-Koninkrijk België
(Kingdom of Belgium)

Area: 30.518 km^2 (11.788 mi^2)
Population: 9.875.716
Population growth per annum: 0,1%
Life expectancy at birth: Males 69 years, females 75 years
Literacy: 98%
Capital with population: Bruxelles (Brussels) 970.346
Other important cities with population: Antwerpen
476.044, Gent 232.620
Language: Flemish (dutch), french, german
Religion: Roman catholic
Currency: Belgian franc = 100 centimes

*The country at "the crossroad of Western Europe" is dominated
by the capital Brussels, Brussels is also the capital of the E.E.C.
The difficulties in uniting Europe are mirrored in the Belgian
nation.The Dutch-speaking Flemings and French-speaking
Wallons stick together against others, but often quarrel
amongst themselvs. Independent 4 Oct 1830.*

⑰ LUXEMBOURG

Grand-Duché de Luxembourg
(Grand Duchy of Luxemburg)

Area: 2.586 km^2 (999 mi^2)
Population: 372.100
Population growth per annum: -0,3%
Life expectancy at birth: Males 68 years, females 75 years
Literacy: 99%
Capital with population: Luxembourg 76.640
Other important cities with population: Esch-sur-Alzette
23.700
Language: Luxemburgish, french, german
Religion: Roman catholic (95%)
Currency: Luxembourg franc = 100 centimes

*Historically Luxembourg has always had strong ties with one
or another of its neighbours while maintaining independence
in form if not in fact. It also formed some sort of a nucleus for
the Coal and Steel Union that evolved into the E.E.C.
Independent 1866.*

⑱ CZECH REPUBLIC

Ceská Republika
(Czech Republic)

Area: 78,864 km^2 (30,448.896mi²)
Population: 10.331.184
Population growth per annum: 0.2%
Life expectancy at birth: Males 69 years, females 76 years
Literacy: 99%
Capital with population: Praha (Prague)
Other important cities with population: Brno 2.058.156,
Ostrava 1.972.200
Language: Czech
Religion: Roman catholic (70%), protestant (15%)
Currency: Koruna = 100 haléru

*In late 60's while trying to implement freedom reforms, the troops
from the Soviet Union and other communist countries invaded
crushing the program. Following demands from the Czech people
for the freedoms granted to the soviet people the Czechoslovak
Communist party ended its domination in 1989. Czech Republic
became independent on 1st Jan 1993.*

⑲ UKRAINE

Area: 603.700 km^2 (233.000 mi^2)
Population: 51.700.000
Population growth per annum: –
Life expectancy at birth: –
Literacy: –
Capital with population: Kyjiv (Kijev) 2.600.000
Other important cities with population: Charkov 1.600.000,
Dnepropetrovsk 1.180.000, Odessa 1.115.000
Language: Ukrainian
Religion: Orthodox, roman catholic
Currency: Rubel = 100 kopek

*The ancient city of Kyjiv – capital of "all Russia" 882-1125 is
now again center of a great country. In Europe only Russia is
larger in size, and only Germany, the UK and Italy have more
inhabitants. For a thousand years Kyjiv has remained one of
the great cities of Christianilty, with e.g. the cathedral of St.
Sophie, founded in 1017. Decl. of Indep.24 Aug 1991.*

⑳ KAZAKHSTAN

Area: 2.717.000 km^2 (1.049.485 mi^2)
Population: 16.500.000
Population growth per annum: –
Life expectancy at birth: –
Literacy: –
Capital with population: Alma-Ata 1.100.000
Other important cities with population: Karaganda
614.000, Tjimkeut 393.000, Semipalatinsk 334.000
Language: Kazakh
Religion: Islam
Currency: Rubel = 100 kopek

*The steppes of Kazakhstan have in many parts become farm-
lands, but names like Betpak-Dala (Hunger Steppe) and Kyzyl-
Kum (Red Sands) mirror the hard living conditions that still
prevail on the treeless, arid lands. In 1961 cosmonaut Jurij
Gagarin reached beyond the horizon of Kazakhstan from
Baykonur Space Center. Decl. of Indep. 16 Dec 1991.*

㉑ MOLDOVA

Republica Moldoveneasca
(Moldavian Repiblic)

Area: 33.700 km^2 (13.000 mi^2)
Population: 4.300.000
Population growth per annum: –
Life expectancy at birth: –
Literacy: –
Capital with population: Chisinau (Kisjinjov) 720.000
Other important cities with population: Tiraspol 182.000,
Beltsy 159.000
Languages: Romanian, russian
Religion: Orthodox
Currency: Rubel = 100 kopek

*The fertile farmlands between the rivers Prut and Dnester have
seen many names, rulers and settlers – from Greek and
Romans to Romanians, Turks and Russians. Since the 15th
century called Bessarabya (after a ruling dynasty) the name of
the land was changed when it become part of the USSR in
1945. Decl . of Independent Aug 1991.*

㉒ FRANCE

République Française
(French Republic)

Area: 543.965 km^2 (210.116 mi^2)
Population: 55.632.000
Population growth per annum: 0,4%
Life expectancy at birth: Males 70 years, females 78 years
Literacy: 99%
Capital with population: Paris 2.188.918,
(Greater Paris 8.706.963)
Other important cities with population: Marseille 878.689,
Lyon 418.476
Language: French
Religion: Roman catholic (80%), islam
Currency: French franc = 100 centimes

*France is one of the great powers of the world. The French
language is still the language of diplomacy. France is culturally
the world's leading nation, and most former French colonies
remain members of the French Commonwealth. France is also
the leading European nation on the space frontier. National
day: 14 july (1789)*

㉓ LIECHTENSTEIN

Fürstentum Liechtenstein
(Principality of Liechtenstein)

Area: 160 km^2 (41 mi^2)
Population: 27.714
Population growth per annum: 1,4 %
Life expectancy at birth: –
Literacy: 100%
Capital with population: Vaduz 4.891
Other important cities with population: Schaan 4.836
Language: German
Religion: Roman catholic
Currency: Swiss franc = 100 rappen (centimes)

*Liechtenstein epitomizes the notion"postage stamp state" –
because of its size and its fame among collectors of stamps. It
is also a surviving stamp-size principality from the times when
Europe was divided among many princes and kings, before
their realms were united into nations. Independent 3 May 1342.*

㉔ SWITZERLAND

Schweizerische Eidgenossenschaft
Confédération Suisse - Confederatione Svizzera
(Swiss Confederation)

Area: 41.293 km^2 (15.950 mi^2)
Population: 6.566.900
Population growth per annum: 0,6%
Life expectancy at birth: Males 72 years, females 78 years
Literacy: 99%
Capital with population: Bern (Berne) 136.300
Other important cities with population: Zürich 346.500,
Basel 171.700, Geneve 160.900
Language: German, french, italian
Religion: Roman catholic (44%), protestant (50%)
Currency: Swiss franc = 100 centimes (rappen)

*The Financial Pole of the world is claimed to be in situated in
some undefined spot in Zürich. Through centuries of neutrality
and economic stability, Switzerland has grown into a global
center of banking. Besides quality watches, tourism somehow
seems to have been invented in this land of few natural
resources. Independent 1 Aug 1291.*

㉕ AUSTRIA

Republik Österreich
(Republic of Austria)

Area: 83.855 km^2 (32.390 mi^2)
Population: 7.575.732
Population growth per annum: 0,1%
Life expectancy at birth: Males 72 years, females 78 years
Literacy: 98%
Capital with population: Wien 1.531.346
Other important cities with population: Graz 243.161,
Linz 199.910
Language: German
Religion: Roman catholic (89%), protestant (6%)
Currency: Schilling = 100 groschen

*Austria is the only state pledged by law and treaties to
neutrality. Vienna, for centuries the capital of the "Holy Roman
Empire", the seat of the Habsburg Emperors, still bears the
imprint of bygone greatness, and remains the cultural capital
of Central Europe. Independent 1276, 1804, 1918, 27 Apr 1945.*

㉖ HUNGARY

Magyar Köztársaság
(Republic of Hungary)

Area: 93.032 km^2 (35.935 mi^2)
Population: 10.604.000
Population growth per annum: -0,2%
Life expectancy at birth: Males 67 years, females 73 years
Literacy: 99%
Capital with population: Budapest 2.104.700
Other important cities with population: Debrecen 217.364,
Miskolc 210.000
Language: Hungarian (Magyar)
Religion: Roman catholic, protestant
Currency: Forint = 100 fillér

*Hungary is in many ways an enclave – a part of Central Europe,
a land of rolling hills and plains (the famous puszta) encircled
by mountain lands, a finno-ugric people surrounded by slavic
neighbours. It is a nation, that rightly takes pride in a thousand
years of fierce fights for freedom, symbolized in the crown of
St.Stephan from 1001, as old as Hungary.*

㉗ ROMANIA

România

Area: 237.500 km^2 (91.738 mi^2)
Population: 22.940.430
Population growth per annum: 0,5%
Life expectancy at birth: Males 68 years, females 73 years
Literacy: 89%
Capital with population: Bucaresti (Bukarest) 1.989.823
Other important cities with population: Constanta 332.676,
Brasov 351.493
Language: Rumanian
Religion: Orthodox (85%)
Currency: Leu = 100 bani

*Rome settled fertile Dacia and made an everlasting imprint. The
frontier province was lost less than two centuries after
conquest, but the people today speak a language based on latin
and the name of the land proclaims it still Roman after almost
two thousand years. Fictious Count Dracula "lived" here, in
Transylvania. Independent 1877.*

㉘ PORTUGAL

República Portuguesa
(Republic of Portugal)

Area: 92.072 km^2 (35.564 mi^2)
Population: 10.350.000
Population growth per annum: 0,6 %
Life expectancy at birth: Males 66 years, females 74 years
Literacy: 86%
Capital with population: Lisboa (Lissabon) 807.937
Other important cities with population: Porto 327.368
Language: Portuguese
Religion: Roman cahtolic
Currency: Escudo = 100 centavos

*In spite of its small size, Portugal managed to become one of
the World's great powers, and to acquire and retain a global
empire for half a millennium. Portugal produces famous wines,
such as madeira and port (from Oporto), and every second
wine bottle in the world is sealed with Portuguese cork.*

㉙ SPAIN

Reino de España
(Kingdom of Spain)

Area: 504.750 km^2 (194.968 mi^2)
Population: 38.996.156
Population growth per annum: 0,4%
Life expectancy at birth: Males 70 years, females 76 years
Literacy: 97%
Capital with population: Madrid 3.100.507
Other important cities with population: Barcelona
1.703.744, Valencia 732.491, Sevilla 655.435
Language: Spanish, catalan, basque, galician
Religion: Roman catholic
Currency: Pesetas = 100 céntimos

*Proud Spain, once one of the World's great powers that sent
the Great Armada to England in a bid to become master of the
oceans, is today still the cultural leader in the Iberic World. It
gave the people such as Cervantes, Loyola, Goya and Picasso.*

㉚ ANDORRA

Principat d'Andorra
(Principality of Andorra)

Area: 468 km^2 (181 mi^2)
Population: 51.400
Population growth per annum: –
Life expectancy at birth: Males 70 years, females 76 years
Literacy: 100%
Capital with population: Andorra la Vella 18.463
Other important cities with population: –
Language: Spanish (59%), catalan (30%)
Religion: Roman catholic
Currency: French franc, spanish peseta

*Conducting trade between Spain and France is and has been
the main business of this Pyrenean principality, jointly ruled by
the Spanish Bishop of Urgel and the Head of State of France.
Outside Andorra some call it smuggling. Tourism also benefits
from the absence of customs duties. Independent 1278.*

㉛ MONACO

Principauté de Monaco
(Principality of Monaco)

Area: 1,95 km^2 (0.75 mi^2)
Population: 27.063
Population growth per annum: -0,3%
Life expectancy at birth: Males 70 years, females 78 years
Literacy: 99%
Capital with population: Monaco
Other important cities with population: –
Language: French, monegasque
Religion: Roman catholic
Currency: French franc = 100 centimes

*Monaco proves that gambling can pay provided you run the
bank! The Monte Carlo Casino has been the Mecca of gamblers
since 1858 and also made Monaco a fashionable tourist resort.
The citizens of microscopic Monaco do not pay income tax.
Independent 1297.*

㉜ SAN MARINO

Repubblica di San Marino
(Republic of San Marino)

Area: 61 km^2 (24 mi^2)
Population: 22.746
Population growth per annum: 1,4%
Life expectancy at birth: –
Literacy: 96%
Capital with population: San Marino 4.363
Other important cities with population: –
Language: Italian
Religion: Roman cahtolic
Currency: Italian lira = 100 centecimi

*The only surviving city state of medieval Italy, San Marino is
still governed by two Capitani Reggenti, democratically elected
for a period of only six months. Sale of postage stamps was
an important industry, but is now dwarfed by the tourist trade.
Over 3.5 million visit San Marino each year. Independent 1263.*

㉝ SLOVENIA

Republika Slovenija
(Republic of Slovenia)

Area: 20.251 km^2 (7.816 mi^2)
Population: 1.999.000
Population growth per annum: 0,3 %
Life expectancy at birth: –
Literacy: –
Capital with population: Ljubljana 305.000
Other important cities with population: Maribor 185.000
Language: Slovenian
Religion: Roman catholic
Currency: Tolar

*Slovenia was part of the "Holy Roman Empire" created by
Charlemagne in the 9th century and part of what remained
until 1919 – and did not suffer from Turkish rule as the rest of
Balkan. The Pastojna caves are Europe's largest, a home for the
blind Olm, adapted to a life in total darkness.
Independent 25 Jul 1991.*

㉞ CROATIA

Republika Hrvatska
(Republic of Croatia)

Area: 56.538 km^2 (21.823 mi^2)
Population: 4.601.000
Population growth per annum: 0,1%
Life expectancy at birth: –
Literacy: –
Capital with populationpopulation: Zagreb 768.000
Other important cities with population: Split 180.000,
Rijeka 193.000, Osijek 158.000
Language: Croatian (serbo-croatian)
Religion: Roman catholic
Currency: Croatian dinar

*The fighting croats have given the world a common word –
with slighly diverging spellings and meaning in different
languages; cravat, cravatte, kravatt – derived from the flamboy-
ant neck- clothes worn by croat mercenaries as a common
"uniform". Croatia and Hungary have for a long time been ruled
as one country. Independent 25 Jul 1991.*

㉟ BOSNIA-HERZEGOVINA

Republika Bosna i Hercegovina
(Republic of Bosnia and Herzegovina)

Area: 51.129 km^2 /19.735 mi^2)
Population: 4.300.000
Population growth per annum: –
Life expectancy at birth: –
Literacy: –
Capital with population: Sarajevo 448.000
Other important cities with population: Banja Luka
183.000, Zenica 132.000
Language: Serbo-croatian
Religion: Islam, roman catholic
Currency: Dinar

*This land is more divided than the hyphenated name indicates:
a miniature version of the former Yugoslavia. The fateful shots
that killed the Arch-duke Franz Ferdinand of Austria and started
the First World War were fired in the powder-keg of Sarajevo
28 Jul 1914. Independent 21 Dec 1991.*

㊱ YUGOSLAVIA

Federativna Republika Jugoslavija
(Socialist Federative Republic of Yugoslavia)

Area: 102.000 km^2 (39.400 mi^2)
Population: 11.200.000
Population growth per annum: –
Life expectancy at birth: –
Literacy: –
Capital with population: Beograd (Belgrad) 1.500.000
Other important cities with population: Nis 643.000,
Novi Sad 257.000, Podgorica 132.000
Language: Serbo-croatian
Religion: Orthodox, islam
Currency: Yugoslavian dinar

*No wonder that a nation-mosaic of combative people's – five –
speaking four different languages, writing in two alphabets and
divided by three different faiths did not survive longer; more of
a miracle that they stuck togheter over 70 years. The name now
denotes a new union of Serbia and Montenegro.*

㊲ MACEDONIA

Area: 25.713 km^2 (9.925 mi^2)
Population: 2.100.000
Population growth per annum: –
Life expectancy at birth: –
Literacy–
Capital with population: Skopje 506.000
Other important cities with population: Tetova 162.000
Language: Makedonian, albanian
Religion: Orthodox
Currency: Makedonian denar

Chaos in historical Macedonia caused the first Balkan War in 1912, and the area was divided. Greece fervently opposes the use of the historical (Greek) name for the newly independent (Slavic) mother part. Not even the firm ground is stable here. The capital Skopje was to 80% devastated by an earthquake in 1963. Independent 9 Sep 1991.

㊳ ITALY
Repubblica Italiana
(Italian Republic)

Area: 301.279 km^2 (116.374 mi^2)
Population: 57.399.108
Population growth per annum: 0,2%
Life expectancy at birth: Males 70 years, females 76 years
Literacy: 98%
Capital with population: Roma (Rome) 2.817.227
Other important cities with population: Milano 1.478.505, Napoli 1.200.958
Language: Italian
Religion: Roman catholic
Currency: Lira = 100 centesimi

All roads lead to Rome, still the Eternal City – the city of the Pope, of the Sistine Chapel, of the Colosseum and innumerable monuments of Imperial Rome. But Italy is also the land of Saint Francis and Leonardo, of Pisa, Venice and Florence – and today of Milan, Torino and Cortina d'Ampezzo. Independent 18 Feb 1861.

㊴ VATICAN CITY STATE
Stato della Città del Vaticano

Area: 0,44 km^2 (0.17 mi^2)
Population: 1.000
Population growth per annum: –
Life expectancy at birth: –
Literacy: –
Capital with population: –
Other important cities with population: –
Language: Italian, latin
Religion: Roman catholic
Currency: Vatian City lira, italian lira = 100 centesimi

The spiritual importance of the Pope is inversely proportionate to the size of his worldly domains, the world's smallest state. Relative to its size it certainly contains greater treasures of art than any other state in the world, such as the Sistine Chapel and the Pietá. Independent 11 Feb 1929.

㊵ ALBANIA
Republika Shqipërisë
(Republic of Albania)

Area: 28.748 km^2 (11.104 mi^2)
Population: 3.080.000
Population growth per annum: 2,1%
Life expectancy at birth: Males 69 years, females 74 years
Literacy: 72%
Capital with population: Tiranë (Tirana) 225.700
Other important cities with population: Durrés 78.700
Language: Albanian
Religion: Islam, atheism
Currency: New Lek = 100 qindarka

In less than spendid isolation after World War Two dogmatical communist leaders turned their land into a vitual "white spot" on the map. Albania is unique also regarding religions; a moslem land declared "the world's first atheist state " with a people that has given us a living christian saint: Mother Theresa. Independent 28 Nov 1912.

㊶ BULGARIA
Republika Bulgaria
(Republic of Bulgaria)

Area: 110.912 km^2 (42.842 mi^2)
Population: 8.973.600
Population growth per annum: 0,1%
Life expectancy at birth: Males 69 years, females 74 years
Literacy: 91%
Capital with population: Sofiya (Sofia) 1.128.859
Other important cities with population: Plovdiv 356.596, Varna 305.891
Language: Bulgarian
Religion: Orthodox (85%), islam (13%)
Currency: Lev = 100 stótinki

Russia helped in 1908 to liberate the Bulgarians from Turkish rule that lasted for over five centuries. The Bulgarians have now liberated themselves from communist rule that lasted for nearly five decades. Europe's "vegetable and fruite garden" was also the tourist "Riviera" for the East block.

㊷ TURKEY
Türkiye Cumhuriyeti
(Republic of Turkey)

Area: 779.452 km^2 (301.077 mi^2)
Population: 50.664.458
Population growth per annum: 2,5%
Life expectancy at birth: Males 58 years, females 63 years
Literacy: 74%
Capital with population: Ankara 2.235.035
Other important cities with population: Istanbul 5.475.982, Izmir 1.489.772
Language: Turkish
Religion: Islam
Currency: Turkish lira = 100 kurus

The land that for centuries served as a link between Europe and Asia now also provides the two continents with a physical link, the huge brige over the Bosporus. The world famous cathedral of Hagia Sofia, built by empreror Justinian 532-537, was turned into a mosque after the fall of Constantinople in 1453.

㊸ GREECE

Elliniki Dimokratia
(Hellenic Republic)

Area: 131.957 km^2 (50.971 mi^2)
Population: 9.990.000
Population growth per annum: 0,3%
Life expectancy at birth: Males 71 years, females 75 years
Literacy: 92%
Capital with population: Athinai (Athéns) 885.737, (Greater-Athéns 3.027.331)
Other important cities with population: Thessaloniki 406.413, Pátrai 141.529
Language: Greek
Religion: Greek orthodox
Currency: Drachma = 100 leptae

The cradle of European civilization is now a member of the E.E.C. and thus takes an active part in shaping the Europe of the future. Greece may well have the world´s largest merchant fleet – even if few sail under Greek flag. Venerable Parthenon, temple of Pallas Athena, still crowns Áthen´s Acropolis. Independent 3 Feb 1830.

㊹ MALTA

Repubblika Ta'Malta
(Republic of Malta)

Area: 316 km^2 (122 mi^2)
Population: 345.705
Population growth per annum: 0,0%
Life expectancy at birth: Males 70 years, females 75 years
Literacy: 67%
Capital with population: Valletta 101.043
Other important cities with population: Birkirkara 20.490
Language: Maltese, english
Religion: Roman catholic
Currency: Maltese Lira = 100 cents = 1000 mils

For unprecedented valour during World War II the people of Malta were collectively awarded the George Cross, Britian´s highest civilian decoration. Malta still proudly carries the cross in its national flag. From 1530 to 1798 Malta was ruled by the Knight Hospitallers – since known as the Knights of Malta. Independent 21 sep 1964.

㊺ SLOVAKIA

Slovenská Republika
(Slovak Republic)

Area : 49.035 km² (18.932mi²)
Population: 5.295.780
Population growth per annum: 0.2%
Life expectancy at birth: Males 68 years, females 74 years
Literacy: 99%
Capital with population: Bratislava 440.421
Other important cities with population: Košice 236.000
Language: Slovak
Religion: Roman catholic
Currency: Koruna=100 haléru

Once part of the Great Moravian Empire, Slovakia has also been ruled by the Magyars and part of the Ottoman Empire. It developed a national identity around 1800's. After WWI united with the Czechs to form independent republic of Czechoslovakia. However the Slovaks resented the Czech power of the new nations economy and government. Gained equal representation in government in 1960's and with the fall of the communist regime became fully independent on 1st Jan 1993.

ASIA

Area: 31.500.000 km² (12.160.000 mi²)
Population: 2.727.000.000
Density of population per km²: 88
(per mi²: 224)

Area: 17.075.000km² (6.595.388mi²)
Population: 147.386.000
Density of population per km²: 8.6
(per mi²: 22.3)

The Asian mainland's nor-
thernmost point is Cape
Chelyuskin at 77° 44′ N.
latitude.

Lowest surface
temperature in the no-
thern hemisphere, −7
C. (−162°F.), was
recorded at Oymyak

Northeastern Siberia has
the most extreme con-
tinental climate in the
world. The variation bet-
ween the warmest month
of Summer (average
temperature of up to
17°C.\(63°F.)) and the
coldest month of Winter
(below −50°C. (−122°F.))
is greater than anywhere
else. Winter here is
colder than in any other
populated spot.

The coniferous forests of
Siberia, the Taiga, are the
most extensive in the
world. The wide-
stretched lowlands rank
second after those of the
Amazon Basin.

There is no clear, natural
boundary between Asia
and Europe which
together form the Eura-
sian mainland. The boun-
dary is usually drawn
along the crest of the
Ural Mountains then
follows the Ural River to
the Caspian Sea then to
the Black Sea via the
Manych Depression and
the Sea of Azov.

Baba Burun at 26° 3′ E.
longitude is the Asian
mainland's westernmost
cape.

① RUSSIA

The Ob drainage system
of 3 million km² (1,158,301 mi²)
is the largest in Asia.

The deepest lake in the
world is Lake Baykal,
1,940 m. (6,363 ft.).

The Caspian Sea
(371,000 km²
(143,243 mi²) is
the largest lake in
the world.

KAZAKHSTAN
②

The deserts and steppes
of Central Asia are the
most extensive area of in-
land drainage in the
world. They cover about
a third of the continent.

⑦ CYPRUS
TURKEY⑥
GEORGIA ③ ①
ARMENIA ④ ⑤ AZER.
⑧ LEBANON ⑨
BAIJ.
SYRIA
⑩ ISRAEL

Asia's highest surface
temperature, 50°C.
(122°F.), has been
recorded at Baghdad.

⑯

UZBEKISTAN

⑲ MONGOLIA

JORDAN
⑪
⑫
IRAQ

⑰
KYRGYZTAN
TURKMENI-
STAN
⑮

The Fedchenko Glacier is
Asia's largest, 1,350 km²
(521 mi²) in size.

The earth's largest va
ty of grass ~ bamboo
can reach up to 40 m
(131 ft.) in length and
up to 30 cm. (12 in.)
thickness in China.

Asia's and the world's
deepest depression is
the Dead Sea in the Jor-
dan Valley, −402 m.
(−1,319 ft.).

⑭
⑬
KUWAIT

TAJIKISTAN
⑱

AFGHANISTAN
㉗

Tibet is the Roof of the
World, 2 million km²
(722,200mi²) above
4,000 m. (13,120 ft.) high.

SAUDI ARABIA
㉓
㉔
BAHRAIN

Mount Everest
(Qomolangma Feng) is
the world's highest moun-
tain, 8,848 m. (29,021 ft.).

C H I N A
㉙

The Arabian Peninsula is
the world's largest and
extends over 2,5 million
km². (965,251 mi²) (larger
than Greenland).

㉕ QATAR
UNITED ㉖
ARAB EMIRATES

PAKISTAN
㉘

NEPAL
㉚

BHUTAN ㉛

The world's heaviest
fall, 26,461 mm.
(1,043 in.) was recor
at Cherrapunji in
1860–61.

㉟ YEMEN
㊱ OMAN

Himalaya is the world's
highest mountain range
with nine of the world's
ten highest peaks and
altogether fourteen
reaching above 8,000 m.
(26,240 ft.).

BANGLA -
DESH㉜

INDIA㊲

㉝
BURMA

㊳ LAOS

THAILAND
㊴

㊵ VIETN

In Summer the east-
bound Southwest Mon-
soon Current replaces
the westerly North
Equatorial Current in the
Indian Ocean, just as the
South West Monsoon
replaces the Northeast
Trade Winds.

㊶
CAMBODIA

㊹ SRI LANKA

㊺ MALDIVES

MALAYSIA
㊻

SINGAPORE
㊼

Cape Buru at 1° 25′N.
latitude is the southern-
most point of the Asian
mainland.

Cape Dezhneva at 169° 45' E. longitude is the most easterly point on the Asian mainland.

Klyuchevskaya Sopka, 4,750 m. (15,580 ft.), is Asia's highest active volcano. The most recent eruption was in 1962.

The northern part of the Sea of Okhotsk is frozen over in February and March

The Sikhote-Alin Range was bombarded in 1947 by the greatest swarm of meteorites known to humankind, over 10,000 meteorites weighing together some 100,000 kg. (220,500 lbs.).

㉔ JAPAN

On the average Tokyo is shaken by an earthquake every week.

㉑ ORTH OREA

OUTH OREA ㉒

ongest river in Asia ourth longest in the , is the Yangtze, km. (3,714 mi.).

The East Asian seas are hit by more than twenty typhoons (tropical storms) during the period September-November every year, the earth's most severely hit region.

WAN

PHILIPPINES ㊷

Borneo, 737,000 km² (284,556 mi²), is Asia's largest island and ranks third in the world.

㊽ NESIA

㉗	AFGHANISTAN	⑨	SYRIA
④	ARMENIA	㉞	TAIWAN
⑤	AZERBAIJAN	⑱	TAJIKISTAN
㉔	BAHRAIN	㊴	THAILAND
㉜	BANGLADESH	⑥	TURKEY
㉛	BHUTAN	⑮	TURKMENISTAN
㊸	BRUNEI	㉖	UNITED ARAB EMIRATES
㉝	BURMA	⑯	UZBEKISTAN
㊶	CAMBODIA	㊵	VIETNAM
㉙	CHINA	㉟	YEMEN
⑦	CYPRUS		
③	GEORGIA		
㊲	INDIA		
㊽	INDONESIA		
⑭	IRAN		
⑫	IRAQ		
⑩	ISRAEL		
⑳	JAPAN		
⑪	JORDAN		
②	KAZAKHSTAN		
⑬	KUWAIT		
⑰	KYRGYZTAN		
㊳	LAOS		
⑧	LEBANON		
㊺	MALAYSIA		
㊾	MALDIVES		
⑲	MONGOLIA		
㉚	NEPAL		
㉑	NORTH KOREA		
㊱	OMAN		
㉘	PAKISTAN		
㊷	PHILIPPINES		
㉕	QATAR		
①	RUSSIA		
㉓	SAUDI ARABIA		
㊼	SINGAPORE		
㉒	SOUTH KOREA		
㊹	SRI LANKA		

① RUSSIA

Rossijskaja Federatsija. Rossija
Russian Federation

Area: 17.075.000 km^2 (6.595.388 mi^2)
Population: 147.400.000
Population growth per annum: –
Life expectancy at birth: –
Literacy: 99%
Capital with population: Moskva (Moscow) 8.970.000
Other important cities with population: S:t Petersburg
5.020.000, Nizjnij Novgorod 1.440.000,
Yekaterinburg (Sverdlovsk) 1.370.000
Language: Russian
Religion: Orthodox
Currency: Rubel = 100 kopek

*Russia alone is almost a continent, with over 10% of the
World's land area, in size equal to South America; the largest
nation of all. Close to 75% of the area is Asiatic (Siberia) but
95% of the population lives west of the Ural Mountains. The
now lost colonial empire of Czars and commissars lasted only
a century, an episode in the millennia of Asiatic History.*

② KAZAKHSTAN

Area: 2.717.000 km^2 (1.049.485 mi^2)
Population: 16.500.000
Population growth per annum: –
Life expectancy at birth: –
Literacy: –
Capital with population: Alma-Ata 1.100.000
Other important cities with population: Karaganda
614.000, Tjimkeut 393.000, Semipalatinsk 334.000
Language: Kazakh, russian
Religion: Islam
Currency: Rubel = 100 kopek

*The steppes of Kazakhstan have in many parts become farm-
lands, but names like Betpak-Dala (Hunger Steppe) and Kyzyl-
Kum (Red Sands) mirror the lack of water and the hard living
conditions that still prevail on the treeless, arid lands. With
cosmonaut Jurij Gagarin mankind in 1961 reached beyond the
horizon of Kazakhstan from Baykonur Space Center.*

③ GEORGIA

Sakartvelos Respublika
(Republic of Georgia)

Area: 69.700 km^2 (26.923 mi^2)
Population: 5.500.000
Population growth per annum: –
Life expectancy at birth: –
Literacy: –
Capital with population: Tbilisi 1.200.000
Other important cities with population: Kutaisi 235.000,
Rustavi 159.000, Batumi 136.000
Language: Georgian, russian
Religion: Orthodox
Currency: Rubel = 100 kopek

*This is Colchis – the Land of the Golden Fleece – the object for
the quest of the Argonauts. The gold has been panned from the
rivers, but the fertile valleys have since lured many conquerors
to Georgia: Roman emperors, Arabic Caliphs, Mongol Khans,
Persian Shahs, Russian Czars – and communist commissars.
Independent 9 Apr 1991.*

④ ARMENIA

Haikakan Hanrapetoutioun (Hajastan)
(Republic of Armenia)

Area: 29.800 km^2 (11.511 mi^2)
Population: 3.700.000
Population growth per annum: –
Life expectancy at birth: –
Literacy: –
Capital with population: Jerevan 1.200.000
Other important cities with population: Kirovakan 159.000,
Leninakan 120.000
Language: Armenian, russian
Religion: Armenian-orthodox
Currency: Rubel = 100 kopek

*Troughout the history the Armenian valleys have been used as
highways by conquering armies. Their history can seldom
recall longer periods of peace or freedom – but notes with
pride that Armenia has been a christian country since AD 300 –
longer than any other nation. Independent 24 Sep 1991.*

⑤ AZERBAIJAN

Azarbaijckan

Area: 86.600 km^2 (33.451 mi^2)
Population: 7.030.000
Population growth per annum: –
Life expectancy at birth: –
Literacy: –
Capital with population: Baku 1.700.000
Other important cities with population: Gjandzja
(Kirovabad) 278.000, Sumgajt 231.000
Language: Azerbaijani, russian
Religion: Islam (shia moslems)
Currency: Rubel = 100 kopek

*Ancient Persians here at Surachana near Baku worshiped the
eternal flames burning over natural oil wells. The Baku area
produced 90% of all oil in Czarist Russia around the turn of the
century, by the Nobel brothers oil company, so the Baku oil has
contributed to the fortune that gave us the Nobel prizes.
Independent 31 Aug 1991.*

⑥ TURKEY

Türkiye Cumhuriyeti
(Republic of Turkey)

Area: 779.452 km^2 (301.077 mi^2)
Population: 50.664.458
Population growth per annum: 2,5%
Life expectancy at birth: Males 58 years, females 63 years
Literacy: 74%
Capital with population: Ankara 2.235.035
Other important cities with population: Istanbul 5.475.982,
Izmir 1.489.772
Language: Turkish
Religion: Islam
Currency: Lira = 100 kurus

*The land that for centuries served as a link between Europe and
Asia now also provides the two continents with a physical link,
the huge bridge over the Bosporus. The world famous
cathedral of Hagia Sofia, built by emperor Justinian 532-537,
was turned into a mosque after the fall of Constantinople in
1453.*

⑦ CYPRUS

Kypriaki Dimokratia-Kibris Cumhuriyeti
(Republic of Cyprus)

Area: 9251 km^2 (3.573 mi^2)
Population: 698.800
Population growth per annum: 1%
Life expectancy at birth: Males 70 years, females 76 years
Literacy: 90% (males 85%, females 96%)
Capital with population: Nikosia 164.500
Other important cities with population: Limassol 118.200
Language: Greek, turkish
Religion: Greek orthodox (80%), islam
Currency: Cyprus pound = 100 cent

The very name of the metal copper is derived from the island's original name, Kypros, as it in ancient times was the World's leading producer of copper. The Greek goddess of love, Aphrodite, was said to have been born here out of the surf. Actually Cyprus itself is a child of the sea, a part of former deep ocean crust lifted high above sea level. Indep. 16 Aug 1960.

⑧ LEBANON

Al-Jumhouriyah al-Lubhaniyah
(Republic of Lebanon)

Area: 10.452 km^2 (4.037 mi^2)
Population: 2.762.000
Population growth per annum: 1,7 %
Life expectancy at birth: Males 66 years, females 71 years
Literacy: 77%
Capital with population: Bayrut 702.000
Other important cities with population: Tripoli 175.000
Language: Arabic
Religion: Islam (57%), christian (43%)
Currency: Lebanese pound = 100 piaster

Since Phoenician times international trade has been the blood of life here at the crossroads of the Levant, populated by fiercely proud clans from all over the Middle East. The lone cedar tree of the flag is almost the last remnant of the mighty forests that once covered Mt. Lebanon. Independent 1 Jun 1944.

⑨ SYRIA

Al-Jumhuriya al-Arabya as-Suriya
(Syrian Arab Republic)

Area: 185.180 km^2 (71.529 mi^2)
Population: 11.300.000
Population growth per annum: 3,6%
Life expectancy at birth: Males 66 years, females 69 years
Literacy: 60%
Capital with population: Damaskus 1.112.214
Other important cities with population: Aleppo 985.413, Homs 346.871
Language: Arabic
Religion: Islam (sunni mosleme), christian
Currency: Syrian pound = 100 piastres

Long before Rome was founded all caravan trails and trade routes "of the World" converged on the capital of Syria, Damascus. Herod, St.Paul and Ibn Battuta as well as Alexander the Great, Julius Ceasar and Genghis Khan have all passed through Damascus. Independent 1 Jan 1944.

⑩ ISRAEL

State of Israel – Medinat Israel

Area: 20.770 km^2 (8.028 mi^2)
Population: 4.406.500
Population growth per annum: 1,6 %
Life expectancy at birth: Males 72 years, females 75 years
Literacy: 92%
Capital with population: Yerushalayim (Jerusalem) 518.200
Other important cities with population: Tel Aviv-Jaffa 1.018.000 , Haifa 596.100
Language: Hebrew, arabic
Religion: Judaism (82%), islam (14%)
Currency: Shekel = 100 agorot

The unprecedented rebirth of a land and a language after two thousand years can be considered a miracle. The fulfillment of ancient prophesies can also be credited to the spirit and the tenacity of the Jewish people. One problem is the fact that three great religions – a majority of mankind – considers Jerusalem a Holy City. Independent 14 May 1948.

⑪ JORDAN

Al Mamlaka al Urduniya al Hashemiyah
(The Hashemite Kingdom of Jordan)

Area: 97.740 km^2 (37.754 mi^2)
(East and West banks)
Population: 3.804.000
Population growth per annum: 1,1%
Life expectancy at birth: Males 62 years, females 66 years
Literacy: 65%
Capital with population: Amman 1.160.000
Other important cities with population: Zarqa 404.500, Irbid 680.200
Language: Arabic
Religion: Islam (90% sunni moslems)
Currency: Jordanian dinar = 1000 fils

Once the rulers of the arid lands east of River Jordan controlled the trade routes across the desert, and accumulated wealth from the incense trade, as can be seen from the glory of the rose-red ruins of Petra. Independent 22 Mar 1946.

⑫ IRAQ

Al-Jumhuriya al'Iraqia
(Republic of Iraq)

Area: 434.924 km^2 (167.997 mi^2)
Population: 17.064.000
Population growth per annum: 2,9%
Life expectancy at birth: Males 58 years, females 63 years
Literacy: 24%
Capital with population: Baghdad 4.868.000
Other important cities with population: al Basrah 1.346.000
Language: Arabic, kurdish
Religion: Islam
Currency: Iraqi dinar = 20 dirhams = 1000 fils

The ancient "Land Between the Rivers", Mesopotamia, is today known as Iraq. The name is said to be derived from a word meaning "origin", a very apt name. Here the wheel and the plow were invented. Here the oldest maps and written records have been found as well as the oldest Codes of Law. Independent 1932.

⑬ KUWAIT
Dowlat al Kuwait
(State of Kuwait)

Area: 17.818 km² (6.883 mi²)
Population: 1.960.000
Population growth per annum: 4,6%
Life expectancy at birth: Males 69 years, females 74 years
Literacy: 70%
Capital with population: Kuwait city 44.335
Other important cities with population: —
Language: Arabic
Religion: Islam (70% sunni moslems)
Currency: Kuwait dinar = 1000 fils

*Kuwait has been known " all over the world " long before it
became associated with oil – or war. Once sturdy dhows sailing
to far away African and East Indian ports brought renown – and
wealth – to Kuwait. The real Sindbad the Sailor may have lived
here. Independent 19 Jun 1961.*

⑭ IRAN
Jomhori-e-Islami-e-Irân
(Islamic Republic of Iran)

Area: 1.648.100 km² (636.607 mi²)
Population: 53.920.000
Population growth per annum: 4,0 %
Life expectancy at birth: Males 58 years, females 59 years
Literacy: 37%
Capital with population: Teheran 6.042.584
Other important cities with population: Mashhad
1.463.508, Esfahan 986.753
Language: Farsi (persian), turkic languages, kurdish
Religion: Islam (shi'i moslems)
Currency: Rial = 100 dinars

*Through milennia Iran (previously called Persia) has
influenced the history and culture of all people. Iran has
nurtured Cyrus, Darius and Xerxes, Zoroaster, Firdawsi and
Omar Khayyam – and ayatollan Khomeini. Iranians invented
polo and developed chess.*

⑮ TURKMENISTAN
Tiorkmenostan

Area: 448.100 km² (173.086 mi²)
Population: 3.500.000
Population growth per annum: –
Life expectancy at birth: –
Literacy: –
Capital with population: Asjchabad 400.000
Other important cities with population: Tjardzjou 161.000,
Marv 89.000
Language: Turkmenian, russian
Religion: Islam
Currency: Rubel = 100 kopek

*The dreaded black sands of the Kara Kum Desert is now
largely covered with green and white cottonfields. This was
made possible by foolishly diverting the water from the Amu-
Darya – a deadly peril to the Aral Sea. In the Kara-Bogaz Gol
the evaporation is made useful through large size salines.
Decl. of independenc Oct 1991*

⑯ UZBEKISTAN
Ozbekiston

Area: 447.000 km² (172.661 mi²)
Population: 19.900.000
Population growth per annum: –
Life expectancy at birth: –
Literacy: –
Capital with population: Taskjent 2.073.000
Other important cities with population: Samarkand
336.000, Buchara 224.000
Language: Uzbekian, russian
Religion: Islam
Currency: Rubel = 100 kopek

*The cultural center of Central Asia. From ancient times famed
cities, Bukhara with carpets and minaretes, the garden city of
Tashkent – and Golden Samarkand, capital of the World's
mightiest empire in the days of Tamerlane – for a while greater
than China. Today Tashkent is biggest in the area.
Independent 31 Aug 1991.*

⑰ KYRGYZTAN

Area: 198.500 km² (76.674 mi²)
Population: 4.300.000
Population growth per annum: –
Life expectancy at birth: –
Literacy: –
Capital with population: Bisjkek (Frunze) 620.000
Other important cities with population: Osj 210.000
Language: Kirghiz, russian
Religion: Islam
Currency: Rubel = 100 kopek

*Kirgizia lies in the very heart of Central Asia, more than 1600
km (995 mi) from the nearest coast (Arabic Sea). No other land
is so isolated from the oceans by mighty mountains and
roadless deserts. Thus there may still be found some of the
World's last wild horses (the Przewalski – horses) that were
discovered first in 1877. Independent 31 Aug 1991.*

⑱ TAJIKISTAN
Tojikiston

Areal: 143.000 km² (55.236 mi²)
Population: 5.500.000
Population growth per annum: –
Life expectancy at birth: –
Literacy: –
Capital with population: Dusjanbe 600.000
Other important cities with population: Chodzjent 153.000
Language: Tadzhik, russian
Religion: Islam (sunni moslems)
Currency: Rubel = 100 kopek

*A large part of the land is dominated by skyhigh mountains,
e.g. Pamir, the "Roof of the World". The formerly highest
mountains of the Soviet Union were named accordingly, Pik
Kommunizma (earlier P. Stalina), Pik Lenina and so on. The
Tadzhiks("The Settled People") have earned fame as good
farmers. Independent 9 Sep 1991*

⑲ MONGOLIA

Bügd Nayramdakh Mongol Ard Uls
(Mongolian People´s Republic)

Area: 1.565.000 km² (604.508 mi²)
Population: 2.017.200
Population growth per annum: 2,6%
Life expectancy at birth: Males 61 years, females 65 years
Literacy: 95%
Capital with population: Ulaanbaatar (Ulan Bator) 500.000
Other important cities with population: Darkhan 80.000
Language: Mongolian
Religion: Buddhism
Currency: Tughrik = 100 mongo

The home of Genghis Khan is now as then a land of unbroken horizons where trees are as rare as people on the windswept grasslands. The Mongols have now exchanged their horses for motor bikes and so only disappear faster out of view. One third of Mongolia is part of the mighty Gobi Desert. Independent 5 Jan 1946.

⑳ JAPAN

Nippon

Area: 377.815 km² (145.938 mi²)
Population: 122.264.000
Population growth per annum: 0,6%
Life expectancy at birth: Males 73 years, females 78 years
Literacy: 99%
Capital with population: Tokyo 8.155.781
Other important cities with population: Yokohama 3.121.601, Nagoya 2.099.564, Kyoto 1.419.390
Language: Japanese
Religion: Buddhist, shintoist, roman catholic
Currency: Yen = 100 sen

Japan has learned to live with earthquakes. Minor tremors are registered more than twice a day, and on average the earth here trembles perceptibly once a week. Only a few cause damage to buildings, as houses here are either very light structures or built to resist even severe shocks.

㉑ NORTH KOREA

Chosun Minchu-chui Inmin Konghwa-guk
(Democratic People´s Republic of Korea)

Area: 120.538 km² (46,560 mi²)
Population: 21.890.000
Population growth per annum: 2,4%
Life expectancy at birth: Males 64 years, females 69 years
Literacy: 85%
Capital with population: P'yongyang 2.639.448
Other important cities with population: Hamhŭng 775.000, Ch'ongjin 754.128
Languages: Korean
Religion: Buddhism (activities discourages), chondism, christian
Currency: Won = 100 chon

Korea is a victim of the 20th century. During the scramble for colonies it was annexed by Japan, and after the Japanese capitulation in 1945 it was divided into two zones of occupation by the U.S.A. and the U.S.S.R. along 38° N lat. The cold war began here and grew into a real war 1950-53. Korea remains divided. Independent 9 Nov 1948.

㉒ SOUTH KOREA

Daehanminkuk Taehan Min'guk
(Republic of Korea)

Area: 99.022 km² (3.825 mi²)
Population: 42.082.128
Population grotwh per annum: 1,2%
Life expectancy at birth: Males 64 years, females 69 years
Litercy: 94%
Capital with population: Soul (Seoul) 9.645.824
Other important cities with population: Pusan 3.516.768, Taegu 2.030.649
Languages: Korean
Religion: Buddhism, confucianism, christian
Currency: Won = 100 chun

In the shadow of China, the Korean people have managed to maintain a national identity – and true independence during most of their history – and also to achieve great cultural feats of their own. Here books were being printed as early as a thousand years ago. Independent 15 Aug 1948.

㉓ SAUDI ARABIA

Al-Mamlaka-al-Arabiya-as-Sa'udiya
(Kingdom of Saudi Arabia)

Area: 2.240.000 km² (865.239 mi²)
Population: 12.006.000
Population growth per annum: 4,0%
Life expectancy at birth: Males 56 years, females 59 years
Literacy: 25%
Capital with population: Riyadh 666.840
Other important cities with population: Jeddah 516.104, Mekkah (Mecca) 366.801
Language: Arabic
Religion: Islam (sunni moslems)
Currency: Riyal = 100 halalah

Like the genie released from Aladdin´s oil lamp, the wealth of oil released from the rocks of the desert have brought fabulous palaces and gardens to its owners. Modern cities, industries, universities and motorways have been created overnight. Independent 20 Sep 1932.

㉔ BAHRAIN

Dawlat al Bahrayn
(State of Bahrain)

Area: 622 km² (240 mi²)
Population: 421.040
Population growth per annum: 2,8%
Life expectancy at birth: Males 66 years, females 69 years
Literacy: 73%
Capital with population: Al Manamah 151.500
Other important cities with population: Al Muharraq 78.000
Language: Arabic
Religion: Islam (sunni moslems 40%, shi´ite moslems 60%)
Currency: Bahrain dinar = 100 fils

The popular joke, that Bahrani gas stations should give free fuel to every buyer of water for coolant was never true but anyhow reflected the lack of water on the oil-rich island, that now is served by a water pipeline following a giant causeway from the mainland. Water is also produced through desalinization plants. Independent 15 Aug 1971.

㉕ QATAR

Dawlat Qatar
(State of Qatar)

Area: 11.437 km^2 (4.418 mi^2)
Population: 371.863
Population growth per annum: 7,2%
Life expectancy at birth: Males 59 years, females 63 years
Literacy: 51%
Capital with population: Al Dawhah 217.294
Other important cities with population: —
Language: Arabic
Religion: Islam
Currency: Riyal = 100 dirhams

A black underground sea of oil has become the source of wealth to Qatar, instead of the Gulf's warm blue waters and its pearl oysters. Independent 1 Sep 1971.

㉖ UNITED ARAB EMIRATES

Ittihad al-Imarat al-Arabiyya

Area: 83.657 km^2 (32.314 mi^2)
Population: 1.600.000
Population growth per annum: -0,5%
Life expectancy at birth: Males 63 years, females 68 years
Literacy: 54%
Capital with population: Abu Dhabi 242.975
Other important cities with population: Dubayy 265.702
Language: Arabic, english
Religion: Islam (sunni moslems)
Currency: UAE dirham = 100 fils

Pearl-fishing and clandestine trade (by some called smuggling) sustained the people on the Trucial Coast after the more lucrative slave trade was abolished by the Perpetual Maritime Truce Treaty, signed by Great Britain and the seven sheiks 1853. Oil has now brought prosperity. Independent 2 Dec 1971.

㉗ AFGHANISTAN

Jamhuria Afghanistan
(Republic of Afghanistan)

Area: 652.090 km^2 (251.881 mi^2)
Population: 18.614.000
Population growth per annum: 2,6%
Life expectancy at birth: Males 43 years, females 44 years
Literacy: 20%
Capital with population: Kabul 1.036.407
Other important cities with population: Kandahar 191.345, Herat 150.497
Language: Pusthu, dari (persian)
Religion: Islam (sunni moslems)
Currency: Afghani = 100 puls

The crossroads of Asia – and once more, a theatre of war. Throughout history, conquering armies have marched through the green valleys beneath Afganistan's forbidding mountains, but no one has ever been able to subjugate its warlike tribes, so fiercely independent, that they were not even united into an emirate before 1747. Independent 1747.

㉘ PAKISTAN

Islami Jamhuriya-e-Pakistan
(Islamic Republic of Pakistan)

Area: 803.943 km^2 (310.537 mi^2)
Population: 102.238.000
Population growth per annum: 3,1%
Life expectancy at birth: Males 55 years, females 54 years
Literacy: 26%
Capital with population: Islamabad 204.364
Other important cities with population: Karachi 5.180.562, Lahore 2.952.689, Faisalabad 1.104.209
Language: Urdu, punjabi, sindhi, pushtu
Religion: Islam (sunni moslems), hindu
Currency: Pakistani rupee = 100 paisa

By peaceful agreement, but through tumultuous upheaval the Islamic nation of Pakistan was created out of parts of former British India. Until 1971 it also comprised Bangladesh 2.000 km. (1.242 mi) away, then known as East Pakistan. Independent 14 Aug 1947.

㉙ CHINA

Zhonghua Renmin Gonghe Guo
(People's Republic of China)

Area: 9.596.961 km^2 (3.706.992 mi^2)
Population: 1.072.220.000
Population growth per annum: 1,1%
Life expectancy at birth: Males 69 years, females 72 years
Literacy: 65%
Capital with population: Beijing (Peking) 5.970.000
Other important cities with population: Shanghai 7.180.000, Tianjin 5.460.000, Shenyang 4.290.000
Language: Mandarinchinese, Shanghai-, Canton-, Fukien-, Hakka-dialects, Tibetan, Vigus (turkic)
Religion: Officially atheist, confucianist, buddhist, taoist
Currency: Yuan = 10 jiao = 100 fen

The lenght of the historical records of China are paralleled only by the Great Wall – one of the greatest human-made structures 4.000 kms (2.500 miles). China is the world's most populous nation, comprising one quarter of all mankind, and will without doubt be one of the superpowers of the future. Independent 1 Oct 1949.

㉚ NEPAL

Nepal Adhirajya
(Kingdom of Nepal)

Area: 147.181 km^2 (56.851 mi^2)
Population: 17.632.960
Population growth per annum: 3,0%
Life expectancy at birth: Males 49 years, females 47 years
Literacy: 21%
Capital with population: Kathmandu 235.160
Other important cities with population: Pátan 79.875
Language: Nepali, indianlanguages
Religion: Hindu (90%), buddhism (5%)
Currency: Nepalese Rupee = 100 paisa

By avoiding involvement in the affairs of the outside world the mountain kingdom of Nepal has like Switzerland managed to remain independent. Nepal shares with China the world's highest peak, Chomolungma, the "Goddess Mother of the World" to the Tibetans, since 1865 also known as Mt. Everest.

③¹ BHUTAN

Druk-yul
(Kingdom of Bhutan)

Area: 46.500 km² (17.961 mi²)
Population: 1.450.000
Population growth per annum: 2,0%
Life expectancy at birth: Males 49 years, females 47 years
Literacy: 5%
Capital with population: Thimphu 15.000
Other important cities with population: —
Language: Dzongkha
Religion: Buddhist (70%), hindu
Currency: Ngultrum = 100 chetrum (Indian rupee also used)

Bhutan's official name Durk Yul translates Land of the Dragon. This is an apt name, as the mountainous former hermit kingdom has many fairy-tale qualities. The only real dragons to be found are those on the national flags.

③² BANGLADESH

Gana Prajatantri Bangladesh
(People's Republic of Bangladesh)

Area: 143.999 km² (55.622 mi²)
Population: 104.100.000
Population growth per annum: 1,9%
Life expectancy at birth: Males 50 years, females 50 years
Literacy: 29%
Capital with population: Dhaka 3.430.312
Other important cities with population: Chittagong 1.391.877, Khulna 646.359
Language: Bengali
Religion: Islam (85%)
Currency: Taka = 100 poisha

The fertile delta lands of Ganges and Brahmaputra, created by floods, have long been more than overpopulated. Troubled by alternating droughts and torrential rains, poor Bangladesh is frequently plagued by hurricanes and devastating tidal floods. Indepedent 20 Dec 1971.

③³ BURMA

Pyidaungsu Myanma Naingngandaw
(Union of Myanmar)

Area: 676.577 km² (261.349 mi²)
Population: 39.840.000
Population growth per annum: 1,8%
Life expectancy at birth: Males 56 years, females 59 years
Literacy: 66%
Capital with population: Rangoon (Yangon) 2.458.712
Other important cities with population: Mandalay 532.985, Moulmein 219.991
Language: Burmese
Religion: Buddhist (85%), hindu, islam
Currency: Kyat = 100 pyas

Burma is still the land of gilded pagodas, where time flows as slowly as the mighty Irrawaddy. In this land of yesterday veteran cars are in everyday use, and elephants haul teak logs to the rivers. Burma's socialists have governed the country since 1948. Independent 4 Jan 1948

③⁴ TAIWAN

Chung-hua Min-Kuo
(Republic of China)

Area: 36.179 km² (13.975 mi²)
Population: 19.700.000
Population growth per annum: 1,1%
Life expectancy at birth: Males 70 years, females 75 years
Literacy: 79%
Capital with population: Taipei 2.637.100
Other important cities with population: Kaohsiung 1.342.797
Language: Chinese (mandarin)
Religion: Buddism
Currency: New Taiwan dollar = 100 cents

The Chinese goverments in Peking and Taipei do agree in one important respect: There is only one China and Taiwan is no more than a Chinese province. The main difference is that the authority of the rulers in Taipei does not extend to any part of ancient, mainland China proper.

③⁵ YEMEN

Al-Jumhuriya al-Yamaniya
(Republic of Yemen)

Area: 531.869 km² (205.301 mi²)
Population: 10.940.266
Population growth per annum: 2,9%
Life expectancy at birth: Males 50 years, females 52 years
Literacy: 53%
Capital with population: San'a 427.150
Other important cities with population: Aden 417.366, Ta'iz 178.043
Language: Arabic
Religion: Islam (shia 50% and sunni 50%)
Currency: Yemen rial = 100 fils, Yemen dinar = 1000 fils

The Roman name "Arabia Felix" ot Lucky Arabia was more apt then than today. The great dams filled up with silt and were destroyed by flood, and incense no longer fetches is weight in gold. Still it is a land of ancient skyscrapers. The 6-7 stories high mud brick houses of Hadramaut seem higher with double rows of windows.

③⁶ OMAN

Saltanat 'Uman
(Sultanate of Oman)

Area: 300.000 km² (115.880 mi²)
Population: 1.334.000
Population growth per annum: 3,0%
Life expectancy at birth: Males 51 years, females 53 years
Literacy: 56%
Capital with population: Masqat 50.000
Other important cities with population: —
Language: Arabic
Religion: Islam
Currency: Rial = 1000 biazas

Like his rival, the King of Portugal, the Sultan of Oman once ruled over a far-flung transocean empire. The red flag of the Sultan flew over forts and trading posts on Asian and African coasts, such as Mombasa and Zanzibar.

(37) INDIA

Bharat
(Republic of India)

Area: 3.166.829 km^2 (1.223.242 mi^2)
Population: 781.374.000
Population growth per annum: 2,0%
Life expectancy at birth: Males 54 years, females 53 years
Literacy: 42%
Capital with population: Delhi 5.714.000
Other important cities with population: Calcutta 9.166.000, Bombay 8.227.000, Madras 4.277.000
Language: Hindi, english
Religion: Hindu, islam
Currency: Rupee = 100 paise

Like the images of Hindu gods that have several eyes, heads and arms (symbolizing their paradoxical nature), the subcontinent and nation of India has many diverse and contradictory features. India is the serene Taj Mahal in cool white marble, and Calcutta with its teeming millions, holy cows and also nuclear power. Independent 26 Jan 1950.

(38) LAOS

Satharanarath Pasathipatai Pasason Lao
(The Lao People's Democratic Republic)

Area: 236.800 km^2 (91.468 mi^2)
Population: 3.799.000
Population growth per annum: 2,7%
Life expectancy at birth: Males 47 years, females 56 years
Literacy: 44%
Capital with population: Vientiane 377.409
Other important cities with population: Savannakhet 50.690, Pakse 44.860, Luang Prabang 44.244
Language: Lao
Religion: Buddhism
Currency: New Kip = 100 at (cents)

Reverence for royalty has always transcended life in Laos. A royal prince led the communists to victory in 1975 and abolished monarchy. Several hundred huge carved burial urns, presumably containing royal remains from prehistoric times, still dot the Plain of Jars. Independent 20 Jun 1954.

(39) THAILAND

Prathes Thai, Muang-Thai
(Kingdom of Thailand)

Area: 513.115 km^2 (198.199 mi^2)
Population: 54.536.000
Population growth per annum: 1,9%
Life expectancy at birth: Males 62 years, females 67 years
Literacy: 88%
Capital with population: Bangkok 5.609.352
Other important cities with population: Chiangmai 101.595
Language: Thai
Religion: Buddhism
Currency: Baht = 100 satangs

Thailand has throughout history managed to survive and maintain independence by deft diplomacy and careful observation of prevailing wind directions. Internally the king retains power in much the same way.

(40) VIETNAM

Công Hòa Xã Hôi Chu Nghja Viêt Nam
(Socialist Republic of Vietnam)

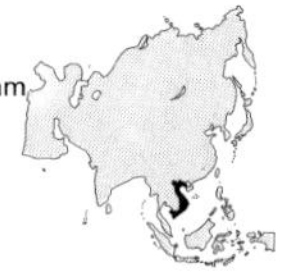

Area: 329.566 km^2 (127.301 mi^2)
Population: 64.000.000
Population growth per annum: 2,4%
Life expectancy at birth: Males 56 years, females 59 years
Literacy: 84%
Capital with population: Hanoi 2.000.000
Other important cities with population: Ho Chi Minh city 4.000.000, Hai Phong 1.279.067
Language: Vietnamese
Religion: Buddhism
Currency: New Dông = 10 xu

The proud and martial Vietnamese of the Red River basin have been called the Prussians of Indo-China. With military aid from the U.S.S.R and captured U.S arms they have now become the strongest military power of South East Asia. Independent 20 Jul 1954.

(41) CAMBODIA

Roat Kampuchea
(State of Cambodia)

Area: 181.035 km^2 (69.928 mi^2)
Population: 7.688.000
Population growth per annum: 0,7%
Life expectancy at birth: Males 47 years, females 50 years
Literacy: 36%
Capital with population: Phnom-Penh 700.000
Other important cities with population: —
Language: Khmer
Religion: Buddhism
Currency: New Riel = 100 sen

Clashing radical idealogies have here just made life worse for everyone. Pleasant Cambodia now lies in ruins just like the mighty remains from its glorious past. Famous Angkor, for over 500 years the capital of all Indochina anyhow was spared further destruction. Independent 7 Nov 1953.

(42) PHILIPPINES

Republika ng Pilipinas
(Republic of Philippines)

Area: 300.000 km^2 (115.880 mi^2)
Population: 58.721.307
Population growth per annum: 2,4%
Life expectancy at birth: Males 63 years, females 67 years
Literacy: 83%
Capital with population: Manila 1.630.485
Other important cities with population: Quezon 1.165.865, Davao 610.375, Cebu 490.281
Language: Filipino, english
Religion: Roman catholic (85%), islam (10%)
Currency: Philippine Peso = 100 centavos

East and West meet in this island natio,n east of the Asian mainland, yet west of the Pacific. The people of this former colony of Spain (1521-1899) and the United States (1899-1942) are of Malayo-Polynesian stock but speak Spanish, English and Pilipino. Most are Roman catholics but some are Moslems. Independent 4 Jul 1946.

㊸ BRUNEI

Negara Brunei Darussalam
(State of Brunei)

Area: 5.765km² (2.227 mi²)
Population: 226.300
Population growth per annum: –
Life expectancy at birth: –
Literacy: 7.8 %
Capital with population: Bandar Seri Begawan 54.000
Other important cities with population: none
Language: Malay, english, chinese
Religion: Islam (63%), buddhist (14%), christian (10%)
Currency: Brunei dollar = 100 cents

A land flowing with oil – where the citizens can use their own money to buy "milk and honey" – as they do not have to pay any income taxes! No wonder the Sultan of Brunei can continue to rule – with broad popular support. Indepedent 31 dec 1983.

㊹ SRI LANKA

Sri Lanka Prajatantrika Samajawadi Janarajaya
(Democratic Socialist Republic of Sri Lanka)

Area: 65.610 km² (25.343 mi²)
Population: 16.361.000
Population growth per annum: 1,6%
Life expectancy at birth: Males 66 years, females 70 years
Literacy: 86%
Capital with population: Colombo 683.000
Other important cities with population: Dehiwala-Mt. Lavinia 191.000, Jaffna 143.000
Language: Sinhala, tamil, english
Religion: Buddhism (70%), hindu (15%), islam, christian
Currency: Sri Lanka rupee = 100 cents

Ceylon is even today a land of legends. On the top of Adam´s peak there is a 1.5 m (5ft.) long foot print, claimed to be left in the rock by Adam (or by Buddha, or Sheva, or St. Thomas according to preference). Independent 4 Nov 1948.

㊺ MALDIVES

Divehi Jumhuriya
(Republic of Maldives)

Area: 298 km² (115 mi²)
Population: 200.000
Population growth per annum: 3,4%
Life expectancy at birth: —
Literacy: 93%
Capital with population: Malé 46.334
Other important cities with population: —
Language: Dhivehi
Religion: Islam (Sunni Moslims)
Currency: Rufiyaa = 100 laaris

In the days when the dhows carried carpets, ivory and slaves over the Indian Ocean, the thousand coral islands of the Maldives lay at the crossroad of the ocean. Now even the names of the atolls. Tiladummati, Fadiffolu, Miladummadulu sound of long lost fame and tales of far away lands. Independent 11 Nov 1968.

㊻ MALAYSIA

Persekutuan Tanah Malaysia
(Federation of Malaysia)

Area: 329.759 km² (127.375 mi²)
Population: 16.968.000
Population growth per annum: 2,6%
Life expectancy at birth: Males 65 years, females 69 years
Literacy: 70%
Capital with population: Kuala Lumpur 919.610
Other important cities with population: George Town (Penang) 248.241, Ipoh 293.849
Language: Bahasa malaysia, english, tamil
Religion: Islam (53%), buddhist (19%), hindu
Currency: Ringgit = 100 sen

In this land reigning rajahs and sultans, each in turn, serve five years as 'Supreme Head of State'. This unusual system of royal rotation has brought unity and stability to this geographically divided nation. In Sarawak the world´s largest cave 700 x 300 m. (2.296 x 984 ft.) has been found. Independent 16 sep 1963.

㊼ SINGAPORE

Hsin-chia-p'o Kung-ho -Kou/Republik Singapura
(Republic of Singapore)

Area: 622 km² (240 mi²)
Population: 2.647.000
Population growth per annum: 2,4 %
Life expectancy at birth: Males 70 years, females 75 years
Literacy: 83%
Capital with population: Singapore 2.647.000
Other important cities with population: none
Language: Chinese, malay, tamil, english
Religion: Buddism, taoism, hindu, christian
Currency: Singapore dollar = 100 cents

A modern City state, living off free entrepot trade and local manufacturing industries requiring skilled labour. Singapore survives without hinderland. Independent 9 Aug 1965.

㊽ INDONESIA

Republik Indonesia
(Republic of Indonesia)

Area: 1.191.443 km² (460.215 mi²)
Population: 170.534.000
Population growth per annum: 2,2 %
Life expectancy at birth: Males 51 years, females 54 years
Literacy: 67 %
Capital with population: Jakarta 7.347.830
Other important cities with population:
Surabaya 2.223.600, Medan 1.805.500, Bandung 1.566.700
Language: Bahasa indonesia
Religion: Islam (87%)
Currency: Rupiah = 100 sen

Panta rei (all flows) ought to be the motto of this nation of over 13.000 islands. No other state has so many active volcanoes. On Java alone there is 27. Here the island volcano of Krakatoa, 1.800 m.(6.000 ft.) high, disintegrated in 1883 in the most catastrophic eruption in history. Indepedent 17 Aug 1945.

OCEANIA

Area: 8,923,000 km² (3,444,278 mi²)
Population: 25,000,000
Density of population per km²: 2.8 (per mi²: 7.4)

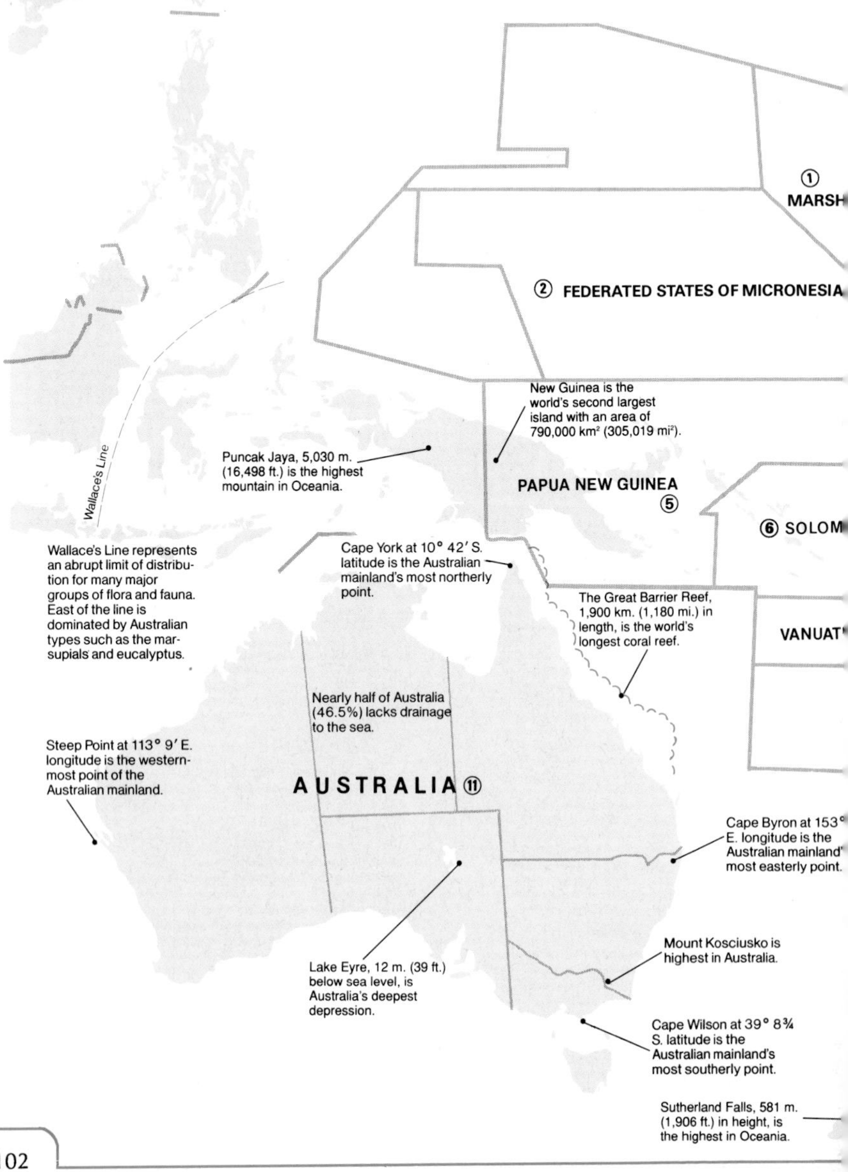

① **MARSH**

② **FEDERATED STATES OF MICRONESIA**

New Guinea is the world's second largest island with an area of 790,000 km² (305,019 mi²).

Puncak Jaya, 5,030 m. (16,498 ft.) is the highest mountain in Oceania.

PAPUA NEW GUINEA ⑤

⑥ **SOLOM**

Wallace's Line

Cape York at 10° 42′ S. latitude is the Australian mainland's most northerly point.

The Great Barrier Reef, 1,900 km. (1,180 mi.) in length, is the world's longest coral reef.

VANUAT

Wallace's Line represents an abrupt limit of distribution for many major groups of flora and fauna. East of the line is dominated by Australian types such as the marsupials and eucalyptus.

Nearly half of Australia (46.5%) lacks drainage to the sea.

Steep Point at 113° 9′ E. longitude is the western-most point of the Australian mainland.

A U S T R A L I A ⑪

Cape Byron at 153° E. longitude is the Australian mainland' most easterly point.

Mount Kosciusko is highest in Australia.

Lake Eyre, 12 m. (39 ft.) below sea level, is Australia's deepest depression.

Cape Wilson at 39° 8¾ S. latitude is the Australian mainland's most southerly point.

Sutherland Falls, 581 m. (1,906 ft.) in height, is the highest in Oceania.

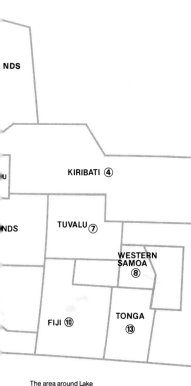

⑪	AUSTRALIA
②	FEDERATED STATES OF MICRONESIA
⑩	FIJI
④	KIRIBATI
①	MARSHALL ISLANDS
③	NAURU
⑫	NEW ZEALAND
⑤	PAPUA NEW GUINEA
⑥	SOLOMON ISLANDS
⑬	TONGA
⑦	TUVALU
⑨	VANUATU
⑧	WESTERN SAMOA

NDS

KIRIBATI ④

U

NDS   TUVALU ⑦

WESTERN
SAMOA
⑧

FIJI ⑩   TONGA
⑬

The area around Lake Taupo is a unique landscape of volcanic features such as bubbling mud cauldrons, hot springs, solfataras and fumaroles. The geyser Waimangu used to be the world's greatest, the column of water could reach as high as 450 m. (1,476 ft.).

NEW
EALAND ⑫

① MARSHALL ISLANDS
Republic of the Marshall Islands

Areal: 181 km²
Population: 40.609
Population growth per annum: –
Life expectancy at birth: –
Literacy: –
Capital with population: Majuro
Other important cities with population: none
Language: English, two native languages , japanese
Religion: Christian
Currency: US dollar

The Word Bikini first became synonymous with the Bomb – and then the name of the teeny-weeny two piece bathing suit – but for inhabitants it became (and is) a paradise lost, all in 1946. On the other islands life has not been so dramatically disrupted. Independent 1986.

② FEDERATED STATES OF MICRONESIA

Area: 702 km² (271 mi²)
Population: 108.600
Population growth per annum: 2,7 %
Life expectancy at birth: Males 64 years, females 68 years
Literacy: 76 %
Capital with population: Kolonia
Other important cities with population: none
Language: English, four native languages
Religion: Protestant, roman catholic
Currency: US dollar

Talking their rightful place in the world of today, the young here still take pride in the ancient culture of their young nation. The World´s hardest currency – the mill-stone-sized coral blocks (up to 3.7 m across) – has never been deva-luated on Yap Island. One of their unwieldy coins still worth a good canoe. Independent 1986.

③ NAURU
Republic of Nauru

Area: 21.3 km² (8 mi²)
Population: 8.042
Population growth per annum: 1,8 %
Life expectancy at birth: –
Literacy: 99 %
Capital with population: No official capital
Other important cities with population: none
Language: Nauruan, english
Religion: Protestant, roman catholic
Currency: Austalian dollar = 100 cents

It is easy to drive around all of Nauru in a car in less time that it takes for an astronaut to circle the Earth, as the total circumference is only 34 km. (21 miles). Independent 31 Jan 1968.

④ KIRIBATI
Ribaberikin Kiribati
(Republic of Kiribati)

Area: 861 km² (332 mi²)
Population: 66.250
Population growth per annum: 1,8 %
Life expectancy at birth: –
Literacy: –
Capital with poplulation: Bairiki 20.000
Other important cities with population: none
Language: Kiribati, english
Religion: Protestant, roman catholic
Currency: Australian dollar = 100 cents

No other nation is spread so thinly as Kiribati, with land size smaller than New York city scattered over an area wider than the contiguous United States! Kiribati always has two days, as it is divided by the dateline. Independent 12 Jul 1979.

⑤ PAPUA NEW GUINEA
Independent State of Papua-New Guinea

Area: 462.840 km² (178.780 mi²)
Population: 3.479.400
Population growth per annum: 2,2%
Life expectancy at birth: Males 57 years, females 56 years
Literacy: 32%
Capital with population: Port Moresby 145.300
Other important cities with population: Lae 76.600
Language: English, numerous local languages
Religion: Animist, protestant, roman catholic
Currency: Kina = 100 toea

The official "Pidgin English" developed here during the last hundred years is quite a new language, using mainly English words. E.g. " Ars bilong diwai" means "roots"(Diwai is a Melanesian word for tree, bilong equals to – and ars is just the very bottom of anything). Independent 16 Sep 1975.

⑥ SOLOMON ISLANDS

Area: 27.556 km² (10.644 mi²)
Population: 290.000
Population growth per annum: 3,4%
Life expectancy at birth: –
Litercy: –
Capital with population: Honiara 24.000
Other important cities with population: none
Languages: English, numerous local languages
Religion: Protestant, roman catholic
Currency: Solomon Island dollar = 100 cents

The Solomon Islands suffered heavily during World War II during the battles of Guadalcanal and the Coral Sea. Yet some islands still profit from the spoils of war by exporting scrap iron. Independent 7 Jul 1978.

⑦ TUVALU

Area: 25 km² (10 mi²)
Population: 8.229
Population growth per annum: 1,6%
Life expectancy at birth: Males 57 years, females 59 years
Literacy: –
Capital with population: Fongafale 2.810
Other important cities with population: none
Language: Tuvaluan, english
Religion: Protestant
Currency: Australian dollar = 100 cents

Tuvalu comprises of nine low coral atolls (formerly also called Lagoon or Ellice islands) in the very centre of the island world of the South Pacific. In spite of the fact that an atoll can measure 10-20 km. (6-12 mi) across its land area is almost negligible. Independent 1 Oct 1978

⑧ WESTERN SAMOA

Malotuto'atasi o Samoa i Sisifo
(Independent state of Western Samoa)

Area: 2.831 km^2 (1.094 mi^2)
Population: 158.940
Population growth per annum: 1,3%
Life expectancy at birth: 63 år
Literacy: 98%
Capital with population: Apia 33.170
Other important cities with population:none
Language: Samoan, english
Religion: Protestant, roman catholic
Currency: Tala = 100 sene

Truly Polynesian Samoa is in many ways an incarnation of the South Sea Islands – complete with beaches and palms and friendly people, but it is at the same time a modern society with TV, colleges, and all the rest. Independent 1 Jan 1962.

⑨ VANUATU

Ripablik blong Vanuatu
(Republic of Vanuatu)

Area: 14.760 km^2 (5.701 mi^2)
Population: 149.400
Population growth per annum: 3,3%
Life expectancy at birth: –
Litercy: 53%
Capital with population: Port Vila 15.000
Other important cities with population: none
Language: Bislama, english, french
Religion: Protestant, roman catholic
Currency: Vatu = 100 centimes

Two colonial powers – France and Great Britain – ruled 1906-80 the former Condominium of the New Hebrides in quaint harmony with strict and sometimes silly divisions of authority. Thus three languages are in common use – a good asset in international context. Independent 30 Jul 1980.

⑩ FIJI

Matanitu Ko Fiti
(Republic of Fiji)

Area: 18.376 km^2 (7.098 mi^2)
Population: 715.375
Population growth per annum: 2%
Life expectancy at birth: Males 70 years, females 75 years
Literacy: 79%
Capital with population: Suva 71.608
Other important cities with population: Lautoka 28.728
Language: English, fijian, hindustani, urdu, chinese
Religion: Christian (53%), hindu (38%)
Currency: Fijian dollar = 100 cents

Volcanic soil, tropical sunshine and gentle trade winds bringing regular rainfall favour suger cane cultivation. Sugar has become the major product of Fiji. Independent 10 Oct 1970.

⑪ AUSTRALIA

Commonwealth of Australia

Area: 7.682.300 km^2 (2.967.421 mi^2)
Population: 16.263.319
Population growth per annum: 1,3%
Life expectancy at birth: Males 70 years, females 76 years
Literacy: 99%
Capital with population: Canberra 285.800
Other important cities with population: Sydney 3.430.600, Melbourne 2.942.000, Brisbane 1.171.300
Language: English, aboriginal languages
Religion: Protestant (61%), roman catholic (26%)
Currency: Australian dollar = 100 cents

The only land that is quite different. Australia, comprises of an entire continent with a quite different fauna and flora – eucalyptus trees and kangaroos, egg-laying mammals and koalas – the living teddy bears. The1,900 km. (1,180 mi) long Great Barrier Reef is the world´s largest coral reef. Independent 1 Jan 1901.

⑫ NEW ZEALAND

Area: 268.046 km^2 (103.537 mi^2)
Population: 3.347.300
Population growth per annum: 0,9%
Life expectancy at birth: Males 70 years, females 76 years
Literacy: 99%
Capital with population: Wellington 351.400
Other important cities with population: Auckland 899.200, Christchurch 333.200
Language: English, maori
Religion: Protestant, roman catholic
Currency: New Zealand dollar = 100 cents

Far from being the opposite of England, green and civilized New Zealand is at the Antipodes seen from Britain – that is exactly at the other side of the earth. On the other hand – from New Zealand England is at the Autipodes. Independent 1931.

⑬ TONGA

Pule'anga Fakatu'i 'o Tonga
(Kingdom of Tonga)

Area: 748 km^2 (289 mi^2)
Population: 95.200
Population growth per annum: 0,4%
Life expectancy at birth: –
Literacy: 99%
Capital with population: Nuku'alofa 28.899
Other important cities with population: none
Language: English, tongan
Religion: Protestant, roman catholic
Currency: Pa'anga = 100 seniti

The " Friendly Islands", Captain Cook's name for Tonga, are not easy to reach due to lack of good harbours. The island of Niuafoou has become known among philatelists as "Tin Can Island" because of the method used to collect and deliver mail. Independent 4 Jun 1970.

AFREICA

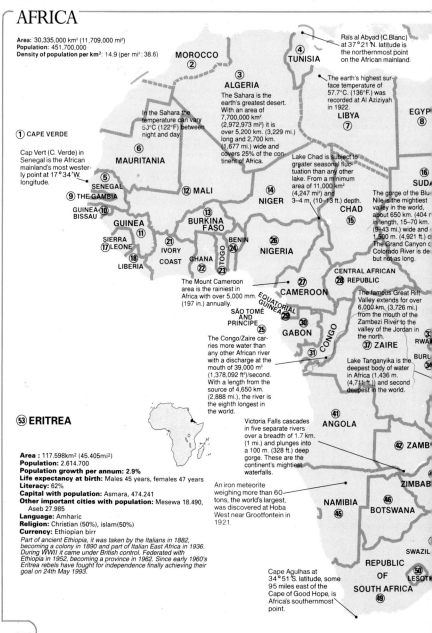

Area: 30,335,000 km² (11,709,000 mi²)
Population: 451,700,000
Density of population per km²: 14.9 (per mi² : 38.6)

MOROCCO ②

TUNISIA ④

Ra's al Abyad (C.Blanc) at 37° 21 'N. latitude is the northernmost point on the African mainland.

ALGERIA ③
The Sahara is the earth's greatest desert. With an area of 7,700,000 km² (2,972,973 mi²) it is over 5,200 km. (3,229 mi.) long and 2,700 km. (1,677 mi.) wide and covers 25% of the continent of Africa.

In the Sahara the temperature can vary 50°C (122°F) between night and day.

The earth's highest surface temperature of 57.7°C. (136°F.) was recorded at Al Aziziyah in 1922.

LIBYA ⑦

EGYPT ⑧

① **CAPE VERDE**

Cap Vert (C. Verde) in Senegal is the African mainland's most westerly point is at 17°34'W. longitude.

MAURITANIA ⑥

Lake Chad is subject to greater seasonal fluctuation than any other lake. From a minimum area of 11,000 km² (4,247 mi²) and 3–4 m. (10–13 ft.) depth.

SUDAN ⑯

⑤ **SENEGAL**
⑨ **THE GAMBIA**
⑩ **GUINEA-BISSAU**
GUINEA ⑪
⑰ **SIERRA LEONE**
⑱ **LIBERIA**

⑫ **MALI**

NIGER ⑭

BURKINA FASO ⑬

CHAD ⑮

The gorge of the Blue Nile is the mightiest valley in the world, about 650 km. (404 mi) in length, 15–70 km. (9–43 mi.) wide and 1,500 m. (4,921 ft.) deep. The Grand Canyon of the Colorado River is deeper but not as long.

IVORY COAST ㉑
GHANA ㉒
TOGO ㉓
BENIN ㉔
NIGERIA ㉖

The Mount Cameroon area is the rainiest in Africa with over 5,000 mm. (197 in.) annually.

CAMEROON ㉗
EQUATORIAL GUINEA ㉙
SÃO TOMÉ AND PRINCIPE ㉕
GABON ㉚
CONGO ㉛

CENTRAL AFRICAN REPUBLIC ㉘

The famous Great Rift Valley extends for over 6,000 km, (3,726 mi.) from the mouth of the Zambezi River to the valley of the Jordan in the north.

ZAIRE ㊲
RWANDA ㉝
BURUNDI ㉞

The Congo/Zaire carries more water than any other African river with a discharge at the mouth of 39,000 m³ (1,378,092 ft³)/second. With a length from the source of 4,650 km. (2,888 mi.), the river is the eighth longest in the world.

Lake Tanganyika is the deepest body of water in Africa (1,436 m. (4,711 ft.) and second deepest in the world.

㊼ **ERITREA**

Area: 117.598km² (45.405mi²)
Population: 2.614.700
Population growth per annum: 2.9%
Life expectancy at birth: Males 45 years, females 47 years
Literacy: 62%
Capital with population: Asmara, 474.241
Other important cities with population: Mesewa 18.490, Aseb 27.985
Language: Amharic
Religion: Christian (50%), islam(50%)
Currency: Ethiopian birr

Part of ancient Ethiopia, it was taken by the Italians in 1882, becoming a colony in 1890 and part of Italian East Africa in 1936. During WWII it came under British control. Federated with Ethiopia in 1952, becoming a province in 1962. Since early 1960's Eritrea rebels have fought for independence finally achieving their goal on 24th May 1993.

④ **ANGOLA**

Victoria Falls cascades in five separate rivers over a breadth of 1.7 km. (1 mi.) and plunges into a 100 m. (328 ft.) deep gorge. These are the continent's mightiest waterfalls.

㊷ **ZAMBIA**

ZIMBABWE

An iron meteorite weighing more than 60 tons, the world's largest, was discovered at Hoba West near Grootfontein in 1921.

NAMIBIA ㊺

BOTSWANA ㊻

SWAZILAND

REPUBLIC OF SOUTH AFRICA ㊾

㊿ **LESOTHO**

Cape Agulhas at 34°51'S. latitude, some 95 miles east of the Cape of Good Hope, is Africa's southernmost point.

The Nile (with Kagera) is the world's longest river (6,690 km. (4,155 mi.)). Some two-thirds of the water in the lower river comes from the Abbysinian Highlands since most of the water from Lake Victoria evaporates in the marshlands of the Sudd.

ERITREA
㊳

DJIBOUTI
⑳

㊵

ETHIOPIA
Ranked the world's hottest place Massawa has an average year round temperature of 30.2°C. (86.4°F.).

Lake Assale in the Danakil Desert is Africa's deepest depression, 174 m. (571 ft.) below sea level.

Ra's Hafun at 51°25'E. longitude is the most easterly point on the African mainland.

㊱ **SOMALIA**

DA

KENYA
㉟

Kilimanjaro is the highest mountain in Africa and one of the world's highest volcanoes. The mountain rises nearly 5,000 m. (16,404 ft.) above the surrounding savanna.

㊵ **SEYCHELLES**

'Victoria (62,940 24,301 mi²)) is a's largest lake and hird largest in the.

NZANIA
㊳

LAWI

㊴

㊱ **COMOROS ISLANDS**

BIQUE

㊽ **MADAGASCAR**

㊷ **MAURITIUS**

Madagascar (587,000 km² (226,641 mi²)) is Africa's largest island and ranks fourth in the world.

ca's highest waterfall a drop of 948 m. 10 ft.) lies on the ela in the Drakensberg. also the world's second est falls.

③ ALGERIA
㊶ ANGOLA
㉔ BENIN
㊻ BOTSWANA
⑬ BURKINA FASO
㉞ BURUNDI
㉗ CAMEROON
① CAPE VERDE
㉘ CENTRAL AFRICAN REP.
⑮ CHAD
㊴ COMOROS ISLANDS
㉛ CONGO
⑳ DJIBOUTI
⑧ EGYPT
㉙ EQUATORIAL GUINEA
㊳ ERITREA
⑲ ETHIOPIA
㉚ GABON
㉒ GHANA
⑪ GUINEA
⑩ GUINEA-BISSAU
㉑ IVORY COAST
㉟ KENYA
㊿ LESOTHO
⑱ LIBERIA
⑦ LIBYA
㊽ MADAGASCAR
㊸ MALAWI
⑫ MALI
⑥ MAURITANIA
㊷ MAURITIUS
② MOROCCO
㊹ MOZAMBIQUE
㊺ NAMIBIA
⑭ NIGER
㉖ NIGERIA
㊾ REPUBLIC OF SOUTH AFRICA
㉝ RWANDA

㉕ SÃO TOMÉ AND PRINCIPE
⑤ SENEGAL
㊵ SEYCHELLES
⑰ SIERRA LEONE
㊱ SOMALIA
⑯ SUDAN
㊿ SWAZILAND
㊳ TANZANIA
⑨ THE GAMBIA
㉓ TOGO
④ TUNISIA
㉜ UGANDA
㊲ ZAIRE
㊷ ZAMBIA
㊼ ZIMBABWE

① CAPE VERDE

República de Cabo Verde
(Republic of Cabo Verde)

Area: 4.033 km² (1.558 mi²)
Population: 334.000
Population growth per annum: 1,4%
Life expectancy at birth: Males 62 years, females 66 years
Literacy: 47%
Capital with population: Cidade de Praia 57.748
Other important cities with population: Mindelo 36.746
Language: Portuguese, crioulo
Religion: Roman Catholic
Currency: Escudo = 100 centavos

Heat and drought are two words that characterize these volcanic islands, named after a cape on the mainland, 580 km. (360 mi.) to the east. Salt is produced by evaporation, an industri with good natural procpects. Independent 5 Jul 1975.

② MOROCCO

Al Mamlaka al-Maghrebia
(Kingdom of Morocko)

Area: 458.730 km² (177.192 mi²)
Population: 23.376.000
Population growth per annum: 2,8%
Life expectancy at birth: Males 58 years, females 62 years
Literacy: 33%
Capital with population: Rabat 1.287.000
Other important cities with population: Dar el Beida (Casablanca) 2.904.000, Marrakech 330.000
Language: Arabic, berber
Religion: Islam (Sunni Moslems)
Currency: Dirham = 100 centimes

East and west meet in Morocco. For the "western" world it is a land of the Near East – and for the "eastern", Islamic world it is a land of the Maghreb, The west.The mosques and palaces of cities such as Marrakech and Fez are famous in the west as well as in the east. Independent 28 Mar 1956.

③ ALGERIA

al-Jumhuria al-Jazairiya
ad-Dimuqratiya ash-Shabiya
(Democratic and Popular Republic of Algeria)

Area: 2.381.741 km² (919.988 mi²)
Population: 23.850.000
Population growth per annum: 3,0%
Life expectancy at birth: Males 59 years, females 61 years
Literacy: 45%
Capital with population: Al Jaza'ir (Algiers) 1.721.607
Other important cities with population: Ouahran (Oran) 663.504, Qacentina (Constantine) 448.578
Language: Arabic, berber
Religion: Islam (sunni moslems)
Currency: Algerian dinar = 100 centimes

Four-fifths of the land is desert. The prosperous and fertile coastal area is just a thin gilt edge along the northern rim of the majestic Sahara. Covering 5200 by 2700 km or 7,7 million km² (2.972.973mi²), the Sahara is the world's largest desert, so that the barren wastes of Algeria comprise of only 25% of the Sahara! Independent 3 Jul 1962.

④ TUNISIA

Al-Jumhuriya at-Tunisiya
(Republic of Tunisia)

Area: 154.300 km² (59.601 mi²)
Population: 7.464.900
Population growth per annum: 3,0%
Life expectancy at birth: Males 60 years, females 63 years
Literacy: 54 %
Capital with population: Tunis 596.654
Other important cities with population: Sfax 231.911 Ariana 98.655
Language: Arabic, french
Religion: Islam
Currency: Tunisian dinar = 100 millimes

A nation with many ties. Ties of history and culture link it forever to all its Mediterranean neighbours, and very strongly to France. Ties of language and blood bind it to the Arabic West, Maghreb. This is also the land of Carthage, that fought Rome for the hegemony of "the world". Independent 20 Mar 1956.

⑤ SENEGAL

République du Sénégal
(Republic of Senegal)

Area: 196.192 km² (75.783 mi²)
Population: 6.982.000
Population growth per annum: 2,2%
Life expectancy at birth: Males 44 years, females 48 years
Literacy: 28%
Capital with population: Dakar 978.553
Other important cities with population: Thiés 126.886 Kaolack 115.679
Language: French, tribal languages
Religion: Islam (90%), christian (5%), animist
Currency: CFA-franc = 100 centimes

The Gateway to West Africa. The leading metropolis of the area, Dakar, is favoured by a magnificent nartural harbour. The location near Cap Vert, the most westerly point of the mainland made Dakar the natural staging post for transatlantic flights to South America until the 1960's. Independent 20 Aug 1960.

⑥ MAURITANIA

al Jumhuria al-Islamiya al Muritaniya
(Islamc Republic of Mauritania)

Area: 1.030.700 km² (398.126 mi²)
Population: 1.894.000
Population growth per annum: 2,2%
Life expectancy at birth: Males 44 years, females 48 years
Literacy: 17%
Capital with population: Nouakchott 500.000
Other important cities with population: none
Language: French, arabic
Religion: Islam
Currency: Ouguiya = 5 khoums

For the Arabs and the Islamic world, Mauritania is the Far West, the Land of the Sunset. Only a fraction of the vast country is habitable, and the lack of water is a severe handicap to any development. Independent 28 Nov 1960.

⑦ LIBYA

Al-Jamahiriya Al-Arabiya Al-Libya
Al-Shabiya Al-Ishtirakiya Al-Uzma
(Socialist People´s Libyan Arab Jamahiriya)

Area: 1.759.540 km² (679.653 mi²)
Population: 3.955.000
Population growth per annum: 4,5%
Life expectancy at birth: Males 58 years, females 62 years
Literacy: 67%
Capital with population: Tripoli 858.000
Other important cities with population: Benghazi 368.000
Misurata 117.000
Language: Arabic
Religion: Islam (Sunni Moslems)
Currency: Libyan dinar = 1000 dirhams

Elusive Libya retains in our times some of the enigmatic features of Africa. The central volcanic area, the Black Hills that are clearly visible on space images of Africa, were recently mapped with the aid of satellite photos. Independent 24 Dec 1951.

⑧ EGYPT

Jumhuriyat Misr al-Arabiya
(Arab Republic of Egypt)

Area: 1.001.449 km² (386.827 mi²)
Population: 50.740.000
Population growth per annum: 2,3%
Life expectancy at birth: Males 58 years, females 61 years
Literacy: 44%
Capital with population: Al Qahira (Cairo) 8.539.000
Other important cities with population: El Iskandariyah (Alexandria) 2.893.000, El Giza 1.670.8000
Language: Arabic
Religion: Islam (sunni moslems 90%)
Currency: Egyptian pound = 100 piastres

The whole of inhabitable Egypt is nothing but an oasis – totally depedent on the water of the Nile. In general the width of the cultivated and settle land is only 3-15 km (2-9 mi). Of the seven wonders of the ancient world Egypt has two, and even if the Pharos has been destroyed, the Pyramids still stand. Independent 28 Feb 1922.

⑨ THE GAMBIA

Republic of the Gambia

Area: 11.295 km² (4.363 mi²)
Population: 788.163
Population growth per annum: 3,5%
Life expectancy at birth: Males 43 years, females 47 years
Literacy: 20%
Capital with population: Banjul 44.188
Other important cities with population: Serekunda 68.433
Language: English, mandinka, wolof, fula
Religion: Islam (85%), christian, animist
Currency: Dalasi = 100 butut

"The land that is the river". The British Empire was built by traders – and for trading a 15-25 km wide strip along the banks of the navigable River Gambia was sufficient. Here Alex Hailey found his roots, and described it in his bestseller. Independent 18 Feb 1965

⑩ GUINEA-BISSAU

Republica da Guiné-Bissau
(Republic of Guinea-Bissau)

Area: 36.125 km² (13.954 mi²)
Population: 943.000
Population growth per annum: 3,5%
Life expectancy at birth: Males 44 years, females 48 years
Literacy: 31%
Capital with population: Bissau 125.000
Other important cities with population: none
Language: Portuguese, crioulo
Religion: Animist, islam (30%), christians(5%)
Currency: Guinea peso = 100 centavos

A new name heralds a new era. For more than 500 years this land was known as Portuguese Guinea. No other land has been a colony for so many years. Guinea Bissau has an exceptional un-African archipelago coast. Independent 24 Sep 1973.

⑪ GUINEA

République de Guinée
(Republic of Guinea)

Area: 245.857 km² (94.967 mi²)
Population: 6.533.000
Population growth per annum: 2,5%
Life expectancy at birth: Males 47 years, females 50 years
Literacy: 28%
Capital with population: Conakry 705.280
Other important cities with population: Kankan 88.760
Language: French, tribal languages
Religion: Islam (69%), animist
Currency: Guinea franc = 100 centimes

The name Guinea rings with a chink of gold – since 1663 when coins were struck in England out of pure 22 carat gold from Guinea. In Britan prices can still be quoted in guineas.Guinea still has natural resources that could bring prosperity to this very poor country. Independent 2 Oct 1958.

⑫ MALI

République du Mali
(Republic of Mali)

Area: 1.240.192 km² (479.046 mi²)
Population: 7.784.000
Population growth per annum: 10,3%
Life expectancy at birth: Males 44 years, females 48 years
Literacy: 17%
Capital with population: Bamako 404.000
Other important cities with population: Segou 65.000
Language: French, bambara
Religion: Islam (65%), animist (30%), christian (5%)
Currency: CFA franc = 100 centimes

Half Sahara and half Sahel, half desert and half savanna land. Mali has been hard hit by years of drought. Once the kings of Mali controlled the trade routes of the Sahara and the minarets of fabled Timbuktu attracted both traders and adventurers to cross the sand seas. Independent 22 Sep 1960.

⑬ BURKINA FASO

République Démocratique Populaire de Burkina Faso
(People's Democratic Republic of Burkina)

Area: 274.122 km² (105.884 mi²)
Population: 8.305.000
Population growth per annum: 2,1%
Life expectancy at birth: Males 44 years, females 48 years
Literacy: 9%
Capital with population: Ouagadougou 442.223
Other important cities with population:
  Bobo–Dioulasso 231.162
Language: French, sudanic tribal languages principally Mossi
Religion: Animist (45%), Islam (30%)
Currency: CFA-franc = 100 centimes

A land at the mercy of the winds. The dreaded dry Harmattan blowing from Sahara is a harbinger of death – the blessed Guinea monsoon from the south an angel of life with its seasonal rain. The savanna lands here depend on a precarious balance between precipitation and evaporation. Independent 5 Aug 1960.

⑭ NIGER

République du Niger
(Republic of Niger)

Area: 1.267.000 km² (489.401 mi²)
Population: 7.249.000
Population growth per annum: 3,3%
Life expectancy at birth: Males 44 years, females 48 years
Literacy: 10%
Capital with population: Niamey 399.100
Other important cities with population: Zinder 82.800
Language: French, hausa
Religion: Islam, animist
Currency: CFA-franc = 100 centimes

A name that is more of an incantation than a description. This is a land-locked, dry and infertile part of Sahara, and the mighty Niger crosses only a narrow corner. The Tuaregs still cross the desert with salt caravans. Independent 3 Aug 1960.

⑮ CHAD

République du Tchad
(Republic of Tchad)

Area: 1.284.000 km² (495.967 mi²)
Population: 5.396.000
Population growth per annum: 2,4%
Life expectancy at birth: Males 42 years, females 44 years
Literacy: 25%
Capital with population: N'djamena 511.700
Other important cities with population: Sarh 124.000
Language: French, arabic, sudanese languages
Religion: Animist (38%), islam (44%), christian (17%)
Currency: CFA-franc = 100 centimes

Land-locked Chad can be called coastal land, as it is part of the Sahel, "the coast" of the sand sea of Sahara. It drains into the shallow central basin of Lake Chad, the ever changing lake that varies from 11.000-50,000 km² (4.200-19.300mi²) and from 3-4m. (10-13 ft.) average depth. Independent 11 Aug 1960.

⑲ SUDAN

Al Jamhuryat es-Sudan al Democratia
(Democratic republic of Sudan)

Area: 2.505.813 km² (967.914 mi²)
Population: 25.560.000
Population growth per annum: 5,6%
Life expectancy at birth: Males 46 years, females 48 years
Literacy: 15%
Capital with population: Al Khartum (Khartoum) 476.218
Other important cities with population: Port Sudan
  206.727
Language: Arabic
Religion: Islam, christian, animist
Currency: Sudanese pound = 100 piastres

In Sudan there are two countries in one. There are the Islamic, Arabic-speaking northern desert lands, and there are the Christian, Nilotic southern savanna lands. In spite of the name, most of the world's gum arabic comes from the acacia forests of Sudan. Independent 1 Jan 1956.

⑰ SIERRA LEONE

The Republic of Sierra Leone

Area: 71.740 km² (27.711 mi²)
Population: 3.875.000
Population growth per annum: 0,7%
Life expectancy at birth: Males 49 years, females 53 years
Literacy: 29%
Capital with population: Freetown 469.776
Other important cities with population: Bo 26.000,
  Kenema 13.000, Makeni 12.000
Language: English, tribal languages
Religion: Animist, christian, islam
Currency: Leone = 100 cents

A new homeland for freed slaves. Under British protection repatriated slaves from Great Britain founded Freetown at one of the few good natural harbours of West Africa back in 1787. Later it was used as a settlement for Africans rescued from slaveships. Independent 27 Apr 1961

⑱ LIBERIA

Republic of Liberia

Area: 111.370 km² (43.019 mi²)
Population: 2.436.000
Population growth per annum: 3,6%
Life expectancy at birth: Males 57 years, females 59 years
Literacy: 35%
Capital with population: Monrovia 425.000
Other important cities with population: Buchanan 24.000
Language: English
Religion: Christian, traditional beliefs
Currency: Liberian dollar = 100 cents

As the name implies. Liberia is a free nation, and has been since it was established in 1822 for freed slaves from USA. In 1847 it became the continent's first independent republic and remained so during the days of the" Scramble for Africa" when this was divided in to colonies. Independent 26 Jul 1847.

⑲ ETHIOPIA

Ityopia
(Ethiopia)

Area: 1.221.900 km² (471. 980 mi²)
Population: 46.184.000
Population growth per annum: 3,2%
Life expectancy at birth: Males 38 years, females 41 years
Literacy: 62%
Capital with population: Addis Abeba 1.412.577
Other important cities with population:
Dire Dawa 98.104
Language: Amharic, other semitic and hamitic languages,
arabic, english
Religion: Orthodox christian (40%), islam (45%)
Currency: Ethiopian birr = 100 cents

*The nation that is an archipelago on dry land. For centuries
Ethiopia was a Christian island in a Moslem sea. It is still an
archipelago of densely populated islands of high plateaus,
separated by deep river gorges and hot lowlands – and a
linguistic archipelago of over 70 ethnic groups.*

⑳ DJIBOUTI

Jumhouriyya Djibouti
(Republic of Djibouti)

Area: 23.200 km² (8.961 mi²)
Population: 484.000
Population growth per annum: 6,8%
Life expectancy at birth: 50 years
Litercy: 20%
Capital with population : Djibouti 290.000
Other important cities with population: none
Language: French, arabic
Religion: Islam
Currency: Djibouti franc = 100 centimes

*The nation is a railway terminal – and vice versa. The entrepot
port would not and could not exist as an independent unity
without the railway to Addis Ababa. This railway was built in
1915 and has since served as the major link between central
Ethiopia and the world. Independent 27 Jun 1977.*

㉑ IVORY COAST

République de Côte d'Ivoire
(Republic of Ivory Coast)

Area: 322.463 km² (124.557 mi²)
Population: 11.634.000
Population growth per annum: 4,5%
Life expectancy at birth: Males 49 years, females 53 years
Literacy: 35%
Capital with population: Abidjan 1.850.000
Other important cities with population: Bouaké 272.640
Language: French, tribal languages
Religion: Islam (23%), christian (12%), indigenuos (63%)
Currency: CFA-franc = 100 centimes

*The Cocoa Coast would be a more apt but less poetic name for
this land. Cocoa and coffee long ago replaced ivory and slaves
as the staples of the Ivory Coast. No nation produces more
cocoa. Other agricultural products are pineapples, bananas
and palm oil. Independent 7 Aug 1960.*

㉒ GHANA

Republic of Ghana

Area: 238.537 km² (92.139 mi²)
Population: 13.812.000
Population growth per annum: 2,5%
Life expectancy at birth: Males 52 years, females 55 years
Literacy: 53%
Capital with population: Accra 964.879
Other important cities with population: Kumasi 348.880,
Tamale 136.828
Language: English, 8 major national languages
Religion: Christian (52%), traditional beliefs, islam(13%)
Currency: New cedi = 100 pesewas

*The former Gold Coast is at the same time a historic truth and a
fitting description. One man and his dreams brought first
independence and then financial ruin to his once prosperous
country. Many foreign flags have flown over Gold Coast –
Portuguese, Swedish, Danish,Dutch, and British.
Independent 6 Mar 1957.*

㉓ TOGO

République Togolaise
(Togolese Republic)

Areal: 56.785 km² (21.934 mi²)
Population: 3.246.000
Population growth per annum: 2,7%
Life expectancy at birth: Males 49 years, females 53 years
Literacy: 41%
Capital with population: Lomé 366.476
Other important cities with population: none
Language: French, kabiye, ewe
Religion: Animist, christian 35%, islam 15%
Currency: CFA-franc = 100 centimes

*An artificial nation. During the scramble for Africa, the
Germans, like all other colonial power just grabbed as much
land as they could regardless of tribal, linguistic and other
natural boundaries. Part of their colonial patchwork finally
emerged as free Togo. Independent 27 Apr 1960.*

㉔ BENIN

République du Benin
(Republic of Benin)

Area: 112.622 km² (43.502 mi²)
Population: 4.444.000
Population growth per annum: 3,2%
Life expectancy at birth: Males 49 years, females 52 years
Literacy: 28%
Capital with population: Porto-Novo 208.258
Other important cities with population: Cotonou 487.020
Language: French, local dialects
Religion: Roman catholic, islam, animist
Currency: CFA-franc = 100 centimes

*Coastal Benin is a country apart – island-studded lagoons that
are neither sea nor land. Here the fishing villages were built on
stilts to escape occasional floods and to give some protection
against slavers. Independent 1 Aug 1960.*

(25) SÃO TOMÉ AND PRINCIPE

Republica democratica de
São Tomé e Principe
(Democatic Republic of
São Tomé and Principe)

Area: 964 km^2 (372 mi^2)
Population: 115.600
Population growth per annum: 2,3%
Life expectancy at birth: Males 64 years, females 67 years
Literacy: 57%
Capital with population: São Tomé 34.907
Other important cities with population: São António 1.000
Language: Portuguese
Religion: Roman catholic
Currency: Dobra = 100 cêntimos

These tropical islands in the cool Benguela current are favoured by fertile volcanic soil. At the turn of the century they were the world's leading producers of cocoa – but now others produce more. Coconuts and coffee are also grown. Independent 12 Jul 1975.

(26) NIGERIA

Federal Republic of Nigeria

Area: 923.768 km^2 (356.821 mi^2)
Population: 105.000.000
Population growth per annum: 3,2%
Life expectancy at birth: Males 51 years, females 54 years
Literacy: 34%
Capital with population: Lagos 1.697.000
(Abuja–proposed capital)
Other important cities with population: Ibadan 1.060.000, Ogbomosho 527.400, Kano 487.100
Language: English, hausa, yoruba, ibo
Religion: Islam, christian
Currency: Naira = 100 kobo

Nigeria is Africa's most populous country in more than one sense. No other can match its over 100 millions and its over 250 linguistic groups (and tribes). It is hard to belive that this prosperous nation once was justly called "The White Man's Grave" (due to the coastal malaria swamps). Independent 1 Oct 1960.

(27) CAMEROON

République du Cameroun
(Republic of Cameroon)

Area: 475.442 km^2 (183.648 mi^2)
Population: 11.082.000
Population growth per annum: 3,2%
Life expectancy at birth: Males 49 years, females 53 years
Literacy: 41%
Capital with population: Yaounde 653.670
Other important cities with population: Douala 1.029.731
Language: English, french, bantu, sudanic
Religion: Islam (22%), roman catholic (21%), protestant (18%), animist (39%)
Currency: CFA-franc = 100 centimes

An ethnic kaleidoscope, the country was a German colony, then two separate League of Nations mandates (French and British) before becoming a unitary republic. There are some two hundred different African ethnic groups. Mt. Cameroon, rising 4,070m.(13,353 ft) from the sea, serves at times as a natural lighthouse, last erupting in 1959. Independent 1 Jan 1960.

(28) CENTRAL AFRICAN REPUBLIC

République Centrafricaine

Area: 622.984 km^2 (240.638 mi^2)
Population: 2.860.000
Population growth per annum: 2,9%
Life expectancy at birth: Males 44 years, females 50 years
Literacy: 33%
Capital with population: Bangui 596.776
Other important cities with population: Bambari 52.092
Language: French, sango
Religion: Animist (57%), roman catholic (20%), protestant (15%)
Currency: CFA-franc = 100 centimes

At this crossroad of Africa the savannas meet the rain forests and the Bantu people mingel with the Nilo-saharan groups and others. Even the rivers are running in opposite directions: the Ubangi towards Congo, the Shari to Lake Chad. Independent 13 Aug 1960.

(29) EQUATORIAL GUINEA

República de Guinea Ecuatorial
(Republic of Equatorial Guinea)

Area: 28.051 km^2 (10.835 mi^2)
Population: 336.000
Population growth per annum: 1,3%
Life expectancy at birth: Males 49 years, females 53 years
Literacy: 37%
Capital with population: Malabo 10.000
Other important cities with population: Bata 17.000
Language: Spanish, fang, english
Religion: Roman catholic (96%)
Currency: CFA-franc = 100 centimes

As an antithesis, a part of the mainland of Africa belongs to the main island of Equatorial Guinea. On Bioko the lingua franca has been pidgin English and on Pagalu Portuguese patois in spite of the fact that spanish was the offical language! Independent 12 Oct 1968.

(30) GABON

République Gabonaise
(Gabonese Republic)

Area: 267.667 km^2 (103.391 mi^2)
Population: 1.226.000
Population growth per annum: 4,2%
Life expectancy at birth: Males 47 years, females 50 years
Literacy: 62%
Capital with population: Libreville 350.000
Other important cities with population: Port–Gentil 123.300
Language: French, bantu dialects, fang
Religion: Roman catholic (65%), animist
Currency: CFA-franc = 100 centimes

Like some brand names Gabon has become almost a household word, because of the widespread use of mahogany plywood for furniture and doors. In addition to timber, Gabon produces oil, manganese and uranium. Independent 17 Aug 1960.

① CONGO

République du Congo
(Republic of the Congo)

Area: 342.000 km² (132.103 mi²)
Population: 2.266.000
Population growth per annum: 3,9%
Life expectancy at birth: Males 49 years, females 53 years
Literacy: 63%
Capital with population: Brazzaville 596.200
Other important cities with population:
 Pointe–Noire 298.014
Language: French, bantu dialects
Religion: Animist (50%), Rroman catholic (30%), protestant
Currency: CFA-franc = 100 centimes

*Without the Congo River there wouldn't be any Congo. the sole reason for establishing the French colony north of the great river was to explore and exploit as much as possible of the basin (in competition with the Belgians).The name of the capital still honours the founding explorer de Brazza.
Independent 15 Aug 1960.*

② UGANDA

Republic of Uganda

Area: 241.139 km² (93.144 mi²)
Population: 15.500.000
Population growth per annum: 3,0%
Life expectancy at birth: Males 56 years, females 59 years
Literacy: 53%
Capital with population: Kampala 458.423
Other important cities with population: none
Language: English,luganda
Religion: Roman catholic, protestant, islam
Currency: New Uganda shilling = 100 cents

Once and future Pearl of Africa? The setting of the gem remains: fertile lands with an abundance of water and magnificent scenery: The fabled Mountains of the Moon,the Ruwenzori, and the source lakes of the Nile with famous waterfalls. With peace can also prosperity be restored in Uganda. Independent 9 Sep 1962.

③ RWANDA

Republika y'u Rwanda
(Republic of Rwanda)

Area: 26.338 km² (10.174 mi²)
Population: 6.710.000
Population growth per annum: 3,1%
Life expectancy at birth: Males 49 years, females 53 years
Literacy: 50%
Capital with population: Kigali 156.650
Other important cities with population: none
Language: French, kinyarwandu
Religion: Animist, roman catholic
Currency: Rwanda franc = 100 centimes

*This tiny nation contains some spectacular features: some of the true sources of the Nile, some of the last mountain gorillas and some active volcanoes in the Virunga Mountains.
Independent 7 Jul 1962.*

㉞ BURUNDI

Republika y'u Burundi
(Republic of Burundi)

Area: 27.834 km² (10.751 mi²)
Population: 5.001.000
Population growth per annum: 2,9%
Life expectancy at birth: Males 44 years, females 47 years
Literacy: 34%
Capital with population: Bujumbura 272.600
Other important cities with population: Gitega 95.300
Language: French, kirundi, kiswahili
Religion: Roman catholic (more than 60%)
Currency: Burundi franc = 100 centimes

*A free colony. The hamiticTutsi established colonial rule over the Hutu – the Bantu majority of the people as early as the 17th century. The Europeans came over two hundred years later and left after seventy years. TheTutsi still rule Burundi.
Independent 1 Jul 1962.*

㉟ KENYA

Jamhuri ya Kenya
(Republic of Kenya)

Area: 582.646 km² (225.057 mi²)
Population: 22.800.000
Population growth per annum: 3,9%
Life expectancy at birth: Males 56 years, females 61 years
Literacy: 59%
Capital with population: Niarobi 827.775
Other important cities with population: Mombasa 341.148, Kisumu 152.643
Language: Kiswahili, english
Religion: Protestant (19%), roman catholic (27%), islam (6%)
Currency: Kenya shilling = 100 cents

*If there is a Safari Land in the world, it must be Kenya. The word safari (from the Arabic word for travel) rings with adventure. Here the adventurer's dreams may still be realized. In parks such as famous Amboseli close-ups of lions can be taken against the background of snow-capped Kilimanjaro.
Independent 12 Dec 1963.*

㊱ SOMALIA

Jamhuriyadda Dimuqradiga Somaliya
(Somali Democratic Republic)

Area: 637.657 km² (246.306 mi²)
Population: 6.220.000
Population growth per annum: -3,1%
Life expectancy at birth: Males 44 years, females 47 years
Literacy: 12%
Capital with population: Muqdisho (Mogadishu) 1.000.000
Other important cities with population: Hargeysa 400.000
Language: Somali, arabic
Religion: Islam (sunni moslems)
Currency: Somali shilling = 100 cents

*Once the land of frankincense and myrrh, now a land of fratricide and famine, as the clans are fighting for power in this droughtridden land of semideserts and dry savannas.
Independent 1 Jul 1960.*

㊲ ZAÏRE
République du Zaire
(Republic of Zaire)

Area: 2.344.885 km^2 (905.752 mi^2)
Population: 32.564.000
Population growth per annum: 1,7%
Life expectancy at birth: Males 44 years, females 48 years
Literacy: 61%
Capital with population: Kinshasa 2.653.558
Other important cities with population:
  Lubumbashi 543.268, Mbuji-Mayi 423.363, Kananga 290.898
Language: French, bantu- och sudanese dialects
Religion: Roman catholic (48%), animist, protestant (13%)
Currency: Zaire = 100 makuta

The heart of Africa. Within Zaire (former Belgian Congo) can be found sophisticated Kinshasa and rain forests with pygmy tribes, uranium and diamond mines as well as leaking river steamers, steaming rain forests but also prosperous farmland – and some 200 different ethic groups. Independent 30 Jun 1960.

㊳ TANZANIA
Jamhuri ya Muungano wa Tanzania
(United Republic of Tanzania)

Area: 945.087 km^2 (365.056 mi^2)
Population: 23.217.000
Population growth per annum: 3,4%
Life expectancy at birth: 52 years
Literacy: 46%
Capital with population: Dar es Salaam 757.346 (Intended capital: Dodoma)
Other important cities with population: Zanzibar 110.669, Mwanza 110.619
Language: Kiswahili, english, tribal languages
Religion: Animist, christian, islam, hindu
Currency: Tanzanian shilling = 100 cents

Arid Tanzania is full of natural wonders: The snow- capped, perfect volcanic cone on Mt. Kilimanjaro, highest in Africa; Lake Victoria: third largest in the World; Lake Tanganyika; second deepest; the Serengeti Plains with the last primeval heards of wild animals: the serene Ngorongoro Crater. Independent 9 Dec 1961.

㊴ COMOROS
Jumhuriyaat al-Qumur al-Ittihadiyah al-Islamiya
(Federal Islamic Republic of the Comoros)

Area: 1.862 km^2 (719 mi^2)
Population: 434.166
Population growth per annum: 6,3%
Life expectancy at birth: Males 48 years, females 52 years
Literacy: 48%
Capital with population: Moroni 20.112
Other important cities with population: none
Language: French, arabic
Religion: Islam
Currency: Comorian-franc = 100 centimes

Essence is the very essence of the economy of the Comoro Islands that produce exotic ilang-ilang, citronella and jasmine essences as well as vanilla extract and cloves. Independent 6 Jul 1975.

㊵ SEYCHELLES
Repiblik Sesel/Republic of Seychelles
(Republic of Seychelles)

Area: 454 km^2 (175 mi^2)
Population: 66.229
Population growth per annum: 0,6%
Life expectancy at birth: 66 år
Litercy: 58%
Capital with population: Victoria 23.334
Other important cities with population: none
Language: Creole, english, french
Religion: Roman catholic, protestant
Currency: Seychelles rupee = 100 cent

The island of the love fruit – the sea (or double) coconut, the world's largest. This gigantic fruit, that may weigh 20-25 kg (50 pounds), contains 3-4 smooth bilobed nuts with obvious, unavoidable associations to the human body. They grow only on the Seychelles, and their origin was long a mystery. Independent 29 Jun 1976.

㊶ ANGOLA
República Popular de Angola
(People's Republic of Angola)

Area: 1.246.700 km^2 (481.559 mi^2)
Population: 9.387.000
Population growth per annum: 2,5%
Life expectancy at birth: Males 45 years, females 48 years
Literacy: 30%
Capital with population: Luanda 1.200.000
Other important cities with population: Huambo 61.885
Language: Portuguese, various bantu languages
Religion: Roman catholic, animist
Currency: Kwanza = 100 lwei

Accessibility shaped the destiny of Angola. In contrast to other parts of Africa there are good harbours here and neither forbidding deserts nor feverish swamps bar the routes to the interior. Thus Angola become one of the first European colonies on the African mainland. Independent 11 Nov 1975.

㊷ ZAMBIA
Republic of Zambia

Area: 752.614 km^2 (290.710 mi^2)
Population: 7.531.119
Population growth per annum: 3,6%
Life expectancy at birth: Males 52 years, females 55 years
Literacy: 76%
Capital with population: Lusaka 818.994
Other important cities with population: Kitwe 449.442, Ndola 418.142
Language: English, bantu dialects
Religion: Christian (70%), animist
Currency: Kwacha = 100 ngwee

A colony for less than 40 years! Here colonial rule was not established until 1924 (as the result of Cecil Rhode's dream of extending British rule from the Cape to Cairo) but by 1964 the winds of change brought freedom to Zambia. The Victoria Fall are Zambia's most famous sight. Independent 24 Oct 1964.

㊸ MALAWI

Dziko la Malawi
(Republic of Malawi)

Area: 118.484 km² (45.766 mi²)
Population: 7.982.607
Population growth per annum: 3,7%
Life expectancy at birth: Males 49 years, females 53 years
Literacy: 41%
Capital with population: Lilongwe 175.000
Other important cities with population: Blantyre 280.000
Language: Chichewa, english
Religion: Animist, christian (50%), islam
Currency: Kwacha = 100 tambala

A self-sufficient land of farmers, striving to build a better future. This is expressed also in their names for the units of currency. One kwacha (dawn) is divided into 100 tambalas (cockerels). Independent 6 Jul 1964.

㊹ MOZAMBIQUE

República de Moçambique
(Republic of Mozambique)

Area: 799.380 km² (308.774 mi²)
Population: 14.907.000
Population growth per annum: 2,6%
Life expectancy at birth: Males 49 years, females 53 years
Literacy: 38%
Capital with population: Maputo 1.006.765
Other important cities with population: Beira 269.700, Nampula 182.553
Language: Portuguese, bantu languages
Religion: Roman catholic, islam, animist
Currency: Metical =100 centavos

Mozambique and South Africa can both benefit from close cooperation as conditions become more peaceful. Mozambique has water-power (Cabora Bassa, 1.4 GW) and a large workforce but few minerals or industries. South Africa needs electricity and has the knowhow needed for developing Mozambique. Independent 15 Jun 1975.

㊺ NAMIBIA

Republic of Namibia

Area: 824.292 km² (318.387 mi²)
Population: 1.252.000
Population growth per annum: 2,8%
Life expectancy at birth: Males 55 years, females 58 years
Literacy: 72%
Capital with population: Windhoek 114.500
Other important cities with population: none
Language: Afrikaans, english, german
Religion: Protestant, roman catholic
Currency: South African rand = 100 cents

The struggle for survival has in many ways always been harder in Namibia than elsewhere. Animals and plants have been forced to adapt to a life without rainfall in large desert areas. The peoples of the land were also for long forced to adapt to a life without freedom, but they have now won the right to decide their own future. Independent 21 Mar 1990.

㊻ BOTSWANA

Republic of Botswana

Area: 582.000 km² (224.808 mi²)
Population: 1.211.816
Population growth per annum: 3,6%
Life expectancy at birth: Males 52 years, females 55 years
Literacy: 41%
Capital with population: Gaborone 110.973
Other important cities with population: Mahalapye 100.902, Serowe 93.008
Language: English, setswana
Religion: Indigenous beliefs, christian (15%)
Currency: Pula =100 theba

Land-locked Botswana lies in the centre of the mountain bowl of southern Africa. Here lies the Kalahari desert and here the Cubango River loses it self in a maze of salt swamps and shallow lakes without outlet, such as famed Lake Ngami. Independent 30 Sep 1966.

㊼ ZIMBABWE

Republic of Zimbabwe

Area: 390.759 km² (150.937 mi²)
Population: 8.870.000
Population growth per annum: 2,7%
Life expectancy at birth: Males 56 years, females 60 years
Literacy: 69%
Capital with population: Harare 656.000
Other important cities with population: Bulawayo 413.800, Chitungwiza 172.500
Language: English, chishona, sindebele
Religion: Christian, animist, islam, hindu
Currency: Zimbabwe dollar = 100 cents

A nation with well-deserved pride. Zimbabwe is named after the impressive ruin-city that also is the firm foundation of the national spirit. These massive stone walls and towers were built more than a thousand years ago by Bantu kings – ancestors to the people of today's Zimbabwe. Independent 18 Apr 1980.

㊽ MADAGASCAR

Repoblika Demokratika n'i Madagaskår
(Democratic Republic of Madagascar)

Area: 587.041 km² (226.755 mi²)
Population: 10.919.000
Population growth per annum: 2,8%
Life expectancy at birth: Males 49 years, females 53 years
Literacy: 67%
Capital with population: Antananrivo 703.000
Other important cities with population: Toamasina 139.000
Language: Malagasay, french
Religion: Animist (57%), christian (40%), islam (3%)
Currency: Malagasy franc = 100 centimes

The fourt largest island of all – and in most aspects an Asian island. Geologically it is a segment of the same block as India, and the population is of Indo-Melanesian stock. The endemic wildlife comprises rare species, such as the bug-eyed-aye-aye and the hedgehog-like tenrec. Independent 26 Jun 1960.

(49) SOUTH AFRICA
Republiek van Suid-Afrika
(Republic of South Africa)

Area: 1.221.037 km^2 (471.647 mi^2)
Population: 29.617.000
Population growth per annum: 2,0%
Life expectancy at birth: Males 63 years, females 66 years
Literacy: Whites 93%, asians 71%, coloureds 75%, africans 32%
Capital with population: Cape Town (legislative) 1.911.521, Pretoria (administrative) 822.925
Other important cities with population: Johannesburg 1.609.408, Durban 982.075, Bloemfontein 232.984
Language: Afrikaans, english
Religion: Protestant, roman catholic
Currency: Rand = 100 cents

Humans have long been their own enemies in South Africa. The original natives, the bushmen, fled into the Kalahari desert at the arrival of the Bantu tribes and the original Dutch boers. The peoples of South Africa have long been forced to live in racial segregation – the infamous Apartheid system that is now being scrapped. Independent 31 May 1910, 1931.

(50) LESOTHO
'Muso oa Lesotho
(Kingdom of Lesotho)

Area: 30.355 km^2 (11.725 mi^2)
Population: 1.670.000
Population growth per annum: 3,0%
Life expectancy at birth: Males 54 years, females 56 years
Literacy: 73%
Capital with population: Maseru 109.382
Other important cities with population: none
Language: Sesotho, english
Religion: Roman catholic (40%), protestant (60%)
Currency: Loti = 100 lisente

For long an encircled nation but not a subjugated land. The free black enclave in South Africa has served as a reminder to its white neighbours that all people are created equal. Independent 4 Oct 1966.

(51) SWAZILAND
Umbuso we Swatini
(Kingdom of Swaziland)

Area: 17.363 km^2 (6.707 mi^2)
Population: 681.059
Population growth per annum: 3,3%
Life expectancy at birth: Males 49 years, females 53 years
Literacy: 68%
Capital with population: Mbabane 38.209
Other important cities with population: Manzini 18.084
Language: Swazi, english
Religion: Protestant, roman catholic, animist
Currency: Lilangeni =100 cents

The proud Swazi people claim a history of five hundred years, but in their country their' rights' are not older than those of their white neigbours on the other side of the Drakensberg Mountains. British protection kept Swaziland out of the Boer's hands. Independent 6 Sep 1968.

NORTH AMERICA

Area: 25,349,000 km^2 (9,785,000 mi^2)
Population: 410,100,000
Density of population per km^2: 16.2
(per mi^2: 41.9)

Cape Prince of Wale
168° 4' W. longitud
the North American
mainland's most wes
point.

Mount McKinley is North
America's highest peak,
6,194 m. (20,322 ft.).

The Malaspina Glacie
covering an area of 3
km^2 (2,385 mi^2), is the
largest on the North
American mainland.

The United States bo
Alaska from Russia in
1867 for $ 7,200,00

(10)	BELIZE
(1)	CANADA
(14)	COSTA RICA
(5)	CUBA
(8)	DOMINICAN REPUBLIC
(11)	EL SALVADOR
(9)	GUATEMALA
(7)	HAITI
(12)	HONDURAS
(6)	JAMAICA
(3)	MEXICO
(13)	NICARAGUA
(15)	PANAMA
(4)	THE BAHAMAS
(2)	UNITED STATES

Snake River Canyon
(Hell's Canyon) on th
boundary between Ida
and Oregon is the wo
deepest ravine 2,400
(7,874 ft.) in depth.

The world's loftiest tre
– up to 111 m. (364 ft.
grow in the redwood f
of California.

Death Valley is the c
nent's deepest depr
sion, 86 m. (282 ft.)
sea level and also th
hottest place (highe
recorded temperatu
56.7°C. (134°F.)).

(52) MAURITIUS

Area: 2.040 km^2 (788 mi^2)
Population: 1.040.000
Population growth per annum: 1,0%
Life expectancy at birth: Males 65 years, females 70 years
Literacy: 79%
Capital with population: Port Louis 139.038
Other important cities with population: Beau-Bassin-Rose Hill 93.061
Language: English, creole
Religion: Hindu (51%), roman catholic (25%), islam (17%)
Currency: Mauritian rupee =100 cents

In relation to size no land on earth has as many different languages – spoken by so many diverse ethnic groups: English (official), Hindi, Creole, Urdu, Tamil, French, Chinese, Arabic and a few African languages. Independent 12 Mar 1968.

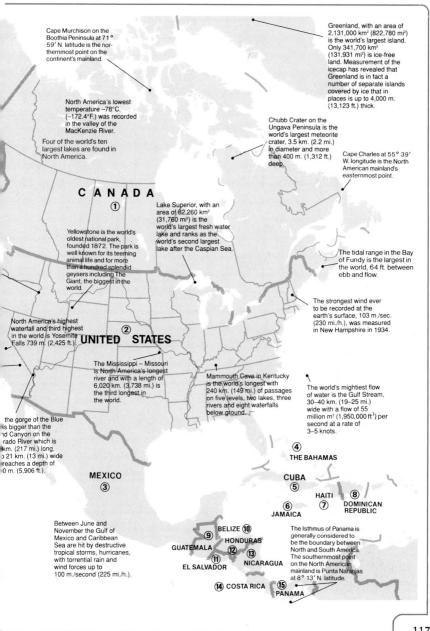

Cape Murchison on the Boothia Peninsula at 71° 59' N. latitude is the northernmost point of the continent's mainland.

North America's lowest temperature −78°C. (−172.4°F.) was recorded in the valley of the MacKenzie River.

Four of the world's ten largest lakes are found in North America.

Greenland, with an area of 2,131,000 km² (822,780 mi²) is the world's largest island. Only 341,700 km² (131,931 mi²) is ice-free land. Measurement of the icecap has revealed that Greenland is in fact a number of separate islands covered by ice that in places is up to 4,000 m. (13,123 ft.) thick.

Chubb Crater on the Ungava Peninsula is the world's largest meteorite crater, 3.5 km. (2.2 mi.) in diameter and more than 400 m. (1,312 ft.) deep.

Cape Charles at 55° 39' W. longitude is the North American mainland's easternmost point.

C A N A D A
①

Lake Superior, with an area of 82,260 km² (31,760 mi²) is the world's largest fresh water lake and ranks as the world's second largest lake after the Caspian Sea.

Yellowstone is the world's oldest national park, founded 1872. The park is well known for its teeming animal life and for more than a hundred splendid geysers including The Giant, the biggest in the world.

The tidal range in the Bay of Fundy is the largest in the world, 64 ft. between ebb and flow.

The strongest wind ever to be recorded at the earth's surface, 103 m./sec. (230 mi./h.), was measured in New Hampshire in 1934.

North America's highest waterfall and third highest in the world is Yosemite Falls 739 m. (2,425 ft.)

②
UNITED   STATES

The Mississippi − Missouri is North America's longest river and with a length of 6,020 km. (3,738 mi.) is the third longest in the world.

Mammouth Cave in Kentucky is the world's longest with 240 km. (149 mi.) of passages on five levels, two lakes, three rivers and eight waterfalls below ground.

The world's mightiest flow of water is the Gulf Stream, 30–40 km. (19–25 mi.) wide with a flow of 55 million m³ (1,950,000 ft³) per second at a rate of 3–5 knots.

the gorge of the Blue is bigger than the nd Canyon on the rado River which is km. (217 mi.) long, 21 km. (13 mi.) wide reaches a depth of 0 m. (5,906 ft.).

④
THE BAHAMAS

MEXICO
③

CUBA
⑤
HAITI   ⑧
⑥   ⑦   **DOMINICAN REPUBLIC**
JAMAICA

Between June and November the Gulf of Mexico and Caribbean Sea are hit by destructive tropical storms, hurricanes, with torrential rain and wind forces up to 100 m./second (225 mi./h.).

BELIZE ⑩
⑨   **HONDURAS**
GUATEMALA   ⑫   ⑬
⑪   **NICARAGUA**
EL SALVADOR

The Isthmus of Panama is generally considered to be the boundary between North and South America. The southernmost point on the North American mainland is Punta Naranjas at 8° 13' N. latitude.

⑭ **COSTA RICA**   ⑮
PANAMA

① CANADA

Area: 9.970.610 km^2 (3.851.320 mi^2)
Population: 25.625.100
Population growth per annum: 0,9%
Life expectancy at birth: Males 70 years, females 77 years
Literacy: 99%
Capital with population: Ottawa 819.263
Other important cities with population: Toronto 3.427.168, Montréal 2.921.357, Vancouver 1.380.729
Language: English, french
Religion: Roman catholic (45%), protestant
Currency: Canadian dollar = 100 cents

A nation that spans a continent, Canada is the world's second largest country. Halifax on the Atlantic is closer to Great Britain than to Vancouver on the Pacific. When the sun rises over Newfoundland it is still midnight in Yukon. The 19.6 m (55 ft) tides in the Bay of Fundy are the world's greatest. Independent 1 Jul 1867

② UNITED STATES OF AMERICA

Area: 9.372.614 km^2 (3.620.334 mi^2)
Population: 245.602.000
Population growth per annum: 0,9%
Life expectancy at birth: Males 69 years, females 77 years
Literacy: 99%
Capital with population: Washington D.C. 626.000
Other important cities with population:
New York 7.262.700, Los Angeles 3.259.340, Chicago 3.009.530
Language: English
Religion: Protestant (55%), Roman catholic (37%), jews (4%)
Currency: US dollar = 100 cents

U.S.A. is a powerful nation. The economic strenght and military might of the nation can hardly be overestimated. It is the world's leading producer of most important commodities: oil, gas, coal, steel, paper. It is also found at the top of most lists of world records and extremes – and especially those of engineering feats. Independent 4 Jul 1776.

③ MEXICO

Estados Unidos Mexicanos
(United Mexican States)

Area: 1.958.201 km^2 (756.389 mi^2)
Population: 82.734.454
Population growth per annum: 2,0%
Life expectancy at birth: Males 65 years, females 70 years
Literacy: 90%
Capital with population: Mexico City 12.932.116
Other important cities with population:
Guadalajara 2.244.715, Monterrey 1.916.472
Language: Spanish
Religion: Roman Catholic
Currency: Mexican pesos = 100 centavos

The centre of power in Central America lies as before in Mexico. In the early 19th century, the Spanish viceroy ruled half of Northern America from here, and today the nation is ranked high among the powers of the Third World. The famous pyramids of Teotihuacán manifest the greatness of Mexico. Independent 16 Sep 1810.

④ THE BAHAMAS

Commonwealth of the Bahamas

Area: 13.939 km^2 (5.384 mi^2)
Population: 207.203
Population growth per annum: 1,7%
Life expectancy at birth: Males 64 years, females 69 years
Literacy: 89%
Capital with population: Nassau 135.437
Other important cities with population: Freeport 24.423
Language: English
Religion: Protestant (48%), Roman catholic (26%)
Currency: Bahamian dollar = 100 cents

A thousand coral reefs and not one but 700 coral islands in the sun. For the industrial eastern USA the beaches of the Bahamas are conveniently close – as Mediterranean shores are to northwestern Europe. Blue underwater caves attract scuba divers. Independent 10 Jul 1973.

⑤ CUBA

República de Cuba
(Republic of Cuba)

Area: 114.524 km^2 (44.237 mi^2)
Population: 10.288.000
Population growth per annum: 0,9%
Life expectancy at birth: Males 71 years, females 74 years
Literacy: 95%
Capital with population: La Habana (Havana) 2.036.799
Other important cities with population: Santiago de Cuba 364.554, Camagüey 265.588
Language: Spanish
Religion: Roman catholic
Currency: Cuban peso = 100 centavos

The Sugar island. Sugar and Cuba are now almost synonymous words, but it is a fact that the sugar cane was imported to Cuba from the Old World by the Spaniards. The Cubans themselves are also descendants of immigrants from the Old World: the Spaniards and their negro slaves. Independent 10 Dec 1898.

⑥ JAMAICA

Area: 10.991 km^2 (4.245 mi^2)
Population: 2.355.400
Population growth per annum: 2,5%
Life expectancy at birth: Males 70 years, females 74 years
Literacy: 96%
Capital with population: Kingston 650.000
Other important cities with population:
Spanish Town 89.097, Montego Bay 70.650
Language: English
Religion: Protestant
Currency: Jamaica dollar = 100 cents

Pirate Island has become Island in the sun and Land of the Rasta – as Fifteen men on a dead man's chest has been replaced by the inspired music of the Rastafarians. The bottle of rum is still avalible. Only scuba divers can today visit infamous Port Royal on the bottom of Kingston Bay. Independent 6 Aug 1962.

⑦ HAITI

Repiblik Dayti/République d'Haiti
(Republic of Haiti)

Area: 27.750 km^2 (10.719 mi^2)
Population: 5.707.000
Population growth per annum: 1,9%
Life expectancy at birth: Males 53 years, females 56 years
Literacy: 35%
Capital with population: Port-au-Prince 738.342
Other important cities with population: none
Language: French, Creole
Religion: Roman catholic, protestant
Currency: Guorde = 100 centimes

Historically the land of voodoo, of mystery and magic. Officially all are Roman catholics, but the undercurrent of ancient African religions is still strong here. Slaves who won their freedom against Spanish, British and French armies created here the world's first Negro republic. Independent 1 Jan 1804.

⑧ DOMINICAN REPUBLIC

República Dominicana

Area: 48.442 km^2 (18.712 mi^2)
Population: 6.708.000
Population growth per annum: 3,6%
Life expectancy at birth: Males 63 years, females 67 years
Literacy: 69%
Capital with population: Santo Domingo 1.313.172
Other important cities with population: Santiago de Los Caballeros 278.638, La Romana 91.571
Language: Spanish
Religion: Roman catholic
Currency: RD-peso = 100 centavos

This is in all but name Columbus' country. Here lie his mortal remains in a lead casket in the cathedral of Santo Domingo. The city that he founded is the oldest European city in the New World, and the island itself carries the name he gave it, Hispaniola – "the Spanish (island)". Independent 27 Feb 1844.

⑨ GUATEMALA

República de Guatemala
(Republic of Guatemala)

Area: 108.889 km^2 (42.060 mi^2)
Population: 8.434.339
Population growth per annum: 2,9%
Life expectancy at birth: Males 62 years, females 65 years
Literacy: 55%
Capital with population: Guatemala 1.500.000
Other important cities with population: Quezaltenango 65.733
Language: Spanish, Indian dialects
Religion: Roman catholic
Currency: Quetzal = 100 centavos

A land of awe inspiring ruins and memories of its brilliant past during the reign of the Mayas – of once glorious cities like Tikal and Uaxactún. It is also a land of melodious place names like Chichicastenango (a famous market town) and Sololá. Independent 1821, 1839.

⑩ BELIZE

Area: 22.963 km^2 (8.870 mi^2)
Population: 175.600
Population growth per annum: –
Life expectancy at birth: 60 years
Literacy: 93%
Capital with population: Belmopan 4.500
Other important cities with population: Belize City 48.400
Language: English, spanish
Religion: Roman catholic (60%), protestant (40%)
Currency: Belizean dollar = 100 cents

Belize is an anomaly – the only British enclave in Latin America. The forests yield valuable timber – mahogany and rosewood – and chicle latex, the original "gum" used for making chewing gum before the development of synthetic gum. Independent 21 Sep 1981.

⑪ EL SALVADOR

República de El Salvador
(Republic of El Salvador)

Area: 21.393 km^2 (8.263 mi^2)
Population: 5.009.000
Population growth per annum: 1,9%
Life expectancy at birth: Males 65 years, females 69 years
Literacy: 72%
Capital with population: San Salvador 462.652
Other important cities with population:
Santa Ana 135.186, San Miguel 86.722
Language: Spanish
Religion: Roman catholic
Currency: Colon = 100 centavos

This is truly the land of volcanoes. The average distance between active volcanoes here is less than 30 km. (19 miles)! Politically the nation has suffered from eruptions of violence, aggravated by outside interference, but peace is returning. Independent 1839, 1841.

⑫ HONDURAS

República de Honduras
(Republic of Honduras)

Area: 112.088 km^2 (43.296 mi^2)
Population: 4.051.400
Population growth per annum: 2,9%
Life expectancy at birth: Males 61 years, females 65 years
Literacy: 57%
Capital with population: Tegucigalpa 640.900
Other important cities with population: San Pedro Sula 429.300, El Progreso 61.100
Language: Spanish
Religion: Roman catholic
Currency: Lempira = 100 centavos

The word banana republic must have been coined with Honduras in mind. Bananas thrive in the fertile volcanic soil and the warm, humid climate of the tropical coastlands. The forest covers impressive Maya ruins, such as Copán. Independent 1821, 5 Nov 1838.

⑬ NICARAGUA

República de Nicaragua
(Republic of Nicaragua)

Area: 127.849 km^2 (49.384 mi^2)
Population: 3.500.000
Population growth per annum: 3,4%
Life expectancy at birth: Males 58 years, females 62 years
Literacy: 58%
Capital with population: Managua 682.111
Other important cities with population: León 100.982
Language: Spanish
Religion: Roman catholic
Currency: New Córdoba = 100 centavos

Nicaragua has been a land of turmoil, plagued by earthquakes, revolutions and counter-revolutions. Through free elections the people has chosen new leaders and peace has been restored. One danger remains: the man-eating sharks of lake Nicaragua, trapped there when a bay was blocked and become a lake. Independent1821, 1838.

⑭ COSTA RICA

República de Costa Rica
(Republic of Costa Rica)

Area: 50.700 km^2 (19.570 mi^2)
Population: 2.816.558
Population growth per annum: 2,8%
Life expectancy at birth: Males 70 years, females 74 years
Literacy: 94%
Capital with population: San José 278.561
Other important cities with population: Alajuela 147.396
Language: Spanish
Religion: Roman catholic
Currency: Colón = 100 centimos

Costa Rica is known as the country that has no army, but a policeforce among the worlds's best equipped ! The lack of generals and colonels is in any case not the only cause for the peaceful, democratic development of the country during the years after 1948. Independent 1821, 1838.

⑮ PANAMA

República de Panama
(Republic of Panama)

Area: 77.082 km^2 (29.774 mi^2)
Population: 2.321.300
Population growth per annum: 2,1%
Life expectancy at birth: Males 69 years, females 74 years
Literacy: 86%
Capital with population: Panama City 389.172
Other important cities with population: Colón 59.840
Language: Spanish
Religion: Roman catholic
Currency: Balboa = 100 centesimos

Panama is known all over the Seven Seas. Few know that the word means 'abundance of fish' but many know the quartered tricolor flag that is flown over many ships (as a flag of 'convenience') – and all know of the Canal that every year carries over 10.000 large ships between the Atlantic and the Pacific. Independent 3 Nov 1903.

SOUTH AMERICA

Area: 17,611,000 km² (6,798,000 mi²)
Population: 278 900,000
Density of population per km²: 15.8 (per mi² : 41.0)

②	ANTIGUA (AND BARBUDA)
⑲	ARGENTINA
⑥	BARBADOS
⑰	BOLIVIA
⑮	BRAZIL
⑯	CHILE
⑩	COLOMBIA
③	DOMINICA
⑬	ECUADOR
⑦	GRENADA
⑪	GUYANA
⑱	PARAGUAY
⑭	PERU
①	SAINT KITTS AND NEVIS
⑤	SAINT LUCIA
④	SAINT VINCENT
⑫	SURINAME
⑨	TRINIDAD AND TOBAGO
⑳	URUGUAY
⑧	VENEZUELA

② ANTIGUA (AND BARBUDA)

① SAINT KITTS-NEVIS

DOMINICA ③

SAINT LUCIA ⑤

BARBADOS

④ SAINT VINCENT ⑥

⑦ GRENADA ⑨ TRINIDAD AND TOBAGO

Punta Gallinas at 12° 28' N. latitude is the most northerly point on the South American mainland.

Discovered in 1935 the Angel Falls in the Roraima Mountains are the highest in the world. The total fall is 980 m. (3,215 ft.) with the greatest single drop of 805 m. (2,641 ft.).

⑧ VENEZUELA

GUYANA

⑩ COLOMBIA

⑪ SURINAME

⑫

The waters from the Amazon can clearly be distinguished 300 km. (186 mi.) out into the Atlantic Ocean.

ECUADOR

20' W. longitude Pariñas is the ̶nmost point on the ̶nd of South ̶ca.

⑬

The Amazon is the longest river in South America (6,570 km. (4,080 mi.) from source to mouth) and is the world's second longest. The drainage basin is the largest in the world and covers 7.05 million km² (2,722,008 mi²) and the river flow is greater than any other (120,000 m² (6,180,000 ft²) per second).

Ocean going ships can reach as far as Iquitos, 3,700 km. (2,298 mi.) from the mouth of the Amazon.

The world's most extensive lowland is part of the Amazon Basin with the largest rain forests, the selvas, covering some 5 million km² (1,930,502 mi²).

⑭ PERU

BRAZIL

⑮

Cabo Branco at 34° 36' W. longitude is the South American mainland's most easterly point.

South America's largest lake in Lago Titicaca, 8,030 km² (3,100 mi²). Situated at 3,812 m. (12,507 ft.) above sea level it is one of the world's highest bodies of water.

South America's highest active volcano is Guallatiri, 6,060 m. (19,882 ft.) (latest eruption in 1959).

In relation to the surroundings the Andes are the world's highest mountain range. Over a distance of 500 km. (311 mi.) the surface drops from peaks around 7,000 m. (22,966 ft.) high to nearly 8,000 m. (26,247 ft.) deep in the Peru-Chile Trench, a difference of over 14,000 m. (45,932 ft.).

⑰ BOLIVIA

PARAGUAY

⑱

The Iguaçu Falls are the mightiest in South America. The falls are divided by forested islands over a width of 3.5 km. (2.2 mi.) with two falls totalling a height of 70 m. (230 ft.).

Calama in the Atacama Desert is probably the driest spot on earth, because no precipitation has ever been recorded there.

South America's highest mountain, Cerro Aconcagua, reaches 6,959 m. (22,831 ft.) above sea level.

ARGENTINA

⑲

⑳ URUGUAY

One of the few passes through the mighty wall of the Andes is the Uspallata (Paso de la Cumbre), 3,842 m. (12,605 ft.) high.

CHILE

⑯

The deepest depression in South America is Salinas Grandes on Peninsula Valdés, 35 m. (115 ft.) below sea level.

Glacier de Patagonia, covering more than 4,000 km² (1,544 mi²), is the continent's largest.

Isla Grande de Tierra del Fuego is the continent's largest island 48,400 km² (18,687 mi²).

Cabo Froward at 53° 54' S. latitude is the South American mainland's southernmost point.

Most southerly point in South America is Cape Horn at 55° 59' S. latitude.

① SAINT KITTS-NEVIS
Federation of Saint Kitts and Nevis

Area: 261 km^2 (101 mi^2)
Population: 43.700
Population growth per annum: 0,1%
Life expectancy at birth: –
Literacy: 97%
Capital with population: Basseterre 14.283
Other important cities with population: none
Language: English
Religion: Protestant
Currency: East Caribbean (EC) dollar = 100 cents

*St. Kitt cultivates tourists and sugar. The pleasant climate in the
trade wind tropics favours both of the main industries. Palms
and beaches correspond to the common " image" of the
Caribbean. Independent 19 Sep 1983.*

② ANTIGUA (AND BARBUDA)
State of Antigua and Barbuda

Area: 442 km^2 (171 mi^2)
Population: 81.500
Population growth per annum: 1,3%
Life expectancy at birth: –
Literacy: 89%
Capital with population: Saint John's 36.000
Other important cities with population: none
Language: English
Religion: Protestant
Currency: East Caribbean (EC) dollar = 100 cents

*Antigua and Barbuda are names known to collectors of stamps,
to naval strategy planners, some students of colonial history
and a few in the suger trade, and of course, to the proud and
independent islanders of the Lesser Antilles.
Independent 1 Nov 1981.*

③ DOMINICA
The Commonwealth of Dominica

Area: 751 km^2 (290 mi^2)
Population: 81.200
Population growth per annum: 1,8%
Life expectancy at birth: Males 57 years, females 59 years
Literacy: 94%
Capital with population: Roseau 8.279
Other important cities with population: none
Language: English, french
Religion: Roman catholic
Currency: East Caribbean (EC) dollar = 100 cents

*Dominica can be called the only Caribbean country among all
the Caribbean lands. Only there still lives a sizeable remnant of
the once dreaded Carib Indians – whose name is perpetuated in
the equally dreadful word cannibal. Independent 3 Nov 1978.*

④ SAINT VINCENT (AND THE GRENADINES)

Area: 389 km^2 (150 mi^2)
Population: 112.614
Population growth per annum: 2,0%
Life expectancy at birth: Males 59 years, females 60 years
Literacy: 96%
Capital with population: Kingstown 28.942
Other important cities with population: none
Language: English
Religion: Protestant, roman catholic
Currency: East Caribbean (E.C.) dollar = 100 cents

*Many different kinds of fruit are grown on the islands –
coconuts, mangoes, avocados, guavas just to mention a few,
but not the pomegranates used for making grenadine syrup (an
ingredient of many cocktailes). Most of the 600 volcanic
Grenadine Islands belong to St. Vincent.
Independent 27 Oct 1979.*

⑤ SAINT LUCIA

Area: 616 km^2 (238 mi^2)
Population: 146.600
Population growth per annum: 2,5%
Life expectancy at birth: Males 69 years, females 76 years
Literacy: 88%
Capital with population: Castries 52.868
Other important cities with population: none
Language: English, french
Religion: Roman catholic
Currency: East Caribbean (EC) dollar = 100 cents

*Bananas, cocoa and coconuts are the chief products of St.
Lucia instead of sugar as on most other Antillean Islands.
A growing number of tourists are discovering the pleasant
beaches of St. Lucia. Independent 22 Feb 1979.*

⑥ BARBADOS

Area: 430 km^2 (166 mi^2)
Population: 253.881
Population growth per annum: 1,4%
Life expectancy at birth: Males 70 years, females 73 years
Literacy: 99%
Capital with population: Bridgetown 7.517
Other important cities with population: none
Language: English
Religion: Protestant
Currency: Barbados dollar = 100 cents

*Tourists and sugar cane thrive here on the most easterly of the
Windward Islands. The gentle trade winds blow with a constant
5-6 m. (16-20 ft.)/s. to keep the surf rolling in and the sky clear
of clouds. Independent 30 Nov 1966.*

⑦ GRENADA

The State of Grenada

Area: 344 km^2 (133 mi^2)
Population: 98.000
Population growth per annum: -1,0%
Life expectancy at birth: 69 years
Literacy: 98%
Capital with population: Saint George's 29.369
Other important cities with population: none
Language: English, french
Religion: Roman catholic
Currency: East Caribbean (EC) dollar = 100 cents

Grenada is one the "spice islands" of the world. It produces more than one third of the nutmeg on the world market. In the world of the super powers Grenada has also had an importance without relation to its tiny size. Independent 7 Feb 1974.

⑧ VENEZUELA

República de Venezuela
(Republic of Venezuela)

Area: 912.050 km^2 (352.295 mi^2)
Population: 18.757.389
Population growth per annum: 2,7%
Life expectancy at birth: Males 66 years, females 72 years
Literacy: 86%
Capital with population: Caracas 3.310.236
Other important cities with population:
  Maracaibo 1.330.215, Valencia 1.180.820
Language: Spanish
Religion: Roman catholic
Currency: Bolivar = 100 centimos

Venice has been called a floating city and Venezuela – "little Venice" – a land floting on oil. Over 4.000 drilling derricks stand now in the shallow waters of the Maracaibo lagoon like the houses on stilts that gave the country its name. In the southeast the Angel Falls, highest in the world, plunge 980 m. / 3.215 ft (805m / 2.641 ft. uninterrupted).Indep.1821, 1830.

⑨ TRINIDAD AND TOBAGO

The Republic of Trinidad and Tobago

Area: 5.128 km^2 (1.981 mi^2)
Population: 1.243.000
Population growth per annum: 1,8%
Life expectancy at birth: Males 68 years, females 74 years
Literacy: 96%
Capital with population: Port of Spain 58.300
Other important cities with population:
  San Fernando 33.100
Language: English
Religion: Roman catholic (34%), protestant (15%), hindu (25%), islam (6%)
Currency: Trinidad and Tobago dollar = 100 cents

A melting pot where everything is transformed. Cultures and traditions, and people from five continents have been mixed and combined under the sun of Trinidad. A different melting pot: an "inexhaustible" lake of asphalt, Pitch Lake, is unique in the world. Independent 31 Aug 1962.

⑩ COLOMBIA

República de Colombia
(Republic of Colombia)

Area: 1.141.748 km^2 (441.020 mi^2)
Population: 27.867.325
Population growth per annum: 1,6%
Life expectancy at birth: Males 63 years, females 67 years
Literacy: 88%
Capital with population: Bogotá 3.982.941
Other important cities with population:
  Medellin 1.468.089, Cali 1.350.565, Barranquilla 899.781
Language: Spanish
Religion: Roman catholic
Currency: Colombian peso = 100 centavos

Colombia may have been the legendary land of El Dorado – the gold-covered king. Today it could be called the land of green gold – as 90 % of all emeralds in the world come from mines in Colombia. However high quality coffee is the country's main export product. Independent 17 Dec 1819.

⑪ GUYANA

Cooperative Republic of Guyana

Area: 214.969 km^2 (83.035 mi^2)
Population: 812.000
Population growth per annum: 0,8%
Life expectancy at birth: Males 67 years, females 72 years
Literacy: 86%
Capital with population: Georgetown 188.000
Other important cities with population: none
Language: English, hindi, urdu, amerindin
Religion: Hindu (34%), protestant (34%),roman catholic (18%), islam (9%)
Currency: Guyana dollar = 100 cents

Guyana is an East Indian country in the West Indies, as the major part of the inhabitants are descendants of immigrants from India. Of all the world's waterfalls only nine are higher than the next 500m. (1.640 ft.) high uninterrupted cascades of the King George VI Falls, north of the Roraima Plateau. Independent 26 May 1966.

⑫ SURINAME

Nieuwe Republick van Suriname
(Republic of Suriname)

Area: 163.820 km^2 (63.278 mi^2)
Population: 415.000
Population growth per annum: 3,2%
Life expectancy at birth: Males 68 years, females 73 years
Literacy: 65%
Capital with population: Paramaribo 103.738
Other important cities with population: none
Language: Dutch, english, spanish
Religion: Hindu (28%), protestant (24%), islam (20%), roman catholic (21%)
Currency: Suriname guilder or florin = 100 cents

A country for $ 24 ? In a deal with Britan in the 15th century the Dutch acquired this former British colony in exchange for New Amsterdam – later better known as the city of New York – in turn bought for $ 24. 90% of today's Surinam is covered with dense rainforest. Independent 25 Nov 1975.

⑬ ECUADOR

República de Ecuador
(Republic of Ecuador)

Area: 270.670 km^2 (104,551 mi^2)

(disputed area 190.807 km^2 not included)
Population: 10.203.722
Population growth per annum: 2,6%
Life expectancy at birth: Males 63 years, females 67 years
Literacy: 80%
Capital with population: Quito 1.093.278
Other important cities with population:
Guayaquil 1.509.108, Cuena 193.012
Language: Spanish, quechua
Religion: Roman catholic
Currency: Sucre = 100 centavos

*A "heavy" ítem in Ecuador´s export statistict is featherweight
balsa timber. TheSpanish word balsa denotes both raft and the
timber, lighter than cork. The Indians used it for building sailing
rafts as early as prehistoric times. The logs for Heyerdahl´s
famous Kon-Tiki were cut in Ecuador in 1947.
Independent 13 May 1830.*

⑭ PERU

República del Perú
(Republic of Peru)

Area: 1.285.216 km^2 (496.437 mi^2)
Population: 21.255.900
Population growth per annum: 2,6%
Life expectancy at birth: Males 59 years, females 63 years
Literacy: 82%
Capital with population: Lima 5.008.400
Other important cities with population: Callao 515.200,
Arequipa 531.829
Language: Spanish, quechua, aymara
Religion: Roman catholic
Currency: Inti = 100 centimos

*The Inca´s land of gold and silver was turned into a land of
guano and fishmeal. The conquistadores stripped the land of
its immense treasures of gold artwork. The stone buildings
of Machu Picchu´s breath-taking eagle´s nest-city still remain –
hidden and forgotten for five centuries until discovered by
Hiram Bingham in 1911. Independent 28 Jul 1821.*

⑮ BRAZIL

República Federativa do Brasil
(Federative Republic of Brazil)

Area: 8.511.965 km^2 (3.287.893 mi^2)
Population: 141.452.200
Population growth per annum: 2,1%
Life expectancy at birth: Males 63 years, females 67 years
Literacy: 74%
Capital with population: Brasilia 1.567.709
Other important cities with population: São
Paulo 10.063.110, Rio de Janiero 5.603.388
Language: Portuguese
Religion: Roman catholic (89%), protestant (7%)
Currency: Cruzeiro = 100 centavos

*Only four countries in the world are larger than Brazil. The
mighty Amazon carries more water than any other river
(120.000 m³/s or 6.180.000ft³/s at the mouth) and is navigable
for ocean going ships up to Iquitos, 3.700 km. (2.298 mi.) from
the sea. Brasilia, created by president Kubitschek and architects
Niemeyer and Costa, became capital in 1960.Indep. 7 Sep 1822*

⑯ CHILE

República de Chile
(Republic of Chile)

Area: 756.945 km^2 (292.383 mi^2)
Population: 12.748.498
Population growth per annum: 1,7%
Life expectancy at birth: Males 65 years, females 70 years
Literacy: 94%
Capital with population: Santiago 4.858.342
Other important cities with population: Viña del
Mar 315.947, Talcahuano 231.356
Language: Spanish
Religion: Roman catholic
Currency: Chilean peso = 100 centavos

*The "narrowest" country in the world, Chile, is nearly twenty-
five times longer than it is wide (175 by 4.300 km. /109 x 2.670
mi.) and stretches from the tropics down to the stormy Cape
Horn in the "Furious Fifties". At Calama in the Atacama Desert
no rainfall has ever been recorded. Independent 18 Sep 1810.*

⑰ BOLIVIA

República de Bolivia
(Republic of Bolivia)

Area: 1.098.581 km^2 (424.346 mi^2)
Population: 6.740.417
Population growth per annum: 2,7%
Life expectancy at birth: Males 47 years, females 51 years
Literacy: 63%
Capital with population: La Paz 1.013.688, Sucre 92.917
Other important cities with population:
Santa Cruz de la Sierra 457.803, Cochabamba 360.446
Language: Spanish, quechua (34%), aymara (25%)
Religion: Roman catholic
Currency: Boliviano = 100 centavos

*Tin mining is the main source of wealth in the land-locked
Bolivia. Most of the population live on the dry, cold tablelands,
higher than many peaks in European Alps. Lake Titicaca,
shared with Peru, is the world´s highest (3.812 m. /12.507 ft.)
navigable body of water. Independent 6 Aug 1825.*

⑱ PARAGUAY

República de Paraguay
(Republic of Paraguay)

Area: 406.752 km^2 (157.115 mi^2)
Population: 4.010.000
Population growth per annum: 2,6%
Life expectancy at birth: Males 64 years, females 69 years
Literacy: 88%
Capital with population: Ascunción 455.517
Other important cities with population: San
Lorenzo 74.359
Language: Spanish, guarani
Religion: Roman catholic
Currency: Guarani = 100 centimos

*Here one man´s will is, and has been, law – by unbroken tradi-
tion from Jesuit times. The Pope was replaced by the King of
Spain, he in turn by the founding dictator "El Supremo" and so
on. General Stroessner (1954-89) has been forced to retire by
General Rodriguez. The Iguaçu falls of the Parana cascade 82 m
over a width of four km through the forest. Indep. 14 May 1811.*

⑲ ARGENTINA

República Argentina
(Argentine Republic)

Area: 2.780.092 km^2 (1.073.859 mi^2)
Population: 31.497.000
Population growth per annum: 1,5%
Life expectancy at birth: Males 66 years, females 73 years
Literacy: 94%
Capital with population: Buenos Aires 2.922.829,
  metropolitan area 9.969.826
Other important cities with population: Córdoba 983.969,
  Rosario 957.301
Language: Spanish
Religion: Roman catholic
Currency: Austral = 100 centavos

*The home of the tango and the gaucho. Argentina is a Europe
in miniature. It is situated on European latitudes (on the
southern hemisphere) and it was populated by settlers from all
over Europe. It has the cotinent's highest peak, Aconcagua and
its lowest spot, Salinas Grandes on the Peninsula Valdés, 35 m.
(115 ft.) below sea level. Independent 25 Mar 1810.*

⑳ URUGUAY

República Oriental del Uruguay
(Eastern Republic of Uruguay)

Area: 176.215 km^2 (68.066 mi^2)
Population: 3.080.000
Population growth per annum: 1,6%
Life expectancy at birth: Males 68 years, females 75 years
Literacy: 94%
Capital with population: Montevideo 1.246.500
Other important cities with population: Salto 77.400,
  Paysandu 75.200
Language: Spanish
Religion: Roman catholic
Currency: New peso = 100 centésimos

*A country of rolling grasslands with grazing cattle and
cultivated fields. As in other agricultural lands, more people
live in the capital than in the all other towns put together.
Independent 25 Aug 1825.*

INDEX

A

Aa Sumayh **56** D 3
Aachen **16** E 4
Aalen **17** F 5
Äänekoski **18** J 3
Aba **55** F 4
Abadab, Jabal **52** F 5
Ābādān **25** E 3
Ābādeh **25** F 3
Abadla **50** E 2
Abaetetuba **73** J 4
Abagnar Qi **35** G 2
Abaiang **46** C 2
Abakaliki **55** F 4
Abakan **32** F 5
Abalak **55** F 2
Abancay **74** B 3
Abariringa **46** D 3
Abarqu **25** F 3
Abarqu, Kavir-e **25** F 3
Abatskoye **27** O 4
Abay **27** O 6
Abaya, Lake **57** F 3
Abaza **32** F 5
Abbai **56** F 2
Abbāsābād **25** G 1
Abbeville **20** D 1
Abbot Ice Shelf **79**
'Abd al Kūrī **57** J 2
Abdulino **26** K 5
Abéché **55** J 3
Abemama **46** C 2
Abengourou **54** D 4
Abeokuta **54** E 4
Aberdeen (S.D., U.S.A.) **66** G 2
Aberdeen (U.K.) **16** C 3
Aberystwyth **16** C 4
Abhā' **53** G 5
Abhar **25** E 1
Abidjan **54** D 4
Abilene **66** G 5
Abkit **33** T 3
Abong Abong, Gunung **38** A 3
Abong Mbang **55** G 5
Abrantes **20** B 4
'Abri **52** E 4
Abruzzo **21** F 3
Abū ad Duhūr **24** B 2
Abū al Bukhush **25** F 4
Abū 'Alī **25** E 4
Abu Dhabi **25** FG 4
Abū Ḥadrīyah **25** E 4
Abū Ḥamad **52** E 5
Abū Jifān **25** E 4

Abū Kamāl **24** C 2
Abū Maṭariq **52** D 6
Abū Mūsa' **25** G 4
Abū Qumayyis, Ra's **25** F 4
Abu Road **36** B 3
Abu Simbel → Abu Sunbul **52** E 4
Abū Sunbul **52** E 4
Abū Ẓaby **25** FG 4
Abū Zanīmah **24** A 3
Abufari **73** F 5
Abunã **74** C 3
Abunã (Rondônia, Brazil) **72** E 5
Abūqrīn **51** J 2
Abuya Myeda **57** F 2
Abyār 'Alī **24** C 4
Abydos **52** E 3
Äbyek **25** F 2
Açailândia **73** J 4
Acaponeta **68** A 3
Acapulco **68** B 4
Acaraú **75** J 1
Acari **75** J 2
Acarigua **72** E 2
Accomac **67** L 4
Accra **54** DE 4
Achao **77** B 7
Achayvayam **33** VW 3
Achelóos **22** B 3
Achinsk **32** EF 4
Acklins Island **69** H 3
Aconcagua, Cerro **76** BC 5
Acopiara **75** J 2
Acorizal **74** E 4
Acre (Brazil) **72** D 5
Acre (Brazil) **74** C 3
Acre (Israel) **24** B 2
Acri **21** G 4
Actaeon Group **47** F 4
Aḑ Ḑafrah **25** F 5
Ad Dahnā' **25** DE 4
Ad Dammām **25** EF 4
Ad Dār al Hamrā' **24** BC 4
Ad Darb **53** G 5
Ad Dawādimī **24** D 4
Ad Dawḥah **25** F 4
Ad Dawr **24** D 2
Ad Dayr **24** A 4
Ad Dibdibah **25** E 3–4
Ad Dilam **25** E 5
Ad Dindar **52** E 6
Ad Dīwanīyah **25** D 3
Ad Duwaym **52** E 6
Adaba **57** F 3
Adak (AK, U.S.A.) **62** B 5
Adak (Sweden) **18** G 2
'Adale **57** H 4

Adam, Mount **77** DE 9
Adamantina **75** F 5
Adamaoua **55** G 4
Adams Bridge **36** C 6
Adamstown **47** G 4
Adana **23** E 3
Adare, Cape **79**
Adavale **43** G 4
Addis Ababa **57** F 3
Addis Zemen **57** F 2
Adelaide **43** F 5
Adelaide Island **79**
Adelaide Peninsula **63** S 2
Adelaide River **42** E 1
Adélie Coast **79**
Aden **53** H 6
Aden, Gulf of **53** H 6
Adi Ugri **57** F 2
Adige **21** F 2
Adıgüzel Barajı **22** C 3
Adirondack Mountains **67** M 3
Adıyaman **23** E 3
Admiralty **62** L 4
Admiralty Islands **44** E 2
Admiralty Mountains **79**
Ado **54** E 4
Ado Ekiti **55** F 4
Adok **56** E 3
Adrano **21** F 4
Adrar **50** E 3
Adrar des Iforas **54** E 1–2
Adré **55** J 3
Adriatic Sea **21** FG 3
Adwa **57** F 2
Adzhar **23** F 2
Adzopé **54** D 4
Aegean Sea **22** C 3
Afao, Mont **51** G 3
Afghanistan **31** GH 4
'Afif **24** D 4–5
Afikpo **55** F 4
Afmadōw **57** G 4
Afognak **62** G 4
African Islands **57** J 5
Afyonkarahisar **22** D 3
Agadez **55** F 2
Agadir **50** D 2
Agana **46** A 2
Agapitovo **27** R 2
Agartala **37** F 3
Agata **32** F 2
Agats **39** J 5
Agattu **62** A 5
Agawa Bay **64** L 6
Agboville **54** D 4
Agdary **32** L 3
Agen **20** D 3

Agepsta **23** F 2
Agha Jāri **25** EF 3
Agordat **57** F 1
Agra **36** C 2
Ağrı **23** F 3
Agrigento **21** F 4
Agrihan **46** A 1
Agrínion **22** B 3
Agto **65** R 2
Água Clara **75** F 5
Aguadulce **72** B 2
Águas Formosas **75** H 4
Agulhas, Cape **58** C 6
Aguscalientes **68** B 3
Ahe **47** F 3
Ahmadabad **36** B 3
Ahmadnagar **36** BC 4
Ahome **66** E 6
Ähtäri **18** H 3
Ähtävänjoki **18** H 3
Ahvāz **25** E 3
Ahvenanmaa **19** GH 3
Aihui **33** N 5
Ailinginae **46** C 2
Ailinglapalap **46** C 2
Aillik **65** Q 4
Ailuk **46** C 2
Aim **33** O 4
Aïn Amenas **51** G 3
Aïn Amguel **51** FG 4
Aïn Beïda **51** G 1
Aïn ben Tili **50** D 3
Aïn Ezzane **51** H 4
Aïn Tiguelguemine **51** F 3
Aioun el Atrouss **50** D 5
Aïr **55** F 2
Airão **73** F 4
Aitape **44** D 2
Aitutaki **47** E 4
Aix-en-Provence **21** E 3
Aiyaíon Pélagos **22** C 3
Aizuwakamatsu **35** M 3
Aj Bogd Uul **34** BC 2
Ajaccio **21** E 3
Ajdābiyā **51** K 2
'Ajmān **25** G 4
Ajmer **36** B 2
Ajo, Cabo de **20** C 3
Ak Dağ **22** C 3
Akademi:, Zaliv **33** P 5
Akcha **31** H 3
Akespe **30** G 1
Akharnaí **22** B 3
Akhisar **22** C 3
Akhtubinsk **26** J 6
Akhtyrka **26** F 5
Akimiski **65** L 5
Akita **35** M 3

Akkabak **31** G 1
Akkajaure **18** G 2
'Akko **24** B 2
Aklavik **62** K 2
Akmenrags **19** H 4
Akobo **56** E 3
Akola **36** C 3
Akosombo Dam **54** E 4
Akpatok **65** O 3
Ákra Akritas **22** B 3
Akra Arnauti **23** D 3
Ákra Maléas **22** B 3
Ákra Spátha **22** B 3
Ákra Taínaron **22** B 3
Akritas, Ákra **22** B 3
Akron **67** K 3
Aksaray **23** D 3
Aksay Kazakzu Zizhixian
34 B 3
Akşehir **22** D 3
Aksha **32** K 5
Akshiy **31** G 1
Akşu (Turkey) **22** D 3
Aksu (China) **31** L 2
Aktasty **27** M 5
Aktogay **27** P 6
Aktyubinsk **27** L 5
Akure **55** F 4
Akureyri **18** B 2
Al Abyaḍ, Ra's **51** G 1
Al 'Alamayn **52** D 2
Al 'Amādīyah **24** D 1
Al 'Amārah **25** E 3
Al 'Aqabah **24** B 3
Al 'Aqaylah **51** J 2
Al Arabīyah as Su'ūdīyah →
Saudi Arabia **53** GH 4
Al 'Arīsh **24** AB 3
Al 'Armah **25** DE 4
Al Arṭāwīyah **25** D 4
Al 'Āshūrīyah **24** D 3
Al 'Awaynāt **51** H 3
Al 'Ayn **25** G 4
Al Bāb **24** B 1
Al Badī' **53** H 4
Al Baḥr al Mayyit **24** B 3
Al Bahrah **25** E 3
Al Barkāt **51** H 4
Al Başrah **25** E 3
Al Batin **25** E 3
Al Baṭinah **53** K 4
Al Bayḍā' **51** K 2
Al Bid' **24** B 3
Al Bi'r **24** B 3
Al Birkah **53** G 4
Al Brayqah **51** JK 2
Al Buḥayrah al Murrah al
Kubrā **24** A 3
Al Fāshir **52** D 6
Al Fatḥah **24** D 2
Al Fawwārah **24** D 4
Al Fayyūm **52** E 3
Al Fuḥayhīl **25** E 3
Al Fujayrah **25** G 4
Al Furāt **24** C 2
Al Fuwayriṭ **25** F 4
Al Ghazālah **24** C 4
Al Ḥaḍhālil **24—25** D 3
Al Ḥadīthah **24** CD 2
Al Ḥamād **24** C 2—3

Al Ḥamrā' **24** C 5
Al Ḥanākīyah **24** C 4
Al Ḥanīsh al Kabīr **53** G 6
Al Ḥarrah (Jordan) **24** BC 2
Al Ḥarrah (Saudi Arabia)
24 C 3
Al Ḥasā' **25** EF 4
Al Ḥasakah **24** C 1
Al Ḥasan **24** D 2
Al Ḥawwārī **51** K 4
Al Ḥayy **25** DE 2
Al Ḥijaz **24** BC 4
Al Ḥillah (Iraq) **25** D 2
Al Ḥillah (Saudi Arabia)
25 E 5
Al Ḥillah (Sudan) **52** D 6
Al Hudaydah **53** G 6
Al Hufrah **24** BC 3—4
Al Hufūf **25** E 4
Al Hūj **24** C 3
Al Ḥusayḥişah **52** E 6
Al Ḥuwaymī **53** H 6
Al Iglim al Janūbīyah
56 DE 3
Al 'Iraq **24** D 2
Al 'Irq **51** K 3
Al 'Isāwiyah **24** B 3
Al Iskandarīyah **52** DE 2
Al Ismā'īlīyah **24** A 3
Al Jafr **24** B 3
Al Jafūrah **25** F 4—5
Al Jaghbūb **51** K 3
Al Jahrah **25** E 3
Al Jalāmīd **24** C 2
Al Jarid, Shaṭṭ **51** G 2
Al Jawf **24** C 3
Al Jayli **52** E 5
Al Jaza'ir **51** F 1
Al Jazīrah **24** CD 2
Al Jiwā' **25** FG 5
Al Jizah **52** E 2
Al Jubayl **25** E 4
Al Julayqah **25** E 4
Al Jumaymah **24** D 3
Al Junaynah **52** C 6
Al Karak **24** B 3
Al Karnak **24** A 4
Al Kāzimīyah **24** D 2
Al Khalīl **24** B 3
Al Khāliş **25** D 2
Al Khārijah **52** E 3
Al Kharj **25** E 5
Al Khartum **52** E 5
Al Kharṭūm Baḥri **52** E 5
Al Khaṣab **25** G 4
Al Khiḍr **25** D 3
Al Khubar **25** F 4
Al Khufayfīyah **25** D 4
Al Khunfah **24** C 3
Al Kir'ānah **25** F 4
Al Kūfah **24** D 2
Al Kufrah **51** K 4
Al Kumayt **25** E 2—3
Al Kuntillah **24** B 3
Al Kūt **25** D 2
Al Kuwayt **25** E 3
Al Labbah **24** D 3
Al Lādhiqīyah **24** B 2
Al Lagowa **52** D 6
Al Lifīyah **24** D 3

Al Lişāfah **25** E 4
Al Lussuf **24** D 3
Al Madīnah **24** C 4
Al Mafraq **24** B 2
Al Maḥallah al Kubrā **52** E 2
Al Mahrah **53** J 5
Al Majann **25** F 5
Al Makhaylī **51** K 2
Al Manadīr **25** G 5
Al Manāmah **25** F 4
Al Manāqil **52** E 6
Al Manşūrah **52** E 2
Al Maqṭa' **25** G 4
Al Marj **51** K 2
Al Mawşil **24** D 1
Al Mayyāh **24** D 4
Al Minyā **52** E 3
Al Mubarraz **25** E 4
Al Mudawwarah **24** B 3
Al Mughayrā' **24** B 3
Al Muharraq **25** F 4
Al Mukallā **53** H 6
Al Murabbā' **24** D 4
Al Musayjid **24** C 4
Al Musayyib **24** D 2
Al Muwayliḥ **24** B 4
Al Nasser **24** A 4
Al Qaḍārif **52** F 6
Al Qadīmah **53** F 4
Al Qāhirah **52** E 2
Al Qalībah **24** B 3
Al Qāmishlī **24** C 1
Al Qanṭarah **24** A 3
Al Qaṭīf **25** E 4
Al Qaṭrānī **24** B 3
Al Qaṭrūn **51** H 3—4
Al Qay'īyah **24** D 4
Al Qayrawān **51** GH 1
Al Qayşūmah **24** D 3
Al Qayşūmah **25** E 3
Al Qunayṭirah **24** B 2
Al Qunfudhah **53** G 5
Al Qurayyah **24** B 3
Al Qurnah **25** E 3
Al Quşayr **24** B 4
Al Qūşūrīyah **24** D 5
Al Quṭayfah **24** B 2
Al Quwārah **24** D 4
Al Quwayīyah **25** D 4
Al Shagra **25** F 4
Al Ubayyid **52** E 6
Al Ugşur **24** A 4
Al Urayq **24** C 3
Al Urdun **24** B 3
Al 'Uwayqilah **24** CD 3
Al 'Uzayr **25** E 3
Al Wajh **24** B 4
Al Warī'ah **25** E 4
Al Widyān **24** C 3
Ala, Monti di **21** E 3
Alabama **67** J 5
Alabama **67** J 5
Alaçam Dağları **22** C 3
Alachakh **33** P 4
Aladağ (Turkey) **23** DE 3
Aladağ (Turkey) **23** F 3
Alagoas **75** J 2
Alagoinhas **75** J 3
Alagón (Spain) **20** C 3
Alajuela **68** F 5

Alakurtti **18** K 2
Alamagan **46** A 1
Alamogordo **66** E 5
Alamos **66** E 6
Åland **19** GH 3
Ålands hav **19** G 4
Alanya **23** D 3
Alaotra, Lac **59** H 3
Alapayevsk **27** M 4
Alaska **62** FH 2
Alaska, Gulf of **62** HJ 4
Alaska Peninsula **62** E 4
Alaska Range **62** GH 3
Alatyr' **26** J 5
Al'Awsajīyah **24** D 4
Alazani **23** G 2
Alba **21** E 3
Alba Iulia **22** B 1
Albacete **20** C 4
Albanel, Lac **65** N 5
Albania **22** AB 2
Albano Laziale **21** F 3
Albany (Australia) **42** B 5
Albany (GA, U.S.A.) **67** K 5
Albany (N.Y., U.S.A.)
67 M 3
Albany (Ontario, Can.)
64 L 5
Albatross Point **45** Q 8
Albert, Lake **56** E 4
Albert Nile **56** E 4
Alberta **63** OP 5
Albi **20** D 3
Albina **73** H 2
Alborán **20** C 4
Ålborg **19** F 4
Albū 'Alī **24** D 2
Albuquerque **66** E 4
Albury **43** H 6
Alcalá **20** B 4
Alcalá **20** C 3
Alcántara, Embalse de
20 B 4
Alcaraz, Sierra de **20** C 4
Alcázar de San Juan **20** C 4
Alciéni **55** G 6
Alcira **20** C 4
Alcolea del Pinar **20** C 3
Alcoy **20** C 4
Aldabra Islands **57** H 6
Aldan **33** N 4
Aldan **33** O 3
Aldanskoye Nagor'ye
33 MN 4
Aleg **50** C 5
Alegrete **76** E 4
Aleksandriya **23** D 1
Aleksandrovsk **27** M 4
Aleksandrovsk-Sakhalinskiy
33 Q 5
Aleksandrovskiy-Savod
32 L 5
Alekseyevka **27** O 5
Alekseyevo **33** R 1
Alençon **20** D 2
Aleppo **24** B 1
Aléria **21** E 3
Alès **20** D 3
Alessandria **21** E 3
Ålestrup **19** E 4

Ålesund **18** E 3
Aleutian Range **62** F 4
Alexander Archipelago
 62 K 4
Alexander Island **79**
Alexandra **44** P 10
Alexandra Falls **63** O 3
Alexandria (Egypt) **52** E 2
Alexandria (LA, U.S.A.)
 67 H 5
Alexandria (MD, U.S.A.)
 67 L 4
Alexandria (Romania)
 22 BC 2
Alexandroúpolis **22** C 2
Aleysk **27** Q 5
Algama **33** N 4
Alganskaya **33** W 3
Algarve **20** B 4
Algeciras **20** B 4
Algeria **50–51** EF 3
Alghero **21** E 3
Algiers **51** F 1
Ali Bayramly **30** DE 3
Ali Sabjeh **57** G 2
Aliåbåd **25** G 3
'Aliåbåd, Küh-e **25** F 2
Aliákmon **22** B 2
Alice River **43** H 3
Alice Springs **42** E 3
Aligarh **36** C 2
Aligüdarz **25** E 2
Aljuq, Küh-e **25** F 3
Aliskerovo **33** V 2
Aliwal North **58** D 6
Allahabad **36** D 2
Allakh-Yun' **33** P 3
Allentown **67** L 3
Alleppey **36** C 6
Alma-Ata **31** K 2
Almada **20** B 4
Almeirim **73** H 4
Almenara **75** H 4
Almendra, Embalse de
 20 B 3
Almería **20** C 4
Al'met'yevsk **26** K 5
Almirante Brown **79**
Almoustarat **54** D 2
Alofi **46** D 4
Alongshan **33** M 5
Alor, Pulau **39** F 5
Alor Setar **38** B 2
Alpena **67** K 2
Alphonse **57** J 6
Alpi Carniche **21** F 2
Alpi Dolomitiche **21** F 2
Alpine **66** F 5
Altamira **73** H 4
Altamont **66** B 3
Altas, Rías **20** B 3
Altay (China) **31** M 1
Altay (Mongolia) **32** G 6
Altay (Russia) **27** R 5
Altay Shan **31** M 1
Altiplanicie Mexicana **68** B 2
Altmark **17** F 4
Alto-Alentejo **20** B 4
Alto Garças **75** F 4
Alto Parnaíba **75** G 2

Alto Río Senguerr **77** B 8
Alto Turi **75** G 1
Alton **67** H 4
Altun Shan **34** AB 3
Alturas **66** B 3
Altynasar **31** G 1
Alva **66** G 4
Alvano, Küh-e **25** E 2
Alvorado **75** G 3
Älvsbyn **18** H 2
Alwar **36** C 2
Alxa Zuoqi **34** DE 3
Alygdzher **32** G 5
Alys-Khaya **33** P 2
Alytus **19** H 5
Amada **52** E 4
Amadeus, Lake **42** E 3
Amadi **56** E 3
Amakinskiy **32** K 1
Amambaí **75** EF 5
Amami-ö-shima **35** J 5
Amangel'dy **27** N 5
Amanzimtoti **59** E 6
Amapá **73** H 3
Amapá **73** H 3
Amarillo **66** F 4
Amaro Leite **75** G 3
Amarti **57** G 2
Amasya **23** E 2
Amazar **32** M 5
Amazonas **72–73** EF 4
Amazonas **73** H 4
Ambala **36** C 1
Ambam **55** G 5
Ambarchik **33** U 2
Ambato **72** C 4
Ambgaon **36** D 3
Ambikapur **36** D 3
Ambilobe **59** H 2
Ambohitralanana **59** J 3
Ambon **39** G 4
Ambositra **59** H 4
Ambovombe **59** H 5
Ambre, Cap d' **59** H 2
Ambrim **45** J 5
Ambur **36** C 5
Amchitka Pass **62** AB 5
Amdo **34** B 4
American Highland **79**
American Samoa **46** D 3
Amery Ice Shelf **79**
Ames **67** H 3
Amga **33** O 3
Amguema **62** B 2
Amguid **51** G 3
Amhara **57** F 2
Amiens **20** D 2
Amindivi Islands **36** B 5
Amirante Islands **57** J 6
Amlia **62** C 5
'Ammän **24** B 3
Ammarfjället **18** G 2
Amo **32** H 3
Åmol **25** F 1
Amorgós **22** C 3
Amos **65** M 6
Amravati **36** C 3
Amritsar **36** C 1
Amsâ'ad **51** K 2

Amsterdam (Netherlands)
 16 DE 4
Amsterdam (N.Y., U.S.A.)
 67 M 3
Amu-Dar'ya **31** G 2
Amukta Pass **62** C 5
Amundsen Gulf **63** N 1
Amundsen-Scott **79**
Amundsen Sea **79**
Amuntai **38** E 4
Amur **33** P 5
Amysakh **32** L 2
An Nabk **24** B 2
An Nabk Abü Qasr **24** C 3
An Nähiyah **24** C 2
An Najaf **24** D 2–3
An' Nakhl **24** AB 3
An Näsiriyah **25** E 3
An Nu'ayrïyah **25** E 2
An Nuhüd **52** D 6
Anabarskoye Ploskogor'ye
 32 J 1–2
Anaco **72** F 2
Anadoli **22–23** CD 3
Anadyr' **33** X 3
Anadyr' **33** X 3
Anadyrskaja Nizmennost'
 33 X 2
Anadyrskiy Zaliv **33** Y 3
Anadyrskoye Ploskogor'ye
 33 VW 2
'Änah **24** D 2
Anaimalai Hills **36** C 5
Anakapalle **36** D 4
Anambas, Kepulauan
 38 C 3
Anamur **23** D 3
Anamur Burnu **23** D 3
Anamuryum **23** D 3
Anantapur **36** C 5
Anapa **23** E 2
Anápolis **75** G 4
Anär **25** G 3
Anatolia **22–23** D 3
Añatuya **76** D 4
Anchorage **62** H 3
Ancohuma **74** C 4
Ancona **21** F 3
Ancud **77** B 7
Anda **35** J 1
Andalucía **20** BC 4
Andaman Islands **37** F 5
Andaman Sea **37** G 5–6
Andarab **31** H 3
Andenes **18** G 2
Anderson (IN, U.S.A.)
 67 J 3–4
Anderson (N.W.T., Can.)
 62 M 2
Anderson (S.C., U.S.A.)
 67 K 5
Andes Mountains **71** C 2–6
Andfjorden **18** G 2
Andhra Pradesh **36** C 4
Andimeshk **25** E 2
Andiria Burun **23** D 3
Andirlangar **31** L 3
Andiyskiy Khrebet **23** G 2
Andizhan **31** J 2
Andkhui **31** H 3

Andong **35** J 3
Andorra **20** D 3
Andorra la Vella **20** D 3
Andöya **18** G 2
Andradina **75** F 5
Andreanof Islands **62** BC 5
Andriba **59** H 3
Ándros **22** C 3
Andros Island **69** G 3
Andújar **20** C 4
Andyngda **32** L 2
Anéfis **54** E 2
Anegada Passage **69** K 4
Aneto, Pico de **20** D 3
Angara **32** F 4
Angarsk **32** H 5
Angaul **32** H 5
Angel Falls **73** F 2
Angeles **39** J 1
Ängelholm **19** F 4
Ångermanälven **18** G 3
Angers **20** C 2
Angical **75** H 3
Angijak Island **65** P 2
Angikuni Lake **63** S 3
Angkor **37** H 5
Anglesey **16** C 4
Angmagssalik **78**
Angoche **59** G 3
Angol **77** B 6
Angola **58** BC 2
Angoulême **20** D 2
Angra do Heroismo **50** A 1
Angu **56** C 4
Anguilla **69** K 4
Anhua **34** F 5
Anhui **35** G 4
Aniak **62** F 3
Aniakchak National
 Monument and Preserve
 62 F 4
Animas Peak **66** E 5
Aniva, Mys **33** Q 6
Anjou **20** C 2
Ankacho **32** J 3
Ankang **34** E 4
Ankara **23** D 2–3
Ankazobe **59** H 3
Anlong **34** E 5
Anlu **34** F 4
Ann Arbor **67** K 3
Ann, Cape **79**
Anna Plains **42** C 2
Annaba **51** G 1
Annai **73** G 3
Annam **37** J 4
Annandale **43** H 3
Annapolis **67** L 4
Annapurna **36** D 2
Annecy **21** E 2
Annobón **55** F 6
Anori **73** F 4
Anqing **35** G 4
Anshan **35** H 2
Anshun **34** E 5
Ansongo **54** E 2
Anta **74** B 3
Antakya **23** E 3
Antalya **22** D 3

Ant – Ass

Antalya Körfezi **22** D 3
Antananarivo **59** H 3
Antarctic Peninsula **79**
Antequera **20** C 4
Anticosti, Île d' **65** P 6
Antigua and Barbuda
 69 KL 4
Antillas Mayores **69** HJ 4
Antiope **46** D 4
Antipodes Islands **79**
Antofagasta **74** B 5
Antofagasta de la Sierra
 76 C 4
Antongil, Baie d' **59** HJ 3
Antonio de Biedma **77** C 8
Antonovo **30** E 1
Antseranana **59** H 2
Antsirabe **59** H 3
Antsohihy **59** H 2
Antwerpen **16** D 4
Anuradhapura **36** D 6
Anxi **34** C 2
Anxiang **34** F 5
Anyang **34** F 3
Anzhero-Sudzhensk **27** R 4
Aomori **35** M 2
Aosta **21** E 2
Aoudaghost **50** C 5
Aoulef el Arab **50–51** F 3
Apaporis **72** D 4
Apataki **47** F 4
Apatity **18** K 2
Apatzingán **68** B 4
Apeldoorn **16** E 4
Api, Tanjung **38** C 3
Apia **46** D 3
Aporé **75** F 4
Aporé **75** F 4
Appalachian Mountains
 67 KM 3–4
Appenino Calabro **21** G 4
Appennino Lucano
 21 G 3–4
Appennino Tosco-Emiliano
 21 F 3
Appleton **67** J 3
Apsheronsk **23** E 2
Apucarana **75** F 5
Apure **72** D 2
Apurimac **74** B 3
Aqär `Atabah **51** H 3
Aqdä **25** F 2
Aquiduauana **74** E 5
Ar Horqin Qi **35** H 2
Ar Radisiyah Bahri **24** A 4
Ar Rahad **52** E 6
Ar Ramädi **24** D 2
Ar Ramlah **24** B 3
Ar Raqqah **24** C 2
Ar Rass **24** D 4
Ar Rawdatayn **25** E 3
Ar Rayhäni **25** G 5
Ar Rifa`i **25** E 3
Ar Rimäl **53** J 4
Ar Riyäd **25** E 4
Ar Rub al Khali **53** HJ 4–5
Ar Rusäfah **24** C 2
Ar Rusayris **52** E 6
Ar Rutbah **24** C 2
Ar Ruways (Qatar) **25** F 4

Ar Ruways (United Arab
 Emirates) **25** F 4
Arabestän **25** E 3
Arabian Sea **9**
Aracaju **75** J 3
Aracati **75** J 1
Araçatuba **75** F 5
Aracena, Sierra de **20** B 4
Araçuai **75** H 4
Arad **22** B 1
Arada **55** J 2
`Arädah **25** F 5
Arafura, Laut **39** HJ 5
Aragarças **75** F 4
Aragon **20** C 3
Aragón **20** C 3
Araguacema **73** HJ 5
Araguaia **73** J 5
Araguaiana **75** F 4
Araguaína **73** J 5
Araguari **75** G 4
Araguatins **73** J 5
Arak (Algeria) **51** F 3
Aräk (Iran) **25** E 2
Arakaka **73** G 2
Arakan Yoma **37** F 3–4
Aral`sk **31** G 1
Aral`skoye More
 30–31 FG 2
Aramac **43** H 3
Arandai **39** H 4
Aranjuez **20** C 3
Aranos **58** B 4
Aranuka **46** C 3
Araouane **54** D 2
Arapiraca **75** J 2
Araquara **75** G 5
Arauá **75** J 3
Arauca **72** D 2
Arauco **77** B 6
Aravalli Range **36** B 2
Araxá **75** G 4
Arbatax **21** E 4
Archer River National Park
 43 G 1
Archipelago Kerimbas
 59 G 2
Archipiélago de Colón
 72 B 6
Archipiélago de la Reina
 Adelaida **77** A 9
Archipiélago de los Chonos
 77 AB 7–8
Arco (U.S.A.) **66** D 3
Arcos **20** B 4
Arcoverde **75** J 2
Arctic Ocean **78**
Arctic Red River **62** L 2
Arctowski **79**
Ardabil **30** D 3
Ardakän **25** FG 2
Årdalstangen **18** E 3
Ardennes **16** E 4
Ardestan **25** F 2
Arecibo **69** J 4
Areia Branca **75** J 1
Arena, Point **66** B 4
Arenápolis **74** E 3
Arendal **19** E 4
Arequipa **74** B 4

Arere **73** H 4
Arezzo **21** F 3
Arga **33** R 2
Argan **34** A 2
Argent, Côte d' **20** C 3
Argentina **77** CD 6
Arges **22** C 2
Argolikós Kólpos **22** B 3
Argungu **55** EF 3
Argyle, Lake **42** D 2
Århus **19** F 4
Arica **74** B 4
Arid, Cape **42** C 5
Arïha **24** B 2
Arinos **74** E 3
Arinos **74** E 3
Aripuanä **73** F 5
Aripuanä **73** F 5
Ariquemes **73** F 5
Ariripina **75** H 2
Arizona (Argentina) **77** C 6
Arizona (U.S.A.) **66** D 5
Arjona **72** C 1
Arka **33** Q 3
Arkalyk **27** N 5
Arkansas **67** H 4
Arkansas **67** H 5
Arkansas City **67** G 4
Arkhangel`sk **26** H 3
Arkhara **33** O 6
Arklow **16** B 4
Arles **21** D 3
Arlington (OR, U.S.A.)
 66 C 2
Arlington (TX, U.S.A.)
 67 G 5
Arlington (VA, U.S.A.)
 67 L 4
Arlit **55** F 2
Arly **54** E 3
Armant **52** E 3
Armavir **23** F 1
Armenia **23** F 2
Armenia (Bolivia) **72** C 3
Armidale **43** J 5
Armstrong **64** K 5
Armyansk **23** D 1
Arnawai **31** J 3
Arnhem **16** E 4
Arnhem, Cape **43** F 1
Arnhem Land **42** EF 1
Aroab **58** B 3
Arorae **46** C 3
Arquipélago dos Bijagós
 54 A 3
Arraias **75** G 3
Arran **16** B 3
Arras **20** D 1
Års **19** E 4
Arsen`yev **35** K 2
Årskogen **18** G 3
Arsuk **65** S 3
Arteaga **68** B 4
Artem **35** K 2
Artemisa **68** F 3
Artigas **75** E 5
Artoli **52** E 5
Artybash **27** R 5
Artyk **33** R 3
Aru, Kepulauan **39** HJ 5

Arua **56** E 4
Aruanä **75** F 3
Aruba, Isla **72** E 1
Arun Qi **33** M 6
Arunachal Pradesh **37** F 2
Aruppukkottai **36** C 6
Arusha **57** F 5
Arvada **66** E 4
Arvayheer **34** D 1
Arvika **19** F 4
Arys` **31** H 2
Arzamas **26** H 4
As Hasäwinah, Jabal **51** H 3
As Sadr (United Arab
 Emirates) **25** G 4
As Sahrä' al Gharbïyah
 52 D 3
As Sahrä' al Janübiyah
 52 D 4
As Sahrä' an Nübiyah
 52 E 4
As Sahrä' ash Sharqïyah
 24 AB 4–5
As Salamiyah **25** E 4
As Sälihïyah **24** C 2
As Sälimïyah **25** E 3
As Salmän **25** D 3
As Salt **24** B 2
As Samäwah **25** D 3
As Sarir **55** K 3
As Silä **25** F 4
As Subü` **52** E 4
As Sulb **25** E 4
As Summän **25** DE 4
As Suwayda` **24** B 2
As Suways **24** A 3
Asahikawa **35** M 2
Asamakka **55** F 2
Asansol **36** E 3
Asba Tafari **57** G 3
Ascensión **74** D 4
Ascension Island **48** A 5
Ascoli Piceno **21** F 3
Aselle **57** F 3
Ash Shabakah **24** D 3
Ash Sharqät **24** D 2
Ash Shatrah **25** E 3
Ash Shihr **53** H 6
Ash Shinafïyah **25** D 3
Ash Shu`aybah **24** CD 3–4
Ash Shu`bah **25** D 3
Ash Shumlül **25** E 4
Asha **27** L 4
Ashdod **24** B 3
Asheville **67** K 4
Ashkhabad **30** F 3
Ashtabula **67** K 3
Ashuanipi **65** O 5
Ashuanipi Lake **65** O 5
Asinara **21** E 3
Asino **27** R 4
Asir, Ra`s **57** J 2
Asmara **57** F 1
Aspermont **66** F 5
Aspiring, Mount **44** P 9
Aspurito **72** E 2
Assa **50** D 3
Assab **57** G 2
Assam **37** F 2
Assiniboia **63** Q 6

Assis **75** F 5
Assisi **21** F 3
Assur **24** D 2
Astakh **33** P 2
Astipálaia **22** C 3
Astrakhan **30** D 1
Asturias **20** B 3
Asuncion (Mariana Is.)
  46 A 1
Asunción (Paraguay) **76** E 4
Aswān **24** A 4
Asyūṭ **52** E 3
Aṭ Ṭafilah **24** B 3
Aṭ Ṭā'if **53** G 4
Aṭ Ṭaysiyah **24** D 3–4
Aṭ Ṭurayf **24** C 3
At Turbah **53** G 6
Atacama, Desierto do
  74 C 5
Atacama, Salar de **74** C 5
Atafu **46** D 3
Atambua **39** F 5
Atar **50** C 4
Atas Bogd Uul **34** C 2
Atasu **27** O 6
'Aṭbarah **52** E 5
Aṭbarah **52** F 5
Atbasar **27** N 5
Ath Thumāmī **25** D 4
Athens **67** K 5
Atherton **43** GH 2
Athínai **22** B 3
Ati **55** H 3
Atico **74** B 4
Atikokan **64** J 6
Atikonak Lake **65** P 5
Atka **33** S 3
Atka Island **62** C 5
Atkarsk **26** H 5
Atlanta **67** JK 5
Atlantic City **67** M 4
Atlantic Ocean **8**
Atlas el Kebir **50** DE 2
Atlas Mountains **50** DF 2
Atlin **62** L 4
Ätran **19** F 4
Atrato **72** C 2
Atsy **39** J 5
Attawapiskat **64** KL 5
Attawapiskat **64** L 5
Attikamagen Lake **65** O 5
Attu **62** A 5
Atuel **77** C 6
Atura **56** E 4
Aua **44** D 2
Auas Mountains **58** B 4
Auburn **67** M 3
Auckland **45** Q 8
Auckland Islands **79**
Aude **20** D 3
Augathella **43** H 4
Augsburg **17** F 5
Augusta (AR, U.S.A.)
  67 H 4
Augusta (GA, U.S.A.)
  67 K 5
Augusta (ME, U.S.A.)
  67 N 3
Augustus, Mount **42** B 3
Auki **45** H 3

Aur **46** C 2
Aurangaband **36** C 4
Aurillac **20** D 3
Aurora **66** F 4
Aus **58** B 5
Ausangate, Nevado **74** B 3
Aust-Agder **19** E 4
Austin (MN, U.S.A.) **67** H 3
Austin (TX, U.S.A.) **66** G 5
Austin, Lake **42** B 4
Australia **42–43** DF 3
Australian Alps **43** H 6
Australian Capital Territory
  43 H 6
Austria **21** F 2
Austvågöy **18** F 2
Auxerre **20** D 2
Auyuittuq National Park
  65 OP 2
Avalon Peninsula **65** R 6
Avanavero **73** G 3
Avarua **47** E 4
Avaz **30** G 4
Ávdhira **22** B 2
Ávej **25** E 2
Ävej, Gardaneh-ye **25** E 2
Avellaneda **76** E 5
Averöya **18** E 3
Avesta **19** G 3
Avignon **21** D 3
Ávila **20** C 3
Avilés **20** B 3
Avola **21** G 4
Awara Plain **57** G 4
Awash **57** G 2
Awash **57** G 3
Awjilah **51** K 3
Axel Heiberg Island **78**
Axiós **22** B 2
Ayabaca **72** BC 4
Ayacucho **74** B 3
Ayaguz **27** Q 6
Ayan **33** P 4
Ayanaka **33** V 3
Ayava **32** H 4
Ayaviri **74** B 3
Aydın **22** C 3
Áyion Óros **22** B 2
Aylmer Lake **63** Q 3
'Ayn al Baydā' **24** BC 2
'Ayn al Ghazāl **51** K 4
'Ayn Sukhnah **24** A 3
'Aynabo **57** H 3
Ayni **31** H 3
Ayon **33** V 2
Ayr (Australia) **43** H 2
Ayr (U.K.) **16** C 3
Aysary **27** O 5
Az Ẓahrān **25** EF 4
Az Zallāq **25** F 4
Az Zarqā' **25** F 4
Az Zarqā' **24** B 2
Az Zāwiyah **51** H 2
Az Zilfī **25** D 4
Az Zugar **53** G 6
Āzādshahr **25** G 1
Azamgarh **36** D 2
Azare **55** G 3
Azelik **55** F 2
Azerbaijan **30** D 2

Aznā **25** E 2
Azores **50** A 1
Azoum **55** J 3
Azov **23** E 1
Azovskoye More **23** E 1
Aztec ruins **66** E 4
Azuero, Península de **72** B 2
Azul **77** E 6
Azur, Côte d' **21** E 3
Azzaba **51** G 1

B

Baʿ qūbah **25** D 2
Bāb al Māndab **53** G 6
Baba Burnu **22** D 2
Baba Burun **22** C 3
Bābā Heydar **25** F 2
Babahoyo **72** C 4
Babai Gaxun **34** D 2
Babanūsah **52** D 6
Babine Lake **63** M 5
Babo **39** H 4
Bābol **25** F 1
Bābol Sar **25** F 1
Babushkin **32** J 5
Babylon **24** D 2
Bacabal **75** GH 1
Bacan, Pulau **39** G 4
Bacău **22** C 1
Back **63** S 2
Bacolod **39** F 1
Bād **25** F 2
Badajoz **20** B 4
Badalona **20** D 3
Badanah **24** C 3
Baden-Baden **17** E 5
Badoumbé **54** B 3
Badr Ḥunayn **24** C 5
Badulla **36** D 6
Badzhal **33** O 5
Bafatá **54** B 3
Baffin Bay **78**
Baffin Island **65** NO 2
Bafia **55** G 5
Bafoussam **55** G 4
Bāfq **25** G 3
Bafra **23** E 2
Bāft **25** G 3
Baga Sola **55** G 3
Bagadzha **32** L 3
Bagalkot **36** C 4
Bagdarin **32** K 5
Bagé **76** F 5
Baghdād **24** D 2
Bāghin **25** G 3
Baghlan **31** H 3
Bagua **72** C 5
Baguio **39** J 1
Baguirmi **55** H 3
Bahama Islands **69** H 3
Bahar Dar **57** F 2
Bahawalpur **31** J 5
Bahía (Argentina) **77** C 8
Bahía (Brazil) **75** H 3
Bahía Blanca **77** D 6
Bahía Blanca **77** D 6
Bahía de Campeche **68** D 4

Bahía de Caráquez **72** B 4
Bahía Grande **77** C 9
Bahía, Islas de la **68** E 4
Bahía Kino **66** D 6
Bahía Laura **77** C 8
Bahía Rosario **66** C 6
Bahía Sebastián Vizcaíno
  66 D 6
Bahías, Cabo dos **77** CD 8
Baḥr al Abyaḍ **52** E 6
Baḥr al Azraq **52** E 6
Baḥr al Jabal **56** E 3
Baḥr ar Rimāl al 'Aẓīm
  52 D 3
Bahraich **36** D 2
Bahrain **25** F 4
Baía de Setúbal **20** B 4
Baia Mare **22** B 1
Baião **73** J 4
Baicheng (Man., China)
  35 H 1
Baicheng (Sink. Uig., China)
  31 L 2
Baie aux Feuilles **65** O 4
Baie d'Antongil **59** HJ 3
Baie-des-Moutons **65** Q 5
Baikal, Lake **32** J 5
Bailang **32** M 6
Baile Átha Cliath **16** B 4
Bailundo **58** B 2
Baimuru **44** D 3
Baing **39** F 6
Baingoin **36** E 1
Baiquan **33** N 6
Bairiki **46** C 2
Bairin Zuoqi **35** GH 2
Baixo-Alentejo **20** B 4
Baiyü **34** C 4
Baja **22** A 1
Baja California Norte **66** C 5
Baja California Sur **66** D 6
Bājah **51** G 1
Bajas, Rías **20** B 3
Bakadzhitsite **22** C 2
Bakel **54** B 3
Baker **46** D 2
Baker Lake (N.W.T., Can.)
  63 S 3
Baker Lake (N.W.T., Can.)
  63 S 3
Bakersfield **66** C 4
Bakharden **30** F 3
Bakhta **27** R 3
Bakhtegān, Daryācheh-ye
  25 FG 3
Bakony **22** A 1
Bakouma **56** C 3
Baku **30** DE 2
Bala **33** O 2
Bala Murghab **31** G 3
Balabac Strait **38** E 2
Ba'labakk, Ra's **24** B 2
Baladiyat 'Adan **53** H 6
Balaghat **36** D 3
Balakhta **32** F 4
Balakovo **26** J 5
Balasore **36** E 3
Balaton **22** A 1
Balbi, Mount **45** F 3
Balclutha **44** P 10

Bald Head **42** B 6
Balde **76** C 5
Baldy Peak **66** E 5
Bale **57** G 3
Baleares, Islas **20** D 3–4
Balearic Islands **20** D 3
Baleia, Ponta da **75** J 4
Baley **32** L 5
Bali **38** DE 5
Bali, Laut **38** E 5
Balıkesir **22** C 3
Balikpapan **38** E 4
Balintang Channel **39** J 1
Balkan Mountains **22** C 2
Balkhash **27** O 6
Balkhash, Ozero **27** OP 6
Balladonia **42** C 5
Ballangen **18** G 2
Ballarat **43** G 6
Ballard, Lake **42** C 4
Balleny Islands **79**
Ballina **43** J 4
Balranald **43** G 5
Balsas **75** G 2
Baltic Sea **19** GH 4
Baltimore **67** L 4
Baltiskaya Grjada
  19 HJ 4–5
Bam **30** F 5
Bamako **54** C 3
Bamba **54** D 2
Bambari **56** C 3
Bambesa **56** D 4
Bambesi **56** E 3
Bamenda **55** G 4
Bamingui **56** C 3
Bamingui-Bangoran, Parc
  National du **56** BC 3
Bamiyan **31** H 4
Bampūr **31** G 5
Ban Kniet **37** J 5
Ban Me Thuot **37** J 5
Ban Na San **37** G 6
Banaba **45** J 2
Banalia **56** D 4
Banana **43** J 3
Banäs, Ra's **24** B 5
Banat **22** B 1
Bancroft **65** M 6
Band Boni **30** F 5
Banda **36** D 2
Banda Aceh **38** A 2
Bandar Abbas **25** G 4
Bandar-e Anzali **30** DE 3
Bandar-e Chārak **25** G 4
Bandar-e Deylam **25** F 3
Bandar-e Khomeyni **25** E 3
Bandar-e Lengeh **25** G 4
Bandar-e Māqām **25** F 4
Bandar-e Moghūyeh
  25 FG 4
Bandar-e Rig **25** F 3
Bandar Seri Begawan
  38 D 3
Bandar Shāh **25** F 1
Bandarlampung **38** C 5
Bandarpunch **36** C 1
Bandau **38** E 2
Bandeira **75** H 5
Bandeirante **75** F 3

Bandırma **22** C 2
Bandundu **56** B 5
Bandundu **56** B 5
Bandung **38** C 5
Banes **69** G 3
Banff National Park **63** O 5
Banfora **54** CD 3
Bangalore **36** C 5
Bangassou **56** C 4
Bangeta, Mount **44** E 3
Banggai, Kepulauan **39** F 4
Bangka, Pulau **38** C 4
Bangko **38** B 4
Bangkok, Bight of **37** H 5
Bangladesh **37** F 3
Bangor (ME, U.S.A.) **67** N 3
  16 B 4
Bangor (N. Ireland, U.K.)
  16 B 4
Bangui **56** B 4
Banhine National Park
  59 E 4
Bani Mazār **52** E 3
Bani Suwayf **52** E 3
Banihal Pass **31** K 4
Bāniyās (Lebanon) **24** B 2
Bāniyās (Syria) **24** B 2
Banja Luka **21** G 3
Banjarmasin **38** DE 4
Banjul **54** A 3
Banks Island (Canada)
  63 N 1
Banks Island (Queensland,
  Austr.) **43** G 1
Banks Islands (Vanuatu)
  45 J 4
Banks Peninsula **45** Q 9
Banks Strait **44** L 9
Bannu **31** J 4
Banská Bystrica **17** G 5
Banyo **55** G 4
Banyuwangi **38** D 5
Banzare Coast **79**
Banzart **51** GH 1
Baoding **34** G 3
Baoji **34** E 4
Baoqing **35** K 1
Baoshan **34** C 5
Baotou **34** E 2
Baqen **34** B 4
Barabinsk **27** P 4
Barabinskaya Step' **27** P 5
Baracaldo **20** C 3
Bārah **52** E 6
Barahona **69** H 4
Barakkul' **27** N 5
Baramula **31** J 4
Baran **36** C 2
Barangbarang **39** F 5
Baranof **62** K 4
Baranovichi **19** J 5
Barão de Capanema **74** E 3
Barão de Melgaço **74** D 3
Barbados **69** K 5
Barbas, Cabo **50** B 4
Barcaldine **43** H 3
Barcellona **21** FG 4
Barcelona **73** F 2
Barcelona (Spain) **20** D 3
Barcelos **73** F 4
Bárdere **57** G 4

Barëda **57** J 2
Bareilly **36** CD 2
Barents Sea **26** GH 2
Barentsovo More **26** GJ 1
Barentu **57** F 1
Bārgå **18** G 2
Barga **36** D 1
Barguzin **32** J 5
Bari **21** G 3
Barīm **53** G 6
Barinas **72** DE 2
Baring, Cape **63** O 2
Barisal **37** F 3
Barisan, Pegunungan **38** B 4
Barito, Sungai **38** D 4
Barkā' **53** K 4
Barkam **34** D 4
Barkly Tableland **43** F 2
Barlee, Lake **42** B 4
Barletta **21** G 3
Barmer **36** B 2
Barnaul **27** Q 5
Barnes Ice Cap **65** N 1–2
Barong **34** C 4
Barotseland **58** C 3
Barquisimeto **72** DE 1
Barra **16** B 3
Barra (Bahía, Brazil) **75** H 3
Barra do Corda **75** G 2
Barra Head **16** B 3
Barracão do Barreto **73** G 5
Barranca (Peru) **72** C 4
Barranca (Peru) **72** C 6
Barrancas **73** F 2
Barranquilla **72** C 1
Barreiras **75** H 3
Barreirinhas **75** H 1
Barreiro **20** B 4
Barreiros **75** JK 2
Barren **37** F 5
Barretos **75** G 5
Barrie **65** LM 7
Barrow (AK, U.S.A.) **62** F 1
Barrow (Argentina) **77** DE 6
Barrow (Rep. of Ireland)
  16 B 4
Barrow Creek **42** E 3
Barrow Island **42** A 3
Barrow, Point **62** FG 1
Barsi **36** C 4
Bartica **73** G 2
Bartın **23** D 2
Bartlesville **67** G 4
Bāruni **36** E 2
Basa'idu **25** G 4
Basauri **20** C 3
Basel **21** E 2
Bashi Haixia **35** H 6
Basilan **39** F 2
Basilan City **39** F 2
Basílio **76** F 5
Baskatong, Réservoir
  65 MN 6
Baskol' **27** P 5
Basra **25** E 3
Bass Strait **44** KL 8
Bassas da India **59** F 4
Basse-Terre **69** K 4
Bassein **37** F 4
Basseterre **69** K 4

Bassin de Rennes **20** C 2
Bastak **25** G 4
Bastia **21** E 3
Bata **55** F 5
Batagay-Alyta **33** O 2
Batalha **20** B 4
Batama **32** H 5
Batang **34** C 4
Batang Hari **38** B 4
Batangas **39** F 1
Bataysk **23** EF 1
Batemans Bay **43** J 6
Batha **55** H 3
Bathurst (Canada) **65** O 6
Bathurst (N.S.W., Austr.)
  43 H 5
Bathurst → Banjul **54** A 3
Bathurst, Cape **62** LM 1
Bathurst Inlet **63** Q 2
Bathurst Inlet **63** Q 2
Bathurst Island (N.T., Austr.)
  42 D 1
Bathurst Island (The Arctic)
  78
Batkanu **54** B 4
Bātlāq-e Gavkhūnī **25** F 2
Batman **23** F 3
Batna **51** G 1
Batoka **58** D 3
Batomga **33** P 4
Baton Rouge **67** H 5
Båtsfjord **18** J 1
Battambang **37** H 5
Battle Creek **67** J 3
Batu **57** F 3
Batu Puteh, Gunung **38** B 3
Batui **39** F 4
Batumi **23** F 2
Baturité **75** J 1
Baubau **39** F 5
Bauchi **55** F 3
Baures **74** D 3
Bauru **75** G 5
Baús **75** F 4
Bavaria **17** F 5
Bavispe **66** E 5
Bawdwin **37** G 3
Baxoi **34** C 4
Bay City **67** K 3
Bay de Verde **65** R 6
Bay of Biscay **20** C 2–3
Bay of Fundy **65** O 6–7
Bay of Plenty **45** R 8
Bayamo **69** G 3
Bayan-Adraga **32** K 6
Bayan-Aul **27** P 5
Bayan Har Shan **34** CD 4
Bayan Har Shankou **34** C 4
Bayan Obo **34** E 2
Bayanbulag **32** G 6
Bayanchandman **32** J 6
Bayanga **56** B 4
Bayanhongor **32** H 6
Bayāz **25** G 3
Bayāzeh **25** G 2
Bayburt **23** F 2
Baydaratskaya Guba **27** N 2
Bayern **17** F 5
Bayji **24** D 2

Baykal, Ozero **32** J 5
Baykal'skiy Khrebet
32 J 4–5
Baykit **32** G 3
Bayonne **20** C 3
Bayovar **72** B 5
Bayram-Ali **31** G 3
Bayreuth **17** F 5
Bayrüt **24** B 2
Baytown **67** H 5–6
Bazar Dyuzi, Gora **30** D 2
Bazarnyy Syzgan **26** J 5
Bazaruto National Park
59 F 4
Bazhong **34** E 4
Bear Island **78**
Beata, Cabo **69** H 4
Beatton River **63** N 4
Beatty **66** C 4
Beaufort **38** E 2
Beaufort **67** K 5
Beaufort Sea **62** JL 1
Beaufort West **58** C 6
Beaumont **67** H 5
Beausejour **63** S 5
Beauvais **20** D 2
Beaver (Sask., Can.) **63** Q 5
Beaver (UT, U.S.A.) **66** D 4
Beawar **36** B 2
Béchar **50** E 2
Bedourie **43** F 3
Be'er Sheva **24** B 3
Beeville **66** G 6
Bega **43** H 6
Begna **19** E 3
Behbehän **25** EF 3
Bei Shan **34** C 2
Bei'an **33** N 6
Beibu Wan **37** J 3
Beida **51** K 2
Beihai **34** E 6
Beijing **35** G 2
Beipiao **35** H 2
Beira **59** EF 3
Beirut **24** B 2
Beitbridge **58** D 4
Beitstad **18** F 3
Beitun **31** M 1
Beja **20** B 4
Bejaïa **51** F 1
Bekdash **30** E 2
Békéscsaba **22** B 1
Bekopaka **59** G 3
Bela **31** H 5
Bela Vista (Brazil) **74** E 5
Bela Vista (Mozambique)
59 E 5
Belarus **19** J 5
Belaya **26** K 4
Belaya Kalitva **23** F 1
Belaya Tserkov **26** F 6
Belcher Islands **65** L 4
Belebey **26** K 5
Belém (Amazonas, Brazil)
72 E 4
Belém (Pará, Brazil) **73** J 4
Belén (Colombia) **72** C 3
Beleuli **30** F 2
Belfast **16** B 4

Belfield **66** F 2
Belfort **21** E 2
Belgaum **36** B 4
Belgium **16** DE 4
Belgorod **26** G 5
Belgorod-Dnestrovskiy
22 CD 1
Belgrade **22** B 2
Beli **55** G 4
Belikh **24** C 1
Belitung, Pulau **38** C 4
Belize **68** E 4
Belize City **68** E 4
Bel'kachi **33** O 4
Bell Ville **76** D 5
Bella Bella **63** M 5
Bellary **36** C 4
Belle Ile **20** C 2
Belle Isle, Strait of **65** Q 5
Belleville (IL, U.S.A.) **67** J 4
Belleville (KS, U.S.A.)
66 G 4
Belleville (Ontario, Can.)
65 M 7
Bellevue (WA, U.S.A.)
66 B 2
Bellin **65** N 3
Bellingham **66** B 2
Bellingshausen **79**
Bellingshausen Sea **79**
Bello **72** C 2
Belluno **21** F 2
Bellyk **32** F 5
Belmonte **75** J 4
Belmopan **68** E 4
Belo Horizonte (Minas
Gerais, Brazil) **75** H 4
Belo Horizonte (Pará, Brazil)
73 H 5
Belo Monta **73** H 4
Belogorsk **33** N 5
Belogor'ye **27** N 3
Beloit **67** J 3
Belorechensk **23** F 2
Belorusskaya Gryada **19** J 5
Belovo **27** R 5
Beloyarovo **33** N 5
Beloye More **26** G 2
Belush'ya Guba **26** K 1
Belyy **26** F 4
Bemidji **67** G 2
Ben Macdhui **16** C 3
Ben Nevis **16** BC 3
Bena Dibile **56** C 5
Benalla **43** H 6
Benares **36** D 2
Bend **66** B 3
Bender Bàyla **57** J 3
Bendery **22** C 1
Bendigo **43** G 6
Benevento **21** FG 3
Bengal **36** E 3
Bengbu **35** G 4
Benghazi **51** JK 2
Bengkulu **38** B 4
Benguela **58** A 2
Benguela Current **9**
Beni (Bolivia) **74** C 3
Beni (Zaire) **56** D 4

Beni Mellal **50** D 2
Beni Ounif **50** E 2
Benidorm **20** CD 4
Benin **54** E 3–4
Benin City **55** F 4
Benjamin Constant **72** D 4
Benson **66** D 5
Bentaeng **39** F 5
Bentiaba **58** A 2
Bentiu **56** E 3
Benue **55** F 4
Benxi **35** H 2
Beograd **22** B 2
Beraketa **59** H 4
Berati **22** A 2
Berau, Teluk **39** H 4
Berbera **57** H 2
Berbérati **56** B 4
Berchogur **30** F 1
Berdichev **19** J 6
Berdigestyakh **33** N 3
Berdyansk **23** E 1
Beregovo **22** B 1
Bereina **44** E 3
Berekum **54** D 4
Berens River **63** S 5
Berezniki **26** L 4
Berezovka (Russia) **27** Q 4
Berezovka (Russia) **32** L 4
Berezovo **27** N 3
Berezovskiy **27** L 5
Bergama **22** C 3
Bergamo **21** EF 2
Bergen (F.R.G.) **17** F 4
Bergen (Norway) **19** DE 3
Bergerac **20** D 3
Bergö **18** H 4
Bergviken **18** G 3
Berhampore **36** E 3
Berhampur **36** D 4
Bering Land Bridge National
Preserve **62** E 2
Bering Sea **62** CD 3–4
Bering Strait **62** CD 2–3
Beringovskiy **33** X 3
Berkakit **33** M 4
Berkeley **66** B 4
Berkner Island **79**
Berlevåg **18** J 1
Berlin **17** F 4
Bermejo **76** C 5
Bermejo (Argentina) **76** D 4
Bermuda Islands **69** K 1
Bern **21** E 2
Bernasconi **77** D 6
Bernburg **17** F 4
Berne **21** E 2
Berner Alpen **21** E 2
Bernina **21** E 2
Bertolínia **75** H 2
Bertoua **55** G 5
Besalampy **59** G 3
Besançon **21** E 2
Besar, Gunung **38** E 4
Beskidy Zachodny **17** GH 5
Beslan **23** F 2
Besna Kobila **22** B 2
Bessarabiya **22** C 1
Bestobe **27** O 5
Bethlehem **58** D 5

Béthune **20** D 1
Betong **37** H 6
Betpak-Dala **27** O 6
Betroka **59** H 4
Betul **36** C 3
Bey Dağlari **22** CD 3
Beyänlü **25** E 1
Beyla **54** C 4
Beyra **57** H 3
Beyşehir Gölü **22** D 3
Béziers **20** D 3
Bhadrakh **36** E 3
Bhadravati **36** C 5
Bhagalpur **36** E 3
Bhamo **37** G 3
Bhandara **36** C 3
Bharuch **36** B 3
Bhatinda **36** BC 1
Bhatpara **36** E 3
Bhavnagar **36** B 3
Bhawanipatna **36** D 4
Bhilwara **36** BC 2
Bhopal **36** C 3
Bhuban **36** E 3
Bhubaneswar **36** E 3
Bhumiphol Dam **37** G 4
Bhusawal **36** C 3
Bhutan **37** F 2
Biak (Indonesia) **39** F 4
Biak (Papua New Guinea)
39 J 4
Biak, Pulau **39** J 4
Biała Podlaska **17** H 4
Białystok **17** H 4
Biankouma **54** C 4
Biaora **36** C 3
Biarritz **20** C 3
Biberach **17** EF 5
Bicuari National Park
58 AB 3
Bida **55** F 4
Bidar **36** C 4
Bidzhan **33** O 6
Bié **58** B 2
Biebrza **17** H 4
Biel **21** E 2
Bielefeld **17** E 4
Bielsko-Biała **17** G 5
Bien Hoa **37** J 5
Bienville, Lac **65** N 4
Bifoum **55** G 6
Big Bend National Park
66 F 6
Big Cypress National
Preserve **67** K 6
Big Spring **66** F 5
Big Trout Lake **64** K 5
Biger **32** G 6
Bighorn **66** E 2
Bight of Bangkok **37** H 5
Bight of Benin **54** E 4
Bigi **56** C 4
Bihać **21** G 3
Bihar **36** E 2
Bihar **36** E 3
Bijapur **36** C 4
Bijeljina **21** G 3
Bijiang **34** C 5
Bikaner **36** B 2
Bikar **46** C 2

Bikin 33 O 6
Bikini 46 C 2
Bilaspur 36 D 3
Bilbao 20 C 3
Bili 56 D 4
Billings 66 E 2
Bilo Gora 21 G 2
Biloela 43 J 3
Biloxi 67 J 5
Binder 32 K 6
Bindura 59 E 3
Binga, Monte 59 E 3
Bingara 43 J 4
Bingham 67 N 2
Binjai 38 A 3
Binnaway 43 H 5
Bintan, Pulau 38 B 3
Bintulu 38 D 3
Bioko 55 F 5
Bi'r Bū Zurayyq 51 K 3
Bi'r Fu'ād 52 D 2
Bir Moghreim 50 C 3
Bi'r Naşīf 24 C 4
Bir Ounane 54 D 1
Bir Rhoraffa 51 G 2
Bi'r Safājah 24 AB 4
Bi'r Shalatayn 52 F 4
Bira 33 P 6
Birao 56 C 2
Biratnagar 36 E 2
Birjand 30 F 4
Birkat Nasser 24 A 5
Birkenhead 16 C 4
Birksgate Range 42 DE 4
Bîrlad 22 C 1
Birmingham (AL, U.S.A.)
    67 J 5
Birmingham (U.K.) 16 C 4
Birnie 46 D 3
Birnin Kebbi 55 E 3
Birnin Kudu 55 F 3
Birobidzhan 33 O 6
Birsilpur 36 B 2
Birsk 26 L 4
Biru 34 B 4
Biscay, Bay of 20 C 2–3
Biscoe Islands 79
Bisekera 33 X 3
Bishkek 31 J 2
Bishop's Falls 65 Q 6
Biskra 51 G 2
Bismarck 66 F 2
Bismarck Archipelago
    44–45 EF 2
Bismarck Range 44 DE 2–3
Bismarck Sea 44–45 EF 2
Bissau 54 A 3
Bissett 63 S 5
Bistriţa 22 B 1
Bitchana 57 F 2
Bitkiné 55 H 3
Bitlis 23 F 3
Bitola 22 B 2
Bitterfontein 58 B 6
Bitterroot Range 66 D 2–3
Bittou 54 DE 3
Biu 55 G 3
Biyang 34 F 4
Biysk 27 R 5
Bizerta 51 GH 1

Bjelašnica 22 A 2
Bjerkvik 18 G 2
Björkö 18 H 3
Björneborg 18 H 3
Björnöya 78
Black Hills 66 F 3
Black River Falls 67 HJ 3
Black Sea 23 DE 2
Blackall 43 H 3
Blackburn, Mount 62 J 3
Blackpool 16 C 4
Blackwell 66 G 4
Blåfjellhatten 18 F 3
Blagoevgrad 22 B 2
Blagoveshchensk 33 N 5
Blaine 67 H 2
Blantyre 59 E 3
Blåskavlen 18 E 3
Blåvands Huk 19 E 4
Blekinge 19 FG 4
Blenheim 45 Q 9
Blida 51 F 1
Bloemfontein 58 D 5
Blois 20 D 2
Blönduós 18 AB 2
Bloomington (IL, U.S.A.)
    67 J 3
Bloomington (IN, U.S.A.)
    67 J 4
Bloomington (MN, U.S.A.)
    67 H 3
Blosseville Coast 78
Blue Ridge 67 KL 4
Bluefields 68 F 5
Bluff Knoll 42 B 5
Blumenau 76 G 4
Blytheville 67 J 4
Bo 54 B 4
Bo Duc 37 J 5
Bo Hai 35 GH 3
Bo River 56 D 3
Bo Trach 37 J 4
Boa Vista (Cape Verde)
    54 B 6
Boa Vista (Roraima, Brazil)
    73 F 3
Boac 39 F 1
Bobai 34 EF 6
Bobo Dioulasso 54 D 3
Bobruysk 19 J 5
Boby, Pic 59 H 4
Boca del Rio 66 E 6
Bôca do Acre 72 E 5
Boca Raton 67 L 6
Bocage Vendéen 20 C 2
Bocaiúva 75 H 4
Bochum 17 E 4
Bodaybo 32 K 4
Bodélé 55 H 2
Boden 18 H 2
Bodensee 21 E 2
Bodö 18 F 2
Boende 56 C 5
Boffa 54 B 3
Boggeragh Mountains
    16 B 4
Bogor 38 C 5
Bogoroditsk 26 G 5
Bogotá 72 D 3
Bogra 36 E 3

Boguchany 32 G 4
Bogué 50 C 5
Bohemia 17 F 5
Bohemia Downs 42 D 2
Böhmerwald 17 F 5
Bohol 39 F 2
Bohol Sea 39 F 2
Bohuslän 19 F 4
Boiaçu 73 F 4
Boise 66 C 3
Boise City 66 F 4
Bojador, Cabo 50 C 3
Bojnürd 30 F 3
Bojuro 76 F 5
Bokatola 56 B 5
Boké 54 B 3
Boknafjorden 19 E 4
Bokora Game Reserve
    56 E 4
Bokpyin 37 G 5
Bokungu 56 C 5
Bolan Pass 31 H 5
Bole (China) 31 L 2
Bole (Ghana) 54 D 4
Bolesławiec 17 G 4
Bolgatanga 54 D 3
Boli 35 K 1
Bolia 56 B 5
Bolívar (Argentina) 77 D 6
Bolívar (Colombia) 72 C 3
Bolivia 74 CD 4
Bollon 43 H 4
Bologna 21 F 3
Bologoye 26 F 4
Bologur 33 O 3
Bolombo 56 C 5
Bolsena, Lago di 21 F 3
Bol'shaya Glushitsa 26 K 5
Bol'sheretsk 33 T 5
Bol'shezemel'skaya Tundra
    26–27 KM 2
Bol'shoy Begichev, Ostrov
    32 KL 1
Bol'shoy Kavkaz 23 FG 2
Bol'shoy Nimnyr 33 MN 4
Bol'shoy Shantar, Ostrov
    33 P 4–5
Bolsón de Mapimi 68 B 2
Bolton 16 C 4
Bolu 22 D 2
Bolzano 21 F 2
Bom Jesus 75 H 2
Bom Jesus da Lapa 75 H 3
Bom Retiro 76 G 4
Boma 55 G 7
Bombay 36 B 4
Bomberai 39 H 4
Bömlo 19 DE 4
Bomongo 56 B 4
Bona, Mount 62 J 3
Bonaparte Archipelago
    42 C 1
Bonavista Bay 65 R 6
Bondo 56 C 4
Bondoweso 38 D 5
Bone, Teluk 39 F 4
Bonete, Cerro 76 C 4
Bongor 55 H 3
Bonito 74 E 5
Bonn 17 E 4

Bonners Ferry 66 C 2
Bonobono 38 E 2
Boola 54 C 4
Boothby, Cape 79
Boothia Peninsula 63 T 2
Boothia, Gulf of 63 T 1
Bophuthatswana 58 C 5
Boquillagas del Carmen
    68 B 2
Bor 22 B 2
Bora-Bora 47 E 4
Borah Peak 66 D 3
Borås 19 F 4
Borasambar 36 D 3
Borazjän 25 F 3
Borba 73 G 4
Bordeaux 20 CD 3
Bordertown 43 G 6
Bordj Bou Arreridj 51 F 1
Bordj Fly Sainte Marie
    50 E 3
Bordj Messouda 51 G 2
Borgä 19 J 3
Börgefjellet 18 F 2
Borislav 17 H 5
Borisoglebsk 26 H 5
Borisov 19 J 5
Borispol 26 F 5
Borja (Bosnia and
    Herzegovina) 21 G 3
Borja (Peru) 72 C 4
Borkou 55 H 2
Borlänge 19 FG 3
Borneo 38 DE 3
Bornholm 19 F 5
Bornu 55 G 3
Borohoro Shan 31 L 2
Boroko 39 F 3
Borolgustakh 32 M 2
Borovichi 26 FG 4
Borroloola 43 F 2
Börselv 18 J 1
Borsippa 24 D 2
Boru 33 Q 1
Borüjen 25 F 3
Borüjerd 25 E 2
Borzya 32 L 5
Bôsăso 57 H 2
Bose 34 E 6
Boshan 35 G 3
Boshnyakovo 33 Q 6
Bosna 21 G 3
Bosnia and Herzegovina
    21 G 3
Bosporus 22 C 2
Bossangoa 56 B 3
Bossembele 56 B 3
Bossemptélé II 56 B 3
Bossier City 67 H 5
Bostandyk 26 J 6
Boston 67 M 3
Botletle 58 C 4
Botoşani 22 C 1
Botswana 58 CD 4
Botucatu 75 G 5
Bou Arfa 50 E 2
Bou Djéhiba 54 D 2
Bou Izakarn 50 D 3
Bou Rjeima 50 BC 5
Bou Saâda 51 F 1

Bouaflé **54** C 4
Bouaké **54** D 4
Bouar **56** B 3
Boubandjida **55** GH 4
Boubandjida National Park **55** GH 4
Boucle de Baoulé, Parc National de la **54** C 3
Bougainville **45** G 3
Bougainville Reef **43** H 2
Bougouni **54** C 3
Bouïra **51** F 1
Boulanouar **50** B 4
Boulder (Australia) **42** C 5
Boulder (U.S.A.) **66** F 3
Boulia **43** F 3
Boulogne-sur-Mer **20** D 1
Boulouli **54** C 2
Boun Neua **37** H 3
Bouna **54** D 4
Boundiali **54** C 4
Boundou **54** B 3
Bountiful **66** D 3
Bounty Islands **79**
Bourem **54** D 2
Bourg **21** E 2
Bourges **20** D 2
Bourgogne **21** DE 2
Bournemouth **16** C 4
Bouvet Island **79**
Bowen (Argentina) **76** C 3
Bowen (Australia) **43** H 2
Bowling Green **67** J 4
Bowman **66** F 2
Bowman Bay **65** MN 2
Boxing **35** G 3
Boyabo **56** B 4
Boyne **16** B 4
Boyuibe **74** D 5
Bozok Platosu **23** DE 3
Brač **21** G 3
Bradenton **67** K 6
Bradford **16** C 4
Bradshaw **42** E 2
Brady **66** G 5
Braga **20** B 3
Bragança **20** B 3
Bragança **73** J 4
Bragina **33** X 3
Brahmaputra **37** F 2
Brăila **22** C 1
Bräk **51** H 3
Brampton **65** L 7
Brandberg **58** A 4
Brandenburg **17** F 4
Brandon **63** S 6
Brandvlei **58** C 6
Brantford **65** L 7
Brasiléia **74** C 3
Brasília **75** G 4
Braşov **22** C 1
Brassey, Mount **42** E 3
Bratislava **17** G 5
Bratsk **32** H 4
Bratskoye Vodokhranilishche **32** H 4
Bratslav **22** C 1
Braunschweig **17** F 4
Brawley **66** C 5
Bray **65** M 2

Brazil **74–75** EG 3
Brazil Current **8**
Brazo Casiquiare **72** E 3
Brazzaville **55** GH 6
Brčko **21** G 3
Brecknock, Península **77** B 9
Breda **16** D 4
Bredbyn **18** G 3
Breiðafjörður **18** A 2
Brejo **75** H 1
Brekken **18** F 3
Bremangerlandet **18** D 3
Bremen **17** E 4
Bremerhaven **17** E 4
Bremerton **66** B 2
Brenner **21** F 2
Brescia **21** F 2
Brest (Belarus) **19** H 5
Brest (France) **20** C 2
Bretagne **20** C 2
Breves **73** H 4
Brevoort Island **65** P 3
Brewton **67** J 5
Bridgeport **67** M 3
Bridger Peak **66** E 3
Bridgetown (Australia) **42** B 5
Bridgetown (Barbados) **69** KL 5
Brighton **16** C 4
Brindisi **21** G 3
Brisbane **43** J 4
Bristol **16** C 4
Bristol Bay **62** EF 4
Bristol Channel **16** C 4
British Columbia **63** MN 4–5
British Isles **8**
Britstown **58** C 6
Brive **20** D 2
Brno **17** G 5
Broadus **66** EF 2
Broadview **63** R 5
Brochet **63** R 4
Broken Hill **43** G 5
Brokhovo **33** ST 4
Brokopondo **73** G 3
Brönnöysund **18** F 2
Brookings **67** G 3
Brookton **42** B 5
Broome **42** C 2
Browne Range Nature Reserve **42** CD 3–4
Brownfield **66** F 5
Brownsville **67** G 6
Brownwood **66** G 5
Bruce Crossing **67** J 2
Bruce, Mount **42** B 3
Brugge **16** D 4
Brumado **75** H 3
Brunei **38** D 2
Brusilovka **26** KL 5
Brusque **76** G 4
Brussels **16** DE 4
Brusset, Erg **55** FG 2
Bruxelles **16** DE 4
Bryan **67** G 5
Bryansk **26** F 5
Bryanskoye **23** G 2

Bryne **19** E 4
Brzeg **17** G 4
Bu Craa **50** C 3
Bu Tu Suay **37** J 5
Bübïyän **25** E 3
Bucaramanga **72** D 2
Buchanan **54** B 4
Bucharest **22** C 2
Buckingham Bay **43** F 1
Buckland **62** E 2
Buco Zau **55** G 6
Bucureşti **22** C 2
Budapest **22** A 1
Budennovsk **23** F 2
Búðardalur **18** A 2
Buenaventura (Colombia) **72** C 3
Buenaventura (Mexico) **66** E 6
Buenavista **66** E 7
Buenos Aires **76** DE 5
Buenos Aires, Lago **77** B 8
Buffalo (N.Y., U.S.A.) **67** L 3
Buffalo (OK, U.S.A.) **66** G 4
Buffalo (S.D., U.S.A.) **66** F 2
Buffalo (WY, U.S.A.) **66** E 3
Buffalo Lake **63** OP 3
Buffalo Narrows **63** Q 4
Bug **17** H 4
Buga **72** C 3
Bugat **32** H 6
Bugorkan **32** J 3
Bugt **33** M 6
Bugul´ma **26** K 5
Buhayrat al Asad **24** C 1–2
Bujumbura **56** D 5
Buka **45** F 3
Bukadaban Feng **34** B 3
Bukavu **56** D 5
Bukhara **31** G 3
Bukit Gandadiwata **39** EF 4
Bukit Masurai **38** B 4
Bukit Sulat **39** G 3
Bukittinggi **38** B 4
Bukoba **56** E 5
Bukukun **32** K 6
Búl, Küh-e **25** F 3
Bulawayo **58** D 4
Buldana **36** C 3
Bulgan **32** H 6
Bulgaria **22** C 2
Buli **39** G 3
Bullahär **57** G 2
Bulo Berde **57** H 4
Bulungu **56** B 5
Bumba **56** C 4
Bumbulan **39** F 3
Bunbury **42** B 5
Bunda **56** E 5
Bunda Bunda **43** G 3
Bundaberg **43** J 3
Bundooma **42** E 3
Bunia **56** E 4
Buorkhaya, Guba **33** O 1
Buorkhaya, Mys **33** O 1
Buqayq **25** E 4
Bür Sa'id **24** A 3
Bür Südän **52** F 3
Buran **27** R 6
Bura´o **57** H 3

Burayḑa **24** D 4
Burdur **22** D 3
Burdwan **36** E 3
Bureinskiy, Khrebet **33** O 5
Bureya **33** O 5
Burgakhcha **33** Q 3
Burgas **22** C 2
Burgaski zaliv **22** C 2
Burgeo **65** Q 6
Burgersdorp **58** D 6
Burgfjället **18** G 3
Burgos (Mexico) **68** C 3
Burgos (Spain) **20** C 3
Burhanpur **36** C 3
Burin Peninsula **65** Q 6
Burkhala **33** RS 3
Burkina Faso **54** D 3
Burlington (CO, U.S.A.) **66** F 4
Burlington (IA, U.S.A.) **67** H 3
Burlington (N.Y., U.S.A.) **67** M 3
Burma **37** FG 3
Burmantovo **27** M 3
Burnie **44** L 9
Burns **66** C 3
Burqin **31** M 1
Burra **43** F 5
Bursa **22** C 2
Buru, Pulau **39** G 4
Burundi **56** DE 5
Buşayrah **24** C 2
Büshehr **25** F 3
Bushman Land **58** B 5
Businga **56** C 4
Busira **56** B 5
Buskerud **19** E 3
Busu Melo **56** C 4
Butang Group **37** G 6
Butaritari **46** C 2
Butembo **56** D 4
Butha Qi **33** M 6
Butt of Lewis **16** B 3
Butte **66** D 2
Button Bay **63** T 4
Button Islands **65** P 3
Butuan **39** G 2
Butung, Pulau **39** F 4
Buy **26** H 4
Büyük Ağrı Dağı **23** F 3
Buzău **22** C 1
Buzuluk **26** K 5
Byblos **24** B 2
Bydgoszcz **17** G 4
Bygdeå **18** H 3
Bygdeträsket **18** H 3
Bykovo **26** J 3
Bykovskiy **33** NO 1
Bylot Island **78**
Byrd Station **79**
Byro **42** B 4
Byrranga, Gory **32** GH 1
Byske **18** H 3
Byskeälven **18** H 2
Bytom **17** G 4
Byuchennyakh **33** QR 3

C

Ca Na **37** J 5
Caaguazu **76** E 4
Cáatingas **75** GH 2
Caazapa **76** E 4
Cabanatuan **39** J 1
Cabezas **74** D 4
Cabimas **72** D 1
Cabinda **55** G 7
Cabo Barbas **50** B 4
Cabo Beata **69** H 4
Cabo Bojador **50** C 3
Cabo Catoche **68** E 3
Cabo Corrientes **72** C 2
Cabo das Correntes **59** F 4
Cabo de Ajo **20** C 3
Cabo de Creus **20** D 3
Cabo de Finisterre **20** B 3
Cabo de Formentor
 20 D 3–4
Cabo de Gata **20** C 4
Cabo de Hornos **77** C 10
Cabo de la Nao **20** D 4
Cabo de Palos **20** C 4
Cabo de Salinas **20** D 4
Cabo de Santa Maria
 (Mozambique) **59** E 5
Cabo de Santa Maria
 (Portugal) **20** B 4
Cabo de São Roque **75** J 2
Cabo de São Vicente **20** B 4
Cabo Delgado **59** G 2
Cabo dos Bahías **77** CD 8
Cabo Frio **75** H 5
Cabo Gracias a Dios
 68 F 4–5
Cabo Norte **73** J 3
Cabo Orange **73** H 3
Cabo Ortegal **20** B 3
Cabo San Antonio
 (Argentina) **77** E 6
Cabo San Antonio (Cuba)
 68 EF 3
Cabo San Diego **77** C 9
Cabo San Lucas **66** E 7
Cabo Santa Elena **68** E 5
Cabo Trafalgar **20** B 4
Cabo Verde **54** AB 6
Cabora Bassa, Lago **59** E 3
Caborca **66** D 5
Cabot Strait **65** Q 6
Cabrera **20** D 4
Cabrera, Sierra de la **20** B 3
Cabruta **72** E 2
Caçador **76** F 4
Čačak **22** B 2
Cáceres (Brazil) **74** E 4
Cáceres (Spain) **20** B 4
Cachi, Nevado de **74** C 5
Cachimbo **73** H 5
Cachoeira **75** J 3
Cachoeira Alta **75** F 4
Cachoeira do Sul **76** F 5
Cachoeiro de Itapemirim
 75 HJ 5
Caconda **58** B 2
Cacula **58** A 2
Cadí, Sierra del **20** D 3
Cadiz (Philippines) **39** F 1

Cádiz (Spain) **20** B 4
Cádiz, Golfo de **20** B 4
Caen **20** C 2
Caetite **75** H 3
Cagayan de Oro **39** F 2
Cagliari **21** E 4
Caguas **69** J 4
Caia **59** F 3
Caibarién **69** G 3
Caico **75** J 2
Caicos Islands **69** H 3
Cailloma **74** B 4
Cairns **43** H 2
Cairo **52** E 2
Caiundo **58** B 3
Cajamarca **72** C 5
Cajazeiras **75** J 2
Cajuapara **73** J 4
Cala Ratjada **20** D 4
Calabar **55** F 4
Calabozo **72** E 2
Calabria **21** G 4
Calabro, Apennino **21** G 4
Calafate **77** B 9
Calais **16** D 4
Calama **74** C 5
Calamar **72** D 3
Calamian Group **39** E 1
Calapan **39** F 1
Calatayud **20** C 3
Calatrava, Campo de **20** C 4
Calbayog **39** FG 1
Calçoene **73** H 3
Calcutta **36** E 3
Caldas **72** C 2
Caldera **76** B 4
Caleta Olivia **77** C 8
Calgary **63** P 5
Cali **72** C 3
Calicut **36** C 5
California **66** BC 3–5
California Current **8**
California, Golfo de
 66 DE 5–7
Calilegua **74** CD 5
Callao **74** A 3
Caltanissetta **21** F 4
Calvi **21** E 3
Cam Ranh **37** J 5
Camagüey **69** G 3
Camaná **74** B 4
Camapuã **75** F 4
Camaquã **76** F 5
Camarat, Cap **21** E 3
Camargo **74** C 5
Camarones **77** C 7
Camaxilo **58** B 1
Cambodia **37** HJ 5
Cambrai **20** D 1
Cambrian Mountains **16** C 4
Cambridge (MA, U.S.A.)
 67 M 3
Cambridge (U.K.) **16** D 4
Cambridge Bay **63** QR 2
Cameia National Park **58** C 2
Cameron **67** H 2
Cameroon **55** FG 4
Cameroon, Mont **55** F 5
Cametá **73** J 4
Camiranga **73** J 4

Camiri **74** D 5
Camocim **75** H 1
Camooweal **43** F 2
Camorta **37** F 6
Camp Century **78**
Campana, Isla **77** A 8
Campbell Island **79**
Campbellton **65** O 6
Campeche **68** D 4
Campeche **68** D 4
Campeche, Bahia de **68** D 4
Campidano **21** E 4
Campina Grande **75** J 2
Campinas **75** G 5
Campo **55** F 5
Campo Corral **72** D 2
Campo de Calatrava **20** C 4
Campo Formoso **75** H 3
Campo Gallo **76** D 4
Campo Grande **75** F 5
Campo Maior **75** H 1
Campos **75** GH 3–4
Campos **75** H 5
Camrose **63** P 5
Can Tho **37** J 6
Canada **62–65**
Cañada Oruro **74** D 5
Canadian River **64** F 4
Çanakkale **22** C 2
Çanakkale Boğazi **22** C 2–3
Canal de la Mona **69** J 4
Canal do Norte **73** H 3
Canal du Midi **20** D 3
Canale di Sicilia **21** F 4
Canale di Malta **21** F 4
Cananea **66** DE 5
Canary Current **8**
Canary Islands **50** B 3
Canaveral, Cape **67** KL 6
Canavieiras **75** J 4
Canberra **43** H 6
Canchas **76** B 4
Candeias **75** J 3
Candelaria **68** D 4
Canéla **75** G 3
Cangamba **58** C 2
Cangombé **58** B 2
Cangyuan **34** C 6
Cangzhou **35** G 3
Caniapiscau, Lac **65** O 5
Canindé **75** J 1
Çankiri **23** D 2
Cann River **43** H 6
Cannanore **36** BC 5
Cannes **21** E 3
Canning Basin **42** C 2
Canoas **76** F 4
Canora **63** R 5
Canosa **21** G 3
Canso **65** P 6
Cantabrian Mountains
 20 BC 3
Cantaura **73** F 2
Canterbury Bight **45** Q 9
Canto do Buriti **75** H 2
Canton (China) **34** F 6
Canton (OH, U.S.A.) **67** K 3
Cap Camarat **21** E 3
Cap Corse **21** E 3
Cap d'Ambre **59** H 2

Cap de Fer **51** G 1
Cap de la Hague **20** C 2
Cap-de-la-Madeleine **65** N 6
Cap Ferret **20** C 3
Cap-Haïtien **69** H 4
Cap Hopes Advance **65** O 3
Cap Lopez **55** F 6
Cap Masoala **59** J 3
Cap Saint-André **59** G 3
Cap Timiris **50** B 5
Cap Vert **54** A 3
Cap Vohimena **59** GH 5
Cap Wolstenholme **65** M 3
Capanema **73** J 4
Capão Bonito **75** G 5
Cape Adare **79**
Cape Agulhas **58** C 6
Cape Ann **79**
Cape Arid **42** C 5
Cape Arid National Park
 42 C 5
Cape Arnhem **43** F 1
Cape Baring **63** O 2
Cape Bathurst **62** LM 1
Cape Bauld **65** QR 5
Cape Boothby **79**
Cape Breton Island **65** Q 6
Cape Canaveral **67** KL 6
Cape Catastrophe **43** F 6
Cape Chapman **63** U 2
Cape Charles **67** L 4
Cape Chelyuskin **78**
Cape Chidley **65** P 3
Cape Coast **54** D 4
Cape Cod **67** N 3
Cape Columbine **58** B 6
Cape Comorin **36** C 6
Cape Cretin **44** E 3
Cape Croker **42** E 1
Cape Cross **58** A 4
Cape Darnley **79**
Cape Dennison **79**
Cape Dorchester **65** M 2
Cape du Couedic **43** F 6
Cape Dyer **65** P 2
Cape Engaño **39** J 1
Cape Farewell **45** Q 9
Cape Fear **67** L 5
Cape Finniss **42** E 5
Cape Flattery **66** AB 2
Cape Freels **65** R 6
Cape Fria **58** A 3
Cape Girardeau **67** J 4
Cape Grim **44** K 9
Cape Guardafui **57** J 2
Cape Harrison **65** Q 5
Cape Hatteras **67** LM 4
Cape Henrietta Maria **65** L 4
Cape Herluf Trolle **65** T 3
Cape Horn **77** C 10
Cape Howe **43** J 6
Cape Jaffa **43** F 6
Cape Kellett **63** M 1
Cape Krusenstern National
 Monument **62** DE 2
Cape Lambert **45** F 2
Cape Lambton **63** MN 1
Cape Leeuwin **42** A 5
Cape Lévêque **42** C 2
Cape Lisburne **62** D 2

Cape Londonderry **42** D 1
Cape Lookout **67** L 5
Cape Low **63** UV 3
Cape Maria van Diemen **45** Q 7
Cape Melville **43** G 1
Cape Mendocino **66** AB 3
Cape Mercy **65** P 3
Cape Meredith **77** D 9
Cape Mohican **62** D 3
Cape Morris Jesup **78**
Cape Naturaliste **42** A 5
Cape Negrais **37** F 4
Cape Newenham **62** E 4
Cape Norvegia **79**
Cape of Good Hope **58** B 6
Cape Otway **43** G 6
Cape Palliser **45** R 9
Cape Palmas **54** C 5
Cape Poinsett **79**
Cape Prince Alfred **63** M 1
Cape Prince of Wales **62** D 2
Cape Providence **44** P 10
Cape Province **58** CD 6
Cape Race **65** R 6
Cape Ray **65** Q 6
Cape Rodney **44** E 4
Cape Sable (Canada) **65** O 7
Cape Sable (FL, U.S.A.) **67** K 6
Cape Saint Francis **58** CD 6
Cape Saint George **45** F 2
Cape Saint Lucia **59** E 5
Cape San Blas **67** J 6
Cape Scott (Australia) **42** D 1
Cape Scott (Canada) **62** M 5
Cape Smith **65** M 3
Cape Town **58** B 6
Cape Van Diemen **42** D 1
Cape Verde **54** AB 6
Cape Wessel **43** F 1
Cape Wrath **16** B 3
Cape Yakataga **62** J 4
Cape York **43** G 1
Cape York Peninsula **43** G 1
Cape Zhelaniya **78**
Capelinha **75** H 4
Capitán Arturo Prat **79**
Capo Carbonara **21** E 4
Capo Circeo **21** F 3
Capo Gallo **21** F 4
Capo Palinuro **21** FG 3
Capo Passero **21** G 4
Capo San Marco **21** E 4
Capo Santa Maria di Leuca **21** G 4
Capo Spartivento **21** E 4
Capo Testa **21** E 3
Capoompeta **43** J 4
Capri **21** F 3
Capricorn Channel **43** J 3
Caprivi Game Park **58** C 3
Caprivi Strip **58** C 3
Car Nicobar **37** F 6
Caracal **22** B 2
Caracaraí **73** F 3
Caracas **72** E 1
Caraga **39** G 2

Carahue **77** B 6
Caratinga **75** H 4
Carauari **72** E 4
Carazinho **76** F 4
Carballo **20** B 3
Carbonara, Capo **21** E 4
Carbonia **21** E 4
Carcassonne **20** D 3
Cárdenas **69** F 3
Cardiff **16** C 4
Cardigan Bay **16** C 4
Careiro **73** G 4
Carey, Lake **42** C 4
Caribbean Sea **69** GJ 4
Caribou Mountains **63** O 4
Carinhanha **75** H 3
Cariparé **75** G 3
Caritianas **73** F 5
Carletonville **58** D 5
Carlisle **16** C 4
Carmila **43** H 3
Carnarvon (Australia) **42** A 3
Carnarvon (S.Africa) **58** C 6
Carnegie **42** C 4
Carnegie, Lake **42** C 4
Carniche, Alpi **21** F 2
Carnot **56** B 3
Carolina **73** J 5
Caroline **47** EF 3
Caroline Islands **46** AB 2
Carondelet **46** D 3
Carora **72** DE 1
Carpathians **22** BC 1
Carpáţii Meridionali **22** B 1–2
Carpentaria, Gulf of **43** F 1
Carpina **75** J 2
Carrick-on-Shannon **16** B 4
Carrillo **68** B 2
Carrizal **72** D 1
Carrizozo **66** E 5
Çarşamba **23** D 3
Carson City **66** C 4
Cartagena (Colombia) **72** C 1
Cartagena (Spain) **20** C 4
Cartago **68** F 6
Carter, Mount **43** G 1
Caruaru **75** J 2
Carvoeiro **73** F 4
Casablanca **50** D 2
Casbas **77** D 6
Cascade Range **66** B 2–3
Cascavel **75** F 5
Caserta **21** F 3
Casey **79**
Casino **43** J 4
Casma **72** C 5
Casper **66** E 3
Caspian Sea **30** DE 2–3
Cassiar **62** L 4
Cassino **21** F 3
Castanhal **73** J 4
Castaño **76** C 5
Castellón **20** D 4
Castelo de Vide **20** B 4
Castelvetrano **21** F 4
Castilla (Chile) **76** B 4
Castilla (Peru) **72** B 5

Castilla la Nueva **20** C 3–4
Castilla la Vieja **20** C 3
Castillos **76** F 5
Castlegar **63** O 6
Castor **63** P 5
Castres **20** D 3
Castries **69** K 5
Castro **77** B 7
Cat Island **69** GH 3
Catalão **75** G 4
Catalonia **20** D 3
Çatalzeytin **23** D 2
Catamarca **76** C 4
Catanduanes **39** F 1
Catanduva **75** G 5
Catania **21** G 4
Catanzaro **21** G 4
Catastrophe, Cape **43** F 6
Catbalogan **39** FG 1
Cateel **39** G 2
Catinzaco **76** C 4
Catoche, Cabo **68** E 3
Catriló **77** D 6
Catrimani **73** F 3
Catwick Islands **37** J 6
Caucasia **72** C 2
Caucasus Mountains **23** F 2
Cauquenes **77** B 6
Caura **73** F 2
Cavalcante **75** G 3
Caxias **75** H 1
Caxias do Sul **76** F 4
Caxito **58** A 1
Cayenne **73** H 3
Cayman Islands **69** FG 4
Ceará **75** J 1
Ceballos **68** B 2
Cebollar **76** C 4
Cebu **39** F 1
Cebu **39** F 2
Čechy **17** E 4
Cedar Falls **67** H 3
Cedar Lake **63** RS 5
Cedar Rapids **67** H 3
Celaya **68** B 3
Celebes **39** EF 4
Celebes Sea **39** F 3
Celje **21** G 2
Celle **17** F 4
Celtic Sea **16** B 4
Cendrawasih **39** H 4
Central African Republic **56** BC 3
Central America **8**
Central Arctic District **63** QR 1
Central, Cordillera (Colombia) **72** C 2–3
Central, Cordillera (Peru) **72** C 5
Central Kalahari Game Reserve **58** C 4
Central Makran Range **31** GH 5
Central Range **44** D 2–3
Central Siberian Plateau **32** GK 3
Central Siberian Plateau **32** GK 3
Cereal **63** P 5

Ceres **75** G 4
Cerf **57** J 6
Cerro Aconcagua **76** BC 5
Cerro Agua Caliente **68** A 2
Cerro Ángel **68** B 3
Cerro Blanco **66** E 6
Cerro Bonete **76** C 4
Cerro Champaquí **76** D 5
Cerro Chirripó **68** F 6
Cerro de la Encantada **66** CD 5
Cerro de Pasco **74** A 3
Cerro de Tocorpuri **74** C 5
Cerro del Toro **76** C 4
Cerro Galán **76** C 4
Cerro Grande **68** B 3
Cerro Las Casilas **66** E 7
Cerro Las Minas **68** E 5
Cerro Marahuaca **72** E 3
Cerro Mariquita **68** C 3
Cerro Mohinora **66** E 6
Cerro Murallón **77** B 8
Cerro Nuevo Mundo **74** C 5
Cerro Ojos del Salado **76** C 4
Cerro San Valentín **77** B 8
Cerro Ventana **66** E 7
Cerro Yavi **72** E 2
Cerro Yucuyácua **68** C 4
Cerro Yumari **72** E 3
Cesano **21** F 3
České Budějovice **17** F 5
Českézemě **17** FG 5
Ceuta **50** D 1
Ceva-i-Ra **46** C 4
Cévennes **20** D 3
Ceyhan **23** E 3
Ceyhan **23** E 3
Ceylânpınar **24** C 1
Ceylon **36** D 6
Chaca **74** B 4
Chachapoyas **72** C 5
Chachro **31** J 5
Chad **55** HJ 3
Chad, Lake **55** G 3
Chädegän **25** F 2
Chadobets **32** G 4
Chagai Hills **31** G 5
Chagda **33** O 4
Chagdo Kangri **36** D 1
Chaghcharän **31** H 4
Chagyl **30** F 2
Chah Bahär **31** G 5
Chahah Burjak **31** G 4
Chaiyaphum **37** H 4
Chakari **58** D 3
Chake Chake **57** FG 6
Chakhansur **31** G 4
Chala **74** B 4
Chalbi Desert **57** F 4
Chalhuanca **74** B 3
Challapata **74** C 4
Chalon-sur-Saône **21** DE 2
Châlons-sur-Marne **21** D 2
Chälús **25** F 1
Chaman **31** H 4
Chamba **36** C 1
Chambéry **21** E 2
Chamical **76** C 5
Chamoli **36** C 1

Champagne **21** DE 2
Champaquí, Cerro **76** D 5
Champdoré, Lac **65** O 4
Chañaral **76** B 4
Chanco **77** B 6
Chandigarh **36** C 1
Chandler **65** P 6
Chandmaní **34** C 1
Chandpur **37** F 3
Chanf **31** G 5
Chang Jiang **35** G 4
Changara **59** E 3
Changchun **35** J 2
Changde **34** F 5
Changji **31** M 2
Changling **35** H 2
Changsha **34** F 5
Changwu **34** E 3
Changzhi **34** F 3
Channel Islands (U.K.)
  16 C 5
Channel Islands (U.S.A.)
  66 C 5
Chany, Ozero **27** P 5
Chaoyang (Guangduog,
  China) **34** G 6
Chaoyang (Liaoning, China)
  35 GH 2
Chaoyangcun **33** MN 5
Chapayev-Zheday **32** L 3
Chapleau **64** L 6
Chapman, Cape **63** U 2
Chapoma **26** GH 2
Chapra **36** DE 2
Chara **32** L 4
Charagua **74** D 4
Charcot Island **79**
Chard **63** P 4
Chardzhou **31** G 3
Chari **55** H 3
Charity **73** G 2
Charkabozh **26** K 2
Charles Peak **42** C 5
Charlesbourg **65** N 6
Charleston (S.C., U.S.A.)
  67 L 5
Charleston (W.V., U.S.A.)
  67 K 4
Charleville **43** H 4
Charlotte **67** KL 4
Charlottesville **67** L 4
Charlottetown **65** P 6
Charlton (Australia) **43** G 6
Charlton (NV, U.S.A.)
  65 LM 5
Charters Towers **43** H 3
Chartres **20** D 2
Charyn **31** K 2
Charyshskoye **27** Q 5
Chasel´ka **27** Q 2
Chatanga **32** K 5
Châteauroux **20** D 2
Châtellerault **20** D 2
Chatham (New Zealand)
  45 S 9
Chatham (Ontario, Can.)
  67 K 3
Chatham Islands **45** S 9
Chattanooga **67** J 5

Chau Phu **37** J 5
Chaumont **21** DE 2
Chaves (Brazil) **73** HJ 4
Chaves (Portugal) **20** B 3
Chayatyn, Khrebet **33** P 5
Chaykovskiy **26** KL 4
Chazhegovo **26** K 3
Cheb **17** F 4
Cheboksary **26** J 4
Chech, Erg **50** E 3−4
Cheduba **37** F 4
Chegga (Algeria) **51** G 2
Chegga (Mauritania) **50** D 3
Chegytun **62** C 2
Cheju **35** J 4
Cheju-do **35** J 4
Chekhov **33** Q 6
Chekunda **33** O 5
Chekuyevo **26** G 3
Chelforó **77** C 6
Cheliff **51** F 1
Chelkar **30** F 1
Chelm **17** H 4
Chelmuzhi **26** G 3
Chelyabinsk **27** M 4
Chelyuskin, Cape **78**
Chemnitz **17** F 4
Chenab **31** J 4
Chenachane **50** E 3
Chengde **35** G 2
Chengdu **34** D 4
Chenxi **34** F 5
Chenzhou **34** F 5
Chepen **72** C 5
Chepes **76** C 5
Cherbourg **20** C 2
Cherchell **51** F 1
Cheremkhovo **32** H 5
Cherepovets **26** G 4
Cherkassy **26** F 6
Cherkessk **23** F 2
Chernigov **26** F 5
Chernovtsy **22** C 1
Chernyakhovsk **19** H 5
Chernyshevskiy **32** K 3
Chernyy Ostrov **32** F 3
Chernyye Brat´ya, Ostrova
  33 S 6
Chernyye Zemli **23** G 1
Cherskiy Range **33** Q 2
Chervonograd **19** HJ 5
Chervonoye, Ozero **19** J 5
Chervonoznamenka **22** D 1
Chesapeake Bay
  Bridge-Tunnel **67** LM 4
Chesterfield, Iles **46** B 4
Chesterfield Inlet **63** T 3
Chesterfield Islands **46** B 4
Chetumal **68** E 4
Cheulik **33** P 2
Cheyenne **66** F 3
Chhatarpur **36** C 3
Chiang Kham **37** H 4
Chiang Mai **37** G 4
Chiang Rai **37** G 4
Chiang Saen **37** H 3
Chiapas **68** D 4
Chiavari **21** E 3
Chiayi **35** H 6
Chiba **35** M 3

Chibagalakh **33** PQ 2
Chibit **27** R 5
Chibougamau **65** N 6
Chicago **67** J 3
Chicapa **58** C 1
Chichagof **62** K 4
Chicheng **35** G 2
Chiclayo **72** C 5
Chico (Argentina) **77** C 7
Chico (Argentina) **77** C 8
Chicoutimi **65** N 6
Chifeng **35** G 2
Chiganak **27** O 6
Chigorodó **72** C 2
Chigubo **59** E 4
Chihli, Gulf of **35** GH 3
Chihuahua **66** E 6
Chik Ballapur **36** C 5
Chikhacheva **33** R 1
Chilabombwe **58** D 2
Childress **66** F 5
Chile **76−77** B 4−6
Chilete **72** C 5
Chilipa de Alvarez **68** C 4
Chillán **77** B 6
Chiloé, Isla de **77** B 7
Chilpancingo **68** BC 4
Chimbay **30** F 2
Chimborazo **72** C 4
Chimbote **72** C 5
Chimkent **31** H 2
Chin **37** F 3
China **34** DF 4
Chinandega **68** E 5
Chincha Alta **74** A 3
Chindu **34** C 4
Chindwin **37** F 3
Chingola **58** D 2
Chinguetti **50** C 4
Chinju **35** J 3
Chipata **59** E 2
Chirchik **31** HJ 2
Chiriguaná **72** D 2
Chishui **34** E 5
Chita **32** K 5
Chitado **58** A 3
Chitato **58** C 1
Chitina **62** J 3
Chitipa **59** E 1
Chitral **31** J 3
Chittagong **37** F 3
Chittaurgarh **36** C 3
Chittoor **36** C 5
Chivasso **21** E 2
Chivay **74** B 4
Chizha **26** H 2
Chkalovo **27** O 5
Chobe National Park **58** C 3
Chodzjent **31** HJ 2
Choele Choel **77** CD 6
Choggia **21** F 2
Choiseul **45** G 3
Chojnice **17** G 4
Cholet **20** C 2
Choluteca **68** E 5
Chomutov **17** F 4
Chon Buri **37** H 5
Chon Thanh **37** J 5
Chona **32** J 3
Ch´ŏngjin **35** JK 2

Ch´ŏngju **35** J 3
Chongqing **34** E 5
Chŏnju **35** J 3
Chorzów **17** G 4
Chos Malal **77** BC 6
Chosica **74** A 3
Chotanagpur **36** DE 3
Chott Melrhir **51** G 2
Choum **50** C 4
Choybalsan **32** K 6
Christchurch **45** Q 9
Christmas Island **38** C 6
Chubut **77** C 7
Chudskoye Ozero **19** J 4
Chukar **32** L 3
Chukchi Sea **62** CD 2
Chuken **33** P 6
Chukotsk Peninsula **78**
Chukotsk Range **78**
Chula Vista **66** C 5
Chulak-Kurgan **31** HJ 2
Chulasa **26** J 3
Chulym **27** QR 4
Chumikan **33** OP 5
Chumphon **37** G 5
Ch´unch´ŏn **35** J 3
Chüplu (Iran) **25** E 1
Chuquibamba **74** B 4
Chuquicamata **74** C 5
Chur **21** E 2
Churchill (Man., Can.)
  63 ST 4
Churchill (Man., Can.) **63** T 4
Churchill, Cape **63** T 4
Churchill Falls **65** P 5
Churchill Lake **63** Q 4
Churchill Mountains **79**
Churu **36** C 2
Churuguara **72** DE 1
Churún Merú **73** F 2
Chusovoy **27** L 4
Chusovskoy **26** L 3
Chute-des-Passes **65** N 6
Chutes de Katende **56** C 6
Chutes de Livingstone
  55 G 7
Chutes Ngaliema **56** D 4
Chuxiong **34** D 5
Chuyengo **32** H 3
Cianjur **38** C 5
Cícero Dantas **75** J 3
Ciechanów **17** H 4
Ciego de Ávila **69** G 3
Ciénaga **72** D 1
Cienfuegos **69** F 3
Cieza **20** C 4
Cihanbeyli Platosu **23** D 3
Cilacap **38** C 5
Cilo Daği **23** F 3
Cimarron **66** G 4
Çimen Daği **23** E 3
Cîmpia Bărăganului
  22 C 1−2
Cîmpia Burnazului **22** C 2
Cîmpina **22** C 1
Cinca **20** D 3
Cincinnati **67** K 4
Cinto, Monte **21** E 3
Circeo, Capo **21** F 3
Circle **62** J 2

Cirebon 38 C 5
Cirque Mountain 65 P 4
Ciskei 58 D 6
Citlaltépetl, Volcán 68 C 4
Citta del Vaticano 21 F 3
Ciudad Acuña 68 B 2
Ciudad Bolívar 73 F 2
Ciudad Camargo 66 E 6
Ciudad de Rio Grande
  68 B 3
Ciudad del Carmen 68 D 4
Ciudad Guayana 73 F 2
Ciudad Guzmán 68 B 4
Ciudad Hidalgo 68 BC 4
Ciudad Juárez 66 E 5
Ciudad Madero 68 C 3
Ciudad Mante 68 C 3
Ciudad Obregón 66 E 6
Ciudad Ojeda 72 D 1
Ciudad Río Bravo 68 C 2
Ciudad-Rodrigo 20 B 3
Ciudad Valles 68 C 3
Ciudad Victoria 68 C 3
Civitanova Marche 21 F 3
Civitavecchia 21 F 3
Cizre 23 F 3
Claire Coast 79
Claire, Lake 63 P 4
Clanwilliam 58 B 6
Clarke Range 43 H 3
Clarksburg 67 KL 4
Clarksville 67 J 4
Clearwater 67 K 6
Clermont 43 H 3
Clermont-Ferrand 20 D 2
Cleveland 67 K 3
Cleveland, Mount 66 D 2
Clinton 63 N 5
Clinton-Colden Lake 63 Q 3
Cloncurry 43 FG 3
Clorinda 76 E 4
Cloud Peak 66 E 3
Clovis 66 F 5
Cluj-Napoca 22 B 1
Cnossus 22 C 3
Coahuila 68 B 2
Coal River 63 M 4
Coari 73 F 4
Coast Mountains
  62−63 LM 4−5
Coast of Labrador
  65 PQ 4−5
Coast Range (Queensland,
  Austr.) 43 J 4
Coast Ranges (U.S.A.)
  66 B 3−4
Coats Island 63 V 3
Coats Land 79
Coatzacoalcos 68 D 4
Cobar 43 H 5
Cobija 74 C 3
Cobquecura 77 B 6
Coburg 17 F 4
Cocachacra 74 B 4
Cochabamba 74 C 4
Cochin 36 C 6
Cochrane 77 B 8
Cocklebiddy 42 D 5
Coco Island 70 B 2
Coco Islands 37 F 5

Cod, Cape 67 N 3
Codó 75 H 1
Cody 66 E 3
Coetivy 57 K 6
Coeur d'Alene 66 C 2
Coff's Harbour 43 J 5
Coihaique 77 B 8
Coimbatore 36 C 5
Coimbra 20 B 3
Cojimies 72 B 3
Cojutepeque 68 E 5
Col de Perthus 20 D 3
Colatina 75 H 4
Cold Bay 62 E 4
Colesberg 58 D 6
Colima 68 B 4
Collier Bay 42 C 2
Collier Ranges National Park
  42 B 3
Collines du Perche 20 D 2
Collinson Peninsula
  63 R 1−2
Cololo, Nevado 74 C 4
Colombia 72 DE 3
Colombo 36 C 6
Colón (Cuba) 69 F 3
Colón (Panamá) 72 C 2
Colón, Archipiélago de
  72 B 6
Colona 42 E 5
Colonia Las Heras 77 C 8
Colorado (Argentina) 77 D 6
Colorado (AZ, U.S.A.)
  66 D 5
Colorado (TX, U.S.A.)
  67 G 5−6
Colorado (U.S.A.) 66 EF 4
Colorado Plateau 66 DE 4
Colorado Springs 66 F 4
Columbia (MO, U.S.A.)
  67 H 4
Columbia (S.C., U.S.A.)
  67 K 5
Columbia (WA, U.S.A.)
  66 BC 2
Columbia Falls 66 D 2
Columbia, Mount 63 O 5
Columbia Mountains
  63 NO 5
Columbia Plateau 66 C 3
Columbine, Cape 58 B 6
Columbus (GA, U.S.A.)
  67 J 5
Columbus (IN, U.S.A.)
  67 J 4
Columbus (MS, U.S.A.)
  67 J 5
Columbus (OH, U.S.A.)
  67 K 4
Columbus (TX, U.S.A.)
  67 G 6
Colville Lake 63 MN 2
Comalcalco 68 D 4
Comandante Luis
  Piedrabuena 77 BC 8−9
Combarbala 76 B 5
Combermere Bay 37 F 4
Commander Islands 78
Committee Bay 63 U 2
Como 21 E 2

Comodoro Rivadavia 77 C 8
Comorin, Cape 36 C 6
Comoros 59 G 2
Compiègne 20 D 2
Con Son 37 J 6
Conakry 54 B 4
Conceição do Araguaia
  73 J 5
Concepción (Bolivia) 74 D 4
Concepción (Chile) 77 B 6
Concepción (Paraguay)
  74 E 5
Concepción del Oro 68 B 3
Concepción del Uruguay
  76 E 5
Conception, Point 66 B 5
Concord 67 M 3
Concórdia (Amazonas,
  Brazil) 72 E 4
Concordia (Argentina)
  76 E 5
Condon 66 C 2
Conejo 66 D 7
Congo 55 H 6
Congo 55 H 6
Connaught 16 B 4
Connecticut 67 M 3
Conrad 66 D 2
Conselheiro Lafaiete 75 H 5
Constanţa 22 C 2
Constantine 51 G 1
Contamana 72 CD 5
Contwoyto Lake 63 PQ 2
Conway Reef 46 C 4
Cooch Bihar 36 E 2
Cook 42 E 5
Cook Inlet 62 G 3
Cook Islands 46 E 3
Cook, Mount 45 Q 9
Cook Mountains 79
Cook Strait 45 QR 9
Cookes Peak 66 E 5
Cooktown 43 H 2
Copenhagen 19 F 4
Copiapó 76 BC 4
Copperbelt 58 D 2
Coppermine 63 OP 2
Coqên 36 E 1
Coquimbo 76 B 4
Coral Harbour 63 UV 3
Coral Sea 46 B 3−4
Coral Sea Islands Territory
  43 HJ 1−2
Corcaigh 16 B 4
Cordillera Cantábrica
  20 BC 3
Cordillera Central (Colombia)
  72 C 2−3
Cordillera Central (Peru)
  72 C 5
Cordillera Central
  (Philippines) 39 J 1
Cordillera Occidental
  72 C 2−3
Cordillera Oriental
  72 CD 2−3
Cordillera Real 72 C 4
Córdoba (Argentina) 76 D 5
Córdoba (Mexico) 68 C 4
Córdoba (Spain) 20 BC 4

Corfu 22 A 3
Corigliano Calabro 21 G 4
Corinth 22 B 3
Corinto 75 H 4
Cork 16 B 4
Çorlu 22 C 2
Cornelio 66 D 6
Cornélio Procópio 75 F 5
Corner Brook 65 Q 6
Cornwall 65 MN 6
Coro 72 E 1
Coroatá 75 H 1
Corocoro 74 C 4
Coromandel Coast 36 D 5
Coromandel Peninsula
  45 R 8
Coronation Gulf 63 P 2
Coronel 77 B 6
Coronel Fabriciano 75 H 4
Coronel Oviedo 76 E 4
Coronel Pringles 77 D 6
Coropuna, Nevado 74 B 4
Corpus Christi 67 G 6
Corrente 75 G 3
Correntes, Cabo das 59 F 4
Correntina 75 GH 3
Corrientes 76 E 4
Corrientes, Cabo 72 C 2
Corse 21 E 3
Corse, Cap 21 E 3
Corsica 21 E 3
Çoruh 23 F 2
Çoruh Dağları 23 F 2
Çorum 23 D 2
Corumbá 74 E 4
Corunna 20 B 3
Corvallis 66 B 3
Cosenza 21 G 4
Cosmoledo Group 57 H 6
Costa Blanca 20 C 4
Costa Brava 20 D 3
Costa de la Luz 20 B 4
Costa de Mosquitos 68 F 5
Costa del Azahar 20 D 3−4
Costa del Sol 20 C 4
Costa Dorada 20 D 3
Costa Rica 68 EF 6
Costa Verde 20 B 3
Cotabato 39 F 2
Cotagaita 74 C 5
Côte d'Argent 20 C 3
Côte d'Azur 21 E 3
Coteau du Missouri 66 FG 2
Cotonou 54 E 4
Cotopaxi 72 C 4
Cottbus 17 F 4
Cotulla 66 G 6
Council Bluffs 67 GH 3
Courland 19 H 4
Coventry 16 C 4
Covington 67 K 4
Cowell 43 F 5
Cowra 43 H 5
Coxim 75 F 4
Cox's Bazar 37 F 3
Cracow 17 H 4
Cradock 58 D 6
Craiova 22 B 2
Cranbrook 42 B 5
Crary Mountains 79

Cratéus **75** H 2
Crato **75** J 2
Crawford **66** F 3
Creil **20** D 2
Cremona **21** F 2
Cres **21** F 3
Crescent City **66** B 3
Crete **22** BC 3
Cretin, Cape **44** E 3
Creus, Cabo de **20** D 3
Creuse **20** D 2
Criciúma **76** G 4
Crimea **23** D 1
Cristmas Island **47** E 2
Crni Drim **22** B 2
Croatia **21** G 2
Crockett **67** G 5
Croker, Cape **42** E 1
Croker Island **42** E 1
Crooked Island Passage
69 GH 3
Crookston **67** G 2
Cross, Cape **58** A 4
Crotone **21** G 4
Crowell **66** G 5
Crown Prince Frederik Island
63 U 2
Crowsnest Pass **63** OP 6
Cruz Alta **76** F 4
Cruz del Eje **76** CD 5
Cruz Grande **68** C 4
Cruzeiro do Oeste **75** F 5
Cruzeiro do Sul **72** D 5
Crystal Brook **43** F 5
Cu Lao Hon **37** J 5
Cuamba **59** F 2
Cuando Cubango **58** BC 3
Cuango **58** B 1
Cuanza **58** B 1
Cuanza Norte **58** AB 1
Cuanza Sul **58** AB 2
Cuauhtémoc **66** E 6
Cuba **69** F 3
Cubango **58** B 3
Cucurpe **66** D 5
Cúcuta **72** D 2
Cuddalore **36** CD 5
Cuddapah **36** C 5
Cudi Daği **23** F 3
Cuenca (Ecuador) **72** C 4
Cuenca (Spain) **20** C 3
Cuencamé de Ceniceros
68 B 3
Cuernavaca **68** BC 4
Cuiabá **74** E 4
Cuito Cuanavale **58** B 3
Culiacán **66** E 7
Cumaná **73** F 1
Cumbal **72** C 3
Cumberland **67** L 4
Cumberland Peninsula
65 OP 2
Cumberland Plateau **67** JK 4
Cumberland Sound **65** O 2
Cunani **73** H 3
Cunene (Angola) **58** A 3
Cunene (Angola) **58** B 3
Cuneo **21** E 3
Cunnamulla **43** H 4
Cupica **72** C 2

Curaçao, Isla **72** E 1
Curacautin **77** B 6
Curcubata, Virful **22** B 1
Curdimurka **43** F 4
Curicó **77** B 5–6
Curimatá **75** H 2–3
Curitiba **76** FG 4
Curtis **46** D 5
Curtis Island **43** J 3
Curuçá **73** J 4
Curumu **73** H 4
Cururupu **73** K 4
Curvelo **75** H 4
Cushing, Mount **63** M 4
Cuttack **36** E 3
Cuvette **55** H 6
Cuxhaven **17** E 4
Cuya **74** B 4
Cuyo Islands **39** F 1
Cuzco **74** B 3
Cyangugu **56** D 5
Cyclades **22** C 3
Cypress Hills **63** PQ 6
Cyprus **23** D 3
Cyrenaica **51** K 2
Czech Republic **17** G 5
Częstochowa **17** G 4

D

Da Hinggan Ling **35** GH 1–2
Da Lat **37** J 5
Da Nang **37** J 4
Da Qaidam **34** C 3
Dabat **57** F 2
Dabbāgh, Jabal **24** B 4
Dabola **54** B 3
Dacca **36** E 3
Dadali **45** G 3
Dadanawa **73** G 3
Daet **39** F 1
Dafeng **35** H 4
Dagabur **57** G 3
Dagana **55** H 3
Dagi **33** Q 5
Dagur **34** C 3
Dahabān **53** F 4
Dahlak Archipelago **57** G 1
Dahongliutan **31** K 3
Dahra **54** A 2
Dahûk **24** D 1
Daintree River National Park
43 G 2
Dairen **35** H 3
Daitō-shotō **35** K 5
Dajarra **43** F 3
Dakar **54** A 3
Dakha **36** E 3
Dakhla **50** B 4
Dakovica **22** B 2
Dala **58** C 2
Dalälven **19** G 3
Dalaman **22** C 3
Dalandzadgad **34** DE 2
Dalarna **19** F 3
Dalby **43** J 4
Dali **34** D 5
Dalian **35** H 3
Dall Lake **62** E 3

Dallas **67** G 5
Dalmā' **25** F 4
Dal'negorsk **35** L 2
Dal'nerechensk **35** K 1
Dal'nyaya **33** Q 6
Dalrymple, Mount **43** H 3
Dalsland **19** F 4
Dalstroy **33** P 3
Daltonganj **36** D 3
Dalwallinu **42** B 5
Daly River **42** E 1
Daly Waters **42** E 2
Daman **36** B 3
Damanhür **52** DE 2
Damara **56** B 3
Damaraland **58** B 4
Damascus **24** B 2
Dämghan **25** FG 1
Damoh **36** C 3
Dampier **42** B 3
Dampier Land **42** C 2
Dan Sai **37** H 4
Dan Xian **34** E 7
Danakil Plain **57** G 2
Danané **54** C 4
Danba **34** D 4
Dandarah **24** A 4
Dandong **35** H 2
Danghe Nanshan **34** C 3
Dangjin Shankou **34** B 3
Dangshan **35** G 4
Danmark **19** E 4
Danmarks Havn **78**
Danube **22** C 1
Danville **67** L 4
Dao Xian **34** F 5
Dapoli **36** B 4
Dar el Beida **50** CD 2
Dar es Salaam **57** F 6
Dar Rounga **56** C 2–3
Dar'a **24** B 2
Dārāb **25** G 3
Daraj **51** H 2
Daran **25** F 2
Daräw **24** A 4
Darband **30** F 4
Darbhanga **36** E 2
Dardanelles **22** C 3
Därfür **52** C 6
Darganata **31** G 2
Darién **72** C 2
Darién, Golfo del **72** C 2
Darjeeling **36** E 2
Darlag **34** C 4
Darling Downs **43** H 4
Darling Range **42** B 5
Darling River **43** G 5
Darlington **16** C 4
Darmstadt **17** E 5
Darnah **51** K 2
Darnley, Cape **79**
Dartmoor **16** C 4
Dartmouth **65** P 7
Darvaza **30** F 2
Darweshan **31** G 4
Darwin **42** E 1
Daryā-ye Māzandarān
30 E 3
Darya-ye Panj **31** J 3

Daryācheh-ye Bakhtegān
25 FG 3
Daryācheh-ye Namak **25** F 2
Daryācheh-ye Tashk
25 FG 3
Dasht-e Kavir **25** FG 2
Dasht-e Lüt **25** G 2
Dasht-e Naomid **30–31** G 4
Date **35** M 2
Datia **36** C 2
Datong (Qin., China) **34** D 3
Datong (Ziz., China) **34** F 2
Datta **33** Q 6
Däuarzan **30** F 3
Daugava **19** H 4
Daugav'pils **19** J 4
Daung Kyun **37** G 5
Dauphin Lake **63** R 5
Dauphin Lake **63** S 5
Dauphiné **21** E 3
Daurskoye **32** F 4
Davangere **36** C 5
Davao **39** G 2
Dävar Panäh **31** G 5
Dāvarzan **25** G 1
Davenport **67** HJ 3
David **72** B 2
Davis (Antarctica) **79**
Davis (CA, U.S.A.) **66** B 4
Davis Inlet **65** P 4
Davis Sea **79**
Davis Strait **65** Q 2
Dawhat as Salwä **25** F 4
Dawson **62** K 3
Dawson Creek **63** N 4
Dawu **34** D 4
Dayangshu **33** M 6
Dayong **34** F 5
Dayr az Zawr **24** C 2
Dayrūt **52** E 3
Dayton **67** K 4
Daytona Beach **67** K 6
Dazhu **34** E 4
Dazja **25** G 2
De Aar **58** C 6
de Gras, Lac **63** P 3
De Kalb **67** J 3
Dead Sea **24** B 3
Deán Funes **76** D 5
Dease Lake **62** L 4
Dease Strait **63** Q 2
Death Valley **66** C 4
Death Valley National
Monument **66** C 4
Débo, Lac **54** D 2
Deboyne Island **45** F 4
Debra Birhan **57** F 3
Debra Markos **57** F 2
Debra Zeit **57** F 3
Debrecen **22** B 1
Decatur (AL, U.S.A.) **67** J 5
Decatur (IL, U.S.A.) **67** J 4
Deccan **36** CD 3–5
Decepción **79**
Dechang **34** D 5
Dédougou **54** D 3
Dedza **59** F 2
Deer Lake **65** Q 6
Deering, Mount **42** D 3
Dêgê **34** C 4

Deh Bid **25** F 3
Deh Shū **31** G 4
Dehdez **25** F 3
Dehra Dun **36** C 1
Dej **22** B 1
Del Campillo **76** D 5
Del City **66** G 4
Delaware **67** L 4
Delegate **43** H 6
Delgado, Cabo **59** G 2
Delgerhaan **32** HJ 6
Delgerhet **34** F 1
Delgertsogt **34** E 1
Delhi **36** C 2
Deličal Daği **22** C 2–3
Delicias **66** E 6
Delijān **25** F 2
Dellys **51** F 1
Delphi **22** B 3
Delta Dunării **22** CD 1
Delta Junction **62** H 3
Demavend, Mount **25** F 2
Demba **56** C 6
Dembia **56** C 3
Dempo, Gunung **38** B 4
Dem´yanovka **27** N 5
Dem´yanskoye **27** N 4
Den Helder **16** D 4
Denali National Park and
    Preserve **62** GH 3
Denau **31** H 3
Denezhkin Kamen´, Gora
    27 L 3
Denison **67** G 5
Denizli **22** C 3
Denkou **34** E 2
Denmark **19** E 4
Denmark Strait **78**
Dennison, Cape **79**
Denpasar **38** E 5
Denton **67** G 5
D´Entrecasteaux Islands
    45 F 3
D´Entrecasteaux, Point
    42 AB 5
Denver **66** F 4
Deogarh **36** D 3
Deolali **36** B 4
Depósita **73** F 3
Deqing **34** F 6
Dera Ismail Khan **31** J 4
Derbent **30** D 2
Derby **42** C 2
Derdap **22** B 2
Dergachi **26** J 5
Dermott **67** H 5
Derudeb **52** F 5
Deryabino **27** Q 1
Derzhavinsk **27** N 5
Des Moines **67** H 3
Désappointement, Îles du
    47 F 3
Desengaño, Punta **77** C 8
Desierto de Sechura **72** B 5
Desierto de Atacama
    74 C 5
Desolación, Isla **77** AB 9
Dessau **17** F 4
Dessye **57** F 2
Detroit **67** K 3

Détroit d´Honguedo **65** P 6
Deutsche Bucht **17** E 4
Deva **22** B 1
Devil´s Island **73** H 2
Devils Lake **66** G 2
Devon Island **78**
Devonport **44** L 9
Devres **23** D 2
Deyang **34** D 4
Deyhuk **30** F 4
Dez Gerd **25** F 3
Dezful **25** E 2
Dezhou **35** G 3
Dhahab **24** B 3
Dhamar **53** G 6
Dhamtari **36** D 3
Dharwar **36** C 4
Dhaulagiri **36** D 2
Dhelfoí **22** B 3
Dhíavlos Zakínthou **22** B 3
Dhírfis Óros **22** B 3
Dhoraji **36** B 3
Dhule **36** B 3
Di Linh **37** J 5
Diable, Île du **73** H 2
Diaca **59** F 2
Diamantina **75** H 4
Diamantina Lakes **43** G 3
Diamond Jenness Peninsula
    63 OP 1
Dianjiang **34** E 4
Dibrugarh **37** FG 2
Dicle **23** F 3
Didiéni **54** C 3
Didyma **22** C 3
Diéma **54** C 3
Dieppe **20** D 2
Dihang **37** G 2
Dijlāh **25** D 2
Dijon **21** E 2
Dıkmen Daği **23** D 2
Dikson **78**
Dilaram **31** G 4
Dilj **21** G 2
Dilling **52** D 6
Dilolo **58** C 2
Dimashq **24** B 2
Dimbokro **54** D 4
Dimitrovgrad **22** C 2
Dimona **24** B 3
Dinagat **39** G 1
Dinajpur **36** E 2
Dinār, Kūh-e **25** F 3
Dinara Planina **21** G 3
Dinder National Park **52** F 6
Dindigul **36** C 5
Ding Xian **34** FG 3
Dingbian **34** E 3
Dingxi **34** D 3
Dinokwe **58** D 4
Dionísio Cerqueira **76** F 4
Diourbel **54** A 3
Dipkarpas **23** D 3
Dipolog **39** F 2
Diré **54** D 3
Diredawa **57** G 3
Dirico **58** C 3
Dirk Hartog Island **42** A 4
Disappointment, Lake
    42 C 3

Dishnä **24** A 4
Disko **78**
Disko Bugt **78**
Disna **19** J 4
District of Columbia **67** L 4
District of Fort Smith **63** P 3
District of Inuvik **62** LM 2
District of Keewatin
    63 TU 2–3
Distrito Federal **75** G 4
Diu **36** B 3
Divändarreh **25** E 1
Divinópolis **75** GH 5
Divo **54** C 4
Dixon Entrance **62** L 5
Diyälä **25** D 2
Diyarbakır **23** F 3
Djado, Plateau du **55** G 1
Djanet **51** G 4
Djelfa **51** F 2
Djibouti **57** G 2
Djibouti **57** G 2
Djougou **54** E 4
Dneprodzerzhinsk **23** D 1
Dnepropetrovsk **23** E 1
Dnestr **22** C 1
Dnestrovskiy Liman **22** D 1
Doba **55** H 4
Dobreta Turnu Severin
    22 B 2
Dobritj **22** C 2
Dobrogea **22** C 2
Dobrowolski **79**
Dobrudzhanska Plato
    22 C 2
Dodecanese **22** C 3
Dodge City **66** F 4
Dodoma **57** F 6
Dogger Bank **16** D 4
Dogondoutchi **55** E 3
Doğu Karadeniz Dağları
    23 EF 2
Doguéraoua **55** F 3
Doha **25** F 4
Dohad **36** B 3
Doi Inthanon **37** G 4
Doilungdêqen **37** F 2
Dôle **21** E 2
Dolo **57** G 4
Dolores **77** E 6
Dolphin and Union Strait
    63 OP 2
Dom Aquino **75** F 4
Doma Peaks **44** D 3
Dombås **18** E 3
Dominica **69** K 4
Dominican Republic
    69 J 3–4
Dompu **39** E 5
Don **26** H 6
Don Benito **20** B 4
Dondo **59** E 3
Dondra Head **36** D 6
Donegal Bay **16** B 4
Donegal Mountains **16** B 4
Donetsk **23** E 1
Donetskiy Kryazh **23** EF 1
Dong Hai **35** HJ 5
Dong Ujimqin Qi **35** G 1
Dongara **42** AB 4

Dongchuan **34** D 5
Dongfang **34** E 7
Dongning **35** K 2
Dongo **58** B 2
Dongoura **54** C 3
Dongping **35** G 3
Dongsheng **34** EF 3
Dongting Hu **34** F 5
Dongxiang **34** G 5
Dönna **18** F 2
Doramarkog **34** C 4
Dorchester, Cape **65** M 2
Dordrecht **16** D 4
Dori **54** D 3
Dornogovï **34** EF 2
Doro (Indonesia) **39** G 3
Döröö Nuur **32** F 6
Dortmund **17** E 4
Dosso **54** E 3
Dothan **67** J 5
Douala **55** FG 5
Douentza **54** D 3
Douglas (AZ, U.S.A.) **66** E 5
Douglas (U.K.) **16** C 4
Douglas (WY, U.S.A.)
    66 EF 3
Doumbouene **55** J 3
Dourados **75** F 5
Douro **20** B 3
Dover (DE, U.S.A.) **67** L 4
Dover (U.K.) **16** D 4
Dover, Strait of **16** D 4
Dovrefjell **18** E 3
Dow Rūd **25** E 2
Dow Sar **25** E 2
Dowlatäbäd **25** G 3
Drake Passage **79**
Drake Strait **77** CD 10
Drakensberg **58** D 5–6
Dráma **22** B 2
Drammen **19** F 4
Drau **21** F 2
Drava **21** G 2
Dresden **17** F 4
Dreux **20** D 2
Drini **22** B 2
Drogobych **17** H 5
Drumheller **63** P 5
Drummondville **65** N 6
Druzhnaya **79**
Druzhnaya II **79**
Dryden **64** J 6
Drysdale River National Park
    42 D 2
Dschang **55** F 4
du Couedic, Cape
    43 F 6
Duaringa **43** H 3
Dubawnt Lake **63** R 3
Dubayy (United Arab
    Emirates) **25** G 4
Dubbo **43** H 5
Dublin **16** B 4
Dubna **26** G 4
Dubno **19** J 5
Dubovskoye **23** F 1
Dubrovitsa **19** J 5
Dubrovnik **21** G 3
Dubrovnoye **27** NO 4
Dubuque **67** H 3

Duc de Gloucester, Îles du
47 F 4
Ducie 47 G 4
Dudhi 36 D 3
Dudinka 27 R 2
Dudley 16 C 4
Duékoué 54 C 4
Duero 20 C 3
Duff Islands 45 J 3
Duga-Zapadnaya, Mys
33 R 4
Dugi Otok 21 F 3
Duisburg 16 E 4
Duitama 72 D 2
Dukán 25 D 2
Dukhán 25 F 4
Dukou 34 D 5
Dukwe 58 D 4
Dulan 34 C 3
Dulga-Kyuyel' 32 K 3
Duluth 67 H 2
Dümä 52 F 2
Dumaguete 39 F 2
Dumfries 16 C 3
Dumont d'Urville 79
Dumpu 44 E 3
Dumyät 52 E 2
Dún Laoghaire 16 B 4
Duna 22 A 1
Dunántúl 22 A 1
Dunărea 22 C 1
Dunaujváros 22 A 1
Dunav 22 B 2
Dunbar 43 G 2
Dundalk 16 B 4
Dundalk Bay 16 B 4
Dundee 16 C 3
Dundgovi 34 E 1
Dunedin 45 Q 10
Dunhua 35 J 2
Dunhuang 34 B 2
Dunkerque 16 D 4
Dunkwa 54 D 4
Dunmarra 42 E 2
Dunqulah al 'Ordi 52 E 5
Duolun 35 G 2
Dura Europos 24 C 2
Durack Range 42 D 2
Durance 21 E 3
Durango (CO, U.S.A.) 66 E 4
Durango (Mexico) 68 AB 3
Duratón 20 C 3
Durban 59 E 5
Durg 36 D 3
Durgapur 36 E 3
Durham 67 L 4
Durmä 25 E 4
Duroy 32 L 5
Durresi 22 A 2
D'Urville Sea 79
Dushan 34 E 5
Dushanbe 31 H 3
Düsseldorf 16 E 4
Dutch Harbor 62 D 5
Duwayhin 25 F 4
Duye 56 D 4
Duyun 34 E 5
Düzce 22 D 2
Dwarka 36 A 3
Dyadmo 32 J 4

Dyrhólaey 18 B 3
Dyurmen'tobe 31 G 1
Dzerzhinsk 26 H 4
Dzhagdy, Khrebet 33 O 5
Dzhalinda 33 M 5
Dzhambul 31 J 2
Dzhankoy 23 D 1
Dzhanybek 26 J 6
Dzhelinde 32 K 1
Dzhetygara 27 M 5
Dzhigudzhak 33 T 3
Dzhirgatal' 31 J 3
Dzhugdzhur Range 33 Q 4
Dzhungarskiy Alatau,
Khrebet 27 PQ 6–7
Dzhunkun 32 K 3
Dzhusaly 31 G 1

E

Eagle 62 J 3
Eagle Pass 66 FG 6
Eagle Peak 66 C 3
East Antarctica 79
East Cape 45 R 8
East China Sea 35 HJ 5
East Falkland 77 E 9
East London 58 D 6
East Point 67 JK 5
East Siberian Sea 78
Easter Island 47 H 4
Eastmain 65 M 5
Eastport 67 N 3
Eau Claire 67 H 3
Eauripik 46 A 2
Ebe 33 Q 3
Eberswalde 17 F 4
Eboli 21 G 3
Ebolowa 55 G 5
Ebon 46 C 2
Ebⁱo 20 C 3
Ebro, Embalse del 20 C 3
Ebyakh 33 S 2
Ech Cheliff 51 F 1
Echmiadzin 23 F 2
Echo Bay 63 O 2
Écija 20 B 4
Ecuador 72 B 4
Edéa 55 FG 5
Edel Land 42 A 4
Edgeöya 78
Edinburgh 16 C 3
Edirne 22 C 2
Edmonds 66 B 2
Edmonton 63 P 5
Edremit 22 C 3
Edward, Lake 56 D 5
Edwards Plateau 66 FG 5–6
Efate 45 J 5
Efes 22 C 3
Egersund 19 E 4
Egilsstaðir 18 C 2
Eglab Dersa 50 E 3
Egmont, Mount 45 Q 8
Eğridir Gölü 22 D 3
Egvekinot 62 B 2
Egypt 52 DE 4
Eiao 47 F 3

Eidfjord 19 E 3
Eifel 16 E 4
Eights Coast 79
Eighty Mile Beach 42 C 2
Eire 16 B 4
Eirunepé 72 DE 5
Eisenach 17 EF 4
Eisenhüttenstadt 17 F 4
Ejin Qi 34 D 2
Ekibastuz 27 P 5
Ekoli 56 C 5
Ekwan 64 L 5
El Adeb Larache 51 G 3
El Alamo 66 C 5
El Banco 72 D 2
El Bayadh 51 F 2
'El Bür 57 H 4
El Cajon 66 C 5
El Cerro 74 D 4
El Cuy 77 C 6
El Difícil 72 D 2
El Diviso 72 C 3
El Djouf 50 D 4
El Dorado (AR, U.S.A.)
67 H 5
El Dorado (KS, U.S.A.)
67 G 4
El Dorado (Mexico) 66 E 7
El Dorado (Venezuela)
73 F 2
El Eulma 51 G 1
El Fasher 52 D 6
El Ferrol del Caudillo 20 B 3
El Goléa 51 F 2
'El Ḥamurre 57 H 3
El Homr 51 F 3
El Jadida 50 D 2
El Kharga   → Al Khārijah
52 E 3
El Maestrazgo 20 CD 3
El Maitén 77 B 7
El Medo 57 G 3
El Messir 55 H 2
El Mirador 68 E 4
El Mreiti 50 D 4
El Obeid 52 E 6
El Oued 51 G 2
El Paso 66 E 5
El Progreso 68 E 4
El Puerto 66 D 6
El Puerto de Santa María
20 B 4
El Salto 68 A 3
El Salvador 68 DE 5
El Sueco 66 E 6
El Tigre (Venezuela) 73 F 2
El Tránsito 76 B 4
El Tunal 76 D 4
El Valle 72 C 2
Elat 24 B 3
Elâzığ 23 E 3
Elba 21 F 3
El'ban 33 P 5
Elbasani 22 A 2
Elbe 17 F 4
Elbert, Mount 66 E 4
Elbeyli 24 B 1
Elbląg 17 G 4
Elbrus 23 F 2

Elburz Mountains 25 FG 1
Elche 20 C 4
Elda 20 C 4
Eldorado 76 EF 4
Eldoret 56 F 4
Elektrostal' 26 G 4
Elemi Triangle 56 EF 4
Elephant Island 79
Elesbão Veloso 75 H 2
Eleuthera Island 69 G 2
El'gakan 33 M 4
Elghena 57 F 1
Elgon, Mount 56 E 4
Elisenvaara 18 J 3
Elista 23 F 1
Elizabeth 43 F 5
Elk 17 H 4
Elk City 66 G 4
Elkhart 67 J 3
Elko 66 C 3
Ellef Ringnes Island 78
Ellensburg 66 B 2
Ellesmere Island 78
Ellice Islands 46 C 3
Elliot (Australia) 42 E 2
Elliot (South Africa) 58 D 6
Ellsworth Land 79
Ellsworth Mountains 79
Elmhurst 67 J 3
Elmira 67 L 3
Eluru 36 D 4
Elvas 20 B 4
Elvira 72 D 5
Ely 66 D 4
Emämrud 25 G 1
Emba 30 F 1
Emba 30 F 1
Embalse de Alcántara
20 B 4
Embalse de Almendra
20 B 3
Embalse de Mequinenza
20 CD 3
Embalse del Ebro 20 C 3
Embarcación 74 D 5
Embarras Portage 63 P 4
Emden 17 E 4
Emel'dzak 33 N 4
Emerald 43 H 3
Emi 32 G 5
Emi Koussi 55 H 2
Empalme 66 D 6
Empedrado 76 E 4
Ems 17 E 4
Encarnación 76 E 4
Enda Salassie 57 F 2
Ende 39 F 5
Enderbury 46 D 3
Enderby Land 79
Endicott Mountains 62 G 2
Engaño, Cape 39 J 1
Engel's 26 J 5
Enggano, Pulau 38 B 5
England 16 CD 4
English Channel 16 C 4–5
Engozero 18 K 2
Enid 66 G 4
Eniwetok 46 B 2
Enkan 33 Q 4
Enköping 19 G 4

Enmore 73 G 2
Ennadai 63 R 3
Ennedi 55 J 2
Enontekiö 18 H 2
Enrekang 39 EF 4
Enschede 16 E 4
Ensenada 66 C 5
Enshi 34 E 4
Entebbe 56 E 4
Entre Ríos 73 H 5
Enugu 55 F 4
Enugu Ezike 55 F 4
Enurmino 62 C 2
Envigado 72 CD 2
Envira 72 D 5
Eolie o Lipari, Isole 21 F 4
Épernay 20 D 2
Ephesus 22 C 3
Epi 45 J 5
Épinal 21 E 2
Équateur 56 BC 4
Equatoria 56 DE 3–4
Equatorial Guinea 55 F 5
Erbil 24 D 1
Erciyas Dağı 23 E 3
Érd 22 A 1
Erechim 76 F 4
Ereentsav 32 L 6
Ereğli 23 D 3
Erenhot 34 F 2
Eresma 20 C 3
Erfurt 17 F 4
Erg Brusset 55 FG 2
Erg Chech 50 E 3–4
Erg de Ténéré 55 G 2
Erg Iguidi 50 DE 3
Ergun He 32 M 5
Ergun Zuoqi 33 M 5
Eriba 52 F 5
Eric 65 O 5
Erie 67 K 3
Erie, Lake 67 K 3
'Erigābo 57 H 2
Erikub 46 C 2
Erimbet 31 G 2
Eritrea 57 FG 2
Ermelo 58 DE 5
Ernest Legouvé 47 E 5
Erode 36 C 5
Erongo 58 B 4
Erongo Mountains 58 B 4
Erozionnyy 33 R 2
Errego 59 F 3
Erromanga 45 J 5
Ertai 31 N 1
Erzgebirge 17 F 4
Erzincan 23 E 3
Erzurum 23 E 3
Erzurum-Kars Yaylâsı 23 F 2
Esbjerg 19 E 4
Esbo 19 H 3
Escanaba 67 J 2
Eschan 33 R 3
Escondido 66 C 5
Escuintla 68 D 5
Esfahan 25 F 2
Eskilstuna 19 G 4
Eskimo Point 63 T 3
Eskişehir 22 D 3
Eslämäbäd 25 E 2

Eslöv 19 F 4
Esmeralda, Isla 77 A 8
Esmeraldas 72 BC 3
España 20 C 4
Esperance 42 C 5
Esperanza 79
Espinal (Bolivia) 74 E 4
Espinal (Colombia) 72 D 3
Espinar 74 B 3
Espírito Santo 75 HJ 4
Espíritu Santo 45 J 5
Esplanada 75 J 3
Espoo 19 H 3
Esquel 77 B 7
Essaouira 50 CD 2
Essen 17 E 4
Essendon, Mount 42 C 3
Estados, Isla de los 77 D 9
Estância 75 J 3
Estelí 68 E 5
Esteros 74 D 5
Estevan 63 R 6
Estonia 19 J 4
Estrecho de le Maire
  77 CD 9–10
Estrecho de Magallanes
  77 B 9
Estrêla, Serra de 20 B 3
Estremadura 20 B 4
Esztergom 22 A 1
Ethiopia 57 FG 3
Ethiopian Plateau 57 FG 3
Etna 21 G 4
Etolin 62 L 4
Etosha National Park 58 B 3
Etosha Pan 58 B 3
Eugene 66 B 3
Eungella National Park
  43 H 3
Euphrates 24 C 2
Eureka 66 B 3
Evansville 67 J 4
Everett 66 B 2
Everett Mountains 65 O 3
Everglades National Park
  67 K 6
Évora 20 B 4
Évreux 20 D 2
Évvoia 22 B 3
Ewasse 45 F 3
Executive Committee Range
  79
Exeter 16 C 4
Exmouth 42 A 3
Extremadura 20 B 4
Eyasi, Lake 56 E 5
Éyl 57 H 3
Eyre 42 D 5
Eyre, Lake 43 F 4
Eyre Peninsula 43 F 5
Eysturoy 16 A 1
Ezop, Gora 33 S 3

F

Fabala 54 C 4
Fabriano 21 F 3
Fada 55 J 2
Faenza 21 F 3

Faeroe Islands 16 A 1
Făgăraş 22 BC 1
Fair Isle 16 C 3
Fairbanks 62 H 3
Fairmont 67 L 4
Fairview 43 G 2
Faisalabad 31 J 4
Faizabad (Afghanistan)
  31 J 3
Faizabad (India) 36 D 2
Fakahina 47 F 4
Fakaofo 46 D 3
Fakarava 47 F 4
Faku 35 H 2
Falagh 56 E 3
Falkenberg 19 F 4
Falkland Islands 77 DE 9
Falkland Sound 77 DE 9
Fall River 67 M 3
Fallon 66 C 4
Falls City 67 G 3
Falmouth 16 B 4
Falster 19 F 5
Falun 19 G 3
Famagusta 23 D 3
Fana 54 C 3
Fangataufa 47 F 4
Fangzheng 35 J 1
Faraday 79
Faradje 56 D 4
Farafangana 59 H 4
Farah 31 G 4
Farallon de Medinilla 46 A 1
Farallon de Pajaros 46 A 1
Faranah 54 B 3
Farasān, Jazā'ir 53 G 5
Faraulep 46 B 2
Farewell, Cape 45 Q 9
Fargo 66 G 2
Faridpur 36 E 3
Färjestaden 19 G 4
Farmington 66 E 4
Fårö 19 G 4
Faro 73 G 4
Farquhar Group 57 J 7
Färs 25 F 3
Fartak, Ra's 53 J 5
Fasā 25 F 3
Fasano 21 G 3
Fastov 26 E 5
Fataka 45 J 4
Fatehgarh 36 CD 2
Fatehpur 36 E 3
Fāurei 22 C 1
Faxaflói 18 A 3
Faxälven 18 G 3
Faya-Largeau 55 H 2
Fayetteville (AR, U.S.A.)
  67 H 4
Fayetteville (N.C., U.S.A.)
  67 L 5
Faysh Khābūr 24 D 1
Fayu 46 B 2
Fazilka 36 B 1
Fdérik 50 C 4
Fear, Cape 67 L 5
Feathertop, Mount 43 H 6
Federated States of
  Micronesia 46 AB 2
Fehmarn 17 F 4
Feijó 72 D 5

Feira de Santana 75 J 3
Feklistova, Ostrov 33 P 4–5
Felipe Carrillo Puerto 68 E 4
Fengcheng 35 H 2
Fengjie 34 E 4
Fengqing 34 CD 6
Fengshui Shan 33 M 5
Feni Islands 45 F 2
Fenoarivo Atsinanana
  59 HJ 3
Fensfjorden 18 DE 3
Fenyang 34 F 3
Feodosiya 23 E 1
Fer, Cap de 51 G 1
Ferfer 57 H 3
Fergana 31 J 2
Fergus Falls 67 G 2
Fergusson 45 F 3
Ferjukot 18 A 3
Ferkéssédougou 54 C 4
Fernando de Noronha Island
  71 G 3
Fernandópolis 75 FG 5
Ferrara 21 F 3
Ferreira Gomes 73 H 3
Ferret, Cap 20 C 3
Fès 50 E 2
Fethiye 22 C 3
Fezzan 51 HJ 3
Fianarantsoa 59 H 4
Fierras 18 G 2
Fiji 46 C 4
Fiji Islands 46 C 4
Filadélfia 74 D 5
Filchner Ice Shelf 79
Fimbul Ice Shelf 79
Fimi 56 B 3
Findlay 67 K 3
Finisterre, Cabo de 20 B 3
Finke 42 E 4
Finke Gorge National Park
  42 E 3
Finke, Mount 42 E 5
Finland 18 J 3
Finniss, Cape 42 E 5
Finnmark 18 H 2
Finnmarksvidda 18 H 2
Finnsnes 18 G 2
Finnveden 19 F 4
Finspång 19 G 4
Fiordland National Park
  44 P 9–10
Firat 23 E 3
Firenze 21 F 3
Firminy 20 D 2
Firozabad 36 C 2
Firth of Forth 16 C 3
Firūz Kūh 25 F 2
Firūzābād 25 F 3
Fisher Strait 63 V 3
Fishguard 16 BC 4
Fiskenæsset 65 R 3
Fitzcarrald 74 B 3
Fitzgerald River National
  Park 42 B 5
Fitzroy Crossing 42 D 2
Fitzroy River (Queensland,
  Austr.) 43 J 3
Fitzroy River (Western
  Australia) 42 C 2

Fiz – Gan

Fizi **56** D 5
Flagstaff **66** D 4
Flamenco **76** B 4
Flåsjön **18** G 3
Flattery, Cape **66** AB 2
Flensburg **17** E 4
Flin Flon **63** R 5
Flinders Chase National Park
  43 F 6
Flinders Island **43** H 6
Flinders Passage **43** H 2
Flinders Range **43** F 5
Flinders Ranges National
  Park **43** FG 5
Flinders River **43** G 2
Flint (Kiribati) **47** E 3
Flint (MI, U.S.A.) **67** K 3
Flisa **19** F 3
Floraville **43** F 2
Florence (AL, U.S.A.) **67** J 5
Florence (Italy) **21** F 3
Florencia **72** C 3
Flores (Azores) **50** A 1
Flores (Guatemala) **68** E 4
Flores (Indonesia) **39** F 5
Flores, Laut **39** EF 5
Flores Sea **39** EF 5
Floriano **75** H 2
Floriano Pleixoto **72** E 5
Florianópolis **76** G 4
Florida (Cuba) **69** G 3
Florida (U.S.A.) **67** K 6
Florida Keys **67** K 7
Floridablanca **72** D 2
Florø **18** E 3
Fluk **39** G 4
Fly River **44** D 3
Foci del Po **21** F 2–3
Focşani **22** C 1
Foggia **21** G 3
Fogo **54** B 7
Foleyet **64** L 6
Folkestone **16** D 4
Fond du Lac **67** J 3
Fongafale **46** CD 3
Fonte Boa **72** E 4
Fonte do Pau-d'Agua **74** E 3
Fonualei **46** D 4
Förde **18** E 3
Forêt d'Ecouves **20** C 2
Forín Linares **74** D 5
Forkas **54** E 3
Forli **21** F 3
Formentera **20** D 4
Formentor, Cabo de
  20 D 3–4
Formosa (Argentina) **76** E 4
Formosa (Goiás, Brazil)
  75 G 4
Formosa (Taiwan) **35** H 6
Formosa, Serra **75** E 3
Formosa Strait **35** GH 5–6
Fornæs **19** F 4
Forrest **42** D 5
Forsayth **43** G 2
Forsnäs **18** G 2
Forssa **19** H 3
Fort-Chimo **65** O 4
Fort Chipewyan **63** P 4
Fort Collins **66** F 3

Fort-de-France **69** K 5
Fort Dodge **67** H 3
Fort Frances **64** J 6
Fort Franklin **63** N 2
Fort-George **65** M 5
Fort Lauderdale **67** L 6
Fort Liard **63** N 3
Fort Mackay **63** P 4
Fort McMurray **63** P 4
Fort Miribel **51** F 3
Fort Morgan **66** F 3
Fort Myers **67** K 6
Fort Nelson **63** N 3
Fort Norman **63** M 3
Fort Peck **66** E 2
Fort Peck Lake **66** E 2
Fort Pierce **67** KL 6
Fort Portal **56** DE 4
Fort Providence **63** N 3
Fort Randell Dam **66** G 3
Fort Resolution **63** OP 3
Fort Rupert **65** M 5
Fort Severn **64** K 4
Fort Shevchenko **30** E 2
Fort Simpson **63** N 3
Fort Smith **67** H 4
Fort Stockton **66** F 5
Fort Vermilion **63** O 4
Fort Wayne **67** J 3
Fort Wellington **73** G 2
Fort William **16** C 3
Fort Worth **66** G 5
Fortaleza **75** J 1
Forth, Firth of **16** C 3
Fortin Coronel Eugenio
  Garay **74** D 5
Fortín Ingavi **74** D 4
Fortín Madrejón **74** E 5
Fortín Ravelo **74** D 4
Fortín Suárez Arana **74** DE 4
Fortune Bay **65** Q 6
Foshan **34** F 6
Fosna **18** F 3
Foso **54** D 4
Fossano **21** E 3
Fossil Bluff **79**
Fougamou **55** G 6
Fougères **20** C 2
Fouladou **54** AB 3
Foumban **55** G 4
Four Mountains, Islands of
  62 CD 5
Fourmies **20** D 1
Fouta Djallon **54** B 3
Fouta Ferlo **54** B 2
Foveaux Strait **44** P 10
Fowlers Bay **42** E 5
Fox Islands **62** D 5
Foxe Basin **63** VW 2
Foxe Channel **65** M 3
Foxe Peninsula **65** M 3
Foz do Breu **72** D 5
Franca **75** H 5
France **20** CD 2
Francis Case, Lake **66** FG 3
Francisco de Orellana
  72 C 4
Francisco Escárcega **68** D 4
Francistown **58** D 4
Francs Peak **66** E 3

Frankfort **67** J 4
Frankfurt am Main **17** E 4
Franklin Mountains
  63 MN 2–3
Franklin Strait **63** S 1
Franz Josef Land **78**
Fraser **63** N 5
Fraser or Great Sandy Island
  43 J 4
Fraser Plateau **63** N 5
Fredericia **19** EF 4
Fredericton **65** O 6
Frederik IX-Land **65** R 2
Frederik VI-Coast **78**
Frederiksdal **65** S 3
Frederikshåb **65** R 3
Frederikshavn **19** F 4
Fredrika **18** G 3
Fredrikstad **19** F 4
Freels, Cape **65** R 6
Freetown **54** B 4
Freiburg **17** E 5
Fréjus **21** E 3
French Guiana **73** H 3
French Polynesia **47** F 4
Fresnillo **68** B 3
Fresno **66** B 4
Freycinet Peninsula **44** L 9
Fria, Cape **58** A 3
Friesland **16–17** E 4
Frio, Cabo **75** H 5
Frisian Islands **16** E 4
Frobisher Bay **65** O 3
Frobisher Bay **65** O 3
Frobisher Lake **63** Q 4
Frolovo **26** H 6
Front Range **66** E 3–4
Fronteiras **75** H 2
Frotín Cañada Oruro **74** D 5
Fröya **18** E 3
Fu'an **35** G 5
Fuding **35** H 5
Fuerte Olimpo **74** E 5
Fuerteventura **50** C 3
Fujian **35** G 5
Fujin **33** O 6
Fujiyama **35** LM 4
Fukui **35** L 3
Fukushima **35** LM 2
Fukushima **35** M 3
Fukuyama **35** K 4
Funchal **50** B 2
Funiu Shan **34** F 4
Funtua **55** F 3
Fuqing **35** G 5
Furancungo **59** E 2
Furmanovka **31** J 2
Furmanovo **26** JK 6
Furneaux Group **44** L 9
Fürth **17** F 5
Fury and Hecla Strait
  64 L 1–2
Fusagasugá **72** D 3
Fushun **35** H 2
Fusong **35** J 2
Futuna (Vanuatu) **45** K 5
Futuna (Wallis and Futuna)
  46 D 3
Fuxin **35** H 2

Fuyang **34** G 4
Fuyuan **34** D 5
Fuyun **31** M 1
Fuzhou **34** G 5
Fyn **19** F 4

G

Gabela **58** A 2
Gabès **51** H 2
Gabon **55** G 6
Gaborone **58** D 4
Gabriel Strait **65** O 3
Gach Särän **25** F 3
Gadag **36** C 4
Gadame **56** E 3
Gäddede **18** F 3
Gadsden **67** J 5
Gaeta **21** F 3
Gaferut **46** A 2
Gafsa → Qafşah **51** G 2
Gagnoa **54** C 4
Gagnon **65** O 5
Gahkom **25** G 3
Gaillimh **16** B 4
Gaimán **77** C 7
Gainesville **67** K 6
Gairdner, Lake **43** F 5
Gakarosa **58** C 5
Gakona **62** H 3
Galadi **57** H 3
Galán, Cerro **76** C 4
Galanino **32** F 4
Galathea Deep **46** D 5
Galaţi **22** C 1
Galatina **21** G 3
Galdhøpiggen **18** E 3
Galena **62** F 3
Galesburg **67** H 3
Galicia (Poland) **17** H 5
Galicia (Spain) **20** B 3
Galimyy **33** T 3
Galka'yo **57** H 3
Galle **36** D 6
Gällivare **18** H 2
Gallo, Capo **21** F 4
Gallup **66** E 4
Galole **57** F 5
Galveston **67** H 6
Gálvez **76** D 3
Galway **16** B 4
Gamba **55** F 6
Gambia **54** A 3
Gambier Islands **47** FG 4
Gamboma **55** H 6
Gamboola **43** G 2
Ganäveh **25** F 3
Gandadiwata, Bukit **39** EF 4
Gandhi Sagar Dam **36** C 3
Gandía **20** C 4
Ganetti **52** E 5
Ganga **36** E 2
Gangan **77** C 7
Gangapur **36** C 3
Gangdisê Shan **36** DE 1
Ganges **36** E 3
Ganina Gar' **32** F 4
Gannett Peak **66** DE 3
Gansu **34** DE 3

Ganta 54 C 4
Ganzhou 34 F 5
Gao 54 D 2
Gao'an 34 G 5
Gaona 76 D 4
Gaoping 34 F 3
Gaoua 54 D 3
Gaoual 54 B 3
Gaozhou 34 F 6
Gap 21 E 3
Garanhuns 75 J 2
Garbokaray 32 G 5
Garbosh, Küh-e 25 EF 2
Garda, Lago di 21 F 2
Gardaneh-ye Ävej 25 E 2
Gardaneh-ye Kandovän
  25 F 1
Gardaneh-ye Khäneh Sorkh
  25 G 3
Gardermoen 19 F 3
Gardez 31 H 4
Gargano, Promontorio del
  21 G 3
Garissa 57 FG 5
Garmisch-Partenkirchen
  17 F 5
Garmsar () 25 F 2
Garonne 20 D 3
Garoua 55 G 4
Garoua Boulai 55 G 4
Garöwe 57 H 3
Garri, Küh-e 25 E 2
Garry Lake 63 R 2
Garwa 36 D 3
Gary 67 J 3
Garze 34 C 4
Gascogne 20 CD 3
Gascoyne Junction 42 B 4
Gashagar 55 G 3
Gashua 55 G 3
Gaspé 65 P 6
Gaspé, Cap de 65 P 6
Gaspé, Péninsule de 65 O 6
Gassi Touil 51 G 2
Gästrikland 19 G 3
Gata, Cabo de 20 C 4
Gata, Sierra de 20 B 3
Gatchina 19 K 4
Gates of the Arctic National
  Park and Preserve 62 G 2
Gauhati 37 F 2
Gauja 19 H 4
Gausta 19 E 4
Gavanka 33 T 4
Gávdhos 22 B 4
Gave de Pau 20 C 3
Gävle 19 G 3
Gävlebukten 19 G 3
Gaya (India) 36 E 3
Gaya (Niger) 54 E 3
Gayndah 43 J 4
Gaza Strip 24 AB 3
Gazelle Peninsula 45 F 2
Gaziantep 23 E 3
Gaziantep Yaylası 23 E 3
Gazimurskiy Zavod 32 L 5
Gazipaşa 23 D 3
Gbarnga 54 C 4
Gdańsk 17 G 4
Gdynia 17 G 4

Gearhart Mountain 66 B 3
Gedi 57 F 5
Gediz 22 C 3
Geelong 43 G 6
Geigar 52 E 6
Geilo 19 E 3
Gejiu 34 D 6
Gela 21 F 4
Gelendzhik 23 E 2
Gelsenkirchen 17 E 4
Gemena 56 B 4
Gemsbok National Park
  58 C 4—5
General Acha 77 D 6
General Alvear 77 C 5—6
General Belgrano II 79
General Belgrano III 79
General Bernardo O'Higgins
  79
General Madariaga 77 E 6
General Pico 77 D 6
General Roca 77 C 6
General San Martin 79
General Santos 39 G 2
Genève 21 E 2
Gengma 34 C 6
Genoa 21 E 3
Genova 21 E 3
Genova, Golfo di 21 E 3
Georg von Neumayer 79
George 65 O 4
George Town (Malaysia)
  38 AB 2
George Town (Tasmania,
  Austr.) 44 L 9
George V Coast 79
George VI Sound 79
Georgetown (Gambia)
  54 B 3
Georgetown (Guyana)
  73 G 2
Georgetown (Queensland,
  Austr.) 43 G 2
Georgia (U.S.A.) 67 K 5
Georgia (U.S.S.R.) 23 F 2
Georgian Bay 65 L 6
Georgiyevsk 23 F 2
Gera 17 F 4
Geraldton 42 A 4
Gerasimovka 27 O 4
Germany 17 F 4
Germi 25 G 2
Gerona 20 D 3
Gêrzê 36 D 1
Gesoa 44 D 3
Getafe 20 C 3
Getz Ice Shelf 79
Geyik Daği 23 D 3
Ghadämis 51 G 2
Ghana 54 D 4
Ghanzi 58 C 4
Ghardaïa 51 F 2
Gharyän 51 H 2
Ghats, Eastern 36 CD 3—5
Ghats, Western 36 BC 4—5
Ghazzah 24 B 3
Gheorghe Gheorghiu-Dej
  22 C 1
Ghimbi 56 F 3
Gibraltar 20 B 4

Gibraltar, Estrecho de
  20 B 4
Gibraltar, Strait of 20 B 4
Gibson Desert 42 C 3
Gifu 35 L 3
Giglio 21 F 3
Gijón 20 B 3
Gila Bend 66 D 5
Gilbert Islands 46 C 2—3
Gilbert River 43 G 2
Gilbués 75 G 2
Giles 42 D 4
Gilgandra 43 H 5
Gillam 63 T 4
Gillette 66 E 3
Gingin 42 B 5
Gingoog 39 G 2
Ginir 57 G 3
Gioia 21 G 3
Giresun 23 E 2
Girne 23 D 3
Gironde 20 C 2
Gisborne 45 R 8
Gitarama 56 DE 5
Giza 52 DE 3
Gizhiga 33 U 3
Gizhiginskaya Guba 33 T 3
Gjandzja 30 D 2
Gjiri i Vlorä 22 A 2
Gjögur 18 B 2
Gjövik 19 F 3
Glacier Bay National Park
  and Preserve 62 K 4
Gladstone 43 J 3
Glåma 19 F 3
Glasgow 16 C 3
Glazov 26 K 4
Glen Canyon National
  Recreation Area 66 D 4
Glendive 66 F 2
Glenhope 45 Q 9
Glennallen 62 H 3
Glenrothes 16 C 3
Glenwood Springs 66 E 4
Glittertind 18 E 3
Gliwice 17 G 4
Głogów 17 G 4
Glomfjord 18 F 2
Glorieuses, Iles 59 H 2
Gloucester 67 M 3
Glubokoye 19 J 4
Glukhov 26 F 5
Goa 36 B 4
Gobabis 58 B 4
Gobi 34 EF 2
Gochas 58 B 4
Godär-e Sorkh 25 G 2
Godar-i-Shah 31 G 5
Godavari 36 D 4
Godavari, Mouths of the
  36 D 4
Gods Lake 63 T 5
Godthåb 65 R 3
Godwar 36 B 2
Goéland, Lac au 65 M 5—6
Goiânia 75 G 4
Goiás (Brazil) 75 G 3
Goiás (Brazil) 75 G 4
Göksu (Turkey) 23 D 3
Göksu (Turkey) 23 E 3

Golan Heights 24 B 2
Gölcük 22 C 2
Gold Coast (Australia)
  43 J 4
Gold Coast (Ghana) 54 DE 5
Golden Hinde 63 M 6
Goldsboro 67 L 4
Goldsworthy 42 B 3
Golets-Inyaptuk, Gora
  32 K 4
Golets-Skalistyy, Gora
  32 LM 4
Golets Skalistyy, Gora
  33 O 4
Golfe de Saint-Malo 20 C 2
Golfe du Lion 20—21 D 3
Golfito 68 F 6
Golfo de California
  66 DE 5—7
Golfo de Chiriquí 72 B 2
Golfo de Guayaquil 72 B 4
Golfo de Honduras 68 E 4
Golfo de los Mosquitos
  72 B 2
Golfo de Panamá 72 C 2
Golfo de Penas 77 B 8
Golfo de Tehuantepec
  68 D 4
Golfo de Valencia 20 D 4
Golfo de Venezuela 72 D 1
Golfo del Darién 72 C 2
Golfo di Genova 21 E 3
Golfo di Salerno 21 F 3
Golfo di Squillace 21 G 4
Golfo di Taranto 21 G 3—4
Golfo San Jorge 77 C 8
Golfo San Matías 77 D 7
Gölgeli Dağları 22 C 3
Golmud 34 B 3
Golovin 62 E 3
Golovnino 35 N 2
Golubovka 27 O 5
Goma 56 D 5
Gombe 55 G 3
Gomel 26 F 5
Gomera 50 B 3
Goméz Palacio 68 B 2
Gomo 36 E 1
Gonäbäd 30 F 4
Gonaïves 69 H 4
Gonam 33 O 4
Gonbad-e Qäbus 30 EF 3
Gonda 36 D 2
Gondar 57 F 2
Gondia 36 D 3
Gongbo' gyamda 34 B 5
Gonghe 34 D 3
Gongpoquan 34 C 2
Good Hope, Cape of
  58 B 6
Goodnews Bay 62 E 4
Goondiwindi 43 HJ 4
Goose Bay 65 P 5
Gora Bazar Dyuzi 30 D 2
Gora Denezhkin Kamen'
  27 L 3
Gora Ezop 33 S 3
Gora Fisht 23 E 2
Gora Golets-Inyaptuk
  32 K 4

Gora Golets-Skalistyy
32 LM 4
Gora Golets Skalistyy
33 O 4
Gora Kamen **32** FG 2
Gora Khil'mi **33** S 1
Gora Khoydype **27** N 2
Gora Konzhakovskiy Kamen'
27 LM 4
Gora Kovriga **26** J 2
Gora Kuytun **27** R 6
Gora Medvezh'ya **33** P 6
Gora Munku-Sardyk
32 GH 5
Gora Narodnaya **27** LM 2
Gora Nelkuchan **33** P 3
Gora Pobeda **33** R 2
Gora Sokhor **32** J 5
Gora Syuge-Khaya **33** P 2
Gora Taklaun **33** Q 3
Gora Tel'pos-Iz **27** L 3
Gora Yamantau **27** L 5
Góra Zamkowa **17** H 4
Gorakhpur **36** D 2
Gorda **66** B 4
Gordion **23** D 3
Gordon **67** H 2
Gordon Downs **42** D 2
Gorgän **25** G 1
Gori **23** F 2
Görlitz **17** F 4
Gorlovka **23** E 1
Gorna Oryakhovitsa **22** C 2
Gorno-Altaysk **27** QR 5
Gornozavodsk **33** Q 6
Gornyak **27** Q 5
Goroka **44** E 3
Goromay **33** Q 5
Gorongosa **59** E 3
Gorongosa National Park
59 E 3
Gorontalo **39** F 3
Gory Byrranga **32** GH 1
Gory Putorana **32** FH 2
Gory Ulutau **31** H 1
Goryn' **19** J 5
Gorzów Wielkopolski
17 G 4
Goshogawara **35** LM 2
Gossi **54** D 2
Gōta kanal **19** F 4
Götaland **19** FG 4
Göteborg **19** F 4
Gothenburg **19** F 4
Gotland **19** G 4
Gotska Sandön **19** GH 4
Göttingen **17** EF 4
Goulburn **43** H 5
Goulimime **50** C 3
Gouré **55** G 3
Gourma-Rarous **54** D 2
Gouro **55** H 2
Gove Peninsula **43** F 1
Governador Valadares
75 H 4
Goya **76** E 4
Gozo **21** F 4
Graaff Reinet **58** C 6
Gračac **21** G 3
Gracias a Dios, Cabo **68** F 5

Grafton **43** J 4
Graham **62** L 5
Graham Land **79**
Grahamstown **58** D 6
Grain Coast **54** BC 4–5
Grajaú **73** J 5
Grampian Mountains **16** C 3
Gran Canaria **50** B 3
Gran Chaco **74** D 5
Gran Sasso d'Italia **21** F 3
Granada (Nicaragua) **68** E 5
Granada (Spain) **20** C 4
Grand Bahama Island **69** G 2
Grand Bassam **54** D 4–5
Grand Canyon **66** D 4
Grand Canyon **66** D 4
Grand Canyon National Park
66 D 4
Grand Coulee **66** C 2
Grand Erg de Bilma **55** GH 2
Grand Erg Occidental
50–51 E 2–3
Grand Erg Oriental
51 G 2–3
Grand Forks **66** G 2
Grand Island **66** G 3
Grand Junction **66** E 4
Grand Marais **67** HJ 2
Grand Passage **45** H 5
Grand Rapids (Man., Can.)
63 S 5
Grand Rapids (MI, U.S.A.)
67 J 3
Grand Rapids (MN, U.S.A.)
67 H 2
Grand Teton **66** D 3
Grande Prairie **63** O 4
Grandin, Lake **63** O 3
Granite City **67** J 4
Granite Peak (MT, U.S.A.)
66 E 2
Granite Peak (NV, U.S.A.)
66 C 3
Granja **75** H 1
Granön **18** G 3
Grants Pass **66** B 3
Granville Lake **63** R 4
Gräsö **19** G 3
Grave, Pointe de **20** C 2
'S-Gravenhage **16** D 4
Gravina **21** G 3
Grayling **67** K 3
Graz **21** G 2
Great Artesian Basin
43 G 3–4
Great Australian Bight
42 DE 5
Great Barrier Island **45** R 8
Great Barrier Reef **43** H 1–2
Great Basin **66** C 3–4
Great Bear Lake **63** NO 2
Great Bitter Lake **24** A 3
Great Dividing Range
43 HJ 3–4
Great Dividing Range
43 HJ 4–6
Great Exuma Island **69** G 3
Great Falls **66** D 2
Great Fisher Bank **16** D 3
Great Inagua Island **69** H 3

Great Indian Desert **36** B 2
Great Karroo **58** C 6
Great Nicobar **37** F 6
Great Plains (Canada)
63 OQ 4–5
Great Plains (U.S.A.)
66 FG 2–4
Great Salt Lake **66** D 3
Great Salt Lake Desert
66 D 3
Great Sandy Desert **42** C 3
Great Slave Lake **63** P 3
Great Victoria Desert **42** D 4
Great Victoria Desert Nature
Reserve **42** DE 4–5
Greater Antilles **69** GJ 3–4
Greece **22** B 3
Greeley **66** F 3
Green Bay **67** J 3
Green Islands **45** F 2
Green River (Papua New
Guinea) **44** D 2
Green River (UT, U.S.A.)
66 D 4
Green River (WY, U.S.A.)
66 DE 3
Greenland **78**
Greenland Sea **78**
Greenock **16** BC 3
Greensboro (GA, U.S.A.)
67 K 5
Greensboro (N.C., U.S.A.)
67 L 4
Greenvale **43** GH 2
Greenville (Liberia) **54** C 4–5
Greenville (MS, U.S.A.)
67 H 5
Greenville (S.C., U.S.A.)
67 K 5
Gregory, Lake **43** F 4
Gregory Range **43** G 2
Greifswald **17** F 4
Grenada **69** K 5
Grenoble **21** E 2
Grey Range **43** G 4
Greymouth **45** Q 9
Grim, Cape **44** K 9
Grímsey **18** B 2
Grimshaw **63** O 4
Grímsstaðir **18** B 2
Grimstad **19** E 4
Grindavik **18** A 3
Griquatown **58** C 5
Grmeč **21** G 3
Grodno **19** H 5
Gröndalen **18** F 3
Grong **18** F 3
Groningen **16** E 4
Groot Vloer **58** C 5
Groot Winter Berg **58** D 6
Groote Eylandt **43** F 1
Grootfontein **58** B 3
Grosseto **21** F 3
Grossglockner **21** F 2
Group, Actaeon **47** F 4
Groznyy **23** G 2
Grudziądz **17** G 4
Grünau **58** B 5
Gruñidera **68** B 3
Gruziya **23** F 2

Grytviken **79**
Guadalajara (Mexico) **68** B 3
Guadalajara (Spain) **20** C 3
Guadalcanal **45** G 3
Guadalquivir **20** C 4
Guadalupe **68** C 2
Guadalupe, Sierra de **20** B 4
Guadarrama, Sierra de
20 C 3
Guadeloupe **69** K 4
Guadeloupe Passage **69** K 4
Guadiana **20** B 4
Guajará Mirim **74** CD 3
Gualeguaychú **76** E 5
Guam **46** A 2
Guaminí **77** D 6
Guan Xian **34** D 4
Guanare **72** E 2
Guandacol **76** C 4
Guangde **35** G 4
Guangdong **34** F 6
Guanghua **34** F 4
Guangshan **34** F 4
Guangxi Zhuangzu Zizhiqu
34 E 6
Guangyuan **34** E 4
Guangzhou **34** F 6
Guantánamo **69** H
Guapí **72** C 3
Guaporé **74** D 3
Guaqui **74** C 4
Guarapuava **76** F 4
Guarda **20** B 3
Guardafui, Cape **57** J 2
Guardal **20** C 4
Guarenas **72** E 1
Guasave **66** E 6
Guasipati **73** F 2
Guatemala **68** D 5
Guatemala **68** DE 5
Guaviare **72** E 3
Guayabal **72** E 2
Guayaquil **72** C 4
Guayaquil, Golfo de **72** B 4
Guaymallén **76** C 5
Guba (Russia) **26** F 3
Guba (Zaire) **58** D 2
Guba Buorkhaya **33** O 1
Gubakha **27** L 4
Gubkin **26** G 5
Gudar, Sierra de **20** C 3
Gudbrandsdalen **18** EF 3
Gudermes **23** G 2
Gudur **36** C 5
Guelta Zemmur **50** C 3
Güera **50** B 4
Guéra **55** H 3
Guéréda **55** J 3
Guernsey **16** C 5
Guerrero **68** B 4
Gügerdt, Küh-e **25** F 2
Gughe **57** F 3
Gui Xian **34** E 6
Guiana Highlands **73** FH 3
Guiding **34** E 5
Guidjiba **55** G 4
Guijá **59** E 4
Guilin **34** F 5
Guinan **34** D 3

Guinea **54** B 3
Guinea-Bissau **54** AB 3
Guinea, Gulf of **55** EF 5
Günes **69** F 3
Guiratinga **75** F 4
Guisanbourg **73** H 3
Guixi **35** G 5
Guiyang **34** E 5
Guizhou **34** E 5
Gujarat **36** B 3
Gujranwala **31** J 4
Gujrat **31** J 4
Gulbarga **36** C 4
Gulf of Aden **53** H 6
Gulf of Alaska **62** HJ 4
Gulf of Boothia **63** T 1
Gulf of Bothnia **18** GH 3
Gulf of Carpentaria **43** F 1
Gulf of Finland **19** H 4
Gulf of Guinea **55** EF 5
Gulf of Khambhat **36** B 3–4
Gulf of Kutch **36** A 3
Gulf of Maine **67** N 3
Gulf of Mannar **36** C 6
Gulf of Martaban **37** G 4
Gulf of Mexico **68** DE 2
Gulf of Ob **27** O 2
Gulf of Oman **53** K 4
Gulf of Papua **44** DE 3
Gulf of Riga **19** H 4
Gulf of Saint Lawrence
　65 P 6
Gulf of Sirt **51** J 2
Gulf of Suez **24** A 3
Gulf of Thailand **37** H 5
Gulf of Tonkin **37** J 4
Gulf of Venice **21** F 2
Gulf Saint Vincent **43** F 6
Gulf Stream **8**
Gulfport **67** J 5
Gulgong **43** H 5
Gulin **34** E 5
Gulistan **31** H 2
Gulu **56** E 4
Guna **36** C 3
Güneydoğu Toroslar
　23 EF 3
Gungu **56** B 6
Guntur **36** D 4
Gunung Abong Abong
　38 A 3
Gunung Batu Puteh
　38 B 3
Gunung Besar **38** E 4
Gunung Binaiya **39** G 4
Gunung Dempo **38** B 4
Gunung Kerinci **38** B 4
Gunung Kinabalu **38** E 2
Gunung Kwoka **39** H 4
Gunung Leuser **38** A 3
Gunung Lokilalaki **39** F 4
Gunung Maling **39** F 3
Gunung Mekongga **39** F 4
Gunung Mulu **38** DE 3
Gunung Mutis **39** F 5
Gunung Saran **38** D 4
Gunung Sorikmerapi **38** A 3
Gunung Tahan **38** B 3
Guoyang **34** G 4
Gurban Obo **34** F 2

Gurbantünggüt Shamo
　31 M 1–2
Gurgan **25** G 1
Guri Dam **73** F 2
Gürlevik Dağı **23** E 3
Gurskoye **33** P 5
Gurupá **73** H 4
Gurupi **75** G 3
Gurvanbulag **32** H 6
Gur´yev **30** E 1
Gusau **55** F 3
Gusinoye Ozero **32** J 5
Gutii, Virful **22** B 1
Guyana **73** G 3
Guyenne **20** CD 3
Guyuan **34** E 3
Guzar **31** H 3
Güzelhisar **22** C 3
Gwalior **36** C 2
Gweru **58** D 3
Gya La **36** E 2
Gyangzê **36** E 2
Gydanskiy Poluostrov
　27 P 1–2
Gympie **43** J 4
Gyöngyös **22** A 1
Györ **22** A 1
Gypsum Point **63** O 3
Gyula **22** B 1

H

Ha Noi **37** J 3
Ha Tinh **37** J 4
Haanja Kõrgustik **19** J 4
Ha´apai Group **46** D 4
Haapsalu **19** H 4
Haarlem **16** D 4
Habay **63** O 4
Habbāniyah **24** D 2
Hachinohe **35** M 2
Hadd, Ra´s al **53** KL 4
Hadejia **55** F 3
Hadejia **55** G 3
Hadera **24** B 2
Hadilik **31** M 3
Hadley Bay **63** Q 1
Hadramawt **53** H 5
Hafar al Bāṭin **25** E 3
Hafirat al ´Aydä **24** C 4
Hafit (Oman) **25** G 4–5
Hafun, Ra´s **57** J 2
Hagemeister **62** E 4
Hagfors **19** F 3
Hague, Cap de la **20** C 2
Hai Phong **37** J 3
Haicheng **35** H 2
Haifa **24** B 2
Haifeng **34** G 6
Haikang **34** EF 6
Haikou **34** F 6–7
Ha´il **24** C 4
Hailar **32** L 6
Hailin **35** J 2
Hailun **33** N 6
Hailuoto **18** H 2
Hainan Dao **34** F 7
Haines **62** K 4
Haines Junction **62** K 3

Haïti **69** H 4
Ḥajārah, Saḥrā´ al
　24–25 D 3
Hajhir, Jabal **57** J 2
Hājjīābād **25** G 3
Hājjīābād-e Māsīleh **25** F 2
Hakkâri Dağları **23** F 3
Hakodate **35** M 2
Halab **24** B 1
Ḥalā´ib **52** F 4
Ḥalbā **24** B 2
Halden **19** F 4
Hale, Mount **42** B 4
Ḥali **53** G 5
Halifax **65** P 7
Hall **62** C 3
Hall Beach **63** V 2
Hall Islands **46** B 2
Hall Peninsula **65** O 3
Halland **19** F 4
Ḥallat´ Ammār **24** B 3
Halle **17** F 4
Halley Bay **79**
Hallingskarvet **19** E 3
Halls Creek **42** D 2
Halmahera **39** G 3
Halmahera, Laut **39** G 4
Halmstad **19** F 4
Hälsingeskogen **18** G 3
Hälsingland **18** G 3
Halti **18** H 2
Ḥalūl **25** F 4
Hamadān **25** E 2
Hamāh **24** B 2
Hamamatsu **35** L 4
Hamar **19** F 3
Hamburg **17** F 4
Häme **18** HJ 3
Hämeenlinna **18** HJ 3
Hämeenselkä **18** H 3
Hamelin Pool **42** A 4
Hamersley Range **42** B 3
Hamersley Range National
　Park **42** B 3
Hamhŭng **35** J 3
Hami **34** B 2
Hamilton (New Zealand)
　45 R 8
Hamilton (Ontario, Can.)
　65 M 7
Hamilton (Victoria, Austr.)
　43 G 6
Hamina [Fredrikshamn]
　19 J 3
Hamm **17** E 4
Hammar, Hawr al (Iraq)
　25 E 3
Hammerfest **18** H 1
Hammond () **67** J 3
Hammur Koke **57** F 3
Hamoyet, Jabal **52** F 5
Hampden **45** Q 10
Ḥamrīn, Jabal **24–25** D 2
Hamuku **39** H 4
Hāmūn-e Jaz Mūriān **30** F 5
Ḥanak **24** B 4
Hanang **56** F 1
Hanceville **63** N 5
Hanchuan **34** F 4
Handan **34** F 3

Handeni **57** F 6
Hanegev **24** B 3
Hanggin Houqi **34** E 2
Hangu **35** G 3
Hangzhou **35** H 4
Hanko **19** H 4
Hanle **31** K 4
Hannover **17** E 4
Hanöbukten **19** FG 4
Hanover **58** C 6
Hanover, Islas **77** AB 9
Hanstholm **19** E 4
Hao **47** F 4
Haparanda **18** H 2
Har Us Nuur **32** F 6
Hara **32** J 6
Ḥaradh **25** E 4
Harar **57** G 3
Harare **59** E 3
Hararge **57** GH 3
Harazê **55** J 4
Harbin **35** J 1
Hardangerfjorden **19** E 3–4
Hardangerjökulen **19** E 3
Hardangervidda **19** E 3
Hardin **66** E 2
Hargeysa **57** G 3
Hari Kurk **19** H 4
Ḥarib **53** H 6
Ḥārim **24** B 1
Härjedalen **18** F 3
Harlingen **67** G 6
Härnösand **18** G 3
Ḥarrat al ´Uwayrid **24** B 4
Ḥarrat Ithnayn **24** C 4
Ḥarrat Khaybar **24** C 4
Harrington Harbour **65** Q 5
Harrisburg **67** L 3
Harrismith **58** D 5
Harrison Bay **62** G 1
Harrison, Cape **65** Q 5
Harstad **18** G 2
Harsvik **18** E 3
Hartford **67** M 3
Hartlepool **16** C 4
Hartz Mountains National
　Park **44** L 9
Harvey **66** G 2
Haryana **36** C 2
Harz **17** F 4
Hasalbag **31** K 3
Hassan **36** C 5
Hassi Bel Guebbour **51** G 3
Hassi Messaoud **51** G 2
Hastings (NE, U.S.A.)
　66 G 3
Hastings (New Zealand)
　45 R 8
Hat Hin **37** H 3
Hat Yai **37** H 6
Hatgal **32** G 5
Hattiesburg **67** J 5
Hatutu **47** F 3
Hauberg Mountains **79**
Haugesund **19** DE 4
Haukipudas **18** HJ 2
Hauraki Gulf **45** R 8
Haut-Zaïre **56** CD 4
Hauterive **65** O 6
Havana **69** F 3

Havern **18** G 3
Havre **66** E 2
Havre-Saint-Pierre **65** P 5
Hawaii **47** E 1
Hawaii **47** E 1
Hawaiian Islands **47** E 1
Hawallī (Kuwait) **25** E 3
Hawke Harbour **65** Q 5
Hawr al Hammar **25** E 3
Hawr as S'adīyah **25** E 2
Hay **43** G 5
Hay River **63** O 3
Hayyā **52** F 5
Hazar Gölü **23** E 3
Hazarajat **31** H 4
He Xian **34** F 6
Hebei **35** G 3
Hebel **43** H 4
Hebi **34** F 3
Hebrides, Inner **16** B 3
Hebrides, Outer **16** B 3
Hebron **65** P 4
Hecate Strait **62** L 5
Hechi **34** E 6
Hechuan **34** E 4
Hedmark **18** F 3
Hefa **24** B 2
Hefei **35** G 4
Hegang **33** NO 6
Heidelberg **17** E 5
Heidenheim **17** F 5
Heilbronn **17** E 5
Heilong Jiang **33** O 6
Heilongjiang **35** JK 1
Heimaey **18** A 3
Heimahe **34** C 3
Heinola **18** J 3
Hejaz **24** B 4
Hekla **18** B 3
Helagsfjället **18** F 3
Helena **66** D 2
Helgeland **18** F 2
Hellas **22** B 3
Hells Canyon **66** C 2
Helmeringhausen **58** B 5
Helong **35** J 2
Helsingborg **19** F 4
Helsingfors **19** J 3
Helsingör **19** F 4
Helsinki **19** J 3
Henan **34** F 4
Henbury **42** E 3
Henderson **47** G 4
Hendijan **25** E 3
Heng Xian **34** E 6
Hengduan Shan **34** C 5
Hengyang **34** F 5
Henik Lakes **63** S 3
Henrietta Maria, Cape
 65 L 4
Henryetta **67** G 4
Henzada **37** G 4
Heraklia **52** F 1
Herat **31** G 4
Hereford **16** C 4
Herlen He **32** L 6
Hermiston **66** C 2
Hermit Islands **44** E 2
Hermon, Mount **24** B 2
Hermosillo **66** D 6

Herning **19** E 4
Herzliyya () **24** B 2
Ḥeydarābād (Iran) **25** D 1
Ḥeydarābād (Iran) **25** G 3
Heyuan **34** F 6
Heze **34** G 3
Hialeah **67** K 6
Hidalgo **68** C 3
Hidalgo del Parral **66** E 6
Hidrolândia **75** G 4
Hierro **50** B 3
High Level **63** O 4
High Prairie **63** O 4
Higuerote **72** E 1
Hiiumaa **19** H 4
Hillsboro **67** G 5
Hilo **47** E 1
Ḥimā Ḍariyah, Jabal **24** C 4
Himachal Pradesh **36** C 1
Himalayas **36—37** CF 1—2
Ḥimş **24** B 2
Hinchinbrook Island **43** H 2
Hindu Kush **31** HJ 3
Hinganghat **36** C 3
Hingol **31** H 5
Hinnöya **18** G 2
Hinton **63** O 5
Hirara **35** J 6
Hirfanlı Barajı **23** D 3
Hirhafok **51** G 4
Hirosaki **35** LM 2
Hiroshima **35** K 4
Hirtshals **19** E 4
Ḥismā **24** B 3
Hispaniola **69** H 4
Hitachi **35** M 3
Hitra **18** E 3
Hiva Oa **47** F 3
Hjälmaren **19** G 4
Hjelmsöya **18** H 1
Ho **54** E 4
Ho Chi Minh **37** J 5
Hoa Binh **37** HJ 3
Hoachanas **58** B 4
Hoai Nhon **37** J 5
Hoare Bay **65** P 2
Hobart **44** L 9
Hobbs **66** F 5
Hoburgen **19** G 4
Hobyä **57** H 3
Hodda **57** J 2
Hodeida **53** G 6
Hodh **50** D 5
Hofsá **18** B 2
Hofsjökull **18** B 3
Höfu **35** K 4
Hoggar **51** F 4
Hohhot **34** F 2
Hoima **56** E 4
Hokkaidö **35** M 2
Hokmäbäd **30** F 3
Holanda **74** C 3
Holguín **69** G 3
Holland **67** J 3
Hollick-Kenyon Plateau **79**
Hollywood (CA, U.S.A.)
 66 C 5
Hollywood (FL, U.S.A.)
 67 L 6
Holstebro **19** E 4

Holyhead **16** C 4
Homäyünshahr **25** F 2
Hombori Tondo **54** D 3
Home Bay **65** O 2
Homosassa **67** K 6
Homs **52** F 2
Hon Panjang **37** H 6
Honavar **36** B 5
Honduras **68** E 5
Hong Kong **34** FG 6
Hongliuhe **34** B 2
Hongor **34** F 1
Honguedo, Détroit d' **65** P 6
Hongyuan **34** D 4
Honiara **45** G 3
Honningsväg **18** J 1
Honolulu **47** E 1
Honshü **35** KL 3
Hood, Mount **66** B 2
Hood Point **42** B 5
Hoover Dam **66** D 4
Hopes Advance, Cap
 65 O 3
Hopin **37** G 3
Hordaland **19** E 3
Horizon Deep **46** D 4
Horlick Mountains **79**
Horn, Cape **77** C 10
Horn Islands **46** D 3
Horn Plateau **63** O 3
Hornavan **18** G 2
Hörnefors **18** G 3
Hornos, Cabo de **77** C 10
Horqin Youyi Qianqi **35** H 1
Horsens **19** EF 4
Horsham **43** G 6
Hosalay **23** D 2
Hose Mountains **38** D 3
Hoseyniyeh **25** E 3
Hospet **36** C 4
Hospitalet de Llobregat
 20 D 3
Hoste, Isla **77** C 10
Hot Springs **67** H 5
Hotagen **18** F 3
Hotan **31** K 3
Hotazel **58** C 5
Hoting **18** G 3
Hottah Lake **63** O 2
Houston **67** G 5
Hovd (Mongolia) **32** F 6
Hovd (Mongolia) **34** D 2
Hövsgöl Nuur **32** H 5
Howe, Cape **43** J 6
Howland **46** D 2
Howrah **36** E 3
Hox Xil Shan **34** AB 3
Hoxud **34** A 2
Hoy **16** C 3
Hrvatska **21** G 2
Hsinchu **35** H 6
Hua Hin **37** GH 5
Huacho **72** C 6
Huainan **35** G 4
Huairen **34** F 3
Huajuapan de León **68** C 4
Huallaga **72** C 5
Huambo (Angola) **58** B 2

Huambo (Angola) **58** B 2
Huanan **35** K 1
Huancabamba **72** C 5
Huancavelica **74** A 3
Huancayo **74** A 3
Huang Hai **35** H 3
Huang He **35** G 3
Huang Xian **35** H 3
Huangshi **34** G 4
Huangyan **35** H 5
Huangzhong **34** D 3
Huánuco **72** C 5
Huara **74** C 4
Huaral **74** A 3
Huaraz **72** C 5
Huarmey **72** C 5
Huascarán, Nevado **72** C 5
Huasco **76** B 4
Huashixia **34** C 3
Huayllay **74** A 3
Hubei **34** F 4
Hubli **36** C 4
Huckitta **42** F 3
Hudat **57** F 4
Ḥuddur Hadama **57** G 4
Huder **33** M 6
Hudiksvall **18** G 3
Hudson **67** M 3
Hudson Bay **64** KL 3—4
Hudson Bay (Sask., Can.)
 63 R 5
Hudson Strait **65** N 3
Hue **37** J 4
Huelva **20** B 4
Huesca **20** C 3
Hughenden **43** G 3
Hugo **67** G 5
Hüich'on **35** J 2
Huihe **32** L 6
Huíla (Angola) **58** AB 2
Huila (Colombia) **72** C 3
Huilai **34** G 6
Huili **34** D 5
Huimin **35** G 3
Huize **34** D 5
Ḥulayfá **24** C 4
Huld **34** E 1
Hull **65** M 6
Huma **33** N 5
Humaitá (Amazonas, Brazil)
 73 F 5
Humaitá (Paraguay) **76** E 4
Humara, Jabal al **52** E 5
Humay **74** A 3
Húnaflói **18** A 2
Hunan **34** F 5
Hunchun **35** K 2
Hunedoara **22** B 1
Hungary **22** A 1
Hüngnam **35** J 3
Hunjiang **35** J 2
Hunsur **36** C 5
Hunter, Ile **45** K 6
Huntington **67** K 4
Huntsville (AL, U.S.A.)
 67 J 5
Huntsville (Ontario, Can.)
 65 M 6
Huntsville (TX, U.S.A.)
 67 G 5

Hunyuan **34** F 3
Huo Xian **34** F 3
Huocheng **31** L 2
Huon Gulf **44** E 3
Huron **66** G 3
Huron, Lake **67** K 3
Hurst **67** G 5
Husum **17** E 4
Hutag **32** H 6
Hutchinson **66** G 4
Hutton, Mount **43** H 4
Hvar **21** G 3
Hveragerði **18** A 3
Hwang Ho **35** G 3
Hwange **58** D 3
Hwange National Park
    58 D 3
Hyargas Nuur **32** F 6
Hyden **42** B 5
Hyderabad (India) **36** C 4
Hyderabad (Pakistan)
    31 H 5
Hyères, Iles d' **21** E 3
Hyesan **35** J 2
Hyvinge **19** H 3
Hyvinkää **19** H 3

I

Iaçu **75** H 3
Ialomiţa **22** C 2
Iaşi **22** C 1
Ibadan **54−55** E 4
Ibagué **72** C 3
Ibaiti **75** F 5
Ibarra **72** C 3
Iberville, Lac d' **65** N 4
Ibi **55** F 4
Ibitiara **75** H 3
Íbiza **20** D 4
Ibiza **20** D 4
Ibotirama **75** H 3
Ibrāhim, Jabal **53** G 4
Ibrim **52** E 4
Içá (Amazonas, Brazil)
    72 E 4
Ica (Peru) **74** A 3
Içana **72** E 3
İçel **23** D 3
Iceland **18** A 3
Ichera **32** J 4
Ichinskaya Sopka **33** T 4
Ico **75** J 2
Icy Cape **62** E 1
Idaho **66** CD 3
Idaho Falls **66** D 3
Idfū **24** A 4
Idhān Awbari **51** H 3
Idhān Murzuq **51** H 4
Ídhi Óros **22** BC 3
Ídhra **22** B 3
Idlib **24** B 2
Idre **18** F 3
Iezerul, Virful **22** B 1
Ifalik **46** A 2
Ifanadiana **59** H 4
Ife **55** E 4
Igarka **27** R 2
Iglesias **21** E 4

Ignace **64** J 6
Ignashino **33** M 5
İğneada **22** C 2
Iguaçu **76** F 4
Iguala **68** C 4
Iguassú Falls **76** F 4
Iguatu **75** J 2
Iguidi, Erg **50** DE 3
Ih Bogd Uul **34** CD 2
Ihosy **59** H 4
Ihtaml **32** H 6
Iivaara **18** J 2
Ijebu Ode **55** E 4
Ijsselmeer **16** E 4
Ijuí **76** F 4
Ikaría **22** C 3
Ikerre **55** F 4
Ikot Ekpene **55** F 4
Ilagan **39** J 1
Ilam **25** E 2
Ilbenge **33** M 3
Ile-à-la-Crosse **63** Q 4
Île d'Anticosti **65** P 6
Ile de France **20** D 2
Ile de la Gonâve **69** H 4
Île de la Madeleine **65** P 6
Ile de Ré **20** C 2
Ile des Noefs **57** J 6
Iles des Pins **45** J 6
Île d'Oléron **20** C 2
Ile d'Ouessant **20** B 2
Île du Diable **73** H 2
Ile d'Yeu **20** C 2
Ile Tidra **50** B 5
Ilebo **56** C 5
Iles Belep **45** H 5
Iles d'Hyères **21** E 3
Îles du Désappointement
    47 F 3
Îles du Duc de Gloucester
    47 F 4
Îles du Roi Georges **47** F 3
Iles Glorieuses (Réunion)
    59 H 2
Iles Loyauté **45** J 6
Îles Palliser **47** F 4
Ilha de Maracá **73** HJ 3
Ilha do Marajó **73** HJ 4
Ilha Grande **72** E 4
Ilha Santa Carolina **59** F 4
Ilhas Selvagens **50** B 2
Ilhéus **75** J 3
Iliamna **62** G 4
Iliamna Lake **62** F 4
Iligan **39** F 2
Ilimsk **32** H 4
Ilinskiy **33** Q 6
Illapel **76** B 5
Illimani, Nevado **74** C 4
Illinois **67** J 3−4
Illizi **51** G 3
Il'men, Ozero **19** K 4
Ilo **74** B 4
Iloilo **39** F 1
Ilomantsi **18** K 3
Ilots de Bass **47** F 4
Ilovlinskaya **26** H 6
Ilubabor **56** EF 3
Ilyichovsk **22** D 1
Ima **32** L 4

Imām al Hamzah **25** D 3
Imandra, Ozero **18** K 2
Imatra **18** J 3
Imbituba **76** G 4
Iméni Gastello **33** R 3
Iméni Mariny **33** R 3
Imgytskoye Boloto **27** O 4
Imi **57** G 3
Imperatriz **73** J 5
Imphal **37** F 3
Imtonzha **33** N 2
In Azaoua **55** F 1
In Gall **55** F 2
In Salah **51** F 3
Inari **18** J 2
Inarijärvi **18** J 2
İnce Burnu **23** D 2
Inch'ŏn **35** J 3
Inchŏpe **59** E 3
Independence **67** H 4
India **36** CD 3
Indian Harbour **65** Q 5
Indian Ocean **9**
Indiana **67** J 3
Indianapolis **67** J 4
Indias Occidentales **69** H 3
Indigirka **33** R 2
Indigirskaya Nizmennost'
    33 QR 2
Indispensable Reefs **46** B 3
Indispensable Strait **45** H 3
Indore **36** C 3
Indramayu **38** C 5
Indus **31** H 6
Înegöl **22** C 2
Ingoda **32** K 5
Ingrid Christensen Coast **79**
Ingul **23** D 1
Inhambane **59** F 4
Inharrime **59** F 4
Inhumas **75** G 4
Inirida **72** E 3
Inkerman **43** G 2
Inn **17** F 5
Inner Hebrides **16** B 3
Inner Mongolia **34** E 2−3
Innisfail **43** H 2
Innokent'yevka **33** P 6
Innsbruck **21** F 2
Inoucdjouac **65** M 4
Insulă Sacalin **22** CD 2
Inta **27** LM 2
Intletovy **27** P 3
Inuvik **62** L 2
Inuvik, District of **62** LM 2
Invercargill **44** P 10
Inverness **16** C 3
Investigator Strait **43** F 6
Inya **27** R 5
Iolotan **31** G 3
Iona National Park **58** A 3
Ionian Islands **22** A 3
Ionian Sea **22** AB 3
Iónioi Nísoi **22** A 3
Iónion Pélagos **22** AB 3
Íos **22** C 3
Iowa **67** H 3
Iowa City **67** H 3
Ipameri **75** G 4
Ipatinga **75** H 4

Ipiales **72** C 3
Ipiaú **75** J 3
Ípiros **22** B 3
Ipixuna **72** D 5
Ipoh **38** B 3
Iporá **75** F 4
Ipswich **16** D 4
Ipu **75** H 1
Iquapé **75** G 5
Iquique **74** B 5
Iquitos **72** D 4
Iracoubo **73** H 2
Irafshan **31** G 5
Iráklion **22** C 3
Iran, Pegunungan **38** D 3
Irapuato **68** B 3
Iraq **24** CD 2
Irbid **24** B 2
Irbit **27** M 4
Irebu **56** B 5
Irecê **75** H 3
Irgiz **31** G 1
Irharen **51** F 4
Irian Jaya **39** HJ 4
Iriba **55** J 2
Iringa **57** F 6
Iriomote-jima **35** H 6
Iriona **68** EF 4
Iriri **73** H 4
Irish Sea **16** BC 4
Irkutsk **32** H 5
Iron Knob **43** F 5
'Irq al Idrisi **51** K 4−5
'Irq al Mazhūr **24** D 4
Irrawaddy **37** G 4
Irrawaddy, Mouths of the
    37 FG 4
Irtuia **73** J 4
Irtysh **27** N 4
Irtysh **27** O 5
Irún **20** C 3
Isabela **72** B 6
Isangi **56** C 4
Ischia **21** F 3
Iseyin **54** E 4
Isfendiyar Dağları **23** D 2
Isha Baydabo **57** G 4
Isherton **73** G 3
Ishigaki **35** H 6
Ishikhly **30** D 3
Ishim **27** N 4
Ishim **27** O 4
Ishimskaya Step' **27** O 5
Ishinomaki **35** M 3
İşiklar Dağı **22** C 2
Isil'kul **27** O 5
Isinga **32** K 5
Isiolo **57** F 4
Isiro **56** D 4
İskenderun **23** E 3
İskenderun Körfezi **23** E 3
Iskitim **27** Q 5
Isla Ángel de la Guarda
    66 D 6
Isla Cedros **66** C 6
Isla de Chiloé **77** B 7
Isla de Cozumel **68** E 3
Isla de Guadelupe **66** C 6
Isla de la Juventud **68** F 3
Isla de los Estados **77** D 9

Isla de Margarita **73** F 1
Isla del Maíz **68** F 5
Isla Grande de Tierra del Fuego **77** C 9
Islamabad **31** J 4
Ísland **18** AB 3
Island Lake **63** T 5
Islands of Four Mountains **62** CD 5
Islas Baleares **20** D 3–4
Islas Canarias **50** B 3
Islas Malvinas **77** DE 9
Islay **16** B 3
Isle **20** D 2
Isle of Man **16** C 4
Isle of Wight **16** C 4
Isles of Scilly **16** B 5
Isole Eolie o Lipari **21** F 4
Isole Ponziane **21** F 3
Isosyöte **18** J 2
Israel **24** B 3
Issano **73** G 2
Issyk-Kul **31** K 2
İstanbul **22** C 2
İstanbul Boğazi **22** C 2
Isteren **18** F 3
Isthmus of Kra **37** G 5
Istmo de Panamá **72** C 2
Istmo de Tehuantepec **68** D 4
Isto, Mount **62** J 2
Istra **21** F 2
Itaberaba **75** H 3
Itabira **75** H 4
Itabuna **75** J 3
Itaguí **72** C 2
Itaituba **73** G 4
Itajaí **76** G 4
Italia **21** FG 3
Italy **21** F 3
Itambé **75** H 4
Itaperucu Mirim **75** H 1
Itaperuna **75** H 5
Itapetinga **75** HJ 4
Itapipoca **75** J 1
Itapiranga **73** G 4
Itapiúna **75** J 1
Itarsi **36** C 3
Itaúnas **75** J 4
Itbäy **52** F 4–5
Itchen Lake **63** P 2
Iténez **74** D 3
Ithaca **67** L 3
Ith/ki **22** B 3
Itivdleg **65** R 2
Ituberá **75** J 3
Ituiutaba **75** G 4
Itumbiara **75** G 4
Iturama **75** F 4
Iturbe **74** C 5
Iturup, Ostrov **33** R 6–7
Itzehoe **17** E 4
Iul'tin **62** B 2
Ivalo **18** J 2
Ivalojoki **18** J 2
Ivanhoe **43** G 5
Ivano-Frankovsk **26** D 6
Ivanovo **26** H 4
Ivittuut **65** S 3
Ivory Coast **54** CD 4

Ivory Coast **54** CD 5
Ivrea **21** E 2
Iwaki **35** M 3
Iwo **55** E 4
Iwŏn **35** J 2
Ixiamas **74** C 3
Izjevsk **26** K 4
Izki **53** K 4
İzmir **22** C 3
İzmir Körfezi **22** C 3
İzmit **22** C 2
Izu-shotö **35** M 4

J

Jabal Abadab **52** F 5
Jabal 'Abd al 'Aziz **24** C 2
Jabal al Humara **52** E 5
Jabal al Lawz **24** B 3
Jabal an Nabi Shu' ayb **53** G 5
Jabal aş Ḩasāwinah **51** H 3
Jabal ash Shaykh **24** B 2
Jabal Dabbāgh **24** B 4
Jabal Hajhir **57** J 2
Jabal Ḩamāṭah **24** B 4
Jabal Hamoyet **52** F 5
Jabal Hamrin **24–25** D 2
Jabal Ḩima Ḍariyah **24** C 4
Jabal Ibrāhīm **53** G 4
Jabal Kātrina **24** AB 3
Jabal Katul **52** D 6
Jabal Lotuke **56** E 4
Jabal Lubnān **24** B 2
Jabal Marrah **52** C 6
Jabal Oda **52** F 4
Jabal Şabir **53** G 6
Jabal Shā'ib al Banāt **24** A 4
Jabal Shammar **24** C 3
Jabal Ţuwayq **25** D 4
Jabalpur **36** CD 3
Jabālyah **24** B 3
Jablah **24** B 2
Jablanica **21** G 3
Jacareacanga **73** G 5
Jaciara **75** F 4
Jaciparaná **73** F 5
Jackpot **66** D 3
Jackson (MS, U.S.A.) **67** H 5
Jackson (TN, U.S.A.) **67** J 4
Jackson, Mount (Antarctica) **79**
Jackson, Mount (Western Australia) **42** B 5
Jacksonville (FL, U.S.A.) **67** K 5
Jacksonville (TX, U.S.A.) **67** GH 5
Jacobabad **31** H 5
Jacobina **75** H 3
Jacona **68** F 4
J.A.D. Jensens Nunatakker **65** S 3
Jadal **55** E 2
Jādū **51** H 2
Jaén **20** C 4
Jaffa, Cape **43** F 6
Jaffna **36** D 6

Jagdalpur **36** D 4
Jaguarão **76** F 5
Jaguarari **75** HJ 3
Jaguariaíva **75** FG 5
Jaguaribe **75** J 2
Jahrom **25** F 3
Jailolo **39** G 3
Jaina **68** D 3
Jaipur **36** C 2
Jakarta **38** C 5
Jakobshavn **78**
Jakobstad **18** H 3
Jalaid Qi **35** H 1
Jalapa Enríquez **68** C 4
Jalgaon **36** C 3
Jalibah **25** E 3
Jalisco **68** B 3
Jālitah **51** G 1
Jalón **20** C 3
Jaluit **46** C 2
Jalula' **25** D 2
Jama **72** B 4
Jamaica **69** G 4
Jamame **57** G 4
Jamari **73** F 5
Jambi **38** B 4
James **66** G 3
James Bay **65** L 5
James Ross Strait **63** S 1–2
Jamestown (N.D., U.S.A.) **66** G 2
Jamestown (N.Y., U.S.A.) **67** L 3
Jamiltepec **68** C 4
Jammu **31** K 4
Jammu and Kashmir **31** K 4
Jamnagar **36** B 3
Jämsä **18** HJ 3
Jamsah **24** A 4
Jamshedpur **36** E 3
Jämtland **18** F 3
Jan Mayen Island **78**
Jandaia **75** FG 4
Janesville **67** J 3
Janjira **36** B 4
Janos **66** E 5
Januária **75** H 4
Japan **35** L 3
Japan, Sea of **35** KL 3
Japurá **72** E 4
Jarābulus **24** C 1
Jaramillo **77** C 8
Jarbah **51** H 2
Jardine River National Park **43** G 1
Jarosław **17** H 4
Jarud Qi **35** H 2
Jarvis **47** E 3
Jasikan **54** E 4
Jasper **67** H 5
Jasper National Park **63** O 5
Jastrzebie Zdrój **17** G 5
Jászberény **22** A 1
Jataí **75** F 4
Jatobal **73** HJ 4
Jaú **75** G 5
Jauja **74** A 3
Java **38** C 5
Java Sea **38** C 5
Jawa **38** CD 5

Jaya, Puncak **39** J 4
Jayapura **44** D 2
Jaza' ir Farasān **53** G 5
Jaza' ir Khurīyā Murīya **53** K 5
Jazīrat Wādī Jimāl **24** B 4
Jbel Toubkal **50** D 2
Jeci **59** EF 2
Jefferson City **67** H 4
Jefferson, Mount **66** C 4
Jēkabpils **19** J 4
Jelenia Góra **17** G 4
Jelgava **19** H 4
Jelow Gir **25** E 2
Jequié **75** H 3
Jequitinhonha **75** H 4
Jerada **50** E 2
Jeremoabo **75** J 3
Jerez de la Frontera **20** B 4
Jerome **66** D 3
Jersey **16** C 5
Jerusalem **24** B 3
Jeypore **36** D 4
Jhang Sadar **31** J 4
Jhansi **36** C 2
Jhelum **31** J 4
Jiamusi **35** K 1
Ji'an **35** J 2
Jiang'an **34** DE 5
Jianghua **34** F 5
Jiangmen **34** F 6
Jiangsu **35** GH 4
Jiangxi **34** G 5
Jiangyou **34** D 4
Jianyang **35** G 5
Jiaozuo **34** F 3
Jiayu **34** F 5
Jiayuguan **34** C 3
Jiddah **53** F 4
Jiekkevarre **18** GH 2
Jieyang **34** G 6
Jigzhi **34** D 4
Jijel **51** G 1
Jijiga **57** G 3
Jilib **57** G 4
Jilin **35** HJ 2
Jilin **35** J 2
Jimma **57** F 3
Jin Xian **35** H 3
Jinan **35** G 3
Jincheng **34** F 3
Jing Xian **34** E 5
Jing Xian **35** G 4
Jingdezhen **35** G 5
Jingning **34** E 3
Jingyuan **34** D 3
Jinhua **35** GH 5
Jining **35** G 3
Jinja **56** E 4
Jinkouhe **34** D 5
Jinping **34** D 6
Jinsha **34** E 5
Jinsha Jiang **34** D 5
Jinshan **35** H 4
Jinxiang **35** G 3–4
Jinzhou **35** H 2
Jiparaná **73** F 5
Jipijapa **72** B 4
Jirjā **52** E 3
Jishou **34** E 5

Jisr ash Shughūr **24** B 2
Jiu **22** B 2
Jiujiang **34** G 5
Jiuquan **34** C 3
Jixi **35** K 1
João Pessoa **75** K 2
Jodhpur **36** B 2
Joensuu **18** JK 3
Jōetsu **35** L 3
Johannesburg **58** D 5
John O'Groat's **16** C 3
Johnsons Crossing **62** L 3
Johnston **46** D 1
Johnstown **67** L 3
Johor Baharu **38** B 3
Joinvile **76** G 4
Joinville Island **79**
Jokkmokk **18** GH 2
Jolo **39** F 2
Jonesboro **67** H 4
Jonglei **56** E 3
Jönköping **19** F 4
Jonquière **65** N 6
Joplin **67** H 4
Jordan **24** B 2–3
Jordan **24** B 3
Jorhat **37** F 2
Joroinen **18** J 3
Jos **55** F 4
Jos Sodarso, Pulau **39** J 5
Joseph Bonaparte Gulf
   42 D 1
Joseph Lake **65** O 5
Jostedalsbreen **18** E 3
Jotunheimen **18** E 3
Ju Xian **35** G 3
Juan de Nova **59** G 3
Juan Fernández Islands
   71 B 6
Juárez **77** E 6
Juàzeiro **75** H 2
Juàzeiro do Norte **75** J 2
Juba (Somalia) **57** G 4
Juba (Sudan) **56** E 4
Jubayl **24** B 2
Jubayt **52** F 5
Júcar **20** C 4
Juchitan de Zaragoza
   68 D 4
Juiz de Fora **75** H 5
Juktån **18** G 2
Julia Creek **43** G 3
Juliaca **74** B 4
Julianatop **73** G 3
Julianehåb **65** S 3
Jullundur **36** C 1
Jumanggoin **34** C 4
Jun Bulen **35** G 1
Jun Xian **34** F 4
Junagadh **36** B 3
Junction **66** G 5
Jundiaí **75** G 5
Juneau **62** L 4
Junee **43** H 5
Junggar Pendi **31** M 1
Junín **76** D 5
Juniyah **24** B 2
Jura (Switzerland) **21** E 2
Jura (U.K.) **16** B 3
Juradó **72** C 2

Jurien Bay **42** A 5
Jürmala **19** H 4
Juruá **72** E 4
Juruena **74** E 3
Juruena **74** E 3
Juruti **73** G 4
Jutaí **72** E 4
Jutland **19** E 4
Juva **18** J 3
Juventud, Isla de la **68** F 3
Jüyom **25** FG 3
Juzur Qarqannah **51** H 2
Jylland **19** E 4
Jyväskylä **18** J 3

K

Kabalo **56** D 6
Kaban'ya **33** P 6
Kabba **55** F 4
Kåbdalis **18** G 2
Kabinda **56** C 6
Kabir Küh **25** E 2
Kabo **56** B 3
Kabompo **58** C 2
Kabondo Dianda **56** CD 6
Kabüd Rāhang **25** E 2
Kabul **31** H 4
Kabwe **58** D 2
Kachikattsy **33** NO 3
Kachin **37** G 2
Kachug **32** J 5
Kadirli **23** E 3
Kadiyevka **23** E 1
Kadoma **58** D 3
Kådugli **52** D 6
Kaduna **55** F 3
Kaédi **50** C 5
Kafue **58** D 2
Kafue **58** D 3
Kafue National Park **58** D 3
Kafura **56** E 5
Kagoshima **35** JK 4
Kagul **22** C 1
Kahemba **56** B 6
Kahoolawe **47** E 1
Kahramanmaraş **23** E 3
Kai Besar, Pulau **39** H 5
Kai, Kepulauan **39** H 5
Kai Xian **34** E 4
Kaifeng **34** FG 4
Kaikoura **45** Q 9
Kaili **34** E 5
Kailu **35** H 2
Kaimur Range **36** D 3
Kainantu **44** E 3
Kainji Dam **55** EF 4
Kainji Reservoir **55** E 3
Kaintragarh **36** D 3
Kaiserslautern **17** E 5
Kaiyuan **34** D 6
Kajaani **18** J 3
Kajaki Dam **31** H 4
Kakhovka **23** D 1
Kakhovskoye
   Vodokhranilishche **23** D 1
Kåki **25** F 3
Kakinada **36** D 4
Kakisa **63** O 3

Kalabagh **31** J 4
Kalach **26** H 5
Kalachinsk **27** O 4
Kalahari **58** C 4
Kalahari Gemsbok National
   Park **58** C 5
Kalai-Khumb **31** J 3
Kalajoki **18** H 3
Kalámai **22** B 3
Kalaong **39** F 2
Kalbarri National Park
   42 A 4
Kaldbakur **18** A 2
Kalehe **56** D 5
Kalemie **56** D 6
Kalevala **18** K 2
Kalewa **37** F 3
Kalga **32** L 5
Kalgoorlie **42** C 5
Kalimantan **38** DE 3
Kaliningrad **19** H 5
Kalisz **17** G 4
Kaliua **56** E 5–6
Kalixälven **18** H 2
Kallsjön **18** F 3
Kalmar **19** G 4
Kalmykovo **30** E 1
Kaloko **56** D 6
Kalole **56** D 5
Kalsubai **36** B 4
Kaltag **62** F 3
Kaluga **26** G 5
Kalumburu **42** D 1
Kama **26** K 4
Kamaishi **35** M 3
Kamanjab **58** B 3
Kamarãn **53** G 5
Kamaria Falls **73** G 2
Kambal'naya Sopka **33** T 5
Kamchatka, Poluostrov
   33 S 4–5
Kamen, Gora **32** FG 2
Kamen-na-Obi **27** Q 5
Kamenets-Podolsky **22** C 1
Kamenjak, Rt **21** F 3
Kamensk-Ural'skiy **27** M 4
Kameshki **33** U 3
Kamet **36** D 1
Kamina **56** D 6
Kamkaly **31** J 2
Kamloops **63** N 5
Kamnrokan **32** K 4
Kampala **56** E 4
Kampar **38** B 3
Kampot **37** H 6
Kamsack **63** R 5
Kamyshin **26** HJ 5
Kanaaupscow **65** M 5
Kanaga **62** B 5
Kananga **56** C 6
Kanangra Boyd National
   Park **43** H 5
Kanazawa **35** L 3
Kanchipuram **36** CD 5
Kandagach **30** F 1
Kandahar **31** H 4
Kandalaksha **18** K 2
Kandalakshskaya Guba
   18 K 2
Kandangan **38** DE 4

Kandavu **46** C 4
Kande **54** E 4
Kandi **54** E 3
Kandy **36** D 6
Kandychan **33** RS 3
Kanem **55** GH 3
Kangalassy **33** N 3
Kangan (Iran) **25** F 4
Kangän (Iran) **30** F 5
Kangar **38** B 2
Kangaroo Island **43** F 6
Kangävar **25** E 2
Kangchenjunga **36** E 2
Kangding **34** D 5
Kangean, Kepulauan **38** E 5
Kangeeak Point **65** P 2
Kangmar **36** E .1
Kangnüng **35** J 3
Kango **55** G 5
Kangping **35** H 2
Kangynin **62** B 2
Kaniama **56** C 6
Kaniet Islands **44** E 2
Kanin Nos, Mys **26** H 2
Kanin, Poluostrov **26** HJ 2
Kankan **54** C 3
Kankesanturai **36** D 6
Kankossa **50** C 5
Kanmaw Kyun **37** G 5
Kannapolis **67** KL 4
Kano **55** F 3
Kanovlei **58** B 3
Kansas **66** G 4
Kansas City **67** H 4
Kansk **32** G 4
Kantang **37** G 6
Kantaralak **37** H 5
Kantchari **54** E 3
Kanye **58** CD 4
Kaohsiung **35** GH 6
Kaolack **54** A 3
Kaoma **58** C 2
Kaouar **55** G 2
Kap Brewster **78**
Kap Farvel **65** T 4
Kapanga **56** C 6
Kapatu **59** E 1
Kapchagay **31** K 2
Kapchagayskoye
   Vodokhranilishche **31** K 2
Kapfenberg **21** G 2
Kapingamarangi **46** B 2
Kapiri Moposhi **58** D 2
Kapisigdlit **65** RS 3
Kapona **56** D 6
Kaposvár **22** A 1
Kapustoye **18** K 2
Kara-Bogaz-Gol,Zaliv **30** E 2
Kara Daģ **23** D 3
Kara-Kala **30** F 3
Kara Sea **27** M 1
Karabekaul **31** G 3
Karabil', Vozvyshennost'
   31 G 3
Karabük **23** D 2
Karabutak **30** G 1
Karachi **31** H 6
Karaga **33** U 4
Karaganda **27** O 6
Karagüney Daĝları **23** DE 2

Karaikkudi **36** C 5
Karaj **25** F 2
Karakelong, Pulau **39** G 3
Karakoram **31** JK 3—4
Karaköse **23** F 3
Karakumy, Peski **30—31** FG 3—4
Karalundi **42** B 4
Karam **32** J 4
Karamagay **31** M 1
Karaman **23** D 3
Karamay **31** L 1
Karasburg **58** B 5
Karasjåkka **18** H 2
Karasu **23** F 3
Karasu-Aras Dağları **23** F 3
Karasuk **27** P 5
Karatau **31** J 2
Karathuri **37** G 5
Karatogay **30** F 1
Karaton **30** E 1
Karaul **27** Q 1
Karaulkel'dy **30** F 1
Karazhingil **27** O 6
Karbalā' **24** D 2
Kardhítsa **22** B 3
Kärdla **19** H 4
Kareliya **18** K 3
Karen **37** G 4
Karesuando **18** H 2
Karganay **33** X 2
Kargat **27** Q 4
Kargopol' **26** G 3
Kari **55** G 3
Kariba Dam **58** D 3
Kariba, Lake **58** D 3
Karibib **58** B 4
Karikal **36** C 5
Karimata, Selat **38** C 4
Karimganj **37** F 3
Karisimbi **56** D 5
Karjala **18** K 3
Karkar **44** E 2
Karkas, Küh-e **25** F 2
Karkinitskiy Zaliv **23** D 1
Karleby **18** H 3
Karlik Shan **34** B 2
Karlovac **21** G 2
Karlovy Vary **17** F 4
Karlshamn **19** FG 4
Karlskoga **19** FG 4
Karlskrona **19** G 4
Karlsruhe **17** E 5
Karlstad **19** F 4
Karlstad **67** G 2
Karluk **62** F 4
Karmøy **19** DE 4
Karnataka **36** C 4
Karong **37** F 2
Karonga **59** E 1
Kárpathos **22** C 3
Kars **23** F 2
Kars Platosu **23** F 2
Karsakpay **31** H 1
Karshi **31** H 3
Karskiye Vorota, Proliv **26—27** L 1
Karskoye More **27** M 1
Kartal **22** C 2
Kartaly **27** LM 5

Karufa **39** H 4
Karwar **36** B 5
Kas Kong **37** H 5
Kasai **56** B 5
Kasai Occidental **56** C 6
Kasai Oriental **56** C 5—6
Kasaji **58** C 2
Kasama **59** E 2
Kasba Lake **63** R 3
Käshän **25** F 2
Kashi **31** K 3
Kashken Teniz **27** O 6
Käshmar **30** F 3
Kasimov **26** H 5
Kaskelen **31** K 2
Kaskinen **18** H 3
Kaskö **18** H 3
Kasongo **56** D 5
Kásos **22** C 3
Kaspiyskiy **23** G 1
Kaspiyskoye More **30** E 1
Kassalá **52** F 5
Kassándra **22** B 2
Kassel **17** E 4
Kastamonu **23** D 2
Kasungu **59** E 2
Kata **32** H 4
Katako-Kombe **56** CD 5
Katangli **33** Q 5
Katawaz **31** H 4
Katende Falls **56** C 6
Kateríni **22** B 2
Katherine **42** E 1
Katherine Gorge National Park **42** E 1
Kathiawar **36** B 3
Kathiri **53** H 5
Katihar **36** E 2
Katmai National Park and Preserve **62** G 4
Katmandu **36** E 2
Katowice **17** G 4
Katrineholm **19** G 4
Katsina **55** F 3
Kattegat **19** F 4
Katul, Jabal **52** D 6
Katyl'ga **27** P 4
Kauai **47** E 1
Kaufbeuren **17** F 5
Kaunas **19** H 5
Kauno Marios **19** H 5
Kavalerovo **35** KL 2
Kaválla **22** B 2
Kavär **25** F 3
Kavendou, Mont **54** B 3
Kavīr, Dasht-e **25** FG 2
Kavīr-e Abarqu **25** F 3
Kavīr-e Namak **25** G 1
Kawa **52** E 5
Kawich Peak **66** C 4
Kawm Umbū **24** A 4
Kaya **54** D 3
Kayah **37** G 4
Kayak **62** J 4
Kayan **38** E 3
Kayes **54** B 3
Kaynar **27** P 6
Kayseri **23** E 3
Kaz Dağı **22** C 3
Kazachinskoye **32** J 4

Kazakhskiy Melkosopochnik **27** NP 6
Kazakhstan **31** FH 1
Kazan' **26** J 4
Kazanlūk **22** C 2
Kazanskoye **27** NO 4
Kazbek **23** F 2
Käzerün **25** F 3
Kazymskaya **27** N 3
Kazymskiy Mys **27** N 3
Kazzān ar Ruşayriş **52** E 6
Ké Macina **54** C 3
Keams Canyon **66** D 4
Keban Gölü **23** E 3
Kebbi **55** E 3
Kebnekaise **18** G 2
Kediat Idjil **50** C 4
Kediri **38** D 5
Kédougou **54** B 3
Keelung **35** H 5
Keetmanshoop **58** B 5
Keewatin, District of **63** TU 2—3
Kefa **57** F 3
Kefallinía **22** B 3
Keimoes **58** C 5
Keitele **18** J 2
Keith **43** G 6
Keketa **44** D 3
Kelang **38** B 3
Keli Hāji Ibrāhīm **25** D 1
Kelkit **23** E 2
Kellett, Cape **63** M 1
Kellog **27** R 3
Kellogg **66** C 2
Kelsey **63** S 4
Kelsey Bay **63** M 5
Keluang **38** B 3
Kem' **18** K 3
Kem' **18** K 3
Kemerovo **27** R 4
Kemi **18** H 3
Kemijärvi **18** J 2
Kemijärvi **18** J 2
Kemijoki **18** J 2
Kemkra **33** P 4
Kempendyayi **32** L 3
Kemps Bay **69** G 3
Kempsey **43** J 5
Kenai **62** G 3
Kenai Fjords National Park **62** H 4
Kenai Mountains **62** G 4
Kenai Peninsula **62** GH 4
Kencha **33** P 3
Kendari **39** F 4
Kendawangan **38** CD 4
Kendyrlik **27** R 6
Kenhardt **58** C 5
Kéniéba **54** B 3
Kenitra **50** D 2
Keniut **33** X 3
Kenmare **66** F 2
Kennedy Range National Park **42** B 3
Keno Hill **62** K 3
Kenora **64** J 6
Kent Peninsula **63** Q 2
Kentau **31** H 2
Kentucky **67** J 4

Kentucky Lake **67** J 4
Kenya **57** F 4
Kenya, Mount **57** F 5
Kepe **18** K 2
Kepulauan Anambas **38** C 3
Kepulauan Aru **39** HJ 5
Kepulauan Banggai **39** F 4
Kepulauan Kai **39** H 5
Kepulauan Kangean **38** E 5
Kepulauan Lingga **38** B 3—4
Kepulauan Mentawai **38** A 4
Kepulauan Natuna **38** C 3
Kepulauan Riau **38** BC 3
Kepulauan Sangihe **39** G 3
Kepulauan Sula **39** FG 4
Kepulauan Talaud **39** G 3
Kepulauan Tanimbar **39** H 5
Kepulauan Togian **39** F 4
Kerala **36** C 5
Kerama-rettō **35** J 5
Kerch' **23** E 1
Kerchenskiy Proliv **23** E 1—2
Kerekhtyakh **33** N 3
Kerema **44** E 3
Kerempe Burnu **23** D 2
Keren **57** F 1
Kerimbas, Archipelago **59** G 2
Kerinci, Gunung **38** B 4
Keriske **33** O 2
Kerki **31** GH 3
Kérkira **22** A 3
Kérkira **22** A 3
Kermadec Islands **46** D 4—5
Kermän **30** F 4
Kermanshäh **25** E 2
Kermänshähän **25** G 3
Kerme Körfezi **22** C 3
Kerulen **32** K 6
Kerzaz **50** E 3
Kestenga **18** K 2
Ketoy, Ostrov **33** S 6
Keuruunselkä **18** HJ 3
Kewanee **67** J 3
Key West **67** K 7
Keyano **65** N 5
Kezhma **32** H 4
Khabarovsk **33** P 6
Khabr, Küh-e **25** G 3
Khäbür **24** C 1
Khachmas **30** D 2
Khairpur **31** J 5
Khäiz, Küh-e **25** F 3
Khakhea **58** C 4
Khakriz **31** H 4
Khalesavoy **27** P 3
Khalīj al 'Aqabah **24** B 3
Khalij as Suways **24** A 3
Khalīj Maşīrah **53** K 5
Khalīj Qābis **51** H 2
Khálki **22** C 3
Khalkidhikí **22** B 2
Khalkís **22** B 3
Khambhat, Gulf of **36** B 3—4
Khamgaon **36** C 3
Khampa (Russia) **32** L 3
Khampa (Russia) **33** M 3
Khän Shaykhün **24** B 2
Khanabad **31** H 3
Khandwa **36** C 3

Khandyga 33 P 3
Khanglasy 27 M 3
Khanh Hung 37 J 6
Khani 32 M 4
Khánia 22 B 3
Khantau 31 J 2
Khanty-Mansiysk 27 N 3
Khanyangda 33 O 4
Khanyardakh 33 N 3
Khao Lang 37 G 6
Khao Luang 37 G 6
Khao Sai Dao Tai 37 H 5
Khappyrastakh 33 M 4
Khara 32 G 5
Kharagpur 36 E 3
Kharan 31 G 5
Kharānaq 25 G 2
Kharānaq, Kūh-e 25 G 2
Kharik 32 H 5
Khärk 25 F 3
Kharoti 31 H 4
Kharstan 33 Q 1
Khartoum 52 E 5
Khasavyurt 23 G 2
Khash 31 G 4
Khāsh 31 G 5
Khash Desert 31 G 4
Khashm Mishraq 25 DE 4
Khaskovo 22 C 2
Khatanga 32 H 1
Khatanga 32 H 1
Khatangskiy Zaliv 32 JK 1
Khataren 33 T 3
Khatyrka 33 X 3
Khawr al Fakkān 25 G 4
Khaybar 24 C 4
Khazzān Jabal al Awliyā'
52 E 5—6
Khe Bo 37 HJ 4
Khemis Miliana 51 F 1
Khenifra 50 D 2
Kherpuchi 33 P 5
Khersan 25 F 3
Kherson 23 D 1
Kheta 32 G 1
Kheta 32 H 1
Kheyrābād 25 G 3
Khibiny 18 K 2
Khil'mi, Gora 33 S 1
Khíos 22 C 3
Khíos 22 C 3
Khirbat Isrīyah 24 BC 2
Khmel'nitskiy 26 E 6
Khodzheyli 30 F 2
Khok Kloi 37 G 6
Khokhropar 31 J 5
Kholmsk 33 Q 6
Khomeyn 25 F 2
Khon Kaen 37 H 4
Khongo 33 S 3
Khor Anghar 57 G 2
Khorāsän 30 F 4
Khorat Plateau 37 H 4
Khordogoy 32 L 3
Khoronnokh 32 LM 2
Khorramābäd 25 E 2
Khorramshahr 25 E 3
Khorsäbäd 24 D 1
Khosrowābād 25 E 3
Khouribga 50 D 2

Khoydype, Gora 27 N 2
Khrebet Bureinskiy 33 O 5
Khrebet Chayatyn 33 P 5
Khrebet Cherskogo
33 P 1—2
Khrebet Dzhagdy 33 O 5
Khrebet Dzhugdzhur
33 OP 4
Khrebet Dzhungarskiy
Alatau 27 PQ 6—7
Khrebet Khugdyunga
32 G 2
Khrebet Kolymskiy 33 SU 3
Khrebet Nuratau 31 H 2
Khrebet Pay-Khoy 27 M 2
Khrebet Sette-Daban 33 P 3
Khrebet Suntar Khayata
33 PQ 3
Khrebet Turana 33 O 5
Khudzhakh 33 R 3
Khugdyungda, Khrebet
32 G 2
Khulkhuta 23 G 1
Khulna 36 E 3
Khurayş 25 E 4
Khurayt 52 D 6
Khuriyā Muriya, Jazā' ir
53 K 5
Khurmalik 31 G 4
Khurramshahr 25 E 3
Khursaniyah 25 E 4
Khuzdar 31 H 5
Khüzestän 25 E 3
Khvāf 30 FG 4
Khvojeh, Kūh-e 25 E 2
Khvor 25 G 2
Khvormüj 25 F 3
Khvoy 30 D 3
Kiambi 56 D 6
Kiantajärvi 18 J 2
Kibangou 55 G 6
Kibwezi 57 F 5
Kichi Kichi 55 H 2
Kidal 54 E 2
Kidira 54 B 3
Kiel 17 F 4
Kielce 17 H 4
Kieta 45 G 3
Kiffa 50 C 5
Kifri 24 D 2
Kigali 56 E 5
Kigilyakh 33 Q 1
Kigoma 56 D 5
Kihnu 19 H 4
Kikiakki 27 Q 3
Kikládhes 22 C 3
Kikori 44 D 3
Kikwit 56 B 6
Kilambé 68 E 5
Kilbuck Mountains 62 F 3
Kilchu 35 J 2
Kili 46 C 2
Kılıç Dağları 22 C 3
Kilimanjaro 57 F 5
Kilindini 57 F 5
Kilis 24 B 1
Kiliya 22 C 1
Killarney 16 B 4
Killeen 66 G 5
Killinek 65 O 3

Kíllini Óros 22 B 3
Kilmarnock 16 C 3
Kil'mez 26 K 4
Kilosa 57 F 6
Kilp-Javr 18 K 2
Kilpisjärvi 18 H 2
Kilwa 56 D 6
Kilwa Masoko 57 F 6
Kimball, Mount 62 J 3
Kimbe Bay 45 F 3
Kimberley (Alb., Canada)
63 O 6
Kimberley (South Africa)
58 CD 5
Kimberley (Western
Australia) 42 D 2
Kimberley Plateau 42 D 2
Kimch'aek 35 J 2
Kimito 19 H 3
Kimparana 54 BC 3
Kinchega National Park
43 G 5
Kinda 56 C 6
Kindia 54 B 4
Kindu 56 D 5
King Christian IX Land 78
King Christian X Land 78
King Frederik VIII Land 78
King Island 43 G 6
King Leopold Ranges
42 CD 2
King Sound 42 C 2
King William Island 63 S 2
King Williams Town 58 D 6
Kingman (AZ, U.S.A.)
66 D 4
Kingman (Pacific Ocean,
U.S.A.) 46 E 2
Kingoonya 43 F 5
Kings Peak 66 DE 3
Kingsmill Group 46 C 3
Kingsport 67 K 4
Kingston (Jamaica) 69 G 4
Kingston (Norfolk Is., Austr.)
46 C 4
Kingston (Ont., Canada)
65 M 7
Kingston-upon-Hull 16 C 4
Kingstown 69 K 5
Kingsville 66 G 5
Kinkala 55 G 6
Kinmaw 37 F 4
Kinnairds Head 16 C 3
Kinoosao 63 R 4
Kinshasa 56 B 5
Kipaka 56 D 5
Kipushi 58 D 2
Kirakira 45 H 4
Kirbey (Russia) 32 H 2
Kirbey (Russia) 32 K 2
Kirensk 32 J 4
Kirghiz Steppe 30—31 FG 1
Kirgiz Step' 30—31 FH 1
Kiribati 46 DE 3
Kırıkhan 23 E 3
Kırıkkale 23 D 3
Kirillovka 23 E 1
Kirishi 19 K 4
Kiritimati 47 E 2
Kirkenes 18 K 2

Kirkjubæjarklaustur 18 B 3
Kırıklareli 22 C 2
Kirkpatrick, Mount 79
Kirksville 67 H 3
Kirkük 24 D 2
Kirkwall 16 C 3
Kirkwood 67 H 4
Kırlangıç Burnu 22 D 3
Kirov 26 F 5
Kirov 26 J 4
Kirovakan 23 F 2
Kirovo Chepetsk 26 K 4
Kirovograd 23 D 1
Kirovsk 18 K 2
Kırşehir 23 D 3
Kiruna 18 H 2
Kisangani 56 D 4
Kishinev 22 C 1
Kisii 56 E 5
Kısılırmak 23 D 2
Kiska 62 A 5
Kislovodsk 23 F 2
Kismäyu 57 G 5
Kisoro 56 DE 5
Kissidougou 54 B 4
Kisumu 56 E 5
Kita 54 C 3
Kitakyushü 35 JK 4
Kitale 56 F 4
Kitami 35 M 2
Kitchener 65 L 7
Kitgum 56 E 4
Kíthira 22 B 3
Kithnos 22 B 3
Kittilä 18 H 2
Kitwe 58 D 2
Kiunga 44 D 3
Kivak 62 C 3
Kivijärvi 18 HJ 3
Kiviöli 19 J 4
Kivu 56 D 5
Kivu, Lake 56 D 5
Kiyev 26 F 5
Kiyevskoye
Vodokhranilishche 26 F 5
Kizel 27 L 4
Kızıl Dağ 23 D 3
Kizlyar 23 G 2
Kizlyarskiy Zaliv 23 G 2
Kizyl-Arvat 30 F 3
Kizyl-Atrek 30 E 3
Kjöllefjord 18 J 1
Kjöpsvik 18 G 2
Klagenfurt 21 F 2
Klaipéda 19 H 4
Klamath Falls 66 B 3
Klerksdorp 58 D 5
Klintsy 26 F 5
Klit 19 E 4
Kłodzko 17 G 4
Klotz, Lac 65 N 3
Kluane National Park 62 K 3
Klukhorskiy Pereval 23 F 2
Klyuchevskaya Sopka
33 U 4
Klyuchi 33 U 4
Knosós 22 C 3
Knox Coast 79
Knoxville 67 K 4

Knud Rasmussen Land **78**
Ko Chang **37** H 5
Ko Kut **37** H 5
Ko Phangan **37** H 6
Ko Phuket **37** G 6
Kobe **35** KL 4
København **19** F 4
Kobenni **50** D 5
Koblenz **17** E 4
Koboldo **33** O 5
Kobrin **19** H 5
Kobuk **62** F 2
Kobuk Valley National Park **62** F 2
Koca Çal **23** D 3
Kocaeli **22** CD 2
Kocasu **22** C 3
Koch **65** M 2
Köchi **35** K 4
Kochikha **32** G 1
Kodi **39** E 5
Kodiak **62** G 4
Kodiak Island **62** G 4
Kodima **26** H 3
Kodžha Balkan **22** C 2
Köes **58** B 5
Koforidua **54** D 4
Kohistan **31** J 3
Kohlu **31** H 5
Kohtla-Järve **19** J 4
Kokalaat **31** G 1
Kokand **31** J 2
Kokchetav **27** N 5
Kokkola **18** H 3
Koko Nor **34** D 3
Kokomo **67** J 3
Kokpekty **27** Q 6
Koksoak **65** O 4
Kokstad **58** D 6
Koktuma **27** Q 6
Kola **18** K 2
Kola **18** K 2
Kola Peninsula **26** G 2
Kolai **31** J 3
Kolar **36** C 5
Kolar Gold Fields **36** C 5
Kolari **18** H 2
Kolbachi **33** M 5
Kolbio **57** G 5
Kolding **19** E 4
Kolesovo **33** S 1
Kolguyev, Ostrov **26** J 2
Kolhapur **36** B 4
Koli **18** J 3
Kolkasrags **19** H 4
Kollumúli **18** C 2
Köln **17** E 4
Kołobrzeg **17** G 4
Kolombangara **45** G 3
Kolomna **26** G 4
Kolomyya **22** C 1
Kolonia **41** E 2
Kolonodale **39** F 4
Kolpakovo **33** T 5
Kolpashevo **27** Q 4
Kol'skiy, Poluostrov **26** G 2
Koluton **27** N 5
Kolwezi **58** D 2
Kolyma **33** T 2
Kolyma Range **33** U 3

Kolymskaya **33** V 2
Kolymskaya Nizmennost'
33 ST 2
Kolymskiy, Khrebet **33** SU 3
Kolymskoye Nagor'ye
33 S 3
Kolyvan' **27** Q 5
Komárno **17** G 5
Komba **56** C 4
Kombolchia **57** FG 2
Komelek **33** O 3
Kommunarsk **23** E 1
Kommunist **33** X 3
Kommunizma, Pik **31** J 3
Komoé, Parc National de la
54 D 4
Komotiní **22** C 2
Kompas Berg **58** C 6
Kompong Cham **37** J 5
Kompong Chhnang **37** H 5
Kompong Som **37** H 5
Kompot **39** F 3
Komsomol'sk-na-Amure
33 P 5
Kona **54** D 3
Kondakova **33** T 2
Kondinin **42** B 5
Kondoa **57** F 5
Kondon **33** P 5
Kondut **42** B 5
Konevo **26** G 3
Kong Frederik VI-Kyst
65 T 3
Kongola **58** C 3
Kongolo **56** D 6
Kongor **56** E 3
Kongur Shan **31** K 3
Koni, Poluostrov **33** S 4
Konin **17** G 4
Konkan **36** B 4
Konkudera **32** K 4
Konosha **26** H 3
Konotop **26** F 5
Konstantinovka **23** E 1
Konstanz **17** E 5
Kontagora **55** F 3
Kontcha **55** G 4
Kontiomäki **18** J 3
Kontum **37** J 5
Konya **20** D 3
Konya Ovası **23** D 3
Konzhakovskiy Kamen',
Gora **27** LM 4
Kootenay National Park
63 O 5
Kópasker **18** B 2
Kopeysk **27** M 5
Köping **19** G 4
Korba **36** D 3
Korça **22** B 2
Korčula **21** G 3
Kord Küy **25** G 1
Kordestán (Iran) **25** E 2
Korea Strait **35** J 4
Korenovsk **23** E 1
Korfovskiy **33** P 6
Korhogo **54** C 4
Korinthiakós Kólpos **22** B 3
Kórinthos **22** B 3
Koriolei **57** G 4

Kōriyama **35** M 3
Korkodon **33** ST 3
Korla **31** M 2
Kormakiti Burnu **23** D 3
Koro **46** C 4
Koro Toro **55** H 2
Köroğlu Dağları **23** D 2
Korosten **19** J 5
Korovin Volcano **62** C 5
Korsakov **33** Q 6
Korsfjorden **19** DE 3
Korshunovo **32** K 4
Koryakskiy Khrebet
33 VW 3
Kos **22** C 3
Kosa Fedotova **23** E 1
Kosciusko, Mount **43** H 6
Košice **17** H 5
Košong **35** J 3
Kosovska Mitrovica **22** B 2
Kossou, Lac de **54** CD 4
Kostino **27** R 2
Kostroma **26** H 4
Koszalin **17** G 4
Kota **36** C 2
Kota Baharu **38** B 2
Kota Kinabalu **38** E 2
Kotaagung **38** B 5
Kotabumi **38** BC 4
Kotel'nich **26** J 4
Kotel'nikovo **23** F 1
Kotel'nyy, Ostrov **33** P 1
Kotikovo **33** Q 6
Kotka **19** J 3
Kotlas **26** J 3
Kotlik **62** E 3
Koto **33** P 6
Kotovsk **22** C 1
Kotu Group **46** D 4
Kotuy **32** H 1
Kotzebue Sound **62** E 2
Koudougou **54** D 3
Koulen **37** H 5
Koumac **45** H 6
Koumbi-Saleh **50** D 5
Koundara **54** B 3
Koungheul **54** AB 3
Kourou **73** H 2
Koutous **55** FG 3
Kouvola **18** J 3
Kova **32** H 4
Kovač **22** A 2
Kovel' **19** HJ 5
Kovrizhka **33** U 3
Kovrov **26** H 4
Kowloon **34** FG 6
Kowt-e Ashrow **31** HJ 4
Koyuk **62** E
Koyukuk **62** F 2
Kozáni **22** B 2
Kozlu **22** D 2
Kozyrevsk **33** T 4
Kragujevac **22** B 2
Kraków **17** GH 4
Kraljevo **22** B 2
Kramfors **18** G 3
Kranj **21** F 2
Krasino **26** K 1
Krasnaya Yaranga **33** X 3
Kraśnik **17** H 4

Krasnodar **23** E 2
Krasnogorsk **33** Q 6
Krasnoje Selo **19** J 4
Krasnokamsk **26** KL 4
Krasnotur'insk **27** M 4
Krasnoural'sk **27** M 4
Krasnovodsk **30** E 2
Krasnoyarsk **32** F 4
Krasnoyarskiy **27** L 5
Krasnyy Chikoy **32** J 5
Krasnyy Luch **23** E 1
Kremenchug **26** F 6
Kresti **26** F 4
Krestovka **26** K 2
Kresty **32** E 1
Kribi **55** F 5
Krichev **26** F 5
Kril'on, Mys **33** Q 6
Krishna **36** C 4
Kristiansand **19** E 3
Kristianstad **19** F 4
Kristiansund **18** E 3
Kristiinankaupunki **18** H 3
Kristineberg **18** G 2
Kristinehamn **19** F 4
Kristinestad **18** H 3
Kríti **22** BC 3
Kritikón Pélagos **22** BC 3
Krivoy Rog **23** D 1
Krk **21** F 2
Krnov **17** G 4
Krokom **18** F 3
Kronotskaya Sopka **33** T 5
Kronotski **33** U 5
Kronotskiy, Mys **33** U 4–5
Kronshtadt **19** J 4
Kroonstad **58** D 5
Kropotkin **23** F 1
Krosno **17** H 5
Krotoszyn **17** G 4
Kruger National Park **59** E 4
Krugersdorp **58** D 5
Krung Thep **37** H 5
Kruševac **22** B 2
Krutinka **27** O 4
Kryazh Kula **33** O 2
Krym **23** D 1
Krymsk **23** E 1–2
Krymskiye Gory **23** D 2
Ksabi **50** E 3
Ksar Chellala **51** F 1
Ksar el Boukhari
51 F 1
Ksar Torchane **50** C 4
Ksen'yevka **32** L 5
Kuala Lumpur **38** B 3
Kuala Terengganu **38** B 2
Kuamut **38** E 2
Kuantan **38** B 3
Kuban' **23** E 1
Kubenskoye, Ozero **26** G 4
Kuching **38** D 3
Kudus **38** D 5
Kudymkar **26** K 4
Kufstein **21** F 2
Kūh-e 'Alīābād **25** F 2
Kūh-e Alijuq **25** F 3
Kūh-e Alvano **25** F 2
Kūh-e Bazmān **30** F 5
Kūh-e Bul () **25** F 3

Küh-e Chehel Dokhtarän 31 G 4
Küh-e Dinär 25 F 3
Küh-e Garbosh 25 EF 2
Küh-e Garri 25 E 2
Küh-e Gugerd 25 F 2
Küh-e Karkas 25 F 2
Küh-e Khabr 25 G 3
Küh-e Khaiz 25 F 3
Küh-e Kharänaq 25 G 2
Küh-e Khvojeh 25 E 2
Küh-e Kükalar 25 F 3
Küh-e Läleh Zär 30 F 5
Küh-e Masähim 25 G 3
Küh-e Safid 25 E 2
Küh-e Sorkh 25 G 2
Küh-e Täbask 25 F 3
Küh-e Taftän 31 G 5
Kühestak 30 F 5
Kühhä-ye Qorüd 25 FG 2–3
Kühhä-ye-Sabalan 30 D 3
Kühhä ye Zagros 25 EF 2–3
Kuhmo 18 J 3
Kuikkavaara 18 J 3
Kuito 58 B 2
Kuiu 62 L 4
Kuivaniemi 18 J 2
Kujani Game Reserve 54 D 4
Kuji 35 M 2
Kükalar, Küh-e 25 F 3
Kula Kangri 37 F 2
Kulakshi 30 F 1
Kulaneh 31 G 5
Kul`chi 33 P 5
Kulgera 42 E 4
Kulinda 32 J 3
Kullen 19 F 4
Kul`sary 30 E 1
Kultay 30 E 1
Kultuk 32 H 5
Kulundinskaya Step` 27 P 5
Kulundinskoye, Ozero 27 PQ 5
Kulyab 31 HJ 3
Kuma (Russia) 18 K 2
Kuma (Russia) 23 G 2
Kumai, Teluk 38 D 4
Kumamoto 35 K 4
Kumanovo 22 B 2
Kumasi 54 D 4
Kumba 55 F 5
Kumbakonam 36 C 5
Kumdah 53 H 4
Kumertau 26 KL 5
Künas 31 L 2
Kunda Hills 36 C 5
Kunduz 31 H 3
Kunene 58 A 3
Kungälv 19 F 4
Kungrad 30 F 2
Kungu 56 B 4
Kungur 26 L 4
Kunlun Shan 31 KM 3
Kunlun Shankou 34 B 3
Kunming 34 D 5
Kunsan 35 J 3
Kuntuk 33 R 4
Kununurra 42 D 2
Kuop 46 B 2
Kuopio 18 J 3

Kuorboaivi 18 J 2
Kuoyka 32 M 1
Kupang 39 F 6
Kupreanof 62 L 4
Kupyansk 26 G 6
Kuqa 31 L 2
Kura 23 G 2
Kurashiki 35 K 4
Kurdufan 52 DE 6
Kürdžhali 22 C 2
Kure 35 K 4
Kuressaare 19 H 4
Kurgan 27 N 4
Kurgan-Tyube 31 H 3
Kuria 46 C 2
Kuria Muria Islands 53 K 5
Kurikka 18 H 3
Kurilovka 26 J 5
Kuril`skiye Ostrova 33 RS 6
Kurmuk 52 E 6
Kurnool 36 C 4
Kuro Siwo 9
Kursk 26 G 5
Kurşunlu Daği 23 E 3
Kuruman 58 C 5
Kuruman 58 C 5
Kurunegala 36 CD 6
Kurupka 62 C 3
Kurzeme 19 H 4
Kuşada Körfezi 22 C 3
Kusaie 46 B 2
Kushchevskaya 23 E 1
Kushiro 35 M 2
Kushka 31 G 3
Kushmurun 27 MN 5
Kuskokwim 62 E 3
Kuskokwim Bay 62 E 4
Kuskokwim Mountains 62 F 3
Kustanay 27 M 5
Küsti 52 E 6
Kütahya 22 C 3
Kutai, Sungai 38 E 4
Kutaisi 23 F 2
Kutch 36 AB 3
Kutch, Gulf of 36 A 3
Kutch, Rann of 36 AB 3
Kutno 17 G 4
Kuusamo 18 J 2
Kuvango 58 B 2
Kuwait 25 E 3
Kuwait 25 E 3
Kuybyshev 27 P 4
Kuybyshevo 33 R 6
Kuybyshevskoye Vodokhranilishche 26 JK 5
Kuygan 27 O 6
Küysanjaq 25 D 1
Kuytun, Gora 27 R 6
Kuyumba 32 G 3
Kuznetsk 26 J 5
Kvalöy 18 H 2
Kvalöya 18 H 1
Kvænangen 18 H 1
Kvarner 21 F 2–3
Kvarnerić 21 F 3
Kverkfjöll 18 B 3

Kvichak Bay 62 F 4
Kvikkjokk 18 G 2
Kwajalein 46 C 2
Kwakoegron 73 G 2
Kwangju 35 J 3
Kwekwe 58 D 3
Kwethluk 62 E 3
Kwikila 44 E 3
Kwoka, Gunung 39 H 4
Kyakhta 32 J 5
Kyancutta 43 F 5
Kyaukme 37 G 3
Kyeintali 37 F 4
Kyle of Lochalsh 16 B 3
Kynnefjäll 19 F 4
Kyoga, Lake 56 E 4
Kyöto 35 L 3
Kyrbykan 33 N 3
Kyren 32 H 5
Kyrgyday 33 M 3
Kyrgyztan 31 JK 2
Kyrta 26 L 3
Kyrynniky 32 L 3
Kyshtovka 27 P 4
Kyshtym 27 M 4
Kystatam 32 M 2
Kytalyktakh 33 OP 2
Kyuekh-Bulung 32 KL 2
Kyushe 30 F 1
Kyüshü 35 K 4
Kyustendil 22 B 2
Kyusyur 33 N 1
Kyzas 27 R 5
Kyzyl 32 F 5
Kyzyldyykan 31 H 1
Kyzylkum, Peski 31 GH 2
Kyzyltau 27 O 6
Kyzylyu 31 H 1
Kzyl-Orda 31 H 2
Kzyltu 27 O 5

L

La Banda 76 D 4
La Carlota 76 D 5
La Ceiba 68 E 4
La Chorrera 72 BC 2
La Coronilla 76 F 5
La Coruña 20 B 3
La Crosse 67 H 3
La Cruz 66 E 7
La Digue 57 K 5
La Dorada 72 D 2
La Estrada 20 B 3
La Fría 72 D 2
La Gran Sabana 73 F 2–3
La Grande 66 C 2
La Habana 69 F 3
La Junta (Bolivia) 74 D 4
La Junta (Mexico) 66 E 6
La Ligua 76 B 5
La Linea 20 B 4
La Loche 63 Q 4
La Mancha 20 C 4
La Mariscala 76 F 5
La Marmora 21 E 4
La Merced 76 C 4
La Montaña 74 B 2–3
La Mosquitia 68 F 4–5
La Oroya 74 A 3

La Palma (Canary Islands) 50 B 3
La Palma (Panamá) 72 C 2
La Paragua 73 F 2
La Paz (Argentina) 76 C 5
La Paz (Argentina) 76 E 5
La Paz (Bolivia) 74 C 4
La Paz (Mexico) 66 D 7
La Piedad 68 D 3
La Plata 76 E 5–6
La Ribera 20 C 3
La Rioja (Argentina) 76 C 4
La Rioja (Spain) 20 C 3
La Roche-sur-Yon 20 C 2
La Rochelle 20 C 2
La Romana 69 J 4
La Ronge 63 Q 4
La Salina 66 D 5
La Serena (Chile) 76 B 4
La Serena (Spain) 20 B 4
La Seyne-sur-Mer 21 E 3
La Spezia 21 EF 3
La Unión 77 B 7
La Vega 69 H 4
Labbezenga 54 E 2
Labé 54 B 3
Labengke, Pulau 39 F 4
Labinsk 23 F 2
Labrador 65 NO 4
Labrador City 65 O 5
Labrador Current 8
Labrador Sea 65 QR 4
Lábrea 73 F 5
Labuhanbajo 39 EF 5
Labytnangi 27 N 2
Lac à l`Eau-Claire 65 MN 4
Lac Alaotra 59 H 3
Lac Albanel 65 N 5
Lac au Goéland 65 M 5–6
Lac Bienville 65 N 4
Lac Caniapiscau 65 O 5
Lac Champdoré 65 O 4
Lac de Gras 63 O 3
Lac de Kossou 54 CD 4
Lac Débo 54 D 2
Lac d`Iberville 65 N 4
Lac Klotz 65 N 3
Lac la Martre 63 O 3
Lac la Ronge 63 R 4
Lac Léman 21 E 2
Lac Mai-Ndombe 56 B 5
Lac Minto 65 N 4
Lac Mistassini 65 N 5
Lac Moero 56 D 6
Lac Naoc ocane 65 NO 5
Lac Sakami 65 M 5
Lac Seul 64 J 5
Lac Upemba 56 D 6
Laccadive Islands 36 B 5
Lacepede Bay 43 F 5
Lachlan River 43 GH 5
Ladoga, Lake 18 K 3
Ladozhskoye Ozero 18 K 3
Ladysmith 58 D 5
Lae (Marshall Is.) 46 C 2
Lae (Papua New Guinea) 44 E 3
Lafayette (IN, U.S.A.) 67 J 3
Lafayette (LA, U.S.A.) 67 H 5

Lafia **55** F 4
Lafiagi **55** EF 4
Laghouat **51** F 2
Lago Agrio **72** C 4
Lago Buenos Aires **77** B 8
Lago Cabora Bassa **59** E 3
Lago de Maracaibo
　72 D 1–2
Lago de Nicaragua **68** E 5
Lago de Poopó **74** C 4
Lago di Bolsena **21** F 3
Lago di Garda **21** F 2
Lago Maggiore **21** E 2
Lago O'Higgins **77** B 8
Lago Posadas **77** B 8
Lago Rogagua **74** C 3
Lago Titicaca **74** C 4
Lago Viedma **77** B 8
Lagoa dos Patos **76** F 5
Lagoa Mangueira **76** F 5
Lagoa Mirim **76** F 5
Lagos **54** E 4
Laguna **76** G 4
Laguna Madre **68** C 2–3
Laguna Mar Chiquita **76** D 5
Laguna Merín **76** F 5
Lagunas (Chile) **74** BC 5
Lagunas (Peru) **72** C 5
Lagune Ndogo **55** G 6
Lagune Nkomi **55** F 6
Lagunillas **74** D 4
Lähijan **25** F 1
Lahore **31** J 4
Lahti **18** J 3
Lai **55** H 4
Lainioälven **18** H 2
Laiyuan **34** F 3
Lajes **76** F 4
Lake Abitibi **65** M 6
Lake Albert **56** E 4
Lake Amadeus **42** E 3
Lake Argyle **42** D 2
Lake Athabasca **63** Q 4
Lake Austin **42** B 4
Lake Baikal **32** J 5
Lake Ballard **42** C 4
Lake Bangweulu **58** D 2
Lake Barlee **42** B 4
Lake Carey **42** C 4
Lake Carnegie **42** C 4
Lake Chad **55** G 3
Lake Charles **67** H 5
Lake Chilwa **59** F 3
Lake City **67** K 5
Lake Claire **63** P 4
Lake Clark National Park and
　Preserve **62** G 3
Lake Disappointment
　42 C 3
Lake Edward **56** D 5
Lake Erie **67** K 3
Lake Eyasi **56** E 5
Lake Eyre **43** F 4
Lake Eyre Basin **43** F 4
Lake Francis Case **66** FG 3
Lake Gairdner **43** F 5
Lake Grandin **63** O 3
Lake Gregory **43** F 4
Lake Huron **67** K 3
Lake Kariba **58** D 3

Lake Kivu **56** D 5
Lake Kyoga **56** E 4
Lake Lefroy **42** C 5
Lake Mackay **42** D 3
Lake Malawi **59** E 2
Lake Manitoba **63** S 5
Lake Maurice **42** E 4
Lake Mc Leod **42** A 3
Lake Melville **65** Q 5
Lake Michigan **67** J 3
Lake Moore **42** B 4
Lake Mweru **56** D 6
Lake Nash **43** F 3
Lake Natron **57** F 5
Lake Nipigon **64** K 6
Lake Nipissing **65** LM 6
Lake Nyasa **59** E 2
Lake Oahe **66** FG 2
Lake of the Ozarks **67** H 4
Lake of the Woods **64** H 6
Lake Okeechobee **67** K 6
Lake Onega **26** G 3
Lake Ontario **67** L 3
Lake Powell **66** D 4
Lake Rebecca **42** C 5
Lake River **65** L 5
Lake Rudolf **57** F 4
Lake Rukwa **56** E 6
Lake Saint Lucia **59** E 5
Lake Sakakawea **66** F 2
Lake Stefanie **57** F 4
Lake Superior **67** J 2
Lake Tana **57** F 2
Lake Tanganyika **56** DE 6
Lake Taupo **45** R 8
Lake Torrens **43** F 5
Lake Turkana **57** F 4
Lake Victoria **56** E 5
Lake Volta **54** DE 4
Lake Winnipegosis **63** RS 5
Lakeland **67** K 6
Lakewood **66** E 4
Lakon **45** J 4
Lakonikos Kólpos **22** B 3
Lakselv **18** J 1
Lakshadweep **36** B 5
Lalara **55** G 5
Lâleli Geçidi **23** E 3
Lalitpur **36** C 3
Lamar **66** F 4
Lamarque **77** C 6
Lamas **72** C 5
Lambaréné **55** FG 6
Lambayeque **72** B 5
Lambert, Cape **45** F 2
Lambert Glacier **79**
Lamberts Bay **58** B 6
Lamezia Terme **21** G 4
Lamía **22** B 3
Lamington National Park
　43 J 4
Lamotrek **46** A 2
Lampang **37** G 4
Lamu **57** G 5
Lancang **34** C 6
Lancang Jiang **34** D 6
Lancaster (CA, U.S.A.)
　66 C 5
Lancaster (U.K.) **16** C 4
Lanciano **21** F 3

Land's End **16** B 4
Landshut **17** F 5
Landskrona **19** F 4
Landsort **19** G 4
Landsortsdjupet **19** G 4
Lang Son **37** J 3
Langjökull **18** B 3
Langkon **38** E 2
Langöya **18** F 2
Langry **33** Q 5
Langzhong **34** E 4
Lansing **67** JK 3
Lanzarote **50** C 3
Lanzhou **34** D 3
Laoag **39** J 1
Laon **20** D 2
Laos **37** HJ 4
Laouni **51** G 4
Lapa **76** G 4
Lapland **18** H 2
Lappajärvi **18** H 3
Lappeenranta **18** J 3
Lappi **18** J 2
Laptev Sea **33** NO 1
Laptevykh, More **32** MN 1
Lapua **18** H 3
L'Aquila **21** F 3
Larache **50** D 1
Laramie Mountains **66** E 3
Laredo **66** G 6
Lårestän **25** FG 4
Lárisa **22** B 3
Larkana **31** H 5
Larlomkriny **27** O 4
Larnaca **23** D 4
Larne **16** B 4
Larrey Point **42** B 2
Larsen Ice Shelf **79**
Läs 'Änöd **57** H 3
Las Cejas **76** D 4
Läs Dawa **57** H 2
Las Flores **77** E 6
Las Lajas **77** BC 5
Las Palmas **50** B 3
Las Plumas **77** C 7
Las Tablas **72** B 2
Las Vegas **66** C 4
Läsh-e Joveyn **31** G 4
Lashio **37** G 3
Lashkar Gäh **31** G 4
Læsö **19** F 4
Latady Island **79**
Latakia **24** B 2
Lätäseno **18** H 2
Latgale **19** J 4
Latgales Augstiene **19** J 4
Latvia **19** J 4
Lau Group **46** D 4
Laughlin Peak **66** F 4
Lauhavuori **18** H 3
Launceston **44** L 9
Laurentian Scarp **65** M 6
Lauria **21** G 4
Lausanne **21** E 2
Laut Arafura **39** HJ 5
Laut Bali **38** E 5
Laut Halmahera **39** G 4
Laut Jawa **38** CD 4
Laut Maluku **39** G 4
Laut, Pulau **38** E 4

Laut Seram **39** GH 4
Laut Sulawesi **39** F 3
Laut Timor **39** G 6
Laval (France) **20** C 2
Laval (Quebec, Can.) **65** N 6
Lävan **25** F 4
Lavka Integralsoyuza **33** V 2
Lawra **54** D 3
Lawton **66** G 5
La'youn **50** C 3
Läzeh **25** F 4
Le Creusot **21** D 2
Le Havre **20** CD 2
Le Maire, Estrecho de
　77 CD 9–10
Le Mans **20** D 2
Le Mars **67** G 3
Le Puy **20** D 2
Leavenworth **67** GH 4
Lebanon (Lebanon) **24** B 2
Lebanon (PA, U.S.A.) **67** L 3
Lebedin **26** F 5
Lebu **77** B 6
Lebyazh'ye **27** P 5
Lecce **21** G 3
Lechang **34** F 5
Leeds **16** C 4
Leeuwarden **16** E 4
Leeuwin, Cape **42** A 5
Leeward Islands (French
　Polynesia) **47** E 4
Leeward Islands (West
　Indies) **69** K 4
Lefroy, Lake **42** C 5
Leganés **20** C 3
Legaspi **39** F 1
Legnago **21** F 2
Legnano **21** E 2
Legnica **17** G 4
Legune **42** D 2
Leichardt River **43** F 2
Leiden **16** D 4
Leipzig **17** F 4
Leirvik **19** E 4
Leiyang **34** F 5
Leka **18** F 2
Lékana **55** G 6
Leksozero, Ozero **18** K 3
Leleque **77** B 7
Léman, Lac **21** E 2
Lemieux Islands **65** P 3
Lemmenjoki **18** J 2
Lemmon **66** F 2
Lemoro **39** F 4
Lena **33** N 1
Lendery **18** K 3
Leninakan **23** F 2
Leningradskaya **79**
Leninka **33** X 3
Leninogorsk (Russia) **26** K 5
Leninogorsk (Russia) **27** Q 5
Leninsk-Kuznetskiy **27** QR 5
Len'ki **27** Q 5
Lenkoran' **30** D 3
Lensk **32** K 3
Lentini **21** F 4
León (Mexico) **68** B 3
León (Nicaragua) **68** E 5
León (Spain) **20** B 3
Leonardville **58** B 4

Leonora 42 C 4
Leopold and Astrid Coast 79
Lepsy 27 P 6
Lérida (Colombia) 72 D 3
Lérida (Spain) 20 D 3
Léros 22 C 3
Lerum 19 F 4
Lerwick 16 C 2
Les Landes 20 C 3
Leskovac 22 B 2
Lesnaya 33 TU 4
Lesosibirsk 32 F 4
Lesotho 58 D 5
Lesozavodsk 35 K 1
L'Esperance Rock 46 D 5
Lesser Antilles 69 K 4–5
Lesser Slave Lake 63 OP 4
Lesser Sunda Islands 39 FG 5
Lestijoki 18 H 3
Lésvos 22 C 3
Leszno 17 G 4
Lethbridge 63 P 6
Lethem 73 G 3
Leticia 72 D 4
Letsok-aw Kyun 37 G 5
Leuser, Gunung 38 A 3
Levante, Riviera di 21 E 3
Lévêque, Cape 42 C 2
Levkás 22 B 3
Lewis 16 B 3
Lewiston (ID, U.S.A.) 66 C 2
Lewiston (ME, U.S.A.) 67 N 3
Lexington 67 K 4
Leyte 39 F 1
Lhari 34 B 4
Lhasa 37 F 2
Lhazhong 36 E 1
Li Xian 34 D 4
Li Xian 34 F 5
Lian Xian 34 F 6
Liancheng 34 G 5
Lianjiang 34 EF 6
Lianyin 33 M 5
Lianyungang 35 GH 4
Liao He 35 H 2
Liaoning 35 H 2
Liard 63 N 3
Liberal 66 F 4
Liberia 54 BC 4
Liberia (Costa Rica) 68 E 5
Libreville 57 F 5
Libya 51 HK 3
Libyan Desert 52 CD 3–4
Licata 21 F 4
Lichinga 59 F 2
Lida 19 J 5
Lidköping 19 F 4
Liechtenstein 21 EF 2
Liége 16 E 4
Lieksa 18 K 3
Lienart 56 D 4
Lienz 21 F 2
Liepäja 19 H 4
Lievestuoreenjärvi 18 J 3
Lifou 45 J 6
Ligurian Sea 21 E 3
Lihir Group 45 F 2

Lihou Reef and Cays 43 J 2
Lijiang 34 D 5
Likasi 58 D 2
Likiep 46 C 2
Likouala 55 H 5
Lille 20 D 1
Lilongwe 59 E 2
Lima (OH, U.S.A.) 67 K 3
Lima (Peru) 74 A 3
Lima (Portugal) 20 B 3
Limassol 23 D 4
Limay Mahuida 77 C 6
Limerick 16 B 4
Limfjorden 19 E 4
Limmen 18 F 3
Limnos 22 C 3
Limoeiro 75 J 2
Limoges 20 D 2
Limon (CO, U.S.A.) 66 F 4
Limón (Costa Rica) 68 F 5
Limousin 20 D 2
Limpopo 59 E 4
Linakhamari 18 K 2
Linares (Chile) 77 B 6
Linares (Mexico) 68 C 3
Linares (Spain) 20 C 4
Lincang 34 D 6
Lincoln (NE, U.S.A.) 67 G 3
Lincoln (U.K.) 16 C 4
Lincoln Sea 78
Lindau 17 E 5
Linden 73 G 2
Lindesnes 19 E 4
Lindi 57 F 6–7
Line Islands 47 E 2–3
Linfen 34 F 3
Lingayen 39 H 1
Lingga, Kepulauan 38 B 3–4
Lingomo 56 C 4
Lingyuan 35 G 2
Linhares 75 J 4
Linhe 34 E 2
Linhpa 37 G 2
Linköping 19 G 4
Linkou 35 K 1
Linosa 21 F 4
Lins 75 G 5
Lintao 34 D 3
Linxi 35 G 2
Linxia 34 D 3
Linyanti 58 C 3
Linyi 35 G 3
Linz 21 F 2
Lion, Golfe du 20–21 D 3
Lipa 39 F 1
Lipari 21 FG 4
Lipetsk 26 GH 5
Lipin Bor 26 G 3
Lisala 56 C 4
Lisboa 20 B 4
Lisburn 16 B 4
Lisburne, Cape 62 D 2
Lishui 35 G 5
Lisichansk 26 G 6
Lisieux 20 D 2
Liski 26 G 5
Lithinon, Ákra 22 B 4
Lithuania 19 H 4
Litke 33 Q 5
Litovko 33 P 6

Little Abaco Island 69 G 2
Little Andaman 37 F 5
Little Colorado 66 D 4
Little Desert National Park 43 G 6
Little Grand Rapids 63 ST 5
Little Nicobar 37 F 6
Little Rock 67 H 5
Litva 19 H 4
Liuzhou 34 E 6
Livengood 62 H 2
Liverpool 16 C 4
Livingston (MT, U.S.A.) 66 D 2
Livingston (Newfoundl., Can.) 65 O 5
Livingstone 58 D 3
Livingstone Falls 55 G 7
Livoniya 19 J 4
Livorno 21 EF 3
Liwale 57 F 6
Liwonde 59 F 2–3
Lizard 16 BC 5
Lizarda 73 J 5
Ljubeli 21 F 2
Ljubljana 21 F 2
Ljungby 19 F 4
Ljusnan 18 G 3
Llallagua 74 C 4
Llano Estacado 66 F 5
Llanos 72 DE 2–3
Llanos de Moxos 74 CD 4
Llullaillaco, Volcán 74 C 5
Lobito 58 A 2
Locarno 21 E 2
Loch Lomond 16 C 3
Loch Ness 16 C 3
Lockhart River Mission 43 G 1
Lod 24 B 3
Lodja 56 C 5
Lodwar 56 F 4
Łodz 17 G 4
Lofoten 18 F 2
Logan, Mount 62 J 3
Logroño 20 C 3
Lohja 19 H 4
Lohjanjärvi 19 H 3
Lohjanselkä 19 H 3
Loholoho 39 F 4
Loire 20 C 2
Loja 72 C 4
Lojo 19 H 3
Lokan tekojärvi 18 J 2
Lokilalaki, Gunung 39 F 4
Lökken 18 E 3
Loks Land 65 P 3
Lokshak 33 O 5
Lolland 19 F 5
Loma Mountains 54 B 4
Lomami 56 C 4
Lomas 74 B 4
Lomas de Zamora 76 E 6
Lombok 38 E 5
Lomé 54 E 4
Lomonosov 19 J 4
Lompoc 66 B 5
Łomža 17 H 4
Loncoche 77 B 6
London (Canada) 65 L 7

London (U.K.) 16 CD 4
Londonderry 77 B 10
Londonderry, Cape 42 D 1
Londrina 75 F 5
Long Beach 66 B 2
Long Island (Papua New Guinea) 44 E 3
Long Island (The Bahamas) 69 G 3
Long Range Mountaines 65 Q 6
Long Valley 66 D 5
Long Xian 34 E 4
Longjiang 33 M 6
Longlac 64 K 6
Longmont 66 F 3
Longreach 43 G 3
Longview (TX, U.S.A.) 67 GH 5
Longview (WA, U.S.A.) 66 B 2
Longxi 34 D 3
Longyan 34 G 5
Longzhou 34 E 6
Lookout, Cape 67 L 5
Lop Buri 37 H 5
Lop Nur 34 B 2
Lopatka 33 T 5
Lopatka, Mys 33 T 5
Lopcha 33 M 4
Lopez, Cap 55 F 6
Lopphavet 18 H 1
Lopydino 26 K 3
Lorca 20 C 4
Lord Howe Island 43 K 5
Lordsburg 66 E 5
Lorestán (Iran) 25 E 2
Loreto (Colombia) 72 D 4
Loreto (Maranhão, Brazil) 73 JK 5
Loreto (Mexico) 66 D 6
Lorient 20 C 2
Lorraine 21 E 2
Los Alamos 66 E 4
Los Ángeles (Chile) 77 B 6
Los Angeles (U.S.A) 66 BC 5
Los Blancos 74 D 5
Los Gatos 66 B 4
Los Lagos 77 B 6
Los Lavaderos 68 C 3
Los Mochis 66 E 6
Los Teques 72 E 1
Los Vilos 76 B 5
Losap 46 C 2
Lošinj 21 F 3
Lost Trail Pass 66 D 2
Lot 20 D 3
Lota 77 B 6
Lotta 18 J 2
Lotuke, Jabal 56 E 4
Loubomo 55 G 6
Louga 54 A 2
Lough Neagh 16 B 4
Louis Trichardt 58 DE 4
Louisiade Archipelago 43 J 1
Louisiana 67 H 5
Louisville 67 J 4
Loukhi 18 K 2

Loum 55 FG 5
Lövånger 18 H 3
Lovech 22 B 2
Lovelock 66 C 3
Lovisa 19 J 3
Lovozero 18 L 2
Lowa 56 D 5
Lowell 67 M 3
Lower California 66 D 6
Lower Tunguska River
32 F 3
Lowestoft 16 D 4
Loyalty Islands 45 J 6
Loyoro 56 E 4
Lozére, Mont 20 D 3
Luacano 58 C 2
Lualaba 56 D 5
Luanda 58 A 1
Luando 58 B 2
Luando 58 B 2
Luando Reserve 58 B 2
Luang Prabang 37 H 4
Luangwa 59 E 2
Luangwa Valley Game
Reserve 59 E 2
Luanshya 58 D 2
Luapala 58 D 2
Lubalo 58 B 1
Lubang Islands 39 EF 1
Lubango 58 A 2
Lubao 56 D 6
Lubbock 66 F 5
Lübeck 17 F 4
Lubefu 56 C 5
Lublin 17 H 4
Lubnän, Jabal 24 B 2
Lubny 26 F 5
Lubumbashi 58 D 2
Lucas 74 E 3
Lucea 69 G 4
Lucena 20 C 4
Lučenec 17 G 5
Lucera 21 G 3
Lucero 66 E 5
Lüchun 34 D 6
Lucknow 36 D 2
Lucusse 58 C 2
Lüda 35 H 3
Lüderitz 58 AB 5
Ludhiana 36 C 1
Ludogorie 22 C 2
Ludvika 19 G 3
Ludwigshafen 17 E 5
Luebo 56 C 6
Luena 58 B 2
Lüeyang 34 E 4
Lufeng 34 G 6
Luga 19 J 4
Luga 19 J 4
Lugano 21 E 2
Luganville 45 J 5
Lugenda 59 F 2
Lugnvik 18 G 3
Lugo 20 B 3
Lugoj 22 B 1
Lugovoy 31 J 2
Luhuo 34 D 4
Luiana 58 C 3
Luimneach 16 B 4

Luís Correia 75 H 1
Luiza 56 C 6
Lukashkin Yar 27 P 3
Lukolela 56 B 5
Luleå 18 H 2
Luleälven 18 H 2
Lüleburgaz 22 C 2
Lumbala Kaquengue 58 C 2
Lumbala N'guimbo 58 C 2
Lumding 37 F 2
Lumsden 44 P 10
Lumut, Tanjung 38 C 4
Lund 17 F 3
Lunda Norte 58 C 1
Lunda Sul 58 C 2
Lundazi 59 E 2
Lüneburg 17 EF 4
Lunkho 31 J 3
Lunovayam 33 U 3
Luntai 31 L 2
Luochuan 34 E 3
Luofu 56 D 5
Luoshan 34 FG 4
Luoyang 34 F 4
Luoyuan 35 GH 5
Lupane 58 D 3
Lupeni 22 B 1
Luputa 56 C 6
Lüq 57 G 4
Luqu 34 D 4
Lusaka 58 D 2
Lusambo 56 C 5
Lushui 34 C 5
Lusk 66 F 3
Lüt, Dasht-e 25 G 2
Luton 16 C 4
Lutsk 19 J 5
Luxembourg 16 E 5
Luxembourg 16 E 5
Luxi 34 C 6
Luxi 34 D 6
Luxor 24 A 4
Luza 26 J 3
Luzern 21 E 2
Luzhai 34 E 6
Luzhou 34 E 5
Luzhskaya Vozvyshennost'
19 J 4
Luzon 39 J 1
Luzon Strait 39 J 1
Lvov 26 D 6
L'vovka 27 P 4
Lyakhovskiye Ostrova
33 P 1
Lynchburg 67 L 4
Lynd 43 G 2
Lynn Lake 63 R 4
Lynx Lake 63 Q 3
Lyon 21 DE 2
Łyso Gory 17 H 4
Lyubertsy 26 G 4

M

Ma'än 24 B 3
Maarianhamina 19 H 3
Ma'arrat an Nu'män 24 B 2
Maastricht 16 E 4
Mabaruma 73 G 2

Mabote 59 E 4
Ma'bús Yúsuf 51 K 3
Mac Kenzie Bay 79
Mac Robertson Land 79
Macadam Plains 42 B 4
Macaíba 75 J 2
Macao 34 F 6
Macapá 73 H 3
Macará 72 B 4
Macas 72 C 4
Macau 75 J 2
Macauley 46 D 4–5
Macdonnell Ranges 42 E 3
Maceió 75 J 2
Macerata 21 F 3
Machala 72 C 4
Machevna 33 W 3
Machilipatnam 36 D 4
Machupicchu 74 B 3
Macia 59 E 5
Mackay 43 H 3
Mackay, Lake 42 D 3
Mackenzie 63 N 3
Mackenzie Bay 62 K 2
Mackenzie King Island 78
Mackenzie Mountains
62–63 LM 2–3
Mackenzie River 43 H 3
Mackinaw City 67 K 2
Macocola 58 B 1
Macomia 59 FG 2
Mâcon (France) 21 D 2
Macon (GA, U.S.A.) 67 K 5
Macquarie Island 79
Madagascar 59 G 3
Mada'in Şälih 24 C 4
Madang 44 E 3
Madaoua 55 F 3
Madeira (Brazil) 73 F 4–5
Madeira (Portugal) 50 B 2
Madeleine, Île de la 65 P 6
Madeniyet 27 P 6
Madhya Pradesh 36 CD 3
Madimba 56 B 5
Madingo-Kayes 55 G 6
Madison 67 J 3
Madiun 38 D 5
Madoi 34 C 4
Madrakah 53 FG 4
Madrakah, Ra's al 53 K 5
Madras 36 D 5
Madre de Dios 74 C 3
Madre Oriental, Sierra
68 BC 2–3
Madura, Pulau 38 D 5
Madurai 36 C 6
Madyan 24 B 4
Maebashi 35 L 3
Maevatanana 59 H 3
Maéwo 45 J 5
Mafeteng 58 D 5
Mafia Island 57 FG 6
Magadan 33 S 4
Magallanes, Estrecho de
77 B 9
Magangué 72 D 2
Magaria 55 F 3
Magdagachi 33 N 5
Magdalena 72 D 1–2
Magdeburg 17 F 4

Magelang 38 C 5
Magellan, Strait of 77 BC 9
Mageröya 18 J 1
Maggiore, Lago 21 E 2
Magnitogorsk 27 L 5
Magwe 37 G 3
Magyarország 22 A 1
Maha Sarakham 37 H 4
Mahabharat Range 36 E 2
Mahabo 59 G 4
Mahadday Wéyne 57 H 4
Mahajan 36 B 2
Mahajanga 59 H 3
Mahalapye 58 D 4
Mahanoro 59 H 3
Maharashtra 36 BC 4
Mahatsanary 59 G 5
Mahbés 50 D 3
Mahbubnagar 36 C 4
Mahd adh Dhahab 24 C 5
Mahḍah 25 G 4
Mahdia 73 G 2
Mahenge 57 F 6
Mahesana 36 B 3
Mahia Peninsula 45 R 8
Mahkene 18 F 3
Mahmud-Raqi 31 HJ 3
Mahmüdäbad 25 F 1
Mahón 20 D 4
Mahuva 36 B 3
Mai-Ndombe, Lac 56 B 5
Maiana 46 C 2
Maiduguri 55 G 3
Maimana 31 G 3
Maine 67 N 2
Mainland (Orkney Is., U.K.)
16 C 3
Mainland (Shetland Is., U.K.)
16 C 2
Maintirano 59 G 3
Mainz 17 E 5
Maio 54 B 6
Maipú 77 E 6
Maipuco 72 D 4
Maitengwe 58 D 4
Maitland 43 J 5
Majuro 46 C 2
Makale 57 F 2
Makambako 56 EF 6
Makarikari 58 D 4
Makarikha 27 L 2
Makarov 33 Q 6
Makarova 32 DE 1
Makassar 39 E 5
Makat 30 E 1
Makaw 37 G 2
Makedhonía 22 B 2
Makedonija 22 B 2
Makeyevka 23 E 1
Makgadikgadi Pan 58 D 4
Makhachkala 30 D 2
Makinsk 27 O 5
Makkah 53 FG 4
Makó 22 B 1
Makokou 55 G 5
Makri 36 D 4
Maksimovka 35 L 1
Makü 30 C 3
Makurdi 55 F 4
Makushino 27 N 4

Makuyuni 57 F 5
Makwa 45 J 2
Malabar Coast 36 BC 5–6
Malabo 55 F 5
Malacca, Strait of 38 B 3
Málaga 20 C 4
Malagasy Republic 59 G 3
Malaimbandy 59 H 4
Malaita 45 H 3
Malakāl 56 E 3
Malang 38 D 5
Malanje 58 B 1
Mälaren 19 G 4
Malargue 77 C 6
Malaspina 77 C 7
Malatya 23 E 3
Malatya Dağları 23 E 3
Malawi 59 E 2
Malāwi (Iran) 25 E 2
Malawi, Lake 59 E 2
Malawi National Park 59 E 2
Malaya 38 B 3
Malaybalay 39 G 2
Malāyer 25 E 2
Malaysia 38 CD 2
Malden 47 E 3
Maldives 36 B 6
Maldonado 76 F 5
Male 29 K 9
Maléas, Ákra 22 B 3
Malegaon 36 B 3
Malei 59 F 3
Malek 56 E 3
Malekula 45 J 5
Maleyevo 32 G 4
Malhada 75 H 3
Mali 54 CD 2–3
Mali Kyun 37 G 5
Malin Head 16 B 3
Maling, Gunung 39 F 3
Mallaig 16 B 3
Mallani 36 B 2
Mallery Lake 63 S 3
Mallorca 20 D 4
Malmö 19 F 4
Maloelap 46 C 2
Mälöy 18 D 3
Malozemel'skaya Tundra 26 JK 2
Malta 21 F 4
Malta (MT, U.S.A.) 66 E 2
Maluku 39 G 4
Maluku, Laut 39 G 3
Malung 19 F 3
Maly Kavkaz 23 FG 2
Malyy Yenisey 32 FG 5
Mama 32 K 4
Mamagota 45 G 3
Mambasa 56 D 4
Mamberamo, Sungai 39 J 4
Mambéré 56 B 4
Mamoré 74 C 3
Mamou 54 B 3
Mamuju 39 E 4
Mamuno 58 C 4
Man 54 C 4
Man, Isle of 16 C 4
Manacapuru 73 F 4
Manado 39 F 3

Managua 68 E 5
Manakara 59 H 4
Manakau 45 Q 9
Manama 25 F 4
Mananara 59 H 3
Manapouri 44 P 10
Manas 31 M 2
Manaus 73 FG 4
Manchester 16 C 4
Manchuria 35 HJ 2
Máncora 72 B 4
Mand 25 F 3
Mandal 19 E 4
Mandal-Ovoo 34 D 2
Mandalay 37 G 3
Mandasor 36 B 3
Mandera 57 G 4
Mandiana 54 C 3
Mandimba 59 F 2
Mandji 55 G 6
Mandla 36 D 3
Mandor 38 C 3
Mandurah 42 B 5
Mandvi 36 A 3
Manfredonia 21 G 3
Manga (Minas Gerais, Brazil) 75 H 3
Manga (Niger/Chad) 55 GH 3
Mangaia 47 E 4
Mangalore 36 B 5
Mangnai 34 B 3
Mangoky 59 G 4
Mangole, Pulau 39 G 4
Mangueira, Lagoa 76 F 5
Mangut 32 K 6
Manhan 32 F 6
Manhattan 67 G 4
Manicaland 59 E 3
Manicoré 73 F 5
Manicouagan 65 O 5
Maniganggo 34 C 4
Manihi 47 F 3
Manila 39 F 1
Manipur 37 F 3
Manisa 22 C 3
Manitoba 63 S 5
Manitoba, Lake 63 S 5
Manitowoc 67 J 3
Manitsoq 65 R 2
Manizales 72 C 2
Manjil 25 E 1
Mankato 67 H 3
Manlay 34 E 2
Manmad 36 BC 3
Mannheim 17 E 5
Manning 63 O 4
Manoa 72 E 5
Manono 56 D 6
Manouane 65 N 6
Manra 46 D 3
Manresa 20 D 3
Mansa 58 D 2
Mansel Island 65 L 3
Mansfield 67 K 3
Manta 72 B 4
Mantecal 72 E 2
Mantova 21 F 2
Manú 74 B 3
Manuae 47 E 4

Manuangi 47 F 4
Manuel Benavides 68 B 2
Manuel Urbano 72 E 5
Manukau 45 Q 8
Manus 44 E 2
Manychskaya Vpadina 23 F 1
Manyoni 56 E 6
Manzanillo (Cuba) 69 G 3
Manzanillo (Mexico) 68 B 4
Manzhouli 32 L 6
Manzil Bū Ruqaybah 51 GH 1
Manzurka 32 J 5
Mao 69 H 4
Maoke, Pegunungan 39 J 4
Maoming 34 F 6
Mapaga 39 EF 4
Mapai 59 F 4
Mapi 39 J 5
Maple Creek 63 Q 6
Mapuera 73 G 4
Maputo 59 F 4
Maquela do Zombo 58 B 1
Maquinchao 77 C 7
Mar del Plata 77 E 6
Maraã 72 E 4
Marabá 73 J 5
Maracaibo 72 D 1
Maracaibo, Lago de 72 D 1–2
Maracaju 75 F 5
Maracay 72 E 1
Marādah 51 J 3
Maradi 55 F 3
Marāgheh 30 D 3
Marahuaca, Cerro 72 E 3
Maramba 58 D 3
Marānd 30 D 3
Maranhão 75 GH 2
Marañón 72 C 4
Marão, Serra do 20 B 3
Marathon 64 K 6
Marawi (Philippines) 39 F 2
Marawi (Sudan) 52 E 5
Marbella 20 C 4
March 21 G 2
Marche 21 F 3
Marcus Baker, Mount 62 H 3
Mardin 23 F 3
Mardin Eşigi 23 F 3
Maré 45 J 6
Marēg 57 H 4
Marganets 23 D 1
Margaret River 42 A 5
Margarita, Isla de 73 F 1
Margaritovo 35 K 2
Margilan 31 J 2
Mari (Burma) 37 G 2
Mari (Papua New Guinea) 44 D 3
Maria (Tuamotu Is.) 47 F 4
Maria (Tubuai Is.) 47 E 4
Maria Theresa 47 E 5
Maria van Diemen, Cape 45 Q 7
Mariampole 19 H 5
Mariana Islands 46 A 1
Marianao 69 F 3

Mariato, Punta 72 B 2
Maribor 21 G 2
Maricourt 65 N 3
Marie Byrd Land 79
Mariehamn 19 H 3
Mariental 58 B 4
Mariestad 19 F 4
Marietta 67 K 5
Mariinsk 27 R 4
Mariinskoye 33 Q 5
Marília 75 G 5
Maringá 75 F 5
Marion (IN, U.S.A.) 67 J 3
Marion (OH, U.S.A.) 67 K 3
Marion Reef 43 J 2
Mariu 44 D 3
Mariupol 23 E 1
Mariyyah 25 F 5
Märjamaa 19 H 4
Marka 57 GH 4
Markha 33 M 3
Marko 18 G 2
Markovo 27 R 3
Marlin 67 G 5
Marmara 22 C 2
Marmara Denizi 22 C 2
Marmara, Sea of 22 C 2
Marmaris 22 C 3
Marne 20 D 2
Maroa 72 E 3
Maroni 73 H 3
Maroua 55 G 3
Marovoay 59 H 3
Marowijne 73 H 3
Marqādah 24 C 2
Marquesas Islands 47 F 3
Marquette 67 J 2
Marrakech 50 D 2
Marree 43 F 4
Marrero 67 H 6
Marrupa 59 F 2
Marsa al' Alam 24 B 4
Marsa 'Umm Ghayj 24 B 4
Marsabit National Reserve 57 F 4
Marsala 21 F 4
Marseille 21 E 3
Marsfjället 18 G 2
Marsh Harbour 69 G 2
Marshall Islands 46 BC 2
Marshalltown 67 H 3
Marta 21 F 3
Martaban, Gulf of 37 G 4
Martigues 21 DE 3
Martin Vaz Islands 71 H 5
Martinique 69 K 5
Marutea 47 F 4
Mary 31 G 3
Maryborough 43 J 4
Maryland 67 L 4
Marystown 65 R 6
Maryville 67 H 3
Masāhim, Küh-e 25 G 3
Masai Steppe 57 F 5
Masaka 56 E 5
Masākin 51 H 1
Masan 35 J 3
Masasi 59 F 2
Masaya 68 E 5
Masbate 39 F 1

159

Mascarene Islands 59 K 6
Maseru 58 D 5
Mashhad 30 F 3
Mashiz 25 G 3
Masindi 56 E 4
Maşirah 53 K 4
Maşirah, Khalīj 53 K 5
Masjed Soleymān 25 E 3
Maskanah 24 B 2
Masoala, Cap 59 J 3
Masohi 39 G 4
Mason City 67 H 3
Masqat 53 K 4
Massachusetts 67 M 3
Massafra 21 G 3
Massangena 59 E 4
Massau 45 E 2
Massava 27 M 3
Massawa 57 F 1
Masset 62 L 5
Massif Central 20 D 2–3
Massif du Pelvoux 21 E 3
Massif du Tsaratanana
    59 H 2
Massinga 59 F 4
Masteksay 30 E 1
Mastuj 31 J 3
Mastung 31 H 5
Mastürah 52 F 4
Masurai, Bukit 38 B 4
Masvingo 59 E 4
Maşyāf 24 B 2
Mata-Utu 46 D 3
Matabeleland 58 D 3–4
Matadi 56 A 6
Matagalpa 68 E 5
Matagami 65 M 6
Matagorda Island 67 G 6
Mataiva 47 F 3
Matam 54 B 2
Matamoros 68 C 2
Matara 36 D 6
Matarani 74 B 4
Mataranka 42 E 1
Matatiele 58 D 6
Matatila Dam 36 C 2
Matay 27 P 6
Matehuala 68 B 3
Matera 21 G 3
Mathura 36 C 2
Matla 36 E 3
Mato Grosso 74 E 3
Mato Grosso 74—75 EF 3
Mato Grosso do Sul
    74—75 EF 4
Matozinhos 20 B 3
Mátra 22 AB 1
Matrüh 52 D 2
Matsu 35 M 2
Matsudo 35 M 3
Matsue 35 K 3
Matsuyama 35 K 4
Matterhorn (Switzerland)
    21 E 2
Matterhorn (U.S.A.) 66 C 3
Matthew, Ile 45 K 6
Matu 38 D 3
Matua, Ostrov 33 S 6
Maturín 73 F 2
Matyushkinskaya 27 P 4

Maubeuge 20 D 1
Maués 73 G 4
Maui 47 E 1
Mauke 47 E 4
Maun 58 C 4
Mauna Kea 47 E 1
Maunoir, Lac 63 MN 2
Maupihaa 47 E 4
Mauralasan 38 E 3
Mauritania 50 CD 5
Mauritius 59 K 6
Mavasjaure 18 G 2
Mavuradonha Mountains
    59 E 3
Mawson 79
Mawson Coast 79
Maxcanu 68 DE 3
May Pen 69 G 4
Mayaguana Island 69 H 3
Mayagüez 69 J 4
Mayamey 25 G 1
Mayapán 68 E 3
Mayd 57 H 2
Maydän 25 D 2
Maykop 23 F 2
Maymakan 33 P 4
Mayna 32 F 5
Maynas 72 C 4
Mayo 62 K 3
Mayo, Mountains of 16 B 4
Mayor-Krest 33 Q 2
Mayotte 59 H 2
Maysk 27 P 4
Mayumba 55 G 6
Mayya 33 O 3
Mazabuka 58 D 3
Mazar 31 K 3
Mazar-i-Sharif 31 H 3
Mazatenango 68 D 5
Mazatlán 68 A 3
Mazomeno 56 D 5
Mazong Shan 34 C 2
Mazowsze 17 H 4
Mazury 17 H 4
Mbabane 59 E 5
Mbakaou Reservoir 55 G 4
Mbala 59 E 1
Mbale 56 E 1
Mbalmayo 55 G 5
Mbamba Bay 59 E 2
Mbandaka 56 B 4
Mbanga 55 F 5
M'banza Congo 58 A 1
Mbanza-Ngungu 56 B 6
Mbeya 56 E 6
Mbinda 55 G 6
Mbini 55 G 5
Mbokou 56 D 3
Mbour 54 A 3
Mbuji-Mayi 56 C 6
Mc Leod, Lake 42 A 3
Mc Murdo 79
Mc Murdo Sound 79
McAllen 66 G 6
McCammon 66 D 3
McComb 67 H 5
McCook 66 F 3
McKean 46 D 3
McKeesport 67 L 3
McKinley, Mount 62 G 3

M'Clintock Channel 63 R 1
M'Clure Strait 63 O 1
Meadow Lake 63 Q 5
Meaux 20 D 2
Mecca 53 FG 4
Mecklenburg 17 F 4
Mecklenburger Bucht 17 F 4
Medan 38 A 3
Medanosa, Punta 77 CD 8
Medellín 72 CD 2
Medelpad 18 G 3
Medford 66 B 3
Medgidia 22 C 2
Medi 56 E 3
Mediaş 22 B 1
Medicine Bow 66 E 3
Medicine Hat 63 P 5
Medigan 27 R 5
Medina 24 C 4
Mediterranean Sea
    15 HL 8–9
Mednogorsk 27 L 5
Medvezhiy Var 32 F 1
Medvezh'ya, Gora 33 P 6
Meekatharra 42 B 4
Meerut 36 C 2
Mega (Ethiopia) 57 F 4
Mega (Indonesia) 39 H 4
Megasani Hill 36 E 3
Meghalaya 37 F 2
Megra 26 H 2
Meguinenza, Embalse de
    20 CD 3
Mehriz 25 G 3
Mehtar Lam 31 J 4
Mei Xian 34 G 6
Meiganga 55 G 4
Meissen 17 F 4
Mejillones 74 B 5
Mékambo 55 G 5
Mekerrhane, Sebkha 51 F 3
Meknès 50 D 2
Mekong 37 J 5
Mekong, Mouths of the
    37 J 6
Mekongga, Gunung 39 F 4
Melaka 38 B 3
Melanesia 45 FJ 2–3
Melbourne (Australia)
    43 G 6
Melbourne (FL, U.S.A.)
    67 KL 6
Melchor Ocampo 68 B 4
Melendiz Daği 23 D 3
Meletsk 32 F 4
Meleuz 26 L 5
Melfort 63 Q 5
Melilla 50 E 1
Melimoyu, Monte
    77 B 7
Melitopol' 23 E 1
Melo 76 F 5
Melrhir, Chott 51 G 2
Melun 20 D 2
Melville 63 R 5
Melville Bay 78
Melville, Cape 43 G 1
Melville Hills 63 N 2
Melville Island (Australia)
    42 E 1

Melville Island (Canada)
    61 G 2
Melville Peninsula 63 V 2
Melyuveyem 33 W 3
Memmingen 17 EF 5
Memphis (Egypt) 52 E 3
Memphis (TN, U.S.A.)
    67 J 4
Mena (U.S.S.R.) 26 F 5
Ménaka 54 E 2
Mendocino, Cape 66 B 3
Mendoza (Argentina) 76 C 5
Mendoza (Peru) 72 C 5
Mengcheng 35 G 4
Mengene Daği 23 F 3
Menghai 34 D 6
Mengzi 34 D 6
Menihek Lakes 65 O 5
Meningie 43 F 6
Menkere 32 M 2
Menominee 67 J 2
Menongue 58 B 2
Menorca 20 D 3
Mentawai, Kepulauan
    38 A 4
Mentawai, Selat 38 A 4
Mentese 22 C 3
Menyuan 34 D 3
Menza 32 J 6
Menzies 42 C 4
Menzies, Mount 79
Mepistskaro 23 F 2
Meppen 17 E 4
Meråker 18 F 3
Merano 21 F 2
Merced 66 B 4
Mercedes (Argentina)
    76 C 5
Mercedes (Argentina)
    76 E 4
Mercedes (Uruguay) 76 E 5
Merchants Bay 65 P 2
Merefa 26 G 6
Merenga 33 T 3
Mergui 37 G 5
Mergui Archipelago 37 G 5
Meriç 22 C 2
Mérida (Mexico) 68 E 3
Mérida (Spain) 20 B 4
Mérida (Venezuela) 72 D 2
Meridian 67 J 5
Mérignac 20 C 3
Merikarvia 18 H 3
Merín, Laguna 76 F 5
Merredin 42 B 5
Merritt Island 67 KL 6
Merseburg 17 F 4
Meru Game Reserve 57 F 4
Merzifon 23 E 2
Mesabi Range 67 H 2
Mesopotamia
    24—25 CD 2–3
Messina 21 FG 4
Messina, Stretto di 21 G 4
Messiniakós Kólpos 22 B 3
Messo 27 P 2
Mesters Vig 78
Meta 72 DE 2
Meta Incognita Peninsula
    65 O 3

Metairie 67 H 5−6
Metán 76 D 4
Metangula 59 EF 2
Metemma 56 F 2
Metlakatla 62 L 4
Metu 56 F 3
Metz 21 E 2
Meuse 21 E 2
Mexicali 66 CD 5
Mexican Hat 66 E 4
Mexico 68 C 3
México City 68 BC 4
Mexico, Gulf of 68 DE 2
Meymeh (Iran) 25 E 2
Meymeh (Iran) 25 F 2
Mezen´ 26 HJ 2
Mezen´ 26 HJ 2
Mezhdurechenskiy 27 N 4
Miami 67 K 6
Miami Beach 67 L 6
Miändowäb 25 D 1
Mïäneh 25 E 1
Mianwali 31 J 4
Mianyang 34 D 4
Miarinarivo 59 H 3
Miass 27 LM 5
Michigan 67 JK 2−3
Michoacán 68 B 4
Michurinsk 26 G 5
Micronesia 46 BC 2−3
Middelburg (South Africa) 58 D 5
Middelburg (South Africa) 58 D 6
Middle Andaman 37 F 5
Midland (MI, U.S.A.) 67 K 3
Midland (TX, U.S.A.) 66 F 5
Midžor 22 B 2
Miekojärvi 18 HJ 2
Mielec 17 H 4
Mieres 20 B 3
Migiurtinia 57 HJ 2
Mijdaḥah 53 H 6
Mikha Tskhakaya 23 F 2
Mikhaylovgrad 22 B 2
Mikhaylovka 26 H 5
Mikínai 22 B 3
Mikindani 59 FG 2
Mikino 33 U 3
Mikkeli 18 J 3
Mîkonos 22 C 3
Milagro 72 C 4
Milan 21 EF 2
Milando Reserve 58 B 1
Milange 59 F 3
Milano 21 E 2
Milâs 22 C 3
Milazzo 21 FG 4
Milcan Tepe 23 E 3
Mildura 43 G 5
Mile 34 D 6
Miles 43 HJ 4
Miles City 66 E 2
Milford Haven 16 B 4
Milgun 42 B 4
Mili 46 C 2
Milk 66 E 2
Millau 20 D 3
Mîlos 22 B 3
Milparinka 43 G 4

Milwaukee 67 J 3
Min Xian 34 D 4
Mina 32 F 5
Mïnä´ ´Abd Alläh 25 E 3
Mïnä´ Sa´üd 25 E 3
Minahassa Peninsula 39 F 3
Minas 76 EF 5
Minas Gerais 75 GH 4
Minas Novas 75 H 4
Minatitlán 68 D 4
Minbya 37 F 3
Mincha 76 B 5
Mindanao 39 FG 2
Mindelo 54 B 6
Mindoro 39 F 1
Mindoro Strait 39 F 1
Mineiros 75 F 4
Mineral´nyye Vody 23 F 2
Minerva Reefs 46 D 4
Minfeng 31 L 3
Mingary 43 G 5
Mingechaur 30 D 2
Mingshui 35 J 1
Mingteke 31 K 3
Minho 20 B 3
Ministro João Alberto 75 F 3
Minna 55 F 4
Minneapolis (KS, U.S.A.) 66 G 4
Minneapolis (MN, U.S.A.) 67 H 3
Minnesota 67 GH 2
Minot 66 F 2
Minqin 34 D 3
Minqing 35 G 5
Minsin 37 G 2
Minsk 19 J 5
Minto 46 B 2
Minusinsk 32 F 5
Miquelon 65 M 6
Mirabad 31 G 4
Miramichi Bay 65 P 6
Miranda 74 E 5
Miranda de Ebro 20 C 3
Miravalles, Volcán 68 F 5
Miri 38 D 3
Miriam Vale 43 J 3
Mirim, Lagoa 76 F 5
Mirnyy 32 K 3
Mirnyy 79
Mirpur Khas 31 H 5
Mirtóon Pélagos 22 B 3
Mirzapur 36 D 2
Mishan 35 K 1
Miskolc 22 B 1
Misool, Pulau 39 H 4
Mişr 52 DE 4
Mişrätah 51 HJ 2
Mişrätah, Ra´s 51 J 2
Mississippi 67 H 5
Mississippi 67 HJ 5
Mississippi Delta 67 J 6
Missoula 66 D 2
Missouri 67 H 4
Missouri 67 H 4
Mistassini, Lac 65 N 5
Misti, Volcán 74 B 4
Misty Fjords National Monument 62 L 4

Mitchell 66 G 3
Mitchell River 43 G 2
Mitilíni 22 C 3
Mitra 55 F 5
Mittellandkanal 17 E 4
Mitú 72 D 3
Mitumba, Monts 56 D 5−6
Miyako 35 M 3
Miyako-rettö 35 H 6
Miyakonojö 35 K 4
Miyaly 30 E 1
Mizdah 51 H 2
Mizen Head 16 AB 4
Mizoram 37 F 3
Mizuho 79
Mizusawa 35 M 3
Mjölby 19 G 4
Mjösa 19 F 3
Mkata 57 F 6
Mkomazi 57 F 5
Mkomazi Game Reserve 57 F 5
Mkushi 58 D 2
Mladá Boleslav 17 F 4
Mljet 21 G 3
Mo i Rana 18 F 2
Moab 66 E 4
Moamba 59 E 5
Moba 56 D 6
Mobaye 56 C 4
Mobile 67 J 5
Mobridge 66 F 2
Moçambique 59 G 3
Mochudi 58 D 4
Mocímboa da Praia 59 G 2
Môco, Morro de 58 AB 2
Moctezuma (Mexico) 66 E 6
Moctezuma (Mexico) 68 B 3
Mocuba 59 F 3
Modena (Italy) 21 F 3
Modena (U.S.A.) 66 D 4
Mogadishu 57 H 4
Mogadouro, Serra do 20 B 3
Mogaung 37 G 2
Mogdy 33 O 5
Mogilev Yn JK 5
Mogilev Podol´skiy 22 C 1
Mogogh 56 E 3
Mogoyn 32 G 6
Mogoytui 32 KL 5
Moguqi 33 M 6
Mohe 33 M 5
Mohican, Cape 62 D 3
Mohon Peak 66 D 5
Mohoro 57 F 6
Mointy 27 O 6
Mojave Desert 66 C 4
Mojiang 34 D 6
Mokp´o 35 J 4
Mokra Gora 22 B 2
Moldaviya 22 C 1
Molde 18 E 3
Moldefjorden 18 E 3
Mole Game Reserve 54 D 4
Molepolole 58 D 4
Mollendo 74 B 4
Molodechno 19 J 5
Molodezhnaya 79
Molokai 47 E 1

Molopo 58 C 5
Moluccas 39 G 4
Mombasa 57 FG 5
Mombetsu 35 M 2
Momboyo 56 B 5
Momskiy Khrebet 33 QR 1−2
Mona, Canal de la 69 J 4
Monaco 21 E 3
Monaghan 16 B 4
Monapo 59 G 2
Monarch Mountain 63 M 5
Monastery of Saint Catherine 24 AB 3
Monchegorsk 18 K 2
Mönchen-Gladbach 16 E 4
Monclova 68 B 2
Moncton 65 O 6
Mondo 55 H 3
Mondragone 21 F 3
Monfalcone 21 F 2
Mong Hpayak 37 G 3
Monga 56 C 4
Monghyr 36 E 2
Mongolia 32 GH 6
Mongolo 32 J 2
Mongu 58 C 3
Mönhhaan 34 F 1
Monkira 43 G 3
Monou 55 J 2
Monreal del Campo 20 C 3
Monroe (LA, U.S.A.) 67 H 5
Monroe (MI, U.S.A.) 67 K 3
Monrovia 54 B 4
Mons 16 D 4
Mont Afao 51 G 3
Mont Blanc 21 E 2
Mont Cameroon 55 F 5
Mont-de-Marsan 20 C 3
Mont Kavendou 54 B 3
Mont Lozére 20 D 3
Mont Panié 45 H 6
Mont Pelat 21 E 3
Mont Tahat 51 G 4
Mont Tembo 55 G 5
Mont Ventoux 21 E 3
Montague 62 H 4
Montana 66 DE 2
Montauban 20 D 3
Montbeliard 21 E 2
Montceau-les-Mines 20 D 2
Monte Alegre 73 H 4
Monte Binga 59 E 3
Monte Carlo 21 E 3
Monte Cinto 21 E 3
Monte Claros 75 H 4
Monte Cristo 74 D 3
Monte d´Oro 21 E 3
Monte Melimoyo 77 B 7
Monte Negro Falls 58 A 3
Monte Quemado 76 D 4
Montecristi 69 H 4
Montecristo 21 F 3
Montego Bay 69 G 4
Montejinnie 42 E 2
Montepuez 59 F 2
Monterado 38 C 3
Monterey 66 B 4
Montería 72 C 2
Montero 74 D 4

Monterrey **68** BC 2
Montes Altos **73** J 5
Montes de Toledo **20** C 4
Montes Universales **20** C 3
Montesilvano **21** F 3
Montevideo **76** EF 5–6
Montgomery **67** J 5
Monti di Ala **21** E 3
Montluçon **20** D 2
Montpelier **67** M 3
Montpéllier **20** D 3
Montréal **65** N 6
Montreux **21** E 2
Montrose **66** E 4
Monts d'Aubrac **20** D 3
Monts Mitumba **56** D 5–6
Monts Nimba **54** C 4
Monts Notre-Dame **65** O 6
Monts Otish **65** N 5
Monts Tamgak **55** F 2
Monts Timétrine **54** D 2
Montserrat **69** K 4
Monza **21** E 2
Moonie **43** J 4
Mooraberree **43** G 4
Moore, Lake **42** B 4
Moorhead **67** G 2
Moorlands **43** F 6
Moose **65** L 5
Moose Jaw **63** Q 5
Moosonee **65** L 5
Mopti **54** D 3
Moquegua **74** B 4
Mora **19** F 3
Moradabad **36** C 2
Moramanga **59** H 3
Morane **47** F 4
Moratuwa **36** C 6
Morava (Czechoslovakia) **17** G 5
Morava (Western Australia) **42** B 4
Morava (Yugoslavia) **22** B 2
Morawhanna **73** G 2
Moray Firth **16** C 3
More Laptevykh **32** MN 1
Möre og Romsdal **18** E 3
Moree **43** H 4
Morelia **68** B 4
Morena, Sierra **20** BC 4
Morenci **66** E 5
Moreno **72** C 5
Moresby **62** L 5
Mori **34** B 2
Morioka **35** M 3
Mornington Island **43** F 2
Moro Gulf **39** F 2
Morobe **44** E 3
Morocco **50** D 2
Morogoro **57** F 6
Morombe **59** G 4
Mörön **32** H 6
Morón (Cuba) **69** G 3
Morón (Spain) **20** B 4
Morón (Venezuela) **72** E 1
Morondava **59** G 4
Moroni **59** G 2
Moroshechnoye **33** T 4
Morotai, Pulau **39** G 3
Morozovsk **23** F 1

Morro de Môco **58** AB 2
Mors **19** E 4
Morshansk **26** H 5
Mörsil **18** F 3
Morskaya **33** X 3
Mortlock Islands **46** B 2
Moruroa **47** F 4
Morven **43** H 4
Morwell **43** H 6
Moscow **26** G 4
Mosel **17** E 4
Moselle **21** E 2
Moshi **57** F 5
Mosjöen **18** F 2
Moskal'vo **33** Q 5
Moskenesöya **18** F 2
Moskva **26** G 4
Mosquera **72** C 3
Mosquitos, Golfo de los **72** B 2
Moss **19** F 4
Mosselbaai **58** C 6
Mossendjo **55** G 6
Mossoró **75** J 2
Mostaganem **50** EF 1
Mostar **21** G 3
Motala **19** G 4
Motihari **36** DE 2
Motril **20** C 4
Motykleyka **33** R 4
Moudjéria **50** C 5
Moul **55** G 2
Moulins **20** D 2
Moulmein **37** G 4
Moundou **55** H 4
Mount Adam **77** DE 9
Mount Augustus **42** B 3
Mount Balbi **45** F 3
Mount Bangeta **44** E 3
Mount Blackburn **62** J 3
Mount Bona **62** J 3
Mount Brassey **42** E 3
Mount Bruce **42** B 3
Mount Brukkaros **58** B 5
Mount Carter **43** G 1
Mount Cleveland **66** D 2
Mount Columbia **63** O 5
Mount Cook **45** Q 9
Mount Cushing **63** M 4
Mount Dalrymple **43** H 3
Mount Deering **42** D 3
Mount Demavend **25** F 2
Mount Douglas **43** H 3
Mount Egmont **45** Q 8
Mount Elbert **66** E 4
Mount Elgon **56** E 4
Mount Elliot **43** H 2
Mount Essendon **42** C 3
Mount Everest **36** E 2
Mount Feathertop **43** H 6
Mount Finke **42** E 5
Mount Forel **78**
Mount Gambier **43** FG 6
Mount Godwin Austin **31** K 3
Mount Hale **42** B 4
Mount Hermon (Lebanon) **24** B 2

Mount Hood **66** B 2
Mount Hutton **43** H 4
Mount Isa **43** F 3
Mount Isto **62** J 2
Mount Jackson (Antarctica) **79**
Mount Jackson (Australia) **42** B 5
Mount Jefferson **66** C 4
Mount Kenya **57** F 5
Mount Kimball **62** J 3
Mount Kirkpatrick **79**
Mount Kosciusko **43** H 6
Mount Livermore **66** F 5
Mount Logan **62** J 3
Mount Magnet **42** B 4
Mount Marcus Baker **62** H 3
Mount McKinley **62** G 3
Mount Menzies **79**
Mount Morgan **43** J 3
Mount Mowbullan **43** J 4
Mount Nurri **43** H 5
Mount Nyiru **57** F 4
Mount Oglethorpe **67** K 5
Mount Olympus **66** B 2
Mount Omatako **58** B 4
Mount Ord **42** D 2
Mount Ossa **44** L 9
Mount Pulog **39** J 1
Mount Queen Bess **63** N 5
Mount Rainier **66** B 2
Mount Ratz **62** L 4
Mount Robson **63** NO 5
Mount Roosevelt **64** M 4
Mount Shasta **66** B 3
Mount Shenton **42** C 4
Mount Sir James MacBrian **62** M 3
Mount Sunflower **66** F 4
Mount Tama **58** A 2
Mount Taylor **66** E 4
Mount Travers **45** Q 9
Mount Victoria (Burma) **37** F 3
Mount Victoria (Papua New Guinea) **44** E 3
Mount Vsevidof **62** D 5
Mount Waddington **63** M 5
Mount Whitney **66** C 4
Mount Wilhelm **44** D 3
Mount Wilson **66** E 4
Mount Wrightson **66** D 5
Mountains of Mayo **16** B 4
Moura **73** F 4
Moussoro **55** H 3
Mouths of the Amazon **73** J 3
Mouths of the Danube **22** CD 1
Mouths of the Indus **36** A 3
Mouths of the Irrawaddy **37** FG 4
Mouths of the Mekong **37** J 6
Mouths of the Orinoco **73** FG 2
Movas **66** E 6
Mowbullan, Mount **43** J 4
Moxico **58** BC 2
Moxos, Llanos de **74** CD 4

Moyale **57** F 4
Moyobamba **72** C 5
Mozambique **59** EF 3
Mozambique Channel **59** FG 3–4
Mozdok **23** FG 2
Mozharka **32** F 5
Mozyr' **19** J 5
Mpanda **56** E 6
Mpika **59** E 2
Msata **57** F 6
Mtsensk **26** G 5
Mtwara **59** G 2
Mu Us Shamo **34** E 3
Muang Nan **37** H 4
Muang Ngao **37** G 4
Muang Phrae **37** H 4
Muar **38** B 3
Muara Teweh **38** D 4
Muaraaman **38** B 4
Mubarak **25** G 4
Mubi **55** G 3
Muchinga Escarpment **59** E 2
Mucojo **59** G 2
Mudanjiang **35** JK 2
Muddy Gap **66** E 3
Mufulira **58** D 2
Muganskaya Step' **30** D 3
Muhagiriya **52** D 6
Muḥammad Qawl **52** F 4
Mühlhausen **17** F 4
Mühlig-Hofmann Mountains **79**
Muhulu **56** D 5
Mui Bai Bung **37** H 6
Muite **59** F 2
Mukachevo **22** B 1
Mukur (Afghanistan) **31** H 4
Mukur (Kazakhstan) **30** E 1
Mulan **35** J 1
Mulanje **59** F 3
Mulata **57** G 3
Mulchén **77** B 6
Mulegé **66** D 6
Mulgrave Island **44** D 4
Mulhacén **20** C 4
Mulhouse **21** E 2
Mull **16** B 3
Mullaittivu **36** D 6
Mullaley **43** HJ 5
Muller, Pegunungan **38** D 3
Mullet Peninsula **16** A 4
Mullewa **42** B 4
Mulligan River **43** F 4
Mulobezi **58** D 3
Multanovy **27** O 3
Mulu, Gunung **38** DE 3
Mulym'ya **27** M 3
Mumra **30** D 1
München **17** F 5
Muncie **67** JK 3
Mundar **33** R 2
Munday **66** G 5
Münden **17** E 4
Munhango **58** B 2
Munich **17** F 5
Munkhafaḍ al Qaṭṭārah **52** D 3

Munku-Sardyk, Gora
  32 GH 5
Munster 16 B 4
Münster 17 E 4
Muntii Rodnei 22 B 1
Munugudzhak 33 U 3
Munzur Silsilesi 23 E 3
Muojärvi 18 J 2
Muong Hiem 37 H 3
Muong Khoua 37 H 3
Muong Lam 37 HJ 4
Muong Sing 37 H 3
Muonio 18 H 2
Mupa National Park 58 B 3
Muqdisho 57 H 4
Mura 21 G 2
Murallón, Cerro 77 B 8
Murana 39 H 4
Murang'a 57 F 5
Murashi 26 J 4
Murat 23 F 3
Murchison River 42 AB 4
Murcia 20 C 4
Murdo 66 F 3
Mureş 22 B 1
Muriaé 75 H 5
Murilo 46 B 2
Murjek 18 H 2
Murmansk 18 K 2
Murmashi 18 K 2
Murom 26 H 4
Muromtsevo 27 P 4
Muroran 35 M 2
Murray Bridge 43 F 6
Murray River 43 G 5
Murrumbidgee River 43 H 5
Murukta 32 H 2
Murwara 36 D 3
Muş 23 F 3
Musala 22 B 2
Musan 35 J 2
Musandam Peninsula
  25 G 4
Muscat 53 K 4
Musgrave 43 G 1
Musgrave Ranges 42 E 4
Mushäsh al 'Ashawri 25 E 4
Müsiän 25 E 2
Muskegon 67 J 3
Muskogee 67 GH 4
Mussende 58 B 2
Mustafa 33 P 3
Müţ 52 D 3
Mutanda 58 D 2
Mutarara 59 F 3
Mutare 59 F 3
Mutoray 32 H 3
Mutshatsha 58 C 2
Muynak 30 F 2
Muzaffarnagar 36 C 2
Muzaffarpur 36 DE 2
Muzhi 27 M 2
Muztag 31 L 3
Muztagata 31 K 3
Mvomero 57 F 6
Mwali 59 G 2
Mwanza 56 E 5
Mweka 56 C 5
Mwinilunga 58 C 2
My Tho 37 J 5

Myakit 33 S 3
Myanmar 37 FG 3
Myaundzha 33 R 3
Mycenae 22 B 3
Myingyan 37 G 3
Myitkyina 37 G 2
Myitta 37 G 5
Myittha 37 G 3
Mymensingh 37 F 3
Mýrdalsjökull 18 B 3
Myrtle Beach 67 L 5
Mys Aniva 33 Q 6
Mys Buorkhaya 33 O 1
Mys Duga-Zapadnaya
  33 R 4
Mys Kanin Nos 26 H 2
Mys Kril'on 33 Q 6
Mys Kronotskiy 33 U 4−5
Mys Kurgalski 19 J 4
Mys Lopatka 33 T 5
Mys Olyutorskiy 33 VW 4
Mys Peschanyy 30 E 2
Mys Pitsunda 23 EF 2
Mys Sarych 23 D 2
Mys Shipunskiy 33 TU 5
Mys Svatoy Nos 33 P 1
Mys Svyatoy Nos 26 GH 2
Mys Taran 19 GH 4−5
Mys Tarkhankut 23 D 1
Mys Taygonos 33 U 3
Mys Terpeniya 33 QR 6
Mys Tolstoy 33 T 4
Mys Uengan 27 N 1
Mys Yelizavety 33 Q 5
Mys Yuzhnyy 33 T 4
Mysore 36 C 5
Mysovaya 33 T 2

N

Na Baek 37 H 4
Naandi 56 D 3
Naantali 19 H 3
Naba 37 G 3
Naberezhnyye Chelny
  26 K 4
Nabī Shu'ayb, Jabal an
  53 G 5
Nabk al Gharbi 24 B 3
Näbul 51 H 1
Näbulus [West Bank] 24 B 2
Nachana 36 B 2
Nådendal 19 H 3
Nadiad 36 B 3
Nador 50 E 1
Nadym 27 O 2
Naftshahr 25 D 2
Nafuce 55 F 3
Nafūd al 'Urayq 24 D 4
Nafūd as Sirr 24−25 D 4
Nafūd as Surrah 53 G 4
Naga 39 F 1
Naga Hills 37 FG 2
Nagaland 37 F 2
Nagano 35 L 3
Nagaoka 35 L 3
Nagasaki 35 J 4
Nagaur 36 B 2

Nagda 36 C 3
Nagercoil 36 C 6
Nago 35 J 5
Nagornyy 33 N 4
Nagoya 35 L 3
Nagpur 36 C 3
Nagqu 34 B 4
Nagykanizsa 22 A 1
Naha 35 J 5
Nahanni National Park
  63 M 3
Nahariyya 24 B 2
Nahävand 25 E 2
Nahr an Nil 24 A 4
Nä'in 25 F 2
Nain 65 P 4
Nairobi 57 F 5
Najafäbäd 25 F 2
Najd 24 CD 4
Najin 35 K 2
Najrän 53 G 5
Nakhichevan' 30 CD 3
Nakhodka 35 K 2
Nakhon Pathom 37 G 5
Nakhon Ratchasima 37 H 5
Nakhon Sawan 37 GH 4
Nakhon Si Thammarat
  37 G 6
Nakina 64 K 5
Nakuru 57 F 5
Nalayh 32 J 6
Nal'chik 23 F 2
Nälüt 51 H 2
Nam Can 37 J 6
Nam Dinh 37 J 3
Namaland 58 B 5
Namanga 57 F 5
Namangan 31 J 2
Namapa 59 G 2
Namaqualand 58 B 5
Namatanai 45 F 2
Nambour 43 J 4
Nametil 59 F 3
Namib Desert 58 AB 3−5
Namib Desert Park 58 AB 4
Namibe 58 A 3
Namibe Reserve 58 A 3
Namibia 58 B 4
Namjagbarwa Feng 34 C 5
Namkham 37 G 3
Namlea 39 G 4
Namling 36 E 2
Namoi River 43 H 5
Namoluk 46 B 2
Namonuito 46 A 2
Namorik 46 C 2
Nampala 54 C 2
Nampula 59 F 3
Namru 36 D 1
Namsang 37 G 3
Namsen 18 F 2−3
Namsos 18 F 3
Namtsy 33 N 3
Namu 46 C 2
Namuli 59 F 3
Namy 33 O 2
Nan Ling 34 EF 5
Nancha 33 N 6
Nanchang 34 G 5
Nanchong 34 E 4

Nancy 21 E 2
Nanda Devi 36 D 1
Nander 36 C 4
Nandyal 36 C 4
Nanfeng 34 G 5
Nang Xian 34 B 5
Nanga Parbat 31 J 3
Nangatayap 38 D 4
Nangong 34 G 3
Nanguneri 36 C 6
Nanjiang 34 E 4
Nanjing 35 G 4
Nanning 34 E 6
Nanping (Fujian, China)
  35 G 5
Nanping (Gansu, China)
  34 D 4
Nansei-shotö 35 J 5
Nantes 20 C 2
Nanton 63 P 5
Nantong 35 H 4
Nanumanga 46 C 3
Nanumea 46 C 3
Nanuque 75 HJ 4
Nanyang 34 F 4
Nanyuki 57 F 4
Nanzhang 34 F 4
Nao, Cabo de la 20 D 4
Naococane, Lac 65 N 5
Napata 52 E 5
Napier 45 R 8
Napier Mountains 79
Naples 21 F 3
Napo 72 D 4
Napoli 21 F 3
Nara (Japan) 35 L 4
Nara (Mali) 54 C 2
Naranjos 68 C 3
Narasun 32 K 5
Narathiwat 37 H 6
Narayanganj 37 F 3
Narbonne 20 D 3
Nares Strait 78
Narew 17 H 4
Narmada 36 B 3
Narodnaya, Gora 27 LM 2
Narrabri 43 HJ 5
Narrogin 42 B 5
Narsarsuaq 65 S 3
Narsimhapur 36 C 3
Narva 19 J 4
Narvik 18 G 2
Narwietooma 42 E 3
Naryn 32 G 5
Näsåker 18 G 3
Nashville 67 J 4
Näsijärvi 18 H 3
Nasik 36 B 3
Näşir 56 E 3
Nassau 69 G 2
Nasser, Birkat 24 A 5
Nässjö 19 F 4
Næstved 19 F 4
Nata 58 D 4
Natal (Brazil) 75 JK 2
Natal (South Africa)
  58−59 E 5
Natashquan 65 P 5
Natchez 67 H 5
Natitingou 54 E 3

Natividade **75** G 3
Natkyizin **37** G 5
Natron, Lake **57** F 5
Natuna, Kepulauan **38** C 3
Naturaliste, Cape **42** A 5
Naupe **72** C 5
Nauru **45** J 2
Naushki **32** J 5
Nauta **72** D 4
Navarino **77** C 10
Navarra **20** C 3
Navia **20** B 3
Navojoa **66** E 6
Navolok **26** G 3
Nawabshah **31** H 5
Náxos **22** C 3
Näy Band **25** F 4
Näy Band, Ra´s-e **25** F 4
Nayarit **68** B 3
Nazaré **20** B 4
Nazareth **72** C 5
Nazca **74** B 3
Naze **35** J 5
Nazerat **24** B 2
Nazilli **22** C 3
Ndali **54** E 4
Ndélé **56** C 3
Ndendé **55** G 6
N´Djamena **55** H 3
Ndogo, Lagune **55** G 6
Ndola **58** D 2
Néapolis **22** B 3
Near Islands **62** A 5
Nebit-Dag **30** E 3
Nebolchi **26** F 4
Nebraska **66** FG 3
Nechako Reservoir **63** M 5
Necochea **77** E 6
Nédéley **55** H 2
Nedong **37** F 2
Neftelensk **32** J 4
Nefteyugansk **27** O 3
Negage **58** B 1
Negelli **57** F 3
Negombo **36** C 6
Negra, Punta **72** B 5
Negrais, Cape **37** F 4
Negritos **72** B 4
Negro, Río () **73** F 4
Negros **39** F 2
Nehávend **25** E 2
Nehbandan **30** FG 4
Nehe **33** MN 6
Nei Monggol Zizhiqu
  34 DG 2
Neijiang **34** E 5
Neiva **72** CD 3
Nejd **24** CD 5
Nekemt **57** F 3
Nelemnoye **33** S 2
Nel´kan **33** P 4
Nelkuchan, Gora **33** P 3
Nellore **36** CD 5
Nel´ma **33** P 6
Nelson (Man., Can.) **63** S 5
Nelson (New Zealand)
  45 Q 9
Nelson Island **62** D 3
Nelspruit **59** E 5
Néma **50** D 5

Neman **19** HJ 5
Nemunas **19** H 4
Nemuro **35** N 2
Nendo **45** J 4
Nengonengo **47** F 4
Nenjiang **33** N 6
Nepa **32** J 4
Nepal **36** D 2
Nepeña **72** C 5
Nerchinsk **32** L 5
Nerekhta **26** H 4
Neringa-Nida **19** H 4
Neriquinha **58** C 3
Nesbyen **19** E 3
Néstos **22** B 2
Netanya **24** B 2
Netherlands **16** DE 4
Netherlands Antilles **69** K 4
Nettilling Lake **65** N 2
Nettuno **21** F 3
Neuchâtel **21** E 2
Neuquén **77** C 6
Nevada **66** C 4
Nevada, Sierra **20** C 4
Nevado Ausangate **74** B 3
Nevado Cololo **74** C 4
Nevado Coropuna **74** B 4
Nevado de Cachi **74** C 5
Nevado de Colima **68** B 4
Nevado Huascarán **72** C 5
Nevado Illimani **74** C 4
Nevado Sajama **74** C 4
Nevado Salluyo **74** C 3
Nevado Yerupajá **74** A 3
Never **33** M 5
Nevers **20** D 2
Nevinnomyssk **23** F 2
Nevşehir **23** D 3
Nev´yansk **27** M 4
New Albany **67** J 4
New Amsterdam **73** G 2
New Bedford **67** M 3
New Bern **67** L 4
New Britain **45** F 3
New Brunswick **65** O 6
New Caledonia **45** H 6
New England **67** MN 3
New Georgia **45** G 3
New Glasgow **65** P 6
New Hampshire **67** M 3
New Hanover **45** F 2
New Hebrides **45** J 5
New Iberia **67** H 6
New Ireland **45** F 2
New Jersey **67** LM 4
New Liskeard **65** LM 6
New Meadows **66** C 2
New Mexico **66** E 5
New Orleans **67** J 5–6
New Plymouth **45** Q 8
New Providence Island
  69 G 3
New Siberian Islands
  78
New South Wales **43** GH 5
New Stuvahok **62** F 4
New York (N.Y., U.S.A.)
  67 M 3
New York (U.S.A.) **67** L 3
New Zealand **45** R 9

Newark (N.J., U.S.A.)
  67 M 3
Newark (OH, U.S.A.) **67** K 3
Newburgh **67** M 3
Newcastle (N.S.W., Austr.)
  43 J 5
Newcastle (WY, U.S.A.)
  66 F 3
Newcastle Waters **42** E 2
Newcastle-upon-Tyne
  16 C 3
Newenham, Cape **62** E 4
Newfoundland **65** Q 5
Newfoundland **65** QR 6
Newman **42** B 3
Newport (OR, U.S.A.)
  66 B 3
Newport (U.K.) **16** C 4
Newport Beach **66** C 5
Newry **42** D 2
Newtonabbey **16** B 4
Neya **26** H 4
Neyriz **25** G 3
Neyshabür **30** F 3
Nezhin **26** F 5
Ngamiland **58** C 3
Ngamring **36** E 2
Ngangla Ringco **36** D 1
Nganglong Kangri **36** D 1
Ngatik **46** B 2
Ngdinga **56** B 6
Ngoc Linh **37** J 4
Ngoko **55** H 5
Ngoring **34** C 3
Nguara **55** H 3
Nha Trang **37** J 5
Nhambiquara **74** E 3
Nia-Nia **56** D 4
Niagara Falls **67** L 3
Niamey **54** E 3
Niangara **56** D 4
Nianzishan **33** M 6
Nias, Pulau **38** A 3
Niassa **59** F 2
Nicaragua **68** EF 5
Nicaragua, Lago de **68** E 5
Nice **21** E 3
Nichalakh **33** QR 1
Nicobar Islands **37** F 6
Nicocli **72** C 2
Nicosia **23** D 3
Nicuadala **59** F 3
Nidelva **19** E 4
Niedere Tauern **21** F 2
Niedersachsen **17** E 4
Niellé **54** C 3
Niemba **56** D 6
Nieuw Amsterdam **73** H 2
Nieuw Nickerie **73** G 2
Nieuwoudtville **58** B 6
Niğde **23** D 3
Niger **55** FG 2
Niger **55** F 4
Niger Delta **55** F 5
Nigeria **55** FG 4
Nihau **47** E 1
Nihiru **47** F 4
Niigata **35** L 3
Nijmegen **16** E 4
Nikel´ **18** K 2

Nikki **54** E 4
Nikolayev **22** D 1
Nikolayevka **27** N 5
Nikolayevo **19** J 4
Nikolayevsk-na-Amure
  33 Q 5
Nikol´sk **26** J 4
Nikol´skiy **31** H 1
Nikopol **23** D 1
Nikpey **25** E 1
Nikšic **22** A 2
Nikumaroro **46** D 3
Nile (Egypt) **24** A 4
Nimba, Monts **54** C 4
Nimbe **55** F 5
Nimes **20** D 3
Nimule **56** E 4
Nincheng **35** G 2
Ningbo **35** H 5
Ningde **35** G 5
Ningdu **34** G 5
Ningxia Huizu Zizhiqu **34** E 3
Ninigo Group **46** A 3
Niokolo Koba, Parc National
  du **54** B 3
Nioro du Sahel **54** C 2
Niort **20** C 2
Niout **50** D 5
Nipigon **64** K 6
Nipigon, Lake **64** K 6
Nipissing, Lake **65** LM 6
Niš **22** B 2
Nisäb **53** H 6
Niterói **75** H 5
Nitiya **33** P 4
Nitra **17** G 5
Niuafo´ou **46** D 4
Niuato Putapu **46** D 4
Niue **46** D 4
Niulakita **46** C 3
Niutao **46** C 3
Nizamabad **36** C 4
Nizhne-Ozernaya **33** U 4
Nizhneangarsk **32** J 4
Nizhneudinsk **32** G 5
Nizhnevartovskoye **27** P 3
Nizhneye Karelina **32** J 4
Nizhniy Novgorod **26** H 4
Nizhniy Pyandzh **31** H 3
Nizhniy Tagil **27** M 4
Nizhnyaya Omka **27** O 4
Nizhnyaya Poyma **32** G 4
Nizhnyaya Tunguska **32** F 3
Nizhnyaya Voch´ **26** K 3
Nizina Podlaska **17** H 4
Nizip **24** B 1
Njazidja **59** G 2
Njunes **18** G 2
Njutånger **18** G 3
Nkayi **55** G 6
Nkhata Bay **59** E 2
Nkolabona **55** G 5
Nkomi, Lagune **55** F 6
Nkongsamba **55** G 5
Nkurenkuru **58** B 3
Noatak National Preserve
  62 F 2
Noefs, Ile des **57** J 6

Nogales **66** D 5
Nogayskiye Step' **23** G 2
Noginsk **26** G 4
Noirmoutier **20** C 2
Nokrek Peak **37** F 1
Nomad **44** D 3
Nome **62** D 3
Nonacho Lake **63** Q 3
Nong Khai **37** H 4
Nonouti **46** C 3
Nord-Kvaløy **18** G 1
Nord-Ostsee-Kanal **17** E 4
Nord-Trøndelag **18** F 3
Nordaustlandet **78**
Nordfriesische Inseln **17** E 4
Norðoyar **16** A 1
Nordkapp **18** J 1
Nordkinn **18** J 1
Nordland **18** F 2
Nordostrundingen **78**
Nordøyane **18** E 3
Nordreisa **18** H 2
Nordvik **32** K 1
Norfolk (NE, U.S.A.) **66** G 3
Norfolk (VA, U.S.A.) **67** L 4
Norfolk Islands **46** C 4
Norge **18** F 2
Nori **27** O 2
Noril´sk **27** R 2
Norman **66** G 4
Normanby Island **43** J 1
Normandie **20** CD 2
Normanton **43** G 2
Norra Storfjället **18** G 2
Norrbotten **18** GH 2
Norrköping **19** G 4
Norrland **18** FG 3
Norrtälje **19** G 4
Norseman **42** C 5
Norsjö **18** G 3
Norsk **33** O 5
North Andaman **37** F 5
North Atlantic Drift **8**
North Battleford **63** Q 5
North Bay **65** M 6
North Bend **66** B 3
North Cape (New Zealand) **45** Q 7
North Cape (Norway) **18** J 1
North Carolina **67** L 4
North Cascades National Park **66** B 2
North Channel **16** B 3–4
North Dakota **66** FG 2
North Fork Pass **62** K 3
North Geomagnetic Pole **78**
North Highlands **66** B 4
North Island **45** Q 8
North Korea **35** K 2
North Lakhimpur **37** F 2
North Las Vegas **66** C 4
North Little Rock **67** H 5
North Magnetic Pole **78**
North Minch **16** B 3
North Platte **66** F 3
North Point **44** L 8
North Pole **78**
North Sea **16** D 3
North Slope **62** FH 2
North Uist **16** B 3

North West Cape **42** A 3
North West Highlands **16** BC 3
Northam **42** B 5
Northampton **16** C 4
Northeast Cape **62** D 3
Northeast Providence Channel **69** G 2
Northern Cook Islands **46** E 3
Northern Dvina River **26** H 3
Northern Indian Lake **63** S 4
Northern Ireland **16** B 4
Northern Mariana Islands **46** B 1
Northern Perimeter Highway **72** D 4–5
Northern Territory **42** E 2–3
Northumberland Islands **43** J 3
Northumberland Strait **65** P 6
Northwest Territories **63** NT 2
Norton Sound **62** E 3
Norvegia, Cape **79**
Norway **18** F 2
Norwegian Sea **15** FH 2
Norwich **16** D 4
Noshiro **35** L 2
Nosovaya **26** K 2
Nosratābād **30** F 5
Nossob **58** C 5
Nosy-Bé **59** H 2
Nosy-Varika **59** H 4
Noteć **17** G 4
Nótioi Sporádhes **22** C 3
Noto-hantō **35** L 3
Notodden **19** E 4
Notre Dame Bay **65** QR 6
Notre Dame, Monts **65** O 6
Nottingham (Ontario, Can.) **65** M 3
Nottingham (U.K.) **16** C 4
Nouadhibou **50** B 4
Nouakchott **50** B 5
Nouméa **45** J 6
Nouvelle-Calédonie **45** H 6
Nova Cruz **75** J 2
Nova Iguaçu **75** H 5
Nova Mambone **59** F 4
Nova Scotia **65** OP 6–7
Nova Vida **74** D 3
Novara **21** E 2
Novaya Kakhovka **23** D 1
Novaya Kazanka **26** J 6
Novaya Zemlya **26** L 1
Novgorod **19** K 4
Novgorodka **19** J 4
Novi Ligure **21** E 3
Novi Pazar **22** B 2
Novi Sad **22** AB 1
Novillero **68** A 3
Novo Hamburgo **76** F 4
Novoaltaysk **27** Q 5
Novobiryusinskiy **32** G 4
Novocherkassk **23** EF 1
Novograd-Volynskiy **19** J 5
Novokazalinsk **31** G 1
Novokocherdyk **27** M 5

Novokuznetsk **27** R 5
Novolazarevskaya **79**
Novomoskovsk (Russia) **26** G 5
Novomoskovsk (Ukraine) **23** E 1
Novopavlovskoye **32** K 5
Novopokrovskaya **23** F 1
Novopolotsk **19** J 4
Novorossiysk **23** E 2
Novorybnoye **32** HJ 1
Novoshakhtinsk **23** E 1
Novosibirsk **27** Q 4
Novotroitskoye **31** J 2
Novoye Ust´ye **33** Q 4
Novoyerudinskiy **32** F 4
Novvy Bug **23** D 1
Novy Uzen´ **30** E 2
Novyy Karymkary **27** N 3
Novyy Port **27** O 2
Novyy Tanguy **32** H 4
Now Shahr **25** F 1
Nowa Sól **17** G 4
Nowbarān **25** E 2
Nowdesheh **25** E 2
Nowgong **37** F 2
Nowra **43** J 5
Nowy Sącz **17** H 5
Nsukka **55** F 4
Ntui **55** G 5
Nuatja **54** E 4
Nubia **52** E 5
Nūbiyah **52** DE 5
Nūbiyah, Aş Şaḩrā´ an **52** E 4
Nueltin Lake **63** S 3
Nueva Esperanza **74** D 4
Nueva Galia **76** C 5–6
Nueva Gerona **68** F 3
Nueva Lubecka **77** BC 7
Nueva Rosita **68** B 2
Nueve de Julio **76** D 6
Nuevo Casas Grandes **66** E 5
Nuevo Laredo **68** BC 2
Nuevo León **68** BC 2
Nuevo Mundo, Cerro **74** C 5
Nuevo Rocafuerte **72** C 4
Nugāl **57** H 3
Nuguria Islands **45** FG 2
Nui **46** C 3
Nukey Bluff **43** F 5
Nukhayb **24** D 2
Nuku Hiva **47** F 3
Nuku´alofa **46** D 4
Nukufetau **46** C 3
Nukulaelae **46** C 3
Nukumanu Islands **45** G 2
Nukunau **46** C 3
Nukunonu **46** D 3
Nukuoro **46** B 2
Nukus **30** F 2
Nullarbor Plain **42** DE 5
Numan **55** G 4
Numbulwar Mission **42** F 1
Numto **27** O 3
Nungnain Sum **35** G 1
Nunivak Island **62** D 3
Nunlygran **62** B 3
Nuntherungie **43** G 5

Nunyamo **62** C 2
Nuoro **21** E 3
Nuqrah **24** C 4
Nuratau, Khrebet **31** H 2
Nuremberg **17** F 5
Nurhak Dağı **23** E 3
Nūrī **52** E 5
Nuristan **31** J 3
Nurmes **18** J 3
Nürnberg **17** F 5
Nurri, Mount **43** H 5
Nushki **31** H 5
Nutak **65** P 4
Nuuk **65** R 3
Nuwaybi´al Muzayyinah **24** B 3
Nyabéssan **55** G 5
Nyakanazi **56** E 5
Nyaksimvol´ **27** M 3
Nyala **52** D 6
Nyamlell **56** D 3
Nyandoma **26** H 3
Nyasa, Lake **59** E 2
Nyazepetrovsk **27** L 4
Nyda **27** O 2
Nyika Plateau **59** E 2
Nyima **36** E 1
Nyiregyháza **22** B 1
Nyiru, Mount **57** F 4
Nykøbing (Denmark) **19** F 5
Nyköping (Sweden) **19** G 4
Nylstroom **58** D 4
Nyngan **43** H 5
Nyuk, Ozero **18** K 3
Nyurba **32** L 3
Nzega **56** E 5
Nzérékoré **54** C 4
Nzwani **59** G 2

O

Oahe Dam **66** F 3
Oahu **47** E 1
Oak Ridge **67** K 4
Oakbank **43** G 5
Oakland (CA, U.S.A.) **66** B 4
Oakland (MD, U.S.A.) **67** L 4
Oakley **66** F 4
Oates Coast **79**
Oaxaca **68** C 4
Oaxaca de Juárez **68** C 4
Ob **27** N 2
Oba **64** L 6
Oban **16** B 3
Obeh **31** G 4
Óbidos **73** G 4
Obihiro **35** M 2
Obil´noye **23** F 1
Obluch´ye **33** O 6
Obodovka **22** C 1
Obruk Platosu **23** D 3
Obshchiy Syrt **26** KL 5
Obskaya Guba **27** O 1–2
Ocala **67** K 6
Ocaña **72** D 2
Occidental, Cordillera **72** C 2–3
Ocean City **67** L 4
Oconee **67** K 5

Oda, Jabal 52 F 4
Odawara 35 L 3–4
Ödemiş 22 C 3
Odendaalsrus 58 D 5
Odense 19 F 4
Oder 17 F 4
Odessa (TX, U.S.A.) 66 F 5
Odessa (Ukraine) 22 D 1
Odienné 54 C 4
Odorheiu Secuiesc 22 C 1
Odzala National Park
   55 GH 5
Oeiras 75 H 2
Oeno 47 G 4
Offenbach 17 E 4
Oficina 73 F 2
Ogaden 57 GH 3
Ōgaki 35 L 3
Ogallala 66 F 3
Ogbomosho 55 E 4
Ogden 66 D 3
Ogilvie Mountains 62 JK 2
Oglat Beraber 50 E 2
Ogoki 64 K 5
Ogooué 55 G 6
Ogradžen 22 B 2
O'Higgins, Lago 77 B 8
Ohio 67 K 3
Ohopoho 58 A 3
Ohrid 22 B 2
Oiapoque 73 H 3
Ōita 35 K 4
Ojo de Agua 76 D 4
Ojos del Salado, Cerro
   76 C 4
Okaba 39 J 5
Okahandja 58 B 4
Okak Islands 65 P 4
Okapa 44 E 3
Okara 31 J 4
Okavango 58 C 3
Okavango Swamp 58 C 3
Okayama 35 K 3–4
Okeanskoye 33 T 5
Okeechobee, Lake 67 K 6
Okha (Russia) 33 Q 5
Okhotsk 33 Q 4
Okhotskiy Perevoz 33 P 3
Okhotskoye More 33 QS 4
Oki-shotō 35 K 3
Okinawa-jima 35 J 5
Oklahoma 66–67 G 4
Oklahoma City 67 G 4
Okondja 55 G 6
Okorukambe 58 B 4
Okstindan 18 F 2
Oktemberyan 23 F 2
Oktyabr'skiy (Russia) 32 F 5
Oktyabr'skiy (Russia)
   33 N 4
Oktyabrskiy 26 K 5
Oktyabr'skoye 27 N 3
Öland 19 G 4
Olanga 18 K 2
Olavarría 77 D 6
Olbia 21 E 3
Old Bahama Channel 69 G 3
Oldenburg (F.R.G.) 17 E 4
Olenegorsk 18 K 2
Olenëk 32 K 2

Olenëkskiy Zaliv 32 M 1
Olenevod 33 WX 3
Oléron, Ile d' 20 C 2
Olifants 59 E 4
Olimarao 46 A 2
Olimbía 22 B 3
Ólimbos 22 B 2–3
Olinda 75 K 2
Ollagüe, Volcán 74 C 5
Olmos 72 C 5
Olomouc 17 G 5
Olonets 18 K 3
Olongapo 39 HJ 2
Oloyskiye Gory 33 U 2
Olsztyn 17 H 4
Olt 22 B 2
Olympia 66 B 2
Olympus 22 B 3
Olympus, Mount 66 B 2
Olyutorka 33 V 3
Olyutorskiy 33 VW 3
Olyutorskiy, Mys 33 V 4
Omaha 67 G 3
Oman 53 JK 4–5
Omatako, Mount 58 B 4
Omboué 55 F 6
Ombu 36 E 1
Omchali 30 E 2
Omdurman 52 E 5
Ōmnōgovi 34 D 2
Omolon 33 T 2
Omolon 33 U 2
Omsk 27 O 4–5
Omutinskiy 27 N 4
Omutninsk 26 K 4
Onawa 67 G 3
Ondangwa 58 B 3
Ondo 55 E 4
Öndörhaan 32 K 6
Onega 26 G 3
Onekotan, Ostrov 33 ST 6
Onezhskoye, Ozero 26 G 3
Ongole 36 D 4
Onilahy 59 G 4
Onitsha 55 F 4
Onkuchakh 32 KL 2
Ono-i-Lau Islands 46 CD 4
Onon 32 L 5
Onotoa 46 C 3
Onslow 42 B 3
Ontario (Canada) 64 JL 5
Ontario (OR, U.S.A.) 66 C 3
Ontario, Lake 67 L 3
Ontojärvi 18 J 3
Ontong Java 45 G 3
Oodnadatta 43 F 4
Ooldea 42 E 5
Oostende 16 D 4
Opasatika 64 L 6
Opis 24 D 2
Opobo 55 F 5
Opochka 19 J 4
Opole 17 G 4
Oporto 20 B 3
Oppland 18 E 3
Oradea 22 B 1
Oran 50 E 1
Orange (France) 21 D 3
Orange (TX, U.S.A.) 67 H 5
Orange, Cabo 73 H 3

Orange Free State 58 D 5
Oranje 58 B 5
Orapa 58 D 4
Orcadas 79
Ord, Mount 42 D 2
Ord River 42 D 2
Ordu 23 E 2
Ordynskoye 27 Q 5
Örebro 19 G 4
Oregon 66 BC 3
Orel 26 G 5
Orem 66 D 3
Orenburg 26 K 5
Orense 20 B 3
Öresund 19 F 4
Organ Peak 66 E 5
Orgeyev 22 C 1
Orhon Gol 32 H 6
Oriental, Cordillera (Bolivia)
   74 BC 3–5
Oriental, Cordillera
   (Colombia) 72 CD 2–3
Orihuela 20 C 4
Orillia 65 M 7
Orinduik 73 F 3
Orinoco 72 E 2
Orissa 36 DE 3
Orissaare 19 H 4
Oristano 21 E 4
Orivesi 18 J 3
Oriximiná 73 G 4
Orizaba 68 C 4
Orkanger 18 E 3
Orkney 58 D 5
Orkney Islands 16 C 3
Orlando 67 K 6
Ormara 31 G 5
Ormoc 39 F 1
Ornö 19 G 4
Örnsköldsvik 18 G 3
Oro, Monte d' 21 E 3
Orocué 72 D 3
Oroluk 46 B 2
Orona 46 D 3
Oroqen Zizhiqi 33 M 5
Oroquieta 39 F 2
Oroville 66 C 2
Orr 67 H 2
Orsa Finnmark 18 F 3
Orsha 19 K 5
Orsk 27 L 5
Ortegal, Cabo 20 B 3
Orto-Ayan 33 NO 1
Ortonville 67 G 2
Orümiyeh 30 D 3
Oruro 74 C 4
Osa 32 H 5
Ōsaka 35 L 4
Osakarovka 27 O 5
Osceola 67 H 3
Osh 31 J 2
Oshkosh 67 J 3
Oshogbo 55 EF 4
Oshtoran Küh 25 E 2
Osijek 21 G 2
Osinovka 27 Q 6
Oskarshamn 19 G 4
Oskoba 32 H 3
Oslo 19 F 4
Oslofjorden 19 F 4

Osmanabad 36 C 4
Osmaneli 22 D 2
Osmaniye 23 E 3
Osnabrück 17 E 4
Osorno 77 B 7
Ossa, Mount 44 L 9
Österdalälven 18 F 3
Österdalen 18 F 3
Östergötland 19 G 4
Östersund 18 FG 3
Östhavet 18 JK 1
Ostrava 17 G 5
Ostroda 17 GH 4
Ostrołeka 17 H 4
Ostrov 19 J 4
Ostrov Bol'shoy Begichev
   32 KL 1
Ostrov Bol'shoy
   Lyakhovskiy 33 Q 1
Ostrov Bol'shoy Shantar
   33 P 4–5
Ostrov Feklistova 33 P 4–5
Ostrov Iturup 33 R 6–7
Ostrov Ketoy 33 S 6
Ostrov Kil'din 18 KL 2
Ostrov Kolguyev 26 J 2
Ostrov Kotel'nyy 33 P 1
Ostrov Malyy Lyakhovskiy
   33 Q 1
Ostrov Matua 33 S 6
Ostrov Onekotan 33 ST 6
Ostrov Paramushir 33 T 5
Ostrov Rasshua 33 S 6
Ostrov Shiashkotan 33 S 6
Ostrov Simushir 33 S 6
Ostrov Urup 33 S 6
Ostrov Vaygach 27 L 1
Ostrov Zav'yalova 33 RS 4
Ostrova Chernyye Brat'ya
   33 S 6
Ostrovnoye 33 U 2
Ostrow Wielkopolski
   17 G 4
Ostrowiec Świetokrzyski
   17 H 4
Ōsumi-shotō 35 JK 4
Otaru 35 M 2
Otavalo 72 C 3
Otavi 58 B 3
Otepää Kõrgustik 19 J 4
Otish, Monts 65 N 5
Otjozondu 58 B 4
Otradnoye 33 T 5
Otta 18 E 3
Ottawa 65 M 6
Ottawa 65 MN 6
Ottumwa 67 H 3
Otway, Cape 43 G 6
Otwock 17 H 4
Ouachita Mountains
   67 GH 5
Ouad Naga 50 B 5
Ouadane 50 C 4
Ouadda 56 C 3
Ouaddaï 55 J 3
Ouagadougou 54 D 3
Ouahigouya 54 D 3
Ouahran → Oran 50 E 1
Oualam 54 E 3

Ouanda-Djallé **56** C 3
Ouangolodougou **54** CD 4
Ouargla **51** G 2
Ouarsenis, Massif de l'
  51 F 1
Ouarzazate **50** D 2
Oubangui **55** H 5
Oudtshoorn **58** C 6
Oued Zem **50** D 2
Ouesso **55** H 5
Ouezzane **50** D 2
Ouham **55** H 4
Oujda **50** E 2
Oulainen **18** HJ 3
Oulu **18** J 2
Oulujärvi **18** J 3
Oulujoki **18** J 3
Oum Chalouba **55** J 2
Oum Hadjer **55** H 3
Ounianga **55** J 2
Ouricuri **75** HJ 2
Ourinhos **75** G 5
Outapi **58** A 3
Outer Hebrides **16** B 3
Outjo **58** B 4
Ouvéa **45** J 6
Ouyen **43** G 5–6
Ovalle **76** B 5
Ovamboland **58** B 3
Oviedo **20** B 3
Owen Stanley Range
  44 E 3
Owensboro **67** J 4
Owerri **55** F 4
Owo **55** F 4
Oxford **16** C 4
Oya Siwo **9**
Oyem **55** G 5
Oyo **54** E 4
Oyón **74** A 3
Oysurdakh **33** S 2
Ozamiz **39** F 2
Ozark Plateau **67** H 4
Ozarks, Lake of the **67** H 4
Ózd **22** B 1
Ozernovskiy **33** T 5
Ozero Balkhash **27** OP 6
Ozero Baykal **32** J 5
Ozero Chervonoye **19** J 5
Ozero Dadynskoye **23** FG 1
Ozero Il'men **19** K 4
Ozero Imandra **18** K 2
Ozero Keret' **18** K 2
Ozero Kubenskoye **26** G 4
Ozero Leksozero **18** K 3
Ozero Manych Gudilo
  23 F 1
Ozero Nyuk **18** K 3
Ozero Onezhskoye **26** G 3
Ozero Pyaozero **18** K 2
Ozero Sasykkol' **27** Q 6
Ozero Segozero **18** K 3
Ozero Seletyteniz **27** O 5
Ozero Sevan **23** G 2
Ozero Syamozero **18** K 3
Ozero Taymyr **32** H 1
Ozero Tengiz **27** N 5
Ozero Verkhneye Kuyto
  18 K 3
Ozero Zaysan **27** Q 6

P

Paamiuut **65** R 3
Paarl **58** B 6
Pacasmayo **72** BC 5
Pachiza **72** C 5
Pachuca **68** C 3–4
Pacific Ocean **8**
Padang **38** B 4
Padang, Pulau **38** B 3
Padangpanjang **38** AB 4
Padangsidempuan **38** A 3
Paddle Prairie **63** O 4
Paderborn **17** E 4
Padilla **74** D 4
Padova **21** F 2
Padre Island **67** G 6
Paducah **67** J 4
Pag **21** F 3
Pagadian **39** F 2
Pagan **46** A 1
Pago-Pago **46** D 3
Pagri **36** E 2
Päijänne **18** J 3
Paisley **16** C 3
Paita **72** B 5
Pak Phanang **37** H 6
Pakin **46** B 2
Pakistan **31** HJ 5
Pakokku **37** F 3
Pakse **37** J 4
Pakwach **56** E 4
Pal Malmal **45** F 3
Palacios **67** G 6
Palangkaraya **38** D 4
Palanpur **36** B 3
Palapye **58** D 4
Palatka **33** S 3
Palauk **37** G 6
Palaw **37** G 5
Palawan **39** E 2
Palawan Passage
  38–39 E 1–2
Palca **74** C 4
Palembang **38** BC 4
Palencia **20** C 3
Palenque **68** D 4
Palermo **21** F 4
Palestine **24** B 2–3
Paletwa **37** F 3
Pali **36** B 2
Palinuro, Capo **21** FG 3
Paljakka **18** J 3
Palk Strait **36** C 5–6
Pallastunturi **18** H 2
Palliser, Cape **45** R 9
Palliser, Îles **47** F 4
Palm Bay **67** KL 6
Palma **20** D 4
Palma Soriano **69** G 3
Palmar Sur **68** F 6
Palmares **75** J 2
Palmas, Cape **54** C 5
Palmeira dos Indios **75** J 2
Palmeirais **75** H 2
Palmer **79**
Palmer Archipelago **79**
Palmer Land **79**
Palmerston **46** E 4
Palmerston North **45** R 9

Palmira **72** C 3
Palmyra (Pacific Ocean,
  U.S.A.) **46** E 2
Palmyra (Syria) **24** C 2
Palmyras Point **36** E 3
Palo Alto **66** B 4
Palo Santo **76** E 4
Paloich **52** E 6
Palopo **39** F 4
Palos, Cabo de **20** C 4
Palu (Indonesia) **39** E 4
Palu (Turkey) **23** EF 3
Pamekasan **38** D 5
Pamir **31** J 3
Pamlico Sound **67** L 4
Pampa **66** F 4
Pampas **76–77** D 5–6
Pamplona **20** C 3
Pan, Tierra del **20** B 3
Pan Xian **34** DE 5
Panaji **36** B 4
Panama **72** C 2
Panamá **72** C 2
Panama Canal **72** B 2
Panama City **67** J 5
Panamá, Golfo de **72** C 2
Panamá, Istmo de **72** C 2
Panay **39** F 1
Pandamatenga **58** D 3
Pandharpur **36** BC 4
Pandivere Kõrgustik **19** J 4
Panevežys **19** H 4
Panggoe **45** G 3
Panhandle **66** F 4
Panié, Mont **45** H 6
Panjao **31** H 4
Panjgur **31** G 5
Panorama **75** F 5
Pantanal de São Lourénço
  74 E 4
Pantanal do Río Negro
  74 E 4
Pantelleria **21** F 4
Paoua **56** B 3
Pápa **22** A 1
Papeete **47** F 4
Papenburg **17** E 4
Papey **18** C 3
Paphos **23** D 4
Papua New Guinea
  44 E 2–3
Pará **73** GH 5
Parabel **27** Q 4
Paracatu **75** H 4
Paracel Islands **37** K 4
Paraguai **74** E 5
Paraguarí **76** E 4
Paraguay **74** DE 5
Paraguay **76** E 4
Paraíba **75** J 2
Parakou **54** E 4
Paramaribo **73** GH 2
Paramirim **75** H 3
Paramushir, Ostrov **33** T 5
Paraná (Argentina) **76** D 5
Paraná (Argentina) **76** E 5
Paraná (Brazil) **75** F 5
Paranaguá **76** G 4
Paranam **73** G 2
Paranavaí **75** F 5

Parangaba **75** J 1
Paraoa **47** F 4
Parbig **27** Q 4
Parc National de la Boucle
  De Baoule **54** C 3
Parc National de la Komoé
  54 D 4
Parc National de
  Sinianka-Minia **55** H 3
Parc National de Taï **54** C 4
Parc National de Wonga
  Wongué **55** FG 6
Parc National de Zakouma
  55 H 3
Parc National du
  Bamingui-Bangoran
  56 BC 3
Parc National du Niokolo
  Koba **54** B 3
Parcs Nationaux du ''W''
  54 E 3
Pardo **75** H 4
Pardubice **17** G 4
Parepare **39** E 4
Parinari **72** D 4
Pariñas, Punta **72** B 4
Parintins **73** G 4
Paris (France) **20** D 2
Paris (TX, U.S.A.) **67** G 5
Parkano **18** H 3
Parker **66** D 5
Parkersburg **67** K 4
Parkes **43** H 5
Parlakimidi **36** D 4
Parlakote **36** D 4
Parma **21** F 3
Parnaguá **75** H 3
Parnaíba **75** H 1
Parnaíba **75** H 1
Parnamirim **75** J 2
Parnarama **75** H 2
Parnassós Óros **22** B 3
Pärnu **19** H 4
Parpaillon **21** E 3
Parral **77** B 6
Parry Islands **78**
Parry Peninsula **63** MN 2
Partille **19** F 4
Partizansk **35** K 2
Paryang **36** D 2
Parys **58** D 5
Pas de Calais **16** D 4
Pasadena **66** C 5
Pascagoula **67** J 5
Pasni **31** G 5
Paso de Indios **77** C 7
Paso de los Libres **76** E 4
Paso de los Vientos
  69 H 3–4
Paso de San Francisco
  76 C 4
Paso del Limay **77** BC 7
Paso Río Mayo **77** B 8
Passau **17** F 5
Passero, Capo **21** G 4
Passo Fundo **76** F 4
Passos **75** G 5
Pasto **72** C 3
Pastos Bons **75** H 2
Patagonia **77** BC 7–9

Pat — Pit

Patan (India) 36 B 3
Patan (Nepal) 36 E 2
Paterson 67 LM 3
Pathankot 36 C 1
Patiala 36 C 1
Pativilca 72 C 6
Patkaglik 31 M 3
Patna 36 E 2
Patnagarh 36 D 3
Patos 75 J 2
Patos, Lagoa dos 76 F 5
Patraikós Kólpos 22 B 3
Patras 22 B 3
Patrocínio 75 G 4
Pau 20 C 3
Pau d'Arco 73 J 5
Paulina Peak 66 B 3
Paulistana 75 H 2
Paulo Afonso 75 J 2
Pavlodar 27 P 5
Pavlof Volcano 62 E 4
Pavlovka 27 O 5
Paxson 62 H 3
Pay-Khoy, Khrebet 27 M 2
Payakumbuh 38 B 4
Paynes Find 42 B 4
Paysandú 76 E 5
Payturma 32 F 1
Pazardžik 22 B 2
Peace River 63 O 4
Peaked Mountain 67 N 2
Pearl 67 J 5
Peary Land 78
Pebane 59 F 3
Pebas 72 D 4
Peć 22 B 2
Pechora 26 K 2
Pechorskoye More 26 KL 2
Pecos 66 F 5
Pecos 66 F 5
Pecos Plains 66 F 5
Pécs 22 A 1
Pedernales 73 F 2
Pedro Afonso 73 J 5
Pedro de Valdivia 74 BC 5
Pedro Juan Caballero 74 E 5
Peel 62 L 2
Peera Peera Poolanna Lake 43 F 4
Pegu 37 G 4
Pegu Yoma 37 G 3–4
Pegunungan Barisan 38 B 4
Pegunungan Iran 38 D 3
Pegunungan Maoke 39 J 4
Pegunungan Muller 38 D 3
Pegunungan Schwaner 38 D 4
Pehuajó 77 D 6
Peixe 75 G 3
Pekalongan 38 C 5
Pekanbaru 38 B 3
Pekin 67 HJ 3
Peking 35 G 2
Pelat, Mont 21 E 3
Peljéšac 21 G 3
Pello 18 H 2
Pelly 62 L 3
Pelly Bay 63 U 2
Pelly Crossing 62 K 3
Pelly Mountains 62 L 3

Peloponnese 22 B 3
Pelopónnisos 22 B 3
Pelotas 76 F 5
Pelvoux, Massif du 21 E 3
Pemangkat 38 C 3
Pematangsiantar 38 A 3
Pemba 59 G 2
Pemba Island 57 FG 6
Pembina 66 G 2
Penas, Golfo de 77 B 8
Pendembu 54 B 4
Penedo 75 J 3
Penglai 35 H 3
Península Brecknock 77 B 9
Península de Azuero 72 B 2
Península de Nicoya 68 E 6
Península de Taitao 77 AB 8
Península Valdés 77 D 7
Peninsule d'Ungava 65 MN 4
Penisola Salentina 21 G 3
Pennine Chain 16 C 4
Pennsylvania 67 L 3
Penny Ice Cap 65 O 2
Penong 42 E 5
Penrhyn 47 E 3
Pensacola 67 J 5
Pensacola Mountains 79
Pentecost 45 J 5
Penza 26 H 5
Penzhinskaya Guba 33 U 3
Penzhinskiy Khrebet 33 VW 3
Peoria 67 J 3
Pereira 72 C 3
Perekop 23 D 1
Pereval Yablonitse 22 BC 1
Pérez 76 C 4
Pergamino 76 D 5
Pergamon 22 C 3
Périgueux 20 D 2
Perm 26 L 4
Pernambuco 75 J 2
Perpignan 20 D 3
Perryville 62 F 4
Persepolis 25 F 3
Perseverancia 74 D 3
Persia 25 F 2
Persian Gulf 25 F 3–4
Perth (Australia) 42 B 5
Perth (U.K.) 16 C 3
Perthus, Col de 20 D 3
Peru 72 C 5
Peru Current 8
Perugia 21 F 3
Pervomaysk 22 D 1
Pervomayskiy 26 H 3
Pervoural'sk 27 L 4
Pesaro 21 F 3
Pescara 21 F 3
Peschanyy, Mys 30 E 2
Peshawar 31 J 4
Peski Karakumy 30–31 FG 3
Peski Kyzylkum 31 GH 2
Peski Sary Ishikotrau 27 P 6
Pessac 20 C 3
Petaluma 66 B 4
Petare 72 E 1
Petauke 59 E 2

Petén 68 D 4
Peter I Island 79
Peterborough (Ontario, Can.) 65 M 7
Peterborough (South Australia) 43 F 5
Petersburg 67 L 4
Petites Pyrénées 20 D 3
Petorca 76 B 5
Petra 24 B 3
Petra Azul 75 H 4
Petrel 79
Petrila 22 B 1
Petrodvorets 19 J 4
Petrolina 75 H 2
Petropavlovsk 27 NO 5
Petropavlovsk-Kamchatskiy 33 T 5
Petrópolis 75 H 5
Petrova Gora 21 G 2
Petrovsk 26 J 5
Petrovsk-Zabaykal'skiy 32 J 5
Petrozavodsk 26 FG 3
Peureulak 38 A 3
Pevek 78
Pforzheim 17 E 5
Phalodi 36 B 2
Phaltan 36 B 4
Phatthalung 37 H 6
Phenix City 67 J 5
Phet Buri 37 G 5
Philadelphia 67 M 4
Philae 52 E 4
Philippines 39 FG 1
Phillipsburg 66 G 4
Phitsanulok 37 H 4
Phnom Aural 37 H 5
Phnom Penh 37 H 5
Phoenix 66 D 5
Phoenix Islands 46 D 3
Phu My 37 J 5
Phu Set 37 J 4
Phu Vinh 37 J 6
Phuket 37 G 6
Phuoc Le 37 J 5
Piara Açu 73 H 5
Piatra Neamț 22 C 1
Piauí 75 H 2
Pibor Post 56 E 3
Pic Boby 59 H 4
Picardie 20 D 2
Pichanal 74 D 5
Pichilemu 77 B 5
Pickle Lake 64 J 5
Pico 50 A 1
Pico Cristóbal Colón 72 D 1
Pico de Aneto 20 D 3
Pico Rondón 73 F 3
Pico Tamacuari 72 E 3
Picos 75 H 2
Pidurutalagala 36 D 6
Piedra Sola 76 E 5
Piedras Negras 68 B 2
Pieksämäki 18 J 3
Pielinen 18 J 3
Pierre 66 FG 3
Pieśt'ány 17 G 5
Pietarsaari 18 H 3
Pietermaritzburg 58 DE 5

Pietersburg 58 D 4
Pigué 77 D 6
Pihtipudas 18 J 3
Pik Kommunizma 31 J 3
Pik Pobedy 31 KL 2
Pikelot 46 A 2
Pikhtovka 27 Q 4
Piła 17 G 4
Pilão Arcado 75 H 3
Pilar (Alagoas, Brazil) 75 J 2
Pilar (Paraguay) 76 E 4
Pilcomayo 74 DE 5
Pilot Peak 66 D 3
Pil'tun 33 Q 5
Pim 27 O 3
Pimenta Bueno 74 D 3
Pimental 73 G 4
Pinaki 47 F 4
Pínar del Rio 68 F 3
Pindaíba 75 F 3
Pindaré Mirim 75 G 1
Pindhos Óros 22 B 2–3
Pine Bluff 67 H 5
Pine Island Bay 79
Pine Pass 63 N 4
Pinerolo 21 E 3
Pinetown 59 E 5
Pingdingshan 34 F 4
Pingdu 35 H 3
Pingelap 46 B 2
Pingle 34 F 6
Pingliang 34 E 4
Pingluo 34 E 3
Pingquan 35 G 2
Pingtung 35 H 6
Pingwu 34 D 4
Pingxiang (China) 34 E 6
Pingxiang (Jiangxi, China) 34 F 5
Pingyang 35 H 5
Pingyao 34 F 3
Pinheiro 73 J 4
Pinnaroo 43 G 6
Pinrang 39 E 4
Pinsk 19 J 5
Pinyug 26 J 3
Piotrków Trybunalski 17 G 4
Pipmouacan, Réservoir 65 N 6
Piracicaba 75 G 5
Piracuruca 75 H 1
Piraiévs 22 B 3
Pirapora 75 H 4
Pires do Río 75 G 4
Pirin 22 B 2
Piripiri 75 H 1
Pirot 22 B 2
Piru 39 G 4
Pisa 21 F 3
Pisac 74 B 3
Pisagua 74 B 4
Pisco 74 A 3
Písek 17 F 5
Pishan 31 K 3
Pit-Gorodok 32 F 4
Pitalito 72 C 3
Pitcairn 47 G 4
Piteå 18 H 2
Pitești 22 B 2

Pitkyaranta **18** K 3
Pitt **45** S 9
Pittsburgh **67** L 3
Pium **75** G 3
Piura **72** B 5
Placentia Bay **65** R 6
Placetas **69** G 3
Plaine des Flandres **20** D 1
Planalto Central **75** G 4
Planalto do Brasil **75** H 4
Planalto do Mato Grosso
　74—75 EF 3—4
Plasencia **20** B 3
Plateau de Millevaches
　20 D 2
Plateau du Djado **55** G 1
Plateau du Tademaït **51** F 3
Plateau Laurentien **65** NQ 5
Plateau of Tibet **36** DE 1
Plateaux **55** H 6
Plateaux de la Marche
　20 D 2
Plato Ustyurt **30** F 2
Platte **66** F 3
Plaza Huincul **77** C 6
Pleasanton **66** G 6
Pleiku **37** J 5
Plentywood **66** EF 2
Pleven **22** B 2
Ploča, Rt **21** G 3
Ploče **21** G 3
Płock **17** GH 4
Ploieşti **22** C 2
Plovdiv **22** BC 2
Plymouth **16** C 4
Plzeň **17** F 5
Po **21** F 3
Pobeda, Gora **33** R 2
Pobedy, Pik **31** KL 2
Pocatello **66** D 3
Pocklington Reef **45** G 4
Poconé **74** E 4
Poços de Caldas **75** G 5
Podgorica **22** A 2
Podgornoye **27** Q 4
Podgornyy **33** R 6
Podol'sk **26** G 4
Podosinovets **26** J 3
Podresovo **27** N 4
Pod'yelanka **32** H 4
Pofadder **58** B 5
Pogibi **33** Q 5
Pohjanmaa **18** J 3
Poinsett, Cape **79**
Point Arena **66** B 4
Point Barrow **62** FG 1
Point Conception **66** B 5
Point Culver **42** CD 5
Point D'Entrecasteaux
　42 AB 5
Point Hope **62** D 2
Point Lake **63** P 2
Pointe-à-Pitre **69** K 4
Pointe de Grave **20** C 2
Pointe de Penmarch
　20 BC 2
Pointe Louis-XIV **65** L 5
Pointe Noire **55** G 6
Poitiers **20** D 2
Poitou **20** CD 2

Pojeierze Pomorskie **17** G 4
Pojezierze Mazurskie **17** H 4
Pokrovsk **33** N 3
Pola de Siero **20** B 3
Poland **17** G 4
Polar Plateau **79**
Polatlı **23** D 3
Pole of Inaccessibility **79**
Polesie Lubelskie **17** H 4
Polesye **19** J 5
Polgovskoye **27** N 4
Polillo Islands **39** J 2
Polist' **19** K 4
Pollensa **20** D 4
Polotsk **19** J 4
Polska **17** G 4
Polson **66** D 2
Poluostrov Buzachi
　30 E 1—2
Poluostrov Kamchatka
　33 S 4—5
Poluostrov Kanin **26** HJ 2
Poluostrov Kol'skiy **26** G 2
Poluostrov Koni **33** S 4
Poluostrov Rybachiy **18** K 2
Poluostrov Taymyr **32** FH 1
Poluostrov Yamal **27** NO 1
Polyarnik **62** B 2
Polyarnyy Ural **27** MN 2
Polynesia **47** EG 2—4
Pombal **75** J 3
Pomerania **17** FG 4
Pomio **46** B 3
Pommersche Bucht **17** F 4
Pomona **66** C 5
Pompei **21** F 3
Pompeyevka **33** O 6
Ponape **46** B 2
Ponca City **67** G 4
Ponce **69** J 4
Pondicherry **36** CD 5
Ponente, Rivera di **21** E 3
Ponferrada **20** B 3
Ponoy **26** H 2
Ponta da Baleia **75** J 4
Ponta Delgada **50** A 1
Ponta do Padrão **58** A 1
Ponta Grossa **76** F 4
Ponta Porã **74—75** EF 5
Ponte Nova **75** H 5
Pontevedra **20** B 3
Pontianak **38** C 4
Pontine Mountains **23** F 2
Ponziane, Isole **21** F 3
Poochera **42** E 5
Pool **55** H 6
Poole **16** C 4
Poona **36** B 4
Poopó **74** C 4
Poopó, Lago de **74** C 4
Poorman **62** F 3
Popacateptl, Volcan **68** C 4
Popayán **72** C 3
Poplar Bluff **67** H 4
Popokabaka **56** B 6
Popondetta **44** E 3
Porangatu **75** G 3
Porbandar **36** A 3
Porco **74** C 4

Pori **18** H 3
Porirua **45** R 9
Porjus **18** H 2
Porlamar **73** F 1
Porpoise Bay **79**
Porsangerhalvöya **18** HJ 1
Porsgrunn **19** EF 4
Port Alberni **63** N 6
Port Alice **63** M 5
Port Arthur (Tasmania,
　Austr.) **44** L 9
Port Arthur (TX, U.S.A.)
　67 H 6
Port au Prince **69** H 4
Port Augusta **43** F 5
Port Blair **37** F 5
Port Blandford **65** R 6
Port Darwin (Falkland Is.,
　U.K.) **77** E 9
Port Darwin (N.T., Austr.)
　42 E 1
Port Gentil **55** F 6
Port Harcourt **55** F 5
Port Hardy **63** M 5
Port Hedland **42** B 3
Port Hope Simpson **65** QR 5
Port Huron **67** K 3
Port Keats **42** D 1
Port Láirge **16** B 4
Port Laoise **16** B 4
Port Lincoln **43** F 5
Port Loko **54** B 4
Port-Louis **59** K 6
Port Moller **62** E 4
Port Moresby **44** E 3
Port Nelson **63** T 4
Port Nolloth **58** B 5
Port-Nouveau-Québec
　65 O 4
Port of Spain **73** F 1
Port Radium **63** O 2
Port Said **24** A 3
Port Saint Johns **58** DE 6
Port Saunders **65** Q 5
Port Sudan → Bür Südan
　52 F 5
Port Wakefield **43** F 5
Portage la-Prairie **63** S 5
Portile de Fier **22** B 2
Portland (ME, U.S.A.)
　67 N 3
Portland (OR, U.S.A.) **66** B 2
Portland (Victoria, Austr.)
　43 G 6
Porto **20** B 3
Pôrto Acre **72** E 5
Pôrto Alegre **76** FG 5
Porto Amboim **58** A 2
Pôrto Artur **75** F 3
Pôrto de Moz **73** H 4
Pôrto Esperidião **74** E 4
Pôrto Grande **73** H 3
Pôrto Jofre **74** E 4
Pôrto Murtinho **74** E 5
Pôrto Nacional **75** G 3
Porto Novo **54** E 4
Pôrto Santana **73** H 3
Pôrto Santo **50** B 2
Pôrto Seguro **75** J 4
Pôrto Valter **72** D 5

Porto-Vecchio **21** E 3
Pôrto Velho **73** F 5
Portoviejo **72** BC 4
Portree **16** B 3
Portsmouth (N.H., U.S.A.)
　67 M 3
Portsmouth (OH, U.S.A.)
　67 K 4
Portsmouth (U.K.) **16** C 4
Portsmouth (VA, U.S.A.)
　67 L 4
Portugal **20** B 3
Portugalete **20** C 3
Porvenir **77** BC 9
Posadas **76** E 4
Posht-e Badam **25** G 2
Positos **74** D 5
Posse **75** G 3
Postavy **19** J 4
Poste-de-la-Baleine **65** M 4
Poste Maurice Cortier
　51 F 4
Postmasburg **58** C 5
Posto Cunambo **72** C 4
Potapovo **27** R 2
Potenza **21** G 3
Potgietersrus **58** D 4
Poti **23** F 2
Potiskum **55** G 3
Potosi **74** C 4
Potrerillos **76** C 4
Potsdam **17** F 4
Pou Bia **37** H 4
Povenets **26** F 2
Póvoa de Varzim **20** B 3
Poza Rica de Hidalgo **68** C 3
Požarevac **22** B 2
Poznań **17** G 4
Pozo Almonte **74** C 5
Prado **75** J 4
Prague **17** FG 4
Praia **54** B 7
Prainha **73** F 5
Praslin **57** K 5
Prato **21** F 3
Praya **38** E 5
Presidencia Roque
　Sáenz-Peña **76** D 4
Presidente Dutra **75** H 2
Presidente Prudente **75** F 5
Presnogor'kovka **27** N 5
Prespansko Jezero **22** B 2
Preston **16** C 4
Pretoria **58** D 5
Priazovskaya
　Vozvyshennost' **23** E 1
Pribilof Islands **62** D 4
Příbram **17** F 5
Prichernomorskaya
　Nizmennost' **23** D 1
Prieska **58** C 5
Prikaspiyskaya Nizmennost'
　30 DE 1
Prikubanskaya Nizmennost'
　23 E 1
Prilep **22** B 2
Priluki **26** H 3
Primavera **79**
Primeira Cruz **75** H 1
Primorsk **19** J 3

Pri – Qim

Primorsko-Akhtarsk **23** E 1
Prince Albert **63** Q 5
Prince Albert Mountains **79**
Prince Albert National Park
  63 Q 5
Prince Albert Peninsula
  63 O 1
Prince Albert Sound
  63 OP 1
Prince Charles Island **65** M 2
Prince Charles Mountains **79**
Prince Edward Island
  (Canada) **65** P 6
Prince Edward Islands
  (Antarctica) **79**
Prince George **63** N 5
Prince of Wales, Cape
  62 D 2
Prince of Wales Island (AK,
  U.S.A.) **62** L 4
Prince of Wales Island
  (Canada) **63** S 1
Prince of Wales Island
  (Queensland, Austr.)
  43 G 1
Prince of Wales Strait
  63 O 1
Prince Patrick Island **78**
Prince Rupert **62** L 5
Prince William Sound
  62 H 3
Princess Astrid Coast **79**
Princess Charlotte Bay
  43 G 1
Princess Martha Coast **79**
Princess Ragnhild Coast **79**
Princess Royal Island
  62 M 5
Príncipe **55** F 5
Pripet Marshes **19** J 5
Pripyat' **19** J 5
Priština **22** B 2
Prizren **22** B 2
Prokhladnyy **23** F 2
Prokhorkino **27** P 4
Prokop'yevsk **27** R 5
Proliv Karskiye Vorota
  26–27 L 1
Proliv Nevel'skogo **33** Q 5
Prome **37** G 4
Promontoire Portland
  65 LM 4
Promontorio del Gargano
  21 G 3
Propria **75** J 3
Protochnoye **27** N 3
Provence **21** E 3
Providence **67** M 3
Providence, Cape **44** P 10
Provideniya **62** C 3
Provo **66** D 3
Prudhoe Bay **62** H 1
Prut **22** C 1
Prydz Bay **79**
Przheval'sk **31** K 2
Pshish **23** E 2
Pskov **19** J 4
Pskovskoye Ozero **19** J 4
Ptich **19** J 5
Pucallpa **72** CD 5

Pucheng **35** G 5
Pudasjärvi **18** J 2
Puebla **68** C 4
Puebla **68** C 4
Pueblo **66** F 4
Pueblo Hundido **76** C 4
Puelches **77** C 6
Puente Alto **76** BC 5
Puente-Genil **20** C 4
Puerto Aisén **77** B 8
Puerto Angel **68** C 4
Puerto Asís **72** C 3
Puerto Ayacucho **72** E 2
Puerto Baquerizo Moreno
  72 B 6
Puerto Barrios **68** E 4
Puerto Cabello **72** E 1
Puerto Cabezas **68** F 5
Puerto Carreño **72** E 2
Puerto Casade **74** E 5
Puerto Chicama **72** BC 5
Puerto Coig **77** C 9
Puerto Colombia **72** C 1
Puerto Cortés **68** E 4
Puerto Cumarebo **72** E 1
Puerto de Villatoro **20** B 3
Puerto Deseado **77** C 8
Puerto Escondido **68** C 4
Puerto Esperanza **76** F 4
Puerto Estrella **72** D 1
Puerto Heath **74** C 3
Puerto Juárez **68** E 3
Puerto la Cruz **73** F 1
Puerto Leguizamo **72** D 4
Puerto Lempira **68** F 4
Puerto Limón **72** D 3
Puerto Madryn **77** C 7
Puerto Magdalena **66** D 7
Puerto Maldonado **74** C 3
Puerto Montt **77** B 7
Puerto Natales **77** B 9
Puerto Nuevo **72** E 2
Puerto Padilla **74** B 3
Puerto Páez **72** E 2
Puerto Patillos **74** B 5
Puerto Patiño **74** C 4
Puerto Plata **69** HJ 4
Puerto Portillo **72** D 5
Puerto Princesa **39** E 2
Puerto Rico (Argentina)
  76 F 4
Puerto Rico (U.S.A.) **69** J 4
Puerto Rondón **72** D 2
Puerto Siles **74** C 3
Puerto Suárez **74** E 4
Puerto Vallarta **68** AB 3
Puerto Varas **77** B 7
Puerto Verlarde **74** D 4
Puerto Villamizar **72** D 2
Puerto Villazón **74** D 3
Puerto Wilches **72** D 2
Puerto Williams **77** C 10
Puertollano **20** C 4
Pugachev **26** J 5
Pukapuka (Cook Is.) **46** DE 3
Pukapuka (French Polynesia)
  47 F 3
Pukaruha **47** F 4
Pukatawagan **63** R 4
Pukch'ŏng **35** J 2

Puksoozero **26** H 3
Pula **21** F 3
Pulap **46** A 2
Pulau Bangka **38** C 4
Pulau Belitung **38** C 4
Pulau Biak **39** J 4
Pulau Bintan **38** B 3
Pulau Buru **39** G 4
Pulau Butung **39** F 4
Pulau Enggano **38** B 5
Pulau Jos Sodarso **39** J 5
Pulau Kai Besar **39** H 5
Pulau Karakelong **39** G 3
Pulau Labengke **39** F 4
Pulau Laut **38** E 4
Pulau Madura **38** D 5
Pulau Mangole **39** G 4
Pulau Misool **39** H 4
Pulau Nias **38** A 3
Pulau Padang **38** B 3
Pulau Roti **39** F 6
Pulau Salawati **39** H 4
Pulau Selaru **39** H 5
Pulau Siberut **38** A 4
Pulau Simeulue **38** A 3
Pulau Taliabu **39** FG 4
Pulau Trangan **39** H 5
Pulau Waigeo **39** H 4
Pulau Wokam **39** H 5
Pulau Yamdena **39** H 5
Pulau Yapen **39** J 4
Puławy **17** H 4
Pullman **66** C 2
Pulog, Mount **39** J 1
Pulozero **18** K 2
Pulusuk **46** A 2
Puna de Atacama **74** C 5–6
Puncak Jaya **39** J 4
Pune **36** B 4
Punjab **36** BC 1
Punkaharju **18** J 3
Puno **74** B 4
Punta Almina **50** D 1
Punta Alta **77** D 6
Punta Arenas **77** B 9
Punta de Europa **20** BC 4
Punta Desengaño **77** C 8
Punta Eugenia **66** C 6
Punta Fijo **72** D 1
Punta Gallinas **72** D 1
Punta Gorda (Belize) **68** E 4
Punta Gorda (Nicaragua)
  68 F 5
Punta Mariato **72** B 2
Punta Medanosa **77** CD 8
Punta Negra **72** B 5
Punta Pariñas **72** B 4
Punta Prieta **66** D 6
Punta Rieles **74** E 5
Puntarenas **68** EF 6
Puqi **34** F 5
Pur **27** P 2
Purdy Islands **44** E 2
Purnea **36** E 2
Purus **73** F 4
Puruvesi **18** J 3
Pusan **35** J 3
Pushchino **33** T 5
Pushkin **19** K 4
Pushkino **26** J 5

Pustoretsk **33** U 3
Putao **37** G 2
Putorana, Gory **32** FH 2
Putumayo **72** D 4
Puulavesi **18** J 3
Puy de Sancy **20** D 2
Puyang **34** G 3
Puyo **72** C 4
Pweto **56** D 6
Pyaozero, Ozero **18** K 2
Pyatigorsk **23** F 2
Pyatistennoy **33** TU 2
Pyawbwe **37** G 3
Pyhäjoki **18** HJ 3
Pyhätunturi **18** J 2
Pyinmana **37** G 4
P'yŏngyang **35** HJ 3
Pyrénées **20** CD 3
Pyshchug **26** J 4

Q

Qâbis **51** H 2
Qâbis, Khalij **51** H 2
Qaʾemshahr **25** F 1
Qafşah **51** G 2
Qagcaka **36** D 1
Qahremānshahr **25** E 2
Qaidam Pendi **34** BC 3
Qalʿ at Dīzah **25** D 1
Qalʿ at Sukkar **25** E 3
Qala-Nau **31** G 4
Qālat **31** H 4
Qalʿat Şālih **25** E 3
Qalīb ash Shuyūkh **25** E 3
Qamalung **34** C 4
Qamdo **34** C 4
Qaminis **51** JK 2
Qanāt as Suways **24** A 3
Qapqal **31** L 2
Qaqortoq **65** S 3
Qarah Dāgh **24** D 1
Qardo **57** H 3
Qarqannah, Juzur **51** H 2
Qasr-e Shīrīn **25** DE 2
Qaşr Farāfirah **52** D 3
Qatar **25** F 4
Qatrūyeh (Iran) **25** G 3
Qattara Depression **52** D 3
Qāyen **30** F 4
Qayyārah **24** D 2
Qazvin **25** F 1
Qeqertasuatsiaat **65** R 3
Qeshm (Iran) **25** G 4
Qeshm (Iran) **25** G 4
Qeys **25** F 4
Qezel Owzan **25** E 1
Qeziʾot **24** B 3
Qianʾan **35** H 1
Qiaowan **34** C 2
Qidong **35** H 4
Qiemo **31** M 3
Qift **24** A 4
Qijiang **34** E 5
Qijiaojing **34** B 2
Qila Ladgasht **31** G 5
Qila Saifullah **31** H 4
Qilian Shan **34** CD 3
Qimen **35** G 5

Qinä 24 A 4
Qing Zang Gaoyuan 36 DE 1
Qingdao 35 H 3
Qinggang 35 J 1
Qinghai 34 C 3
Qinghai Hu 34 D 3
Qingjiang (Jiangsu, China) 35 G 4
Qingjiang (Jiangxi, China) 34 G 5
Qingyang 34 E 3
Qinhuangdao 35 GH 3
Qinling Shan 34 EF 4
Qinzhou 34 E 6
Qionghai 34 F 7
Qionglai 34 D 4
Qiqihar 33 M 6
Qira 31 L 3
Qirjat Yam 24 B 2
Qitai 31 M 2
Qitaihe 35 K 1
Qiyang 34 F 5
Qog Ul 35 G 2
Qolleh-ye Damāvand 25 F 2
Qom 25 F 2
Qomsheh 25 F 2—3
Qoşbeh-ye Naşşār 25 E 3
Qotbābād 25 G 4
Qotur 30 C 3
Qu Xian 35 G 5
Quan Phu Quoc 37 H 5
Quang Ngai 37 J 4
Quanzhou (Fujian, China) 35 G 6
Quanzhou (Guangxi Zhuangzu Zizhiqu, China) 34 F 5
Qu'Appelle 63 R 5
Quartu Sant' Elena 21 E 4
Qüchän 30 F 3
Québec 65 N 5
Québec 65 N 6
Quebracho Coto 76 D 4
Queen Bess, Mount 63 N 5
Queen Charlotte Islands 62 KL 5
Queen Charlotte Sound 62 LM 5
Queen Elizabeth Islands 78
Queen Fabiola Mountains 79
Queen Mary Coast 79
Queen Maud Gulf 63 R 2
Queen Maud Land 79
Queen Maud Mountains 79
Queensland 43 GH 3
Queenstown (South Africa) 58 D 6
Queenstown (Tasmania, Austr.) 44 L 9
Quelimane 59 F 3
Quembo 58 B 2
Querétaro 68 BC 3
Queshan 34 F 4
Quesnel 63 N 5
Quetta 31 H 4
Quevedo 72 C 4
Quezaltenango 68 D 5
Quezon City 39 J 2
Qui Nhon 37 J 5
Quibala 58 AB 2

Quibdó 72 C 2
Quiçama National Park 58 A 1
Quiculungo 58 B 1
Quilabamba 74 B 3
Quilacollo 74 C 4
Quillaicillo 76 B 5
Quillota 76 B 5
Quilon 36 C 6
Quilpie 43 G 4
Quimilí 76 D 4
Quimper 20 C 2
Quincy 67 H 4
Quines 76 C 5
Quintana Roo 68 E 3—4
Quito 72 C 4
Quixadá 75 J 1
Qujing 34 D 5
Qulansiyah 57 J 2
Qulbān Layyah 25 E 3
Qurnat aş Şawdā' 24 B 2
Qūs 24 A 4
Qusaybah 24 C 2
Qusum 34 B 5

R

Raab 21 G 2
Raahe 18 H 3
Rába 22 A 1
Raba 39 E 5
Rabak 52 E 6
Rabat 50 D 2
Rabaul 45 F 2
Rabyānah 51 K 4
Rabyānah, Ramlat 51 JK 4
Race, Cape 65 R 6
Rach Gia 37 HJ 5—6
Racine 67 J 3
Radhanpur 36 B 3
Radisson 65 M 5
Radomsko 17 G 4
Rae 63 O 3
Ra's-e Näy Band 25 F 4
Raevavae 47 F 4
Rafaela 76 D 5
Rafah 24 B 3
Rafhā 24 D 3
Rafsanjän 25 G 3
Raga 56 D 3
Rahimyar Khan 31 J 5
Raiatea 47 E 4
Raichur 36 C 4
Raiganj 36 E 2
Raigarh 36 D 3
Rainbow Peak 66 C 3
Rainier, Mount 66 B 2
Rainy Lake 64 J 6
Raipur 36 D 3
Raj Nandgaon 36 D 3
Rajada 75 H 2
Rajahmundry 36 D 4
Rajakoski 18 J 2
Rajapalaiyam 36 C 6
Rajasthan 36 BC 2
Rajgarh 36 C 3
Rajkot 36 B 3
Rajshahi 36 E 3
Rakahanga 46 E 3

Rakitnoye 19 J 5
Rakulka 26 HJ 3
Raleigh 67 L 4
Ralik Chain 46 C 2
Ramādah 51 H 2
Ramea 65 Q 6
Rāmhormoz 25 E 3
Ramlat Hagolan 24 B 2
Ramlat Rabyänah 51 JK 4
Rampur 36 C 2
Ramree 37 F 4
Ramsgate 16 D 4
Rancagua 76 B 5
Ranchi 36 E 3
Randers 19 F 4
Randijaure 18 G 2
Rangkasbitung 38 C 5
Rangoon 37 G 4
Rangpur 36 E 2
Rankin Inlet 63 T 3
Rann of Kutch 36 AB 3
Rantauprapat 38 AB 3
Ranua 18 J 2
Raoul 46 D 4
Rapa 47 F 4
Rapa Nui 47 H 4
Raper, Cape 65 O 2
Rapid City 66 F 3
Raraka 47 F 4
Rarotonga 47 E 4
Ra's Abū Madd 24 B 4
Ra's Abū Qumayyis 25 F 4
Rås al Abyaḍ 24 BC 5
Ra's al Abyaḍ 51 G 1
Ra's al Ḥadd 53 KL 4
Ra's al Khafji 25 E 3
Ra's al Khaymah 25 G 4
Ra's al Madrakah 53 K 5
Ra's al Mish'äb 25 E 3
Ra's as Saffānīyah 25 E 3
Ra's ash Shaykh 24 B 3
Ra's Asîr 57 J 2
Ra's aţ Ţīb 51 H 1
Ra's az Zawr 25 E 4
Ra's Banäs 24 B 5
Ra's Barīdī 24 B 4
Ras Dashan 57 F 2
Ra's Fartak 53 J 5
Ra's Ghärib 24 A 3
Ra's Häfün 57 J 2
Ra's Mişrätah 51 J 2
Ra's Muḥammad 24 B 4
Rasht 25 E 1
Raskoh 31 G 5
Rasshua, Ostrov 33 S 6
Rasskazovo 26 H 5
Rastigaissa 18 J 1
Råstojaure 18 H 2
Rat Buri 37 G 5
Rat Islands 62 A 5
Ratak Chain 46 C 2
Ratangarh 36 B 2
Ratlam 36 C 3
Ratnagiri 36 B 4
Ratnapura 36 D 6
Ratta 27 Q 3
Ratz, Mount 62 L 4
Raufarhöfn 18 B 2
Raúl Leoni, Represa 73 F 2
Rauma 18 H 3

Raumo 18 H 3
Raupelyan 62 C 2
Raurkela 36 D 3
Ravahere 47 F 4
Ravänsar 25 E 2
Rävar 25 G 3
Ravenna 21 F 3
Ravenshoe 43 GH 2
Räwah 24 CD 2
Rawaki 46 D 3
Rawalpindi 31 J 4
Rawanduz 25 D 1
Rawlinna 42 D 5
Rawlins 66 E 3
Rawson 77 D 7
Raychikhinsk 33 N 6
Raymond 66 B 2
Räzän 25 E 2
Razan 25 E 2
Razdan 23 F 2
Razgrad 22 C 2
Ré, Ile de 20 C 2
Real, Cordillera 72 C 4
Realico 76 D 6
Reao 47 G 4
Rebbenesöy 18 G 1
Rebecca, Lake 42 C 5
Reboly 18 K 3
Recife 75 K 2
Recifs d'Entrecasteaux 45 H 5
Reconquista 76 DE 4
Red Bluff 66 B 3
Red Deer 63 P 5
Red Deer River 63 P 5
Red Lake 63 J 5
Red Lake 64 J 5
Red River (LA, U.S.A.) 67 H 5
Red River (MN, U.S.A.) 67 G 2
Red Sea 52 F 3—4
Red Water 63 P 5
Redding 66 B 3
Redenção da Gurguéia 75 H 2
Redoubt Volcano 62 G 3
Reef Islands 45 J 4
Regensburg 17 F 5
Reggane 50 EF 3
Reggio di Calabria 21 G 4
Reggio nell'Emilia 21 F 3
Reghin 22 B 1
Regina (Brazil) 73 H 3
Regina (Canada) 63 R 5
Registan 31 GH 4
Rehoboth 58 B 4
Reims 20 D 2
Reindeer Lake 63 R 4
Reinoksfjellet 18 G 2
Reitoru 47 F 4
Rekinniki 33 U 3
Reliance 63 Q 3
Remansão 73 HJ 4
Remanso 75 H 2
Rembang 38 D 5
Renascença 72 E 4
Renfrew 65 M 6
Rengo 76 B 5
Rennell 45 H 4

Ren—Rum

Rennes **20** C 2
Rennie Lake **63** Q 3
Reno **66** B 4
Renton **66** B 2
Replot **18** H 3
Represa Raúl Leoni **73** F 2
Republic of Ireland **16** B 4
Repulse Bay **63** U 2
Requena **72** D 4
Réservoir Baskatong
  65 MN 6
Réservoir Cabonga **65** M 6
Réservoir Decelles **65** M 6
Réservoir Gouin **65** MN 6
Réservoir Pipmouacan
  65 N 6
Reshteh-ye Kūhhā-ye Alborz
  25 F 1
Resistencia **76** DE 4
Reşiţa **22** B 1
Resolution Island **65** P 3
Réunion **59** K 6
Reus **20** D 3
Revilla Gigedo Islands
  61 G 8
Rewari **36** C 2
Rey **25** F 2
Reykjahlíð **18** B 2
Reykjanes **18** A 3
Reykjavik **18** A 3
Reynosa **68** C 2
Rezé **20** C 2
Rēzekne **19** J 4
Rhein **16** E 4
Rhinelander **67** J 2
Rhinmal **36** B 2
Rhode Island **67** M 3
Rhodes **22** C 3
Rhodope Mts **22** BC 2
Rhondda **16** C 4
Rhône **21** D 3
Rías Altas **20** B 3
Rías Bajas **20** B 3
Ribeirão Prêto **75** G 5
Riberalta **74** C 3
Richard's Bay **59** E 5
Richland **66** C 2
Richmond (Queensland,
  Austr.) **43** G 3
Richmond (VA, U.S.A.)
  67 L 4
Richmond Hill **65** M 7
Riding Mountain National
  Park **63** R 5
Rietavas **19** H 4
Riga **19** H 4
Riga, Gulf of **19** H 4
Rihand Dam **36** D 3
Riihimäki **19** HJ 3
Riiser-Larsen Ice Shelf **79**
Riiser-Larsen Peninsula **79**
Rijau **55** F 3
Rijeka **21** F 2
Riley **66** C 3
Rimatara **47** E 4
Rimini **21** F 3
Rîmnicu Sărat **22** C 1
Rîmnicu Vîlcea **22** B 1–2
Rimouski **65** O 6
Rinchinlhümbe **32** G 5

Rinconada **74** C 5
Ringgold Isles **46** D 4
Ringvassöy **18** G 2
Rio Balsas **68** B 4
Río Branco (Acre, Brazil)
  72 E 5
Río Branco (Roraima, Brazil)
  73 F 3
Río Bravo del Norte
  66 EF 5–6
Río Chico **77** C 8
Río Claro **75** G 5
Río Colorado **77** D 6
Río Cuarto **76** CD 5
Rio das Mortes **75** F 3
Río de Janeiro **75** H 5
Río de Janeiro **75** H 5
Río de la Plata **76** E 5–6
Rio de Oro **50** BC 4
Río Gallegos **77** C 9
Río Grande (Argentina)
  77 C 9
Río Grande (Bahía, Brazil)
  75 H 3
Río Grande (Brazil) **75** G 4
Río Grande (Río Grande do
  Sul, Brazil) **76** F 5
Rio Grande (TX, U.S.A.)
  66 G 6
Rio Grande de Santiago
  68 B 3
Río Grande do Norte **75** J 2
Río Grande do Sul **76** EF 4
Río Grande o'Guapay
  74 D 4
Río Lagartos **68** E 3
Río Mulatos **74** C 4
Rio Negro (Argentina)
  77 D 6–7
Río Negro (Brazil) **73** F 4
Rio Negro, Pantanal do
  74 E 4
Río Turbio Mines **77** B 9
Río Verde **75** F 4
Río Verde de Mato Grosso
  75 F 4
Ríobamba **72** C 4
Rioja **72** C 5
Riom **20** D 2
Ríosucio **72** C 2
Ritzville **66** C 2
Rivadavia **76** B 4
Rivas **68** E 5
Rivera (Argentina) **77** D 6
Rivera (Uruguay) **76** E 5
Riverina **43** GH 5
Riverside **66** C 5
Riverton **63** S 5
Riviera di Levante **21** E 3
Riviera di Ponente **21** E 3
Rivoli **21** E 2
Riwoqê **34** C 4
Riyadh **25** E 4
Rize **23** F 2
Rizhao **35** G 3
Rizhskiy Zaliv **19** H 4
Rjuven **19** E 4
Rkiz **50** B 5
Roan Plateau **66** E 4
Roanne **20** D 2

Robāt-e Khān **25** G 2
Robert Butte **79**
Robinson River **43** F 2
Robore **74** E 4
Rocha **76** F 5
Rochefort **20** C 2
Rocher River **63** P 3
Rocher Thomasset **47** F 3
Rochester (MN, U.S.A.)
  67 H 3
Rochester (N.Y., U.S.A.)
  67 L 3
Rock Hill **67** K 5
Rock Island **67** H 3
Rock Springs **66** E 3
Rockefeller Plateau **79**
Rockford **67** J 3
Rockhampton **43** HJ 3
Rockport **66** B 4
Rocky Mount **67** L 4
Rocky Mountain House
  63 O 5
Rocky Mountains
  61 FH 4–6
Rodeo **68** B 2
Rodez **20** D 3
Ródhos **22** C 3
Ródhos **22** C 3
Rodina **32** G 4
Rodopi **22** BC 2
Roebourne **42** B 3
Roebuck Bay **42** C 2
Roes Welcome Sound
  63 U 2–3
Rogagua, Lago **74** C 3
Rogaland **19** E 4
Rogers Peak **66** D 4
Rohtak **36** C 2
Roi Georges, Îles du **47** F 3
Rolleston **43** H 3
Roma (Italy) **21** F 3
Roma (Queensland, Austr.)
  43 H 4
Romaine **65** P 5
Roman **22** C 1
Romania **22** BC 1
Romanovka **32** K 5
Romans-sur-Isère **21** E 2
Rome (Italy) **21** F 3
Rome (OR, U.S.A.) **66** C 3
Romny **26** F 5
Roncador, Serra do **75** F 3
Ronda **20** BC 4
Rondane **18** EF 3
Rondón, Pico **73** F 3
Rondônia **74** D 3
Rondonópolis **75** F 4
Rong Xian **34** F 6
Rongan **34** E 5
Ronge, Lac la **63** R 4
Rongelap **46** C 2
Rongerik **46** C 2
Rongjiang **34** E 5
Rönne **19** F 4
Ronne Ice Shelf **79**
Ronneby **19** G 4
Roosevelt Island **79**
Roosevelt, Mount **63** M 4
Roper River **42** E 1
Roraima (Brazil) **73** F 3

Roraima (Venezuela) **73** F 2
Röros **18** F 3
Rörvik **18** F 3
Rosario (Argentina) **76** D 5
Rosário (Maranhão, Brazil)
  75 H 1
Rosario (Mexico) **68** A 3
Rosario de Lerma **76** C 4
Roseau **69** K 4
Roseburg **66** B 3
Rosenheim **17** F 5
Rosetown **63** Q 5
Rosignol **73** G 2
Roşiori de Vede **22** C 2
Roskilde **19** F 4
Roslavl' **26** F 5
Ross Ice Shelf **79**
Ross Island **79**
Ross River **62** L 3
Ross Sea **79**
Rossano **21** G 4
Rossel Island **45** F 4
Rosslare **16** B 4
Rosso **50** B 5
Rossosh **26** G 5
Rostock **17** F 4
Rostov **26** G 4
Rostov-na-Donu **23** EF 1
Roswell **66** F 5
Rota **46** A 2
Rothera **79**
Rotorua **45** R 8
Rotterdam **16** D 4
Rotuma **46** C 3
Rouen **20** D 2
Rovaniemi **18** J 2
Rovdino **26** H 3
Rovereto **21** F 2
Rovigo **21** F 2
Rovno **19** J 5
Rowley **65** M 2
Roxas **39** F 1
Roy Hill **42** C 3
Rozhdestvenskoye **26** J 4
Roztocze **17** H 4
Rt Kamenjak **21** F 3
Rt Ploča **21** G 3
Rtishchevo **26** H 5
Ruacana Falls **58** AB 3
Ruaha National Park **56** E 6
Ruapehu **45** R 8
Rubtsovsk **27** Q 5
Ruby **62** F 3
Rudall River National Park
  42 C 3
Rudbar **31** G 4
Rudnyy **27** M 5
Rudolf, Lake **57** F 4
Rufiji **57** F 6
Rufino **76** D 5
Rufisque **54** A 3
Rügen **17** F 4
Ruijin **34** G 5
Rujm al Mudhari **24** C 2
Rukwa, Lake **56** E 6
Rum Jungle **42** E 1
Rumädah **53** G 6
Rumphi **59** E 2

Rundu **58** B 3
Ruoqiang **34** A 3
Rupert **65** M 5
Rurrenabaque **74** C 3
Rurutu **47** E 4
Rusakovo **33** U 4
Ruse **22** C 2
Rushan **31** J 3
Russas **75** J 1
Russia **26** FH 4
Russkaya (Antarctica) **79**
Russkaya (Russia) **35** L 1
Rustavi **23** G 2
Rustenburg **58** D 5
Rutenga **59** E 4
Ruvuma **59** F 2
Ruwenzori National Park
  56 DE 5
Ruzayevka **26** H 5
Ružomberok **17** G 5
Rwanda **56** DE 5
Ryazan' **26** G 5
Ryazhsk **26** G 5
Rybachiy, Poluostrov **18** K 2
Rybinsk **26** G 4
Rybinskoye
  Vodokhranilishche **26** G 4
Rybnik **17** G 4
Rybnitsa **22** C 1
Ryn Peski **26** J 6
Ryukyu Islands **35** J 5
Rzeszów **17** H 4

S

S. Ambrosio Island
  71 C 5
S. Félix Island **7ı** B 5
Sa Dec **37** J 5
Sa Madre Occidental
  68 AB 2—3
Sa´ādatābād (Iran) **25** F 3
Sa´ādatābād (Iran) **30** F 5
Saalfeld **17** F 4
Saarbrücken **17** E 5
Saaremaa **19** H 4
Saariselkä **18** J 2
Šabac **22** A 2
Sabadell **20** D 3
Sabah **38** E 2
Sabanalarga **72** C 1
Sabaya **74** C 4
Sabhā **51** H 3
Sabinas **68** B 2
Şabir, Jabal **53** G 6
Sabkhat al Bardawil **24** A 3
Sable, Cape (Canada)
  65 O 7
Sable, Cape (FL, U.S.A.)
  67 K 6
Sable Island **65** P 7
Sæbö **18** A 2
Sabonkafi **55** F 3
Sabrina Coast **79**
Sachs Harbour **63** N 1
Sachsen **17** F 4
Sacramento **66** B 4
Sacramento Mountains
  66 E 5

Sacramento Valley
  66 B 3—4
Sad Bi´Ar **24** B 2
Sad Kharv **25** G 1
Şa´dah **53** G 5
Sadiya **37** G 2
Sado-shima **35** L 3
Sadon **23** F 2
Şafāqis **51** H 2
Safi **50** D 2
Safid, Kūh-e (Iran) **25** E 2
Safonovo (Russia) **26** F 4
Safonovo (Russia) **26** J 2
Safonovo (Russia) **33** X 3
Şafwān **25** E 3
Saga **36** E 2
Sagaing **37** G 3
Sagar **36** C 3
Sagastyr **33** N 1
Sage **66** D 3
Saglouc **65** M 3
Sagres **20** B 4
Sagua la Grande **69** G 3
Sagunto **20** C 4
Sagwon **62** H 2
Sahagún **72** C 2
Sahara **50—51** EG 4
Saharanpur **36** C 2
Sahiwal **31** J 4
Sahlabad **30** F 4
Sahrā´ al Hajārah **24—25** D 3
Sahuayo de Diaz **68** B 4
Said Bundas **56** C 3
Sa´īdābād (Iran) **25** G 3
Saigon **37** J 5
Saihan Toroi **34** D 2
Saimaa **18** J 3
Sa´in Dezh **25** E 1
Saindak **31** G 5
Saint Alban's **65** Q 6
Saint Anthony **65** QR 5
Saint Arnaud **43** G 6
Saint-Brieuc **20** C 2
Saint Cloud **67** H 2
Saint Croix **69** JK 4
Saint-Denis (France) **20** D 2
Saint-Denis (Réunion)
  59 K 6
Saint-Dizier **21** DE 2
Saint-Elie **73** H 3
Saint-Étienne **20** D 2
Saint Francis, Cape **58** CD 6
Saint George (Queensland,
  Austr.) **43** H 4
Saint George (UT, U.S.A.)
  66 D 4
Saint George, Cape **45** F 2
Saint George's **69** K 5
Saint-Georges **65** NO 6
Saint George's Channel
  (Papua New Guinea)
  45 F 2—3
Saint George's Channel
  (United Kingdom) **16** B 4
Saint Helena **48** B 6
Saint-Jean **65** N 6
Saint Jérôme **65** N 6
Saint John **65** O 6
Saint John's (Antigua)
  69 K 4

Saint John's (Canada)
  65 R 6
Saint Johns (AZ, U.S.A.)
  66 E 5
Saint Joseph **67** H 4
Saint Kitts and Nevis **69** K 4
Saint Lawrence Island
  62 C 3
Saint Lawrence River **65** O 6
Saint Léonard **65** O 6
Saint Louis (MO, U.S.A.)
  67 H 4
Saint-Louis (Senegal)
  54 A 2
Saint Lucia **69** K 5
Saint Lucia, Cape **59** E 5
Saint Lucia, Lake **59** E 5
Saint-Malo **20** C 2
Saint Marys **45** L 9
Saint Matthias Group **45** E 2
Saint-Nazaire **20** C 2
Saint Paul (MN, U.S.A.)
  67 H 3
Saint-Paul (Réunion) **59** K 6
Saint Petersburg **19** K 4
Saint Petersburg **67** K 6
Saint Pierre et Miquelon
  65 Q 6
Saint-Quentin **20** D 2
Saint Thomas **65** L 7
Saint Vincent **69** K 5
Saint Vincent, Gulf **43** F 6
Saint Vincent Passage
  69 K 5
St. Gallen **21** E 2
St. Marys **62** E 3
Sainte-Thérèse **65** MN 6
Saintes **20** C 2
St. Peter and St. Paul Rocks
  71 G 2
S:t Pierre **65** Q 6
St Moritz **21** E 2
St. Austell **16** C 4
Saipan **46** A 1
Sajama, Nevado **74** C 4
Sakai **35** L 4
Sakākah **24** C 3
Sakami, Lac **65** M 5
Sakaraha **59** G 4
Sakarya **22** D 2
Sakata **35** L 3
Såkevare **18** G 2
Sakhalin **33** Q 5
Sakhalinskiy Zaliv **33** Q 5
Sakht Sar **25** F 1
Saksaul'skiy **31** G 1
Sal **54** B 6
Sala y Gómes **47** H 4
Salaca **19** H 4
Salada **68** D 4
Salado (Argentina) **76** D 4
Salado (Argentina) **77** C 6
Salaga **54** D 4
Salālah **53** J 5
Salamá **68** D 4
Salamanca **20** B 3
Salamat **55** J 3
Salar de Atacama **74** C 5
Salar de Uyuni **74** C 5
Salavat **26** L 5

Salaverry **72** C 5
Salawati, Pulau **39** H 4
Saldanha **58** B 6
Sale (Australia) **43** H 6
Salé (Morocco) **50** D 2
Şāleḥābād **25** E 2
Salekhard **27** N 2
Salem **36** C 5
Salem **66** B 3
Salentina, Penisola
  21 G 3—4
Salerno, Golfo di **21** F 3
Saletekri **36** D 3
Salida **66** E 4
Salihli **22** C 3
Salina (KS, U.S.A.) **66** G 4
Salina (UT, U.S.A.) **66** D 4
Salinas (CA, U.S.A.) **66** B 4
Salinas (Ecuador) **72** B 4
Salinas, Cabo de **20** D 4
Salinas de Hidalgo **68** B 3
Salinas Grandes **76** CD 4—5
Salinópolis **73** J 4
Salisbury **65** M 3
Salisbury → Harare **59** E 3
Salling **19** E 4
Salluyo, Nevado **74** C 3
Salmäs **30** C 3
Salmon Mountains **66** B 3
Salo **19** H 3
Salon-de-Provence **21** E 3
Salonga National Park
  56 C 5
Salonica **22** B 2
Salpausselkä **18** J 3
Sal´sk **23** F 1
Salso **21** F 4
Salt Lake **43** F 3
Salt Lake City **66** D 3
Salt Range **31** J 4
Salta **74** C 5
Saltdalselva **18** G 2
Salten **18** G 2
Saltillo **68** B 2
Salto **76** E 5
Salue Timpaus, Selat **39** F 4
Salumbar **36** B 3
Salvador **75** J 3
Salwä **25** F 4
Salwā Baḥrī **24** A 4
Salween **37** G 4
Salzach **21** F 2
Salzburg **21** F 2
Salzgitter **17** F 4
Sam Neua **37** H 3
Samagaltay **32** G 5
Samak, Tanjung **38** C 4
Samangan **31** H 3
Samar **39** G 1
Samara **26** K 5
Samarinda **38** E 4
Samarkand **31** H 3
Sāmarrā´ **24** D 2
Samarskoye **27** Q 6
Samauma **72** E 5
Sambaliung **38—39** E 3
Sambalpur **36** D 3
Sambava **59** J 2
Sambor (Kampuchea)
  37 J 5

Sam – San

Sambor (Russia) **17** H 5
Samfya **58** D 2
Samka **37** G 3
Samoa Islands **46** D 3
Samokov **22** B 2
Sámos **22** C 3
Samothráki **22** C 2
Sampit **38** D 4
Samsang **36** D 1
Samsun **23** E 2
Samthar **36** C 2
Samus' **27** QR 4
Samut Prakan **37** H 5
Samut Songkhram **37** H 5
San **54** D 3
San' a' **53** G 5
San Andrés **69** F 5
San Andrés Tuxtla **68** D 4
San Angelo **66** F 5
San Antonia de Cortés
  68 E 4–5
San Antonio (Chile) **76** B 5
San Antonio (Portugal)
  50 A 1
San Antonio (TX,U.S.A.)
  66 G 6
San Antonio, Cabo
  (Argentina) **77** E 6
San Antonio, Cabo (Cuba)
  68 F 3
San Antonio Oeste **77** D 7
San Bernardino **66** C 5
San Bernardo **76** BC 5
San Blas, Cape **67** J 6
San Borja **74** C 3
San Carlos (Nicaragua)
  68 F 5
San Carlos (Philippines)
  39 F 1
San Carlos de Bariloche
  77 B 7
San Carlos del Zulia **72** D 2
San Casme **76** E 4
San Cristóbal (Argentina)
  76 D 5
San Cristóbal (Dominican
  Rep.) **69** HJ 4
San Cristobal (Galápagos Is.,
  Ecuador) **72** B 6
San Cristobal (Solomon Is.)
  45 H 4
San Cristóbal (Venezuela)
  72 D 2
San Cristóbal de las Casas
  68 D 4
San Diego **66** C 5
San Diego, Cabo **77** C 9
San Dimitri Point **21** F 4
San Dona di Piave **21** F 2
San Felípe (Chile)
  76 B 5
San Felípe (Colombia)
  72 E 3
San Felipe (Venezuela)
  72 E 1
San Fernando (Chile) **77** B 5
San Fernando (Mexico)
  68 C 3
San Fernando (Spain)
  20 B 4

San Fernando (Trinidad and
  Tobago) **73** F 1
San Fernando de Apure
  72 E 2
San Fernando de Atabapo
  72 E 3
San Francisco (Argentina)
  76 D 5
San Francisco (CA, U.S.A.)
  66 B 4
San Francisco de Macorís
  69 HJ 4
San Francisco del Rincón
  68 B 3
San Francisco, Paso de
  76 C 4
San Gregorio **77** B 9
San Ignacio **74** D 4
San Ignacio (Bolivia) **74** C 3
San Ignacio (Paraguay)
  76 E 4
San Isidro **76** DE 5
San Jacinto **72** C 2
San Javier **74** D 4
San Joaquín **74** D 3
San Joaquin Valley **66** BC 4
San Jorge, Golfo **77** C 8
San Jose (CA, U.S.A.)
  66 B 4
San José (Costa Rica)
  68 F 6
San José de Chiquitos
  74 D 4
San José de Jáchal **76** C 5
San José de Mayo **76** E 5
San José del Cabo **66** E 7
San José del Guaviare
  72 D 3
San Juan (Argentina) **76** C 5
San Juan (Dominican Rep.)
  69 H 4
San Juan (Peru) **74** A 4
San Juan (Puerto Rico)
  69 J 4
San Juan (Venezuela) **72** E 2
San Juan Bautista Tuxtepec
  68 C 4
San Juan del Norte **68** F 5
San Juan, Rio **68** F 5
San Julián **77** C 8
San Justo **76** D 5
San Lorenzo **72** C 3
San Luis (Argentina) **76** C 5
San Luís (Venezuela) **72** E 1
San Luis Obispo **66** B 4
San Luis Potosi **68** B 3
San Luis Rio Colorado
  66 D 5
San Marco, Capo **21** E 4
San Marino **21** F 3
San Marino **21** F 3
San Martín **72** D 3
San Martín de los Andes
  77 B 7
San Mateo **66** B 4
San Matías **74** E 4
San Matías, Golfo **77** D 7
San Miguel (Bolivia) **74** D 3
San Miguel (El Salvador)
  68 E 5

San Miguel de Allende
  68 BC 3
San Miguel de Huachi
  74 C 4
San Miguel de Tucumán
  76 C 4
San Miguel del Padrón
  69 F 3
San Nicolás (Argentina)
  76 D 5
San Nicolás (Mexico) **68** B 2
San Onofre **72** C 2
San Pablo **77** C 9
San Pedro (Argentina)
  74 D 5
San Pedro (Mexico) **68** B 2
San Pedro (Paraguay) **74** E 5
San Pedro de Arimena
  72 D 3
San Pedro Sula **68** E 4
San Quintin **66** C 5
San Rafael (Argentina)
  76 C 5
San Remo **21** E 3
San Salvador **68** E 5
San Salvador [Watling Is.]
  69 GH 3
San Salvador de Jujuy
  74 C 5
San Sebastian (Argentina)
  77 C 9
San Sebastián (Spain)
  20 C 3
San Severo **21** G 3
San Valentin, Cerro **77** B 8
Sanae **79**
Sanaga **55** G 5
Sanandaj **25** E 2
Sanâw **53** J 5
Sanchor **36** B 3
Sancti Spíritus **69** G 3
Sand Hills **66** F 3
Sandakan **38** E 2
Sandaré **54** B 3
Sandnes **19** E 4
Sandnessjöen **18** F 2
Sandoa **56** C 6
Sandoy **16** A 1
Sandviken **19** G 3
Sandy Lake **64** J 5
Sandykachi **31** G 3
Sangar **33** N 3
Sangatolon **33** R 3
Sangay, Volcán **72** C 4
Sangha **55** GH 5
Sangha **55** H 5
Sangihe, Kepulauan **39** G 3
Sangli **36** B 4
Sanhe **32** M 5
Sanikiluaq **65** M 4
Sanjawi **31** H 4
Sankt Gotthard-Pass **21** E 2
Sankt Pölten **21** G 2
Sankuru **56** C 5
Sanlúcar de Barrameda
  20 B 4
Sannär **52** E 6
Sannikova **78**
Sanok **17** H 5
Sansanding **54** C 3

Sant' Antioco **21** E 4
Santa Ana (CA, U.S.A.)
  66 C 5
Santa Ana (El Salvador)
  68 DE 5
Santa Ana (Mexico) **66** D 5
Santa Ana (Solomon Is.)
  45 H 4
Santa Barbara **66** B 5
Santa Bárbara do Sul **76** F 4
Santa Carolina, Ilha **59** F 4
Santa Catalina **76** C 4
Santa Catarina **76** F 4
Santa Clara (CA, U.S.A.)
  66 B 4
Santa Clara (Cuba) **69** F 3
Santa Clara (Mexico) **66** E 6
Santa Clotilde **72** D 4
Santa Cruz (Argentina)
  77 C 9
Santa Cruz (Bolivia) **74** D 4
Santa Cruz (CA, U.S.A.)
  66 B 4
Santa Cruz de Mudela
  20 C 4
Santa Cruz de Tenerife
  50 B 3
Santa Cruz do Sul **76** F 4
Santa Cruz, Isla **72** B 6
Santa Cruz Islands **45** J 4
Santa Elena **72** B 4
Santa Elena, Cabo **68** E 5
Santa Fé (Argentina) **76** D 5
Santa Fe (N.M., U.S.A.)
  66 E 4
Santa Filomena **75** G 2
Santa Helena **73** JK 4
Santa Inés, Isla **77** B 9
Santa Isabel (Argentina)
  77 C 6
Santa Isabel (Solomon Is.)
  45 G 3
Santa Maria (CA, U.S.A.)
  66 B 4
Santa Maria (Portugal)
  50 A 1
Santa María (Río Grande do
  Sul, Brazil) **76** F 4
Santa Maria, Cabo de
  (Mozambique) **59** E 5
Santa Maria, Cabo de
  (Portugal) **20** B 4
Santa Maria di Leuca, Capo
  21 G 4
Santa Maria dos Marmelos
  73 F 5
Santa Marta **72** D 1
Santa Rita (Colombia)
  72 D 3
Santa Rita (Venezuela)
  72 E 2
Santa Rosa (Argentina)
  77 CD 6
Santa Rosa (CA, U.S.A.)
  66 B 4
Santa Rosa (N.M., U.S.A.)
  66 F 5
Santa Rosa (Río Grande do
  Sul, Brazil) **76** F 4
Santa Rosalia **66** D 6

174

Santa Sylvina **76** D 4
Santa Teresa **75** G 3
Santana do Livramento **76** EF 5
Santander (Colombia) **72** C 3
Santander (Spain) **20** C 3
Santarém **73** H 4
Santiago (Chile) **76** BC 5
Santiago (Haiti) **69** H 4
Santiago (Panamá) **72** B 2
Santiago da Cacém **20** B 4
Santiago de Compostela **20** B 3
Santiago del Estero **76** CD 4
Santo André **75** G 5
Santo Ângelo **76** F 4
Santo Antão **54** A 6
Santo António de Jesus **75** J 3
Santo Antônio do Içá **72** E 4
Santo Domingo (Dominican Rep.) **69** J 4
Santo Domingo (Mexico) **66** D 6
Santo Tomás **68** F 5
Santos **75** G 5
São Borja **76** E 4
São Carlos **75** G 5
São Domingos **75** G 3
São Felix **75** F 3
São Felix do Xingu **73** H 5
São Francisco **75** J 2
São Francisco do Sul **76** G 4
São João **75** G 5
São João del Rei **75** H 5
São João do Piauí **75** H 2
São José do Río Prêto **75** FG 5
São José dos Campos **75** G 5
São Leopoldo **76** F 4
Sao Lourénco, Pantanal de **74** E 4
São Luís **75** H 1
São Mateus **75** J 4
São Miguel **50** A 1
São Miguel do Araguaia **75** F 3
São Nicolau **54** B 6
São Paulo (Brazil) **75** FG 5
São Paulo (Brazil) **75** G 5
São Paulo de Olivença **72** E 4
São Raimundo Nonato **75** H 2
São Romão **75** G 4
São Roque, Cabo de **75** J 2
São Sebastião **75** GH 5
São Tiago **54** B 6
São Tomé **55** F 5
São Tomé **55** F 5
São Tomé and Principe **55** F 5
São Vicente (Cape Verde) **54** A 6
São Vicente (Sao Paulo,Brazil) **75** G 5
São Vicente, Cabo de **20** B 4

Saône **21** D 2
Sape **39** E 5
Sapele **55** F 4
Sapporo **35** M 2
Sapulut **38** E 3
Sáqand **25** G 2
Saqqez **25** E 1
Sar Dasht **25** D 1
Sara Buri **37** H 5
Sarafjagär **25** F 2
Sarajevo **21** G 3
Saraktash **26** L 5
Saralzhin **30** E 1
Saran' **27** O 6
Saran, Gunung **38** D 4
Saranpaul' **27** M 3
Saransk **26** J 5
Sarapul **26** K 4
Sarasota **67** K 6
Saratok **38** D 3
Saratov **26** HJ 5
Sarawak **38** D 3
Saräya **24** B 2
Sarbáz **31** G 5
Sarco **76** B 4
Sardegna **21** E 3
Sardinia **21** E 3
Sarek National Park **18** G 2
Sarektjåkkå **18** G 2
Sargodha **31** J 4
Sarh **55** H 4
Sarigan **46** A 1
Sarıoğlan **23** E 3
Sarīr Tibisti **51** J 4
Sariwon **35** J 3
Sarkand **27** P 6
Sarmi **39** J 4
Sarmiento **77** C 8
Sarnia **64** L 7
Saroako **39** F 4
Saronikós Kólpos **22** B 3
Saros Körfezi **22** C 2
Saroto **27** N 2
Sarpinskaya Nizmennost' **23** G 1
Sartyn`ya **27** M 3
Sarvestän **25** F 3
Sary-Ozek **31** K 2
Sary-Tash **31** J 3
Saryassiya **31** H 3
Saryg-Sep **32** G 5
Sasaram **36** D 3
Sasebo **35** J 4
Saskatchewan **63** Q 5
Saskatchewan **63** R 5
Saskatoon **63** Q 5
Saskylakh **32** KL 1
Sason Dağları **23** F 3
Sasovo **26** H 5
Sassari **21** E 3
Sassuolo **21** F 3
Sastre **76** D 5
Sasykkol', Ozero **27** Q 6
Satara **33** NO 2
Satawal **46** A 2
Satawan **46** B 2
Satipo **74** B 3
Satka **27** L 4
Satna **36** D 3
Satpura Range **36** C 3

Sattahip **37** H 5
Satu Mare **22** B 1
Sauce **76** E 5
Sauda Nathil **25** F 4
Sauðarkrókur **18** B 2
Saudi Arabia **53** GH 4
Sault Sainte Marie **64** L 6
Saumarez Reef **43** J 3
Saurimo **58** C 1
Sava **22** AB 2
Savai`i **46** D 3
Savannah **67** K 5
Savant Lake **64** JK 5
Save **59** E 4
Säveh **25** F 2
Savo **18** J 3
Savoie **21** E 2
Savonlinna **18** J 3
Sawäkin **52** F 5
Sawbä **56** E 3
Sawdiri **52** D 6
Sawhäj **52** E 3
Saydä **24** B 2
Sayhut **53** J 5
Saywün **53** H 5
Sazin **31** J 3
Sbaa **50** E 3
Scafell Pike **16** C 4
Scaife Mountains **79**
Scammon Bay **62** D 3
Scandinavia **9**
Scarborough **16** C 4
Schefferville **65** O 5
Schenectady **67** M 3
Schleswig **17** E 4
Schleswig-Holstein **17** E 4
Schouten Islands **44** D 2
Schwaner, Pegunungan **38** D 4
Schwarzwald **17** E 5
Schwatka Mountains **62** F 2
Schwedt **17** F 4
Schweinfurt **17** F 4
Schwenningen **17** E 5
Schwerin **17** F 4
Sciacca **21** F 4
Scicli **21** F 4
Scilly, Isles of **16** B 5
Scoresby Sound **78**
Scoresbysund **78**
Scotia Sea **79**
Scotland **16** C 3
Scott **79**
Scott, Cape **42** D 1
Scott Island **79**
Scott Reef **42** C 1
Scottsdale (AZ, U.S.A.) **66** D 5
Scottsdale (Tasmania, Austr.) **44** L 9
Sea of Azov **23** E 1
Sea of Crete **22** BC 3
Sea of Japan **35** KL 3
Sea of Okhotsk **33** R 4
Seabra **75** H 3
Seattle **66** B 2
Sebkha Azzel Matti **50** F 3
Sebkha Mekerrhane **51** F 3
Sebkha Oumm ed Droûs Telli **50** C 4

Sebkhet Oumm ed Droûs Guebli **50** C 4
Sechura **72** B 5
Sedan **21** DE 2
Seddenga **52** DE 4
Seeheim **58** B 5
Sefadu **54** B 4
Sefrou **50** E 2
Segesta **21** F 4
Segezha **18** K 3
Ségou **54** C 3
Segovia **20** C 3
Segozero, Ozero **18** K 3
Segre **20** D 3
Seguam **62** C 5
Seguin **66** G 6
Segura **20** C 4
Seiland **18** H 1
Seinäjoki **18** H 3
Seine **20** D 2
Seke **56** E 5
Sekoma **58** C 4
Sekondi-Takoradi **54** D 5
Selaru, Pulau **39** H 5
Selassi **39** H 4
Selat Karimata **38** C 4
Selat Makassar **38** E 4
Selat Mentawai **38** A 4
Selat Salue Timpaus **39** F 4
Selatan, Tanjung **38** D 4
Selawik **62** F 2
Seldovia **62** G 4
Selemdzhinsk **33** O 5
Selenge (Mongolia) **32** H 6
Selenge (Mongolia) **32** J 6
Selenge (Zaire) **56** B 5
Seletyteniz, Ozero **27** O 5
Selfjord **19** E 4
Selgon **33** P 6
Selinunte **21** F 4
Selizharovo **26** F 4
Selma **67** J 5
Selous Game Reserve **57** F 6
Selvagens, Ilhas **50** B 2
Selvänä **30** C 3
Selwyn Lake **63** R 3–4
Selwyn Mountains **62** LM 3
Semara **50** C 3
Semarang **38** D 5
Sembé **55** G 5
Semiozernoye **27** M 5
Semipalatinsk **27** Q 5
Semisopochnoi **62** AB 5
Semitau **38** D 3
Semmering **21** G 2
Semnän **25** F 2
Semporna **39** E 3
Sena Madureira **72** E 5
Senador Pompeu **75** J 2
Sendai **35** M 3
Sêndo **34** C 4
Senegal **54** AB 3
Sénégal **54** B 3
Senftenberg **17** F 4
Senhor do Bonfim **75** H 3
Senja **18** G 2
Senjavin Group **46** B 2
Senneterre **65** M 6
Sens **20** D 2

Sen−Sie

Senta **22** B 1
Sentinel Peak **63** N 5
Seoni **36** C 3
Seoul **35** J 3
Sepik River **44** D 2
Sept-Îles **65** O 5
Şerafettin Dağları **23** F 3
Serakhs **31** G 3
Seram **39** G 4
Seram, Laut **39** GH 4
Serang **38** C 5
Serdobsk **26** HJ 5
Seremban **38** B 3
Serengeti National Park **56** EF 5
Sergino **27** N 3
Sergipe **75** J 3
Sergiyev Posad **26** G 4
Seroglazovka **23** G 1
Serov **27** M 4
Serowe **58** D 4
Serpa **20** B 4
Serpukhov **26** G 5
Serra Acarai **73** G 3
Serra Bonita **75** G 4
Serra da Estrêla **20** B 3
Serra do Cachimbo **73** G 5
Serra do Estrondo **73** J 5
Serra do Marão **20** B 3
Serra do Mogadouro **20** B 3
Serra do Navio **73** H 3
Serra do Roncador **75** F 3
Serra do Tombador **74** E 3
Serra dos Carajás **73** H 4−5
Serra dos Gradaús **73** H 5
Serra dos Parecis **74** D 3
Serra Formosa **75** E 3
Serra Talhada **75** J 2
Sérrai **22** B 2
Serrezuela **76** C 5
Serrinha **75** J 3
Serrota **20** BC 3
Seruai **39** J 4
Serule **58** D 4
Sesfontein **58** A 3
Sesheke **58** C 3
Sesibi **52** E 4
Seskarö **18** H 2
Sestroretsk **19** J 3
Sète **20** D 3
Sete Lagoas **75** H 4
Sétif **51** G 1
Settat **50** D 2
Sette-Daban, Khrebet **33** P 3
Setúbal **20** B 4
Setúbal, Baía de **20** B 4
Seumanyam **38** A 3
Sevan, Ozero **23** G 2
Sevarujo **74** C 4
Sevastopol' **23** D 2
Sever **33** V 3
Severn **64** K 4
Severnaya Dvina **26** H 3
Severnaya Zemlya **78**
Severnoye **27** P 4
Severnyy Anyuyskiy Khrebet **33** UW 2
Severo-Kuril'sk **33** ST 5

Severo Sibirskaya Nizmennost' **32** FK 1
Severodvinsk **26** G 3
Severomorsk **18** K 2
Sevier Desert **66** D 4
Sevilla **20** B 4
Sevrey **34** D 2
Seward (AK, U.S.A.) **62** H 3
Seward (NE, U.S.A.) **66** G 3
Seward Peninsula **62** E 2
Sewell **76** B 5
Seychelles **57** J 5
Seyhan **23** E 3
Seymchan **33** S 3
Sfax **51** H 2
Sfîntu Gheorghe **22** C 1
Shaanxi **34** E 4
Shaba **56** CD 6
Shache **31** K 3
Shaddādi **24** C 1
Shadrinsk **27** M 4
Shahdol **36** D 3
Shaḥḥāt **51** K 2
Shahjahanpur **36** C 2
Shahmirzad **25** F 2
Shahr Kord **25** F 2
Sha'ib al Banāt, Jabal **24** A 4
Sha'ib Hasb **24** D 3
Sha'ib Nisāh **25** E 4
Shakhrisyabz **31** H 3
Shakhterskiy **33** X 3
Shakhtinsk **27** O 6
Shakhty **23** F 1
Shaki **54** E 4
Shalgiya **27** O 6
Shalkar **26** K 5
Shām, Jabal ash **53** K 4
Shamattawa **63** T 4
Shāmīyah **24** C 2
Shammar, Jabal **24** CD 4
Shamrock **66** F 4
Shan **37** G 3
Shandan **34** D 3
Shandi **52** E 5
Shandong **35** G 3
Shandong Bandao **35** H 3
Shangcheng **34** FG 4
Shangdu **34** F 2
Shanghai **35** H 4
Shanghang **34** G 5
Shangqiu **34** G 4
Shangrao **35** G 5
Shangzhi **35** J 1
Shanh **32** H 6
Shankou **34** B 2
Shannon **16** B 4
Shannon, Mouth of the **16** AB 4
Shanshan **34** B 2
Shantarskiye Ostrova **33** P 4
Shantou **34** G 6
Shanxi **34** F 3
Shaoguan **34** F 6
Shaowu **35** G 5
Shaoxing **35** H 5
Shaoyang **34** F 5
Shaqrā' **53** H 6

Sharāf **24** D 3
Shark Bay **42** A 4
Sharm ash Shaykh **24** AB 4
Shary **24** D 4
Shashamanna **57** F 3
Shashi **34** F 4
Shasta, Mount **66** B 3
Shatt al 'Arab **25** E 3
Shaṭṭ al Jarīd **51** G 2
Shaviklde **23** G 2
Shawinigan **65** N 6
Shaybārā **24** B 4
Shaykh ' Uthmān **53** H 6
Shaykh Şa'd **25** DE 2
Shchara **19** J 5
Shchel'yayur **26** K 2
Shchuchinsk **27** N 5
Sheboygan **67** J 3
Shedin Peak **63** M 4
Sheffield **16** C 4
Shekhawati **36** C 2
Sheki **30** D 2
Shelburne **65** OP 7
Shelby **66** D 2
Sheldon Point **62** D 3
Shelikhova, Zaliv **33** T 3−4
Shelikof Strait **62** G 4
Shellharbour **43** J 5
Shenandoah National Park **67** L 4
Shendam **55** F 4
Shenmu **34** F 3
Shenton, Mount **42** C 4
Shenyang **35** H 2
Shepetovka **19** J 5
Shepparton **43** H 6
Sherbro Island **54** B 4
Sherbrooke **65** N 6
Sheridan **66** E 3
Sherridon **63** R 4
Shetland Islands **16** C 2
Shevchenko **30** E 2
Shevli **33** O 5
Sheya **32** L 3
Sheyang **35** H 4
Sheyenne **66** G 2
Shiashkotan, Ostrov **33** S 6
Shīb Kūh **25** F 3−4
Shibarghan **31** H 3
Shibazhan **33** N 5
Shijiazhuang **34** F 3
Shikarpur **31** H 5
Shikoku **35** K 4
Shilka **32** L 5
Shilkan **33** R 4
Shilla **36** C 1
Shillong **37** F 2
Shimanovsk **33** N 5
Shimizu **35** L 4
Shindand **31** G 4
Shingshal **31** K 3
Shiping **34** D 6
Shipunovo **27** Q 5
Shipunskiy, Mys **33** TU 5
Shiquanhe **36** C 1
Shīr Kūh **25** FG 3
Shirabad **31** H 3
Shirase Glacier **79**
Shīrāz **25** F 3
Shire **59** F 2

Shirikrabat **31** G 2
Shishaldin Volcano **62** E 5
Shishou **34** F 5
Shiveluch, Sopka **33** U 4
Shivpuri **36** C 2
Shizuoka **35** L 4
Shkodra **22** A 2
Sholapur **36** C 4
Shoptykul' **27** P 5
Shorawak **31** H 4
Shoshone **66** E 3
Shoshoni **66** E 3
Shouguang **35** G 3
Showa **79**
Shqiperia **22** AB 2
Shreveport **67** H 5
Shrewsbury **16** C 4
Shuangliao **35** H 2
Shuangyashan **35** K 1
Shucheng **35** G 4
Shuicheng **34** DE 5
Shule **31** K 3
Shumagin Islands **62** F 4−5
Shumerlya **26** J 4
Shuo Xian **34** F 3
Shurinda **32** K 4
Shūshtar **25** E 2
Shuwak **52** F 6
Si Xian **35** G 4
Siah-Chashmeh **30** C 3
Siahan Range **31** GH 5
Sialkot **31** J 4
Siargao **39** G 2
Šiauliai **19** H 4
Sibay **27** L 5
Šibenik **21** G 3
Siberut, Pulau **38** A 4
Sibirskoye Ploskogorye, Sredne **32** FK 2−3
Sibiti **55** G 6
Sibiu **22** B 1
Sibolga **38** A 3
Sibsagar **37** FG 2
Sibu **38** D 3
Sibuyan Sea **39** F 1
Sicasica **74** C 4
Sichuan **34** CE 4
Sicilia **21** F 4
Sicilia, Canale de **21** F 4
Sicily **21** F 4
Sicuani **74** B 3
Siderno **21** G 4
Sidi-bel-Abbès **50** E 1
Sidney **66** F 3
Sidon **24** B 2
Siedlce **17** H 4
Siegen **17** E 4
Siena **21** F 3
Sierra Colorada **77** C 7
Sierra de Alcaraz **20** C 4
Sierra de Aracena **20** B 4
Sierra de Gata **20** B 3
Sierra de Gredos **20** B 3
Sierra de Guadalupe **20** B 4
Sierra de Guadarrama **20** C 3
Sierra de Gúdar **20** C 3
Sierra de la Cabrera **20** B 3
Sierra del Cadí **20** D 3
Sierra Leone **54** B 4

Sierra Madre **68** D 4
Sierra Madre del Sur
   68 BC 4
Sierra Mojada **68** B 2
Sierra Morena **20** BC 4
Sierra Nayarit **68** B 3
Sierra Nevada (Spain)
   20 C 4
Sierra Nevada (U.S.A.)
   66 BC 3–4
Sierra Pacaraima **73** F 3
Sierra Parima **73** F 3
Sierra Vizcaíno **66** D 6
Sífnos **22** B 3
Sighetul Marmaţiei **22** B 1
Signy Island **79**
Siguiri **54** C 3
Siilinjärvi **18** J 3
Siirt **23** F 3
Sikar **36** C 2
Sikasso **54** C 3
Sikerin **33** Q 2
Sikhote-Alin **33** P 6
Sikkim **36** E 2
Siktyakh **33** N 2
Silchar **37** F 3
Silesia **17** G 4
Silet **51** F 4
Silifke **23** D 3
Siliguri **36** E 2
Silistra **22** C 2
Siljan **19** F 3
Silkeborg **19** E 4
Siltou **55** H 2
Silver City **66** E 5
Simanggang **38** D 3
Simav **22** C 2
Simenga **32** J 3
Simeulue, Pulau **38** A 3
Simferopol' **23** D 2
Simla **36** C 1
Simojärvi **18** J 2
Simplicio Mendes **75** H 2
Simpson Desert **43** F 3
Simpson Desert National
   Park **43** F 4
Simrishamn **19** F 4
Simushir, Ostrov **33** S 6
Sinä´ **24** A 3
Sinai **24** A 3
Sinäwan **51** H 2
Sincelejo **72** C 2
Sind **31** H 5
Sinda **33** P 6
Singapore **38** BC 3
Singaraja **38** E 5
Singida **56** E 5
Singleton **43** J 5
Sinianka-Minia, Parc
   National du **55** H 3
Sinjaja **19** J 4
Sinjär **24** C 1
Sinkiang Uighur **31** L 3
Sinnamary **73** H 2
Sinop **23** E 2
Sinskoye **33** N 3
Sintang **38** D 3
Sinüiju **35** HJ 2
Sioux City **67** G 3
Sioux Falls **67** G 3

Siping **35** H 2
Sipiwesk **63** S 4
Siple Station **79**
Sir Edward Pellew Group
   43 F 2
Sir James MacBrian, Mount
   62 M 3
Siracusa **21** G 4
Sireniki **62** C 3
Siret **22** C 1
Sirgän **31** H 5
Sirino **21** G 3
Sirr, Nafūd as **24**–**25** D 4
Sirsa **36** C 2
Sirt **51** J 2
Sirt, Gulf of **51** J 2
Sisak **21** G 2
Sisophon **37** H 5
Sisseton **66** G 2
Sistema Iberico **20** C 3
Sistemas Béticos **20** C 4
Sistig-Khem **32** FG 5
Sitapur **36** D 2
Sittwe **37** F 3
Sivaki **33** N 5
Sivas **23** E 3
Sivash **23** D 1
Siverek **23** E 3
Siwah **52** F 3
Siwalik Range **36** CD 1–2
Siwan **36** D 2
Sjælland **19** F 4
Sjövegan **18** G 2
Skagen **19** F 4
Skagern **19** F 4
Skagerrak **19** E 4
Skagway **62** K 4
Skåne **19** F 4
Skarsöy **18** E 3
Skarstind **18** E 3
Skarżysko-Kamienna **17** H 4
Skeldon **73** G 2
Skeleton Coast Park **58** A 3
Skellefteå **18** H 3
Skellefteälven **18** G 2
Skien **19** E 4
Skierniewice **17** H 4
Skiftet **19** H 3
Skikda **51** G 1
Skíros **22** B 3
Skjoldungen **65** T 3
Sklad **32** M 1
Skópelos **22** B 3
Skopi **22** C 3
Skopje **22** B 2
Skövde **19** F 4
Skovorodino **33** M 5
Skye **16** B 3
Slantsy **19** J 4
Śląsk **17** G 4
Slatina **22** B 2
Slave Coast **54** E 4
Slave River **63** P 3–4
Slavgorod **27** P 5
Slavonski Brod **21** G 2
Slavuta **19** J 5
Slavyansk **26** G 6
Sligo **16** B 4
Sliven **22** C 2
Slobodka **22** C 1

Slobodskoy **26** K 4
Slonim **19** J 5
Slovakia **17** GH 5
Slovechno **19** J 5
Slovenia **21** FG 2
Slovensko **17** GH 5
Sluch´ **19** J 5
Słupsk **17** G 4
Slutsk **19** J 5
Småland **19** G 4
Smallwood Réservoir
   65 P 5
Smela **26** F 6
Smidovich **78**
Smirnykh **33** Q 6
Smith **63** P 4
Smithton **44** L 9
Smokey Dome **66** CD 3
Smoky Cape **43** J 5
Smoky Hill **66** F 4
Smöla **18** E 3
Smolensk **26** F 5
Smooth Rock Falls **65** L 6
Snake **66** C 2
Snezhnoye **33** W 2
Snoul **37** J 5
Snowdon **16** C 4
Snowdrift **63** P 3
Sobolevo **33** T 5
Sobral **75** H 1
Sochi **23** E 2
Society Islands **47** EF 4
Socorro (N.M., U.S.A.)
   66 E 5
Socotra **57** J 2
Sodankylä **18** J 2
Soddu **57** F 3
Söderhamn **18** G 3
Södermanland **19** G 4
Södertälje **19** G 4
Sofiya **22** B 2
Sofiysk **33** O 5
Sofporog **18** K 2
Sog Xian **34** B 4
Sogamoso **72** D 2
Sogn og Fjordane **18** E 3
Sognefjorden **18** E 3
Söke **22** C 3
Sokodé **54** E 4
Sokółka **17** H 4
Sokolov **17** F 4
Sokosti **18** J 2
Sokoto **55** EF 3
Sol´-Iletsk **26** L 5
Solberg **18** G 3
Soldatovo **33** V 3
Soledad **72** D 1
Soligorsk **19** J 5
Solikamsk **26** L 4
Solimões **72** E 4
Solitaire **58** B 4
Solomon Islands **45** GH 3
Solomon Sea **45** F 3
Solov´yevsk **32** L 5
Solyanka **32** M 3
Somalia **57** GH 3–4
Somerset **43** G 1
Somme **20** D 1
Somport, Puerto **20** C 3
Sonakh **33** P 5

Sönderborg **19** EF 5
Söndre Strömfjord **65** RS 2
Song Hong **37** H 3
Songea **59** F 2
Songhua Jiang **35** J 1
Songnim **35** J 3
Songo **59** E 3
Sonmiani **31** H 5
Sonneberg **17** F 4
Sonoita **66** D 5
Sonoma Peak **66** C 3
Sonora **66** D 6
Sonoran Desert **66** D 5
Sonqor **25** E 2
Sonsonate **68** DE 5
Sopka Shiveluch **33** U 4
Sopochnaya Karga **32** DE 1
Sopron **22** A 1
Sopur **31** J 4
Sor Mertvyy Kultuk **30** E 1
Sör Rondane Mountains **79**
Sör-Tröndelag **18** F 3
Sora **21** F 3
Soria **20** C 3
Sorikmerapi, Gunung
   38 A 3
Sorkh, Kuh-e **25** G 2
Sorkheh **25** F 2
Sorolen **27** P 6
Sorong **39** H 4
Soroti **56** E 4
Söröya **18** H 1
Sorsatunturi **18** J 2
Sorsele **18** G 2
Sorsogon **39** F 1
Sortavala **18** K 3
Sosnogorsk **26** KL 3
Sosnovo-Ozerskoye **32** K 5
Sosnovyy Bor **27** Q 3
Sosyka **23** EF 1
Sotkamo **18** J 3
Sotra **19** D 3
Sotsial **27** P 6
Souanké **55** G 5
Soudan **43** F 3
Souk Ahras **51** G 1
Söul **35** HJ 3
Soumenselkä **18** H 3
Soure **73** J 4
Souris **63** R 6
Sousa **75** J 2
Sousse **51** H 1
South Africa **58** CD 6
South Andaman **37** F 5
South Atlantic Ocean **79**
South Australia **42**–**43** EF 4
South Bend (IN, U.S.A.)
   67 J 3
South Bend (WA, U.S.A.)
   66 B 2
South Carolina **67** K 5
South China Sea **38** CD 2
South Dakota **66** FG 3
South East Cape **44** L 9
South Geomagnetic Pole **79**
South Georgia **79**
South Island **44** P 9
South Korea **35** JK 3

South Magnetic Pole **79**
South Orkney Islands **79**
South Pacific Ocean **79**
South Platte **66** F 3
South Pole **79**
South Sandwich Islands **79**
South Saskatchewan
　63 PQ 5
South Shetland Islands **79**
South Shields **16** C 3–4
South Uist **16** B 3
South Wellesley Islands
　43 F 2
Southampton **16** C 4
Southampton Island
　63 UV 3
Southend **63** R 4
Southend-on-Sea **16** D 4
Southern Alps **45** Q 9
Southern Cook Islands
　47 E 4
Southern Cross **42** B 5
Southern Uplands **16** C 3
Southwest Cape **44** P 10
Soven **76** C 5
Sovetsk **26** J 4
Sovetskaya Gavan' **33** PQ 6
Sovetskaya Rechka **27** Q 2
Sozimskiy **26** K 4
Spain **20** BC 4
Spanish Town **69** G 4
Sparks **66** C 4
Spartanburg **67** K 5
Spartí **22** B 3
Spartivento, Capo **21** E 4
Spassk Dal'niy **35** K 2
Spátha, Ákra **22** B 3
Spearfish **66** F 3
Spence Bay **63** T 2
Spencer Gulf **43** F 5
Spicer Islands **65** M 2
Spitsbergen **78**
Split **21** G 3
Spokane **66** C 2
Spooner **67** H 2
Springbok **58** B 5
Springfield (CO, U.S.A.)
　66 F 4
Springfield (IL, U.S.A.)
　67 HJ 4
Springfield (MA, U.S.A.)
　67 M 3
Springfield (MO, U.S.A.)
　67 H 4
Springfield (OR, U.S.A.)
　66 B 3
Springs **58** D 5
Squillace, Golfo di **21** G 4
Srbija **22** B 2
Sredinnyy Khrebet
　33 TU 4–5
Sredna Gora **22** B 2
Sredne Sibirskoye
　Ploskogor'ye **32** FK 2–3
Srednekolymsk **33** S 2
Sredniy **33** S 4
Srednyaya Itkana **33** U 3
Sremska Mitrovica **22** A 2
Sri Lanka **36** D 6
Srikakulam **36** D 4

Srinagar **31** K 4
Staaten River National Park
　43 G 2
Stafford **16** C 4
Stalowa Wola **17** H 4
Stamford **67** M 3
Standerton **58** D 5
Stanke Dimitrov **22** B 2
Stanley **77** E 9
Stanley Falls **56** D 4
Stanley Mission **63** R 4
Stanovka **27** O 4
Stanovoy Khrebet
　32–33 LN 4
Stanovoy Nagor'ye **32** KL 4
Stara Planina **22** BC 2
Stara Zagora **22** C 2
Staraya Russa **19** K 4
Staraya Vorpavla **27** N 3
Starbuck **47** E 3
Stargard Szczecinski **17** G 4
Starodub **26** F 5
Starogard Gdański **17** G 4
Staryy Oskol **26** G 5
Staten Island **77** D 9
Stavanger **19** DE 4
Stavropol' **23** F 1
Stavropolka **27** N 5
Stavropol'skaya
　Vozvyshennost' **23** F 1
Steen River **63** O 4
Stefanie, Lake **57** F 4
Stefansson Island **63** Q 1
Steinkjer **18** F 3
Steinkopf **58** B 5
Stellenbosch **58** B 6
Stenon **22** C 3
Stepanakert **30** D 3
Sterlitamak **26** KL 5
Steubenville **67** K 3
Stevenson Entrance **62** G 4
Stewart (AK, U.S.A.)
　62 M 4
Stewart (Canada) **62** KL 3
Stewart (New Zealand)
　44 P 10
Stewart Crossing **62** K 3
Stewart Island **44** P 10
Stewart Islands **45** H 3
Steyr **21** F 2
Stillwater **67** G 4
Štip **22** B 2
Stirling Range National Park
　42 B 5
Stjørdal **18** F 3
Stockholm **19** G 4
Stockton **66** B 4
Stockton Plateau **66** F 5
Stöde **18** G 3
Stoke-on-Trent **16** C 4
Stony Rapids **63** Q 4
Stony River **62** F 3
Storån **18** G 4
Storavan **18** G 2
Stornoway **16** B 3
Storö **19** E 4
Storsjön **18** F 3
Storuman **18** G 2
Storvigelen **18** F 3
Stöttingfjället **18** G 3

Strait of Belle Isle **65** Q 5
Strait of Bonifacio **21** E 3
Strait of Dover **16** D 4
Strait of Hormuz **25** G 4
Strait of Magellan **77** BC 9
Strait of Makassar **38** E 4
Strait of Malacca **38** B 3
Straits of Florida **67** KL 6–7
Stralsund **17** F 2
Strand **58** B 6
Stranraer **16** B 4
Strasbourg **21** E 2
Stratford **66** F 4
Straubing **17** F 5
Streaky Bay **42** E 5
Strelka-Chunya **32** H 3
Stretto di Messina **21** G 4
Streymoy **16** A 1
Strömsund **18** G 3
Stryy **26** D 6
Stung Treng **37** J 5
Sturt Desert **43** G 4
Sturt National Park **43** G 4
Stuttgart **17** E 5
Stykkishólmur **18** A 2
Styr' **19** J 5
Subayhah **24** C 3
Suceava **22** C 1
Sucre **74** CD 4
Sudan **52** DE 6
Sudbury **65** L 6
Suddie **73** G 2
Sudety **17** G 4
Suðuroy **16** A 1
Suez **24** A 3
Suez Canal **24** A 3
Şuhār **53** K 4
Sühbaatar **34** F 1
Suhl **17** F 4
Suide **34** F 3
Suining **35** G 4
Suizhong **35** H 2
Sukabumi **38** C 5
Sukaraja **38** D 4
Sukhana **32** L 2
Sukhona **26** H 4
Sukhumi **23** F 2
Sukkertoppen **65** R 2
Sukkur **31** H 5
Suksukan **33** S 3
Sula, Kepulauan **39** FG 4
Sulaiman Range **31** H 4–5
Sulaimāniya **25** D 2
Sulanheer **34** E 2
Sulat, Bukit **39** G 3
Sulawesi **39** EF 4
Sulb **52** E 4
Sulitelma **18** G 2
Sullana **72** B 4
Sultan Dağları **22–23** D 3
Sulu Archipelago **39** F 2–3
Sulu Sea **39** EF 2
Sumarokovo **27** R 3
Sumatera **38** AB 3–4
Sumaúma **73** G 3
Šumava **17** F 5
Sumba **39** EF 5
Sumbawa **38** E 5
Sumbawanga **56** E 6
Sumbe **58** A 2

Sümber **34** E 1
Sumburgh Head **16** C 3
Sumgait **30** DE 2
Summel **24** D 1
Summit Lake **63** N 4
Sumperk **17** G 5
Sumter **67** KL 5
Sumy **26** G 5
Suna **56** E 6
Sunda Islands **9**
Sundarbans **36–37** EF 3
Sunderland **16** C 4
Sündiren Dağları **22** D 3
Sundsvall **18** G 3
Sunflower, Mount **66** F 4
Sungai Barito **38** D 4
Sungai Kampar **38** B 3
Sungai Kutai **38** E 4
Sungai Mamberamo **39** J 4
Sunnan **18** F 3
Sunndalsfjorden **18** E 3
Suokonmäki **18** H 3
Suolahti **18** J 3
Suomenselkä **18** J 3
Suomi **18** J 3
Suoyarvi **18** K 3
Superior **67** H 2
Süphan Dağı **23** F 3
Şür **24** B 2
Surabaya **38** D 5
Surakarta **38** CD 5
Surat (India) **36** B 3
Surat (Queensland, Austr.)
　43 H 4
Surat Thani **37** GH 6
Suratgarh **36** B 2
Surendranagar **36** B 3
Surgut **27** O 3
Surgutikha **27** R 3
Surigao **39** G 2
Surin **37** H 5
Suriname **73** G 3
Sürïyah **24** BC 2
Surtsey **18** A 3
Surud Ad **57** H 2
Survey Pass **62** FG 2
Susa **25** E 2
Süsah **51** H 1
Süsangerd **25** E 3
Susques **74** C 5
Susuman **33** R 3
Sutlej **31** J 4
Sutton **62** H 3
Sutun'ya **33** O 2
Suva **46** C 4
Suva Gora **22** B 2
Suva Planina **22** B 2
Suwałki **17** H 4
Suwon **35** J 3
Suzhou **35** GH 4
Suzun **27** Q 5
Svalbard **78**
Svartisen **18** F 2
Svatoy Nos, Mys **33** P 1
Svealand **19** FG 4
Sveg **18** F 3
Svendborg **19** F 4
Sverige **18** G 3
Svetlogorsk **19** J 5
Svetlograd **23** F 1

Svetlyy 33 N 4
Svetozarevo 22 B 2
Svir' 26 F 3
Svobodnyy 33 N 5
Svolvær 18 FG 2
Svyatoy Nos, Mys 26 GH 2
Swain Reefs 43 J 3
Swains 46 D 3
Swakopmund 58 A 4
Swan Hill 43 G 6
Swan River 63 R 5
Swansea 16 C 4
Swaziland 59 E 5
Sweden 18 G 3
Swellendam 58 C 6
Świdnik 17 H 4
Swift Current 63 Q 5
Swinoujście 17 F 4
Switzerland 21 E 2
Syadaykharvuta 27 OP 2
Syalakh 33 MN 2
Syamozero, Ozero 18 K 3
Syangannakh 33 R 2
Syðri-Hagangur 18 B 2
Sydney (New Brunswick,
    Can.) 65 Q 6
Sydney (N.S.W., Austr.)
    43 J 5
Syktyvkar 26 JK 3
Sylhet 37 F 3
Syr-Dar'ya 31 H 2
Syracuse 67 L 3
Syria 24 BC 2
Syrian Desert 24 C 2
Syuge-Khaya, Gora 33 P 2
Syurkum 33 Q 5
Syzran 26 J 5
Szczecin 17 F 4
Szczecinek 17 G 4
Szeged 22 A 1
Székesféhérvár 22 A 1
Szekszárd 22 A 1
Szentes 22 B 1
Szolnok 22 B 1
Szombathely 22 A 1

T

Ta' izz 53 G 6
Taarom 43 HJ 4
Tabacal 74 D 5
Ţabaqah 24 C 2
Tabas 25 G 2
Tabasco 68 D 4
Tabatinga 72 E 4
Tabelbala 50 E 3
Tabelbalet 51 G 3
Tabeng 37 H 5
Tabiteuea 46 C 3
Tabla 54 E 3
Table Mountain 58 B 6
Tábor (Czechoslovakia)
    17 F 5
Tabor (Russia) 33 R 1
Tabora 56 E 6
Tabou 54 C 5
Tabriz 30 D 3
Tabuaeran 47 E 2
Tabūk 24 B 3

Tacheng 31 L 1
Tacloban 39 F 1
Tacna 74 B 4
Tacoma 66 B 2
Tacuarembó 76 E 5
Tademaït, Plateau du 51 F 3
Tadoule Lake 63 S 4
Taegu 35 J 3
Taejŏn 35 J 3
Tagama 55 F 2
Taganrog 23 E 1
Taganrogskiy Zaliv 23 E 1
Tagounite 50 D 3
Taguatinga 75 G 3
Taguenout Haggueret
    54 D 1
Tagula Island 43 J 1
Tahan, Gunung 38 B 3
Tahat, Mont 51 G 4
Tahiti 47 F 4
Tahoua 55 EF 3
Tahrūd 30 F 5
Tahtali Dağlari 23 E 3
Tahuata 47 F 3
Taï, Parc National de 54 C 4
Taibus Qi 34 FG 2
Taichung 35 H 6
Tailai 35 H 1
Taimba 32 G 3
Tainan 35 GH 6
Taínaron, Ákra 22 B 3
Taipei 35 H 6
Taiping 38 B 3
Taipu 75 J 2
Taitao, Península de
    77 AB 8
Taitung 35 H 6
Taivalkoski 18 J 2
Taiwan 35 H 6
Taiwan Haixia 35 GH 5--6
Taiyuan 34 F 3
Tajikistan 31 HJ 3
Tajito 66 D 5
Tájo 20 B 4
Tajrish 25 F 2
Tajumulco, Volcán 68 D 4
Tak 37 G 4
Takāb 25 E 1
Takamatsu 35 K 4
Takatshwane 58 C 4
Takeo 37 H 5
Takestan 25 E 1
Takht-e Soleiman 25 F 1
Takhta-Bazar 31 G 3
Takijuq Lake 63 P 2
Takla Landing 63 M 4
Takla Makan 31 L 3
Taklaun, Gora 33 Q 3
Taklimakan Shamo 31 LM 3
Takua Pa 37 G 6
Talak 55 EF 2
Talakan 33 O 6
Talandzha 33 O 6
Talara 72 B 4
Talaud, Kepulauan 39 G 3
Talavera de la Reina 20 C 4
Talawdi 52 E 6
Talaya (Russia) 32 G 4
Talaya (Russia) 33 S 3
Talca 77 B 6

Talcahuano 77 B 6
Taldy-Kurgan 27 P 6
Talence 20 C 3
Taliabu, Pulau 39 FG 4
Talimardzhan 31 H 3
Taliqan 31 H 3
Taliwang 38 E 5
Talkalakh 24 B 2
Talkeetna 62 G 3
Tall 'Afar 24 D 1
Tall aş Şuwār 24 C 2
Tall Kayf 24 D 1
Tall Kūshik 24 CD 1
Tallahassee 67 K 5
Tallinn 19 HJ 4
Talo 57 F 2
Taltal 76 B 4
Tama, Mount 58 A 2
Tamale 54 D 4
Tamanrasset 51 G 4
Tamaulipas 68 C 3
Tambacounda 54 B 3
Tambalan 38 E 3
Tambisan 39 E 2
Tambo 43 H 3
Tambov 26 H 5
Tamch 32 F 6
Tamchaket 50 C 5
Tame 72 D 2
Tamel Aike 77 B 8
Tamgak, Monts 55 F 2
Tamil Nadu 36 C 5
Tammerfors 18 H 3
Tampa 67 K 6
Tampere 18 H 3
Tampico 68 C 3
Tamu 37 F 3
Tamworth 43 J 5
Tana (Kenya) 57 F 5
Tana (Norway) 18 J 1
Tana (Vanuatu) 45 J 5
Tana, Lake 57 F 2
Tanaga 62 B 5
Tanami 42 D 2
Tanami Desert 42 E 2
Tanami Desert Wildlife
    Sanctuary 42 E 3
Tanana 62 G 2
Tanana 62 H 3
Tanch'ŏn 35 J 2
Tandaho 57 G 2
Tandil 77 E 6
Tane-ga-shima 35 K 4
Tang-e Karam 25 F 3
Tanga 57 F 5--6
Tanganyika, Lake 56 DE 6
Tanger 50 D 1
Tangerang 38 C 5
Tanggula Shan 34 BC 4
Tanggula Shankou 34 B 4
Tanghe 34 F 4
Tangier → Tanger 50 D 1
Tangmai 34 C 4
Tangshan 35 G 3
Tangyuan 35 J 1
Tanimbar, Kepulauan 39 H 5
Tanjung Api 38 C 3
Tanjung Lumut 38 C 4
Tanjung Samak 38 C 4
Tanjung Selatan 38 D 4

Tanjung Vals 39 J 5
Tanjungbalai 38 AB 3
Tanjungredeb 38 E 3
Tanjungselor 38 E 3
Tannu Ola 32 F 5
Ţanţa 52 E 2
Tanzania 56--57 EF 6
Tao'an 35 H 1
Taolanaro 59 H 5
Taoudenni 54 D 1
Taoyuan 35 H 5
Tapachula 68 D 5
Tapajós 73 G 4
Tapurucuara 72 E 4
Taquari (Brazil) 74 E 4
Taquari (Brazil) 75 F 4
Tara 27 O 4
Ţarābulus (Lebanon) 24 B 2
Ţarābulus (Libya) 51 H 2
Taracuá 72 E 3
Tarakan 38 E 3
Tarakki 31 H 4
Taranto 21 G 3
Taranto, Golfo di 21 G 3--4
Tarapoto 72 C 5
Tarasovo 26 J 2
Tarata 74 C 4
Tarauacá 72 D 5
Tarawa 46 C 2
Tarbes 20 D 3
Taree 43 J 5
Tareya 32 F 1
Tarfaya 50 C 3
Ţarīf 25 F 4
Tarija 74 D 5
~Tarim Liuchang 34 A 2
Tarin Kowt 31 H 4
Tarkhankut, Mys 23 D 1
Tarko-Sale 27 P 3
Tarkwa 54 D 4
Tarlac 39 J 1
Tarma 74 A 3
Tarn 20 D 3
Tärnaby 18 G 2
Tarnobrzeg 17 H 4
Tarnów 17 H 4
Taroudant 50 D 2
Tarragona 20 D 3
Tarrasa 20 D 3
Tarsū Mūsa 51 J 4
Tarsus 23 D 3
Tart 34 B 3
Tartagal 74 D 5
Tartu 19 J 4
Ţarţus 24 B 2
Tarutung 38 A 3
Tas-Tumus 33 O 1
Tashanta 27 R 6
Tashauz 30 F 2
Tashk, Daryācheh-ye
    25 FG 3
Tashkent 31 H 2
Tashtagol 27 R 5
Tasikmalaya 38 C 5
Tasman Bay 45 Q 9
Tasman Sea 44 NO 8
Tasmania 44 L 9
Tassili N-Ajjer 51 G 3
Tasüj 30 D 3
Tatabánya 22 A 1

Tatakoto **47** F 4
Tatarbunary **22** C 1
Tatarsk **27** P 4
Tatarskiy Proliv **33** Q 6
Tatry **17** H 5
Taubaté **75** GH 5
Taumaturgo **72** D 5
Taunggon **37** G 3
Taungup **37** F 4
Taunton **16** C 4
Tauranga **45** R 8
Tavatuma **33** T 3
Tavda **27** N 4
Taverner Bay **65** N 2
Tavolara **21** E 3
Tavoy **37** G 5
Tawau **38** E 3
Tawitawi Group **39** F 2
Ţawüq **24** D 2
Tawzar **51** G 2
Taxco de Alarcón **68** C 4
Taxkorgan **31** K 3
Tay **16** C 3
Tayga **27** QR 4
Taygonos, Mys **33** U 3
Taylor **62** DE 2
Tayma' **24** C 4
Taymyr **32** F 2
Taymyr, Ozero **32** H 1
Taymyr, Poluostrov **32** FH 1
Tayshet **32** G 4
Taytay **39** E 1
Taz **27** P 2
Taza **50** E 2
Täzah Khurmātū **24** D 2
Tazovskiy **27** P 2
Tbilisi **23** F 2
Tcholliré **55** G 4
Teba **39** J 4
Tébessa **51** G 1
Tebingtinggi **38** A 3
Tebulos Mta **23** G 2
Tecer Dağlari **23** E 3
Tecka **77** B 7
Tecomán **68** B 4
Tecuci **22** C 1
Tedzhen **30** FG 3
Tefé **73** F 4
Tegal **38** C 5
Tegre **57** FG 2
Tegucigalpa **68** E 5
Tegyul'te-Tërde **33** O 3
Tehrän **25** F 2
Tehuacán **68** C 4
Teiga Plateau **52** D 5
Tejo **20** B 4
Tekeli **31** K 2
Tekes **31** L 2
Tekirdağ **22** C 2
Tel Aviv-Yafo **24** B 2–3
Telegraph Creek **62** L 4
Telemaco Borba **75** F 5
Telemark **19** E 4
Telén **77** C 6
Teles Pires **73** G 5
Teli **32** F 5
Tell al 'Amärna **52** E 3
Tello **76** C 5
Telok Anson **38** B 3
Tel'pos-Iz, Gora **27** L 3

Teluk Berau **39** H 4
Teluk Bone **39** F 4
Teluk Cendrawasih **39** HJ 4
Teluk Kumai **38** D 4
Teluk Tomini **39** F 4
Telukbatang **38** CD 4
Témacine **51** G 2
Tematangi **47** F 4
Tembenchi **32** G 3
Tembo **56** B 6
Tembo, Mont **55** G 5
Temirtau **27** O 5
Temiscaming **65** M 6
Temoe **47** G 4
Tempa **78**
Temple **67** G 5
Temuco **77** B 6
Tena **72** C 4
Tenali **36** D 4
Tenasserim **37** G 5
Ténéré **55** FG 2
Tenerife **50** B 3
Tengchong **34** C 5
Tengiz, Ozero **27** N 5
Teniente Marsh **79**
Teniente Matienzo **79**
Tenke **32** L 3
Tennant Creek **42** E 2
Tennessee **67** J 4
Tenojoki **18** J 2
Tenterfield **43** J 4
Teófilo Otoni **75** H 4
Tepatitlán **68** B 3
Tepic **68** B 3
Teraina **47** E 2
Teramo **21** F 3
Tercan **23** F 3
Terceira **50** A 1
Teresina **75** H 2
Teressa **37** F 6
Terhazza **50** D 4
Termez **31** H 3
Ternate **39** G 3
Terni **21** F 3
Ternopol' **26** E 6
Terpeniya, Mys **33** QR 6
Terpeniya, Zaliv **33** Q 6
Terpugovo **27** N 4
Terrace **62** M 5
Terracina **21** F 3
Terracy Bay **64** K 6
Tessalit **54** E 1
Tessenei **57** F 1–2
Testa, Capo **21** E 3
Tete **59** E 3
Tétouan **50** D 1
Tetovo **22** B 2
Tevere **21** F 3
Teverya **24** B 2
Tēwo **34** D 4
Texarkana **67** H 5
Texas **66** FG 5
Texas City **67** H 6
Teya **32** F 3
Teykovo **26** GH 4
Teyuareh **31** G 4
Teziutlán **68** C 4
Tezpur **37** F 2
Thailand **37** GH 4
Thakhek **37** HJ 4

Thames **16** C 4
Thana **36** B 4
Thangoo **42** C 2
Thanh Hoa **37** J 4
Thanjavur **36** C 5
Thap Sakae **37** GH 5
Thar Desert **36** B 2
Thargomindah **43** G 4
Thásos **22** B 2
Thaton **37** G 4
The Alps **21** EF 2
The Bahamas **69** GH 2
The Everglades **67** K 6
The Gambia **54** A 3
The Granites **42** E 3
The Gulf **25** EF 3–4
The Hague **16** D 4
The Johnston Lakes **42** C 5
The Pas **63** R 5
The Wash **16** D 4
Thebes **24** A 4
Thermaïkos Kólpos
  22 B 2–3
Thessalía **22** B 3
Thessaloníki **22** B 2
Thiès **54** A 3
Thimphu **36** E 2
Thio (Ethiopia) **57** G 2
Thio (New Caledonia) **45** J 6
Thíra **22** C 3
Þjórsá **18** B 3
Thompson **63** S 4
Thompson Falls **66** C 2
Thon Buri **37** GH 5
Thonon **21** E 2
Thráki **22** C 2
Thrakikón Pélagos **22** BC 2
Three Forks **66** D 2
Three Kings Islands **45** Q 7
Three Pagodas Pass **37** G 4
Thule **78**
Thunder Bay **64** K 6
Thung Song **37** G 6
Thurston Island **79**
Thy **19** E 4
Ti-n Zaouâtene **51** F 4
Tiandong **34** E 6
Tiangua **75** H 1
Tianjin **35** G 3
Tianjun **34** C 3
Tianmen **34** F 4
Tiaret **51** F 1
Tiber **21** F 3
Tibesti **55** H 1
Tibet **36** E 1
Tibet, Plateau of **36** DE 1
Tibistī, Sarir **51** J 4
Tichla **50** B 4
Tidjikdja **50** C 5
Tidra, Île **50** B 5
Tieli **35** J 1
Tielongtan **31** K 3
Tientsin **35** G 3
Tierra de Campos **20** BC 3
Tierra del Fuego, Isla Grande
  de **77** C 9
Tierra del Pan **20** B 3
Tigil' **33** T 4
Tigris **25** D 2
Tiguent **50** B 5

Tihämat **53** G 5
Tijuana **66** C 5
Tikal **68** E 4
Tikhoretsk **23** F 1
Tikhvin **26** F 4
Tiksi **33** N 1
Tilcara **74** C 5
Tilichiki **33** V 3
Tillabéri **54** E 3
Tillamook **66** B 2
Tillia **55** E 2
Timanskiy Kryazh
  26 JL 2–3
Timaru **45** Q 9
Timashevskaya **23** E 1
Timbauba **75** J 2
Timbuktu → Tombouctou
  54 D 2
Timétrine **54** D 2
Timétrine, Monts **54** D 2
Timia **55** F 2
Timimoun **50** F 3
Timir-Atakh-Tas **33** S 2
Timiris, Cap **50** B 5
Timişoara **22** B 1
Timkapaul' **27** M 3
Timmiarmiut **65** T 3
Timmins **65** L 6
Timor, Laut **39** G 6
Timor Sea **39** G 6
Timote **76** D 6
Tinaca Point **39** G 2
Tindouf **50** D 3
Tinfouchy **50** D 3
Tingri **36** E 2
Tini Wells **52** C 6
Tinian **46** A 2
Tinogasta **76** C 4
Tínos **22** C 3
Tinsukia **37** G 2
Tirän **24** B 4
Tirana **22** AB 2
Tiraspol' **22** C 1
Tire **22** C 3
Tirgovişte **22** C 2
Tîrgu Jiu **22** B 1
Tîrgu Mureş **22** BC 1–2
Tirich Mir **31** J 3
Tîrnăveni **22** B 1
Tirol **21** F 2
Tirso **21** E 3
Tiruchchirappalli **36** C 5
Tirunelveli **36** C 6
Tirupati **36** C 5
Tiruvannamalai **36** C 5
Tisdale **63** R 5
Tisza **22** B 1
Tiszántúl **22** B 1
Titicaca, Lago **74** C 4
Titov Veles **22** B 2
Titovo Užice **22** A 2
Titusville **67** K 6
Tiveden **19** F 4
Tizatlan **68** C 4
Tizi Ouzou **51** F 1
Tizimín **68** E 3
Tiznit **50** D 3
Tjåhumas **18** G 2
Tkhach **23** F 2
Tkvarcheli **23** F 2

Tlemcen **50** E 2
Toaca, Virful **22** C 1
Toamasina **59** H 3
Toba & Kakar Ranges
  31 H 4
Tobago, Isla **73** F 1
Tobermorey **43** F 3
Tobol **27** M 5
Tobol **27** N 4
Tobol´sk **27** N 4
Tobseda **26** K 2
Tocantina **73** J 5
Tocantins **73** J 4
Tocapilla **74** B 5
Tocorpuri, Cerro de **74** C 5
Togiak **62** E 4
Togian, Kepulauan **39** F 4
Togni **52** F 5
Togo **54** E 4
Togtoh **34** F 2
Togyz **31** G 1
Tohma **23** E 3
Toijala **18** H 3
Tok **62** J 3
Tokara-rettō **35** J 5
Tokat **23** E 2
Tokelau Islands **46** D 3
Tokko **32** L 4
Tokmak (Georgia) **31** K 2
Tokmak (Ukraine) **23** E 1
Toksun **31** M 2
Toktogul **31** J 2
Toku-no-shima **35** J 5
Tokur **33** O 5
Tokushima **35** K 4
Tōkyō **35** L 3
Toledo (OH, U.S.A.) **67** K 3
Toledo (Spain) **20** C 4
Toledo, Montes de **20** C 4
Toli **31** L 1
Toliara **59** G 4
Tolima **72** C 3
Tolstoy, Mys **33** T 4
Toltén **77** B 6
Toluca **68** C 4
Tol´yatti **26** J 5
Tomakomai **35** M 2
Tomaszów Mazowiecki
  17 H 4
Tomatlán **68** AB 4
Tombigbee **67** J 5
Tombouctou **54** D 2
Tomé **77** B 6
Tomelloso **20** C 4
Tomini, Teluk **39** F 4
Tomkinson Ranges **42** D 4
Tomma **18** F 2
Tommot **33** N 4
Tompa **32** J 4
Tomsk **27** R 4
Tonantins **72** E 4
Tondano **39** FG 3
Tonekābon **25** F 1
Tonga **46** D 4
Tonga (Sudan) **56** E 3
Tonga Islands **46** D 4
Tongariro National Park
  45 R 8
Tongatapu Group **46** D 4
Tongchuan **34** E 3

Tonghai **34** D 6
Tonghe **35** J 1
Tongliao **35** H 2
Tongoy **76** B 5
Tongren **34** D 3
Tongren **34** E 5
Tongtian He **34** C 4
Tongyu **35** H 2
Tongzi **34** E 5
Tonj **56** D 3
Tonk **36** C 2
Tonle Sap **37** H 5
Tonopah **66** C 4
Tönsberg **19** F 4
Toompine **43** G 4
Toowoomba **43** J 4
Topeka **67** G 4
Topolinyy **33** P 3
Topozero, Ozero **18** K 2
Toraya **74** B 3
Torbat-e Heydariyeh
  30 FG 3
Torbay **16** C 4
Torbino **26** F 4
Torey **32** H 5
Tori **56** E 3
Torino **21** E 2
Torneälven **18** H 2
Torneträsk **18** H 2
Tornio **18** H 2
Toro, Cerro del **76** C 4
Torom **33** P 5
Toronto **65** M 7
Toropets **26** F 4
Tororo **56** E 4
Toros Dağlari **23** D 3
Torquato Severo **76** F 5
Torralevega **20** C 3
Torrens Creek **43** H 3
Torrens, Lake **43** F 5
Torrente **20** C 4
Torreón **68** B 2
Torres Strait **43** G 1
Torrington **66** F 3
Torshavn **16** A 1
Tortkuduk **27** O 5
Tortosa **20** D 3
Torud **25** G 2
Toruń **17** G 4
Toscana **21** F 3
Tosontsengel **32** G 6
Tostuya **32** K 1
Totma **26** H 4
Totness **73** G 2
Totoras **76** D 5
Totten Glacier **79**
Tottori **35** K 3
Toubkal, Jbel **50** D 2
Touggourt **51** G 2
Toulouse **20** D 3
Toungoo **37** G 4
Touraine **20** D 2
Tourcoing **20** D 1
Tourine **50** C 4
Tours **20** D 2
Towakaima **73** G 2
Townsend **66** D 2
Townsville **43** H 2
Toyama **35** L 3
Toygunen **62** C 2

Toyohashi **35** L 4
Toyota **35** L 3
Trabzon **23** F 2
Trafalgar, Cabo **20** B 4
Trāghan **51** H 3
Trang **37** G 6
Trangan, Pulau **39** H 5
Transantarctic Mountains
  79
Transilvania **22** B 1
Transkei **58** D 6
Transtrandsfjällen **18** F 3
Transvaal **58** D 5
Trapani **21** F 4
Trat **37** H 5
Traun **21** F 2
Travers, Mount **45** Q 9
Trebisacce **21** G 4
Treinta y Tres **76** EF 5
Trelew **77** CD 7
Trelleborg **19** F 4
Tremonton **66** D 3
Trenčín **17** G 5
Trenel **77** D 6
Trenque Lauquen **77** D 6
Trento **21** F 2
Trenton **67** M 3
Trepassey **65** R 6
Tres Arroyos **77** D 6
Tres Cerros **77** C 8
Tres Esquinas **72** CD 3
Três Lagoas **75** F 5
Tres Puentes **76** BC 4
Treviso **21** F 2
Triabunna **44** L 9
Trialetskiy Khrebet **23** F 2
Trichur **36** C 5
Trier **16** E 5
Trieste **21** F 2
Trikala **22** B 3
Trincomalee **36** D 6
Trindade Island **71** G 5
Trinidad (Bolivia) **74** D 3
Trinidad (Colombia) **72** D 2
Trinidad (Cuba) **69** G 3
Trinidad (Uruguay) **76** E 5
Trinidad and Tobago
  73 FG 1
Trinidad, Isla **73** F 1
Trinity Islands **62** G 4
Trinkitat **52** F 5
Tripoli (Lebanon) **24** B 2
Tripoli (Libya) **51** J 2
Tripolitania **51** HJ 2
Tripura **37** F 3
Tristan da Cunha **10** G 5
Trivandrum **36** C 6
Trnava **17** G 5
Trobriand or Kiriwina Islands
  45 F 3
Trois-Pistoles **65** O 6
Trois Rivières **65** N 6
Troitsk (Kazakhstan) **27** M 5
Troitsk (Russia) **32** F 4
Troitsko-Pechorsk **26** L 3
Trollhättan **19** F 4
Trollheimen **18** E 3
Trollhetta **18** E 3
Trolltindane **18** E 3
Tromelin **49** H 6

Troms **18** G 2
Tromsö **18** G 2
Trondheim **18** F 3
Trondheimsfjorden **18** F 3
Troodos **23** D 4
Trout Peak **66** E 3
Trout River **65** O 6
Troy (AL, U.S.A.) **67** J 5
Troy (Turkey) **22** C 3
Troy Peak **66** C 4
Troyan **22** B 2
Troyes **20** D 2
Trujillo (Peru) **72** C 5
Trujillo (Venezuela) **72** D 2
Truk Islands **46** B 2
Truro **65** P 6
Truth or Consequences [Hot
  Springs] **66** E 5
Truva **22** C 3
Trysilfjellet **18** F 3
Tsaratanana, Massif du
  59 H 2
Tsavo National Park **57** F 5
Tselinograd **27** O 5
Tsenhermandal **32** JK 6
Tsenogora **26** J 3
Tsentralno Tungusskoye
  Plato **32** GH 3–4
Tsetseg **32** F 6
Tsetserleg (Mongolia)
  32 G 6
Tsetserleg (Mongolia)
  32 H 6
Tshane **58** C 4
Tshesebe **58** D 4
Tshikapa **56** C 6
Tsiafajavona **59** H 3
Tsimlyanskoye
  Vodokhranilishche **23** F 1
Tsingtao **35** H 3
Tsingtao **35** H 3
Tsipanda **33** P 4
Tskhinvali **23** F 2
Tsodilo Hills **58** C 3
Tsuchiura **35** M 3
Tsumeb **58** B 3
Tsumkwe **58** C 3
Tsuruoka **35** L 3
Tuamotu Archipelago
  47 F 4
Tuan **37** H 3
Tuapse **23** E 2
Tuba **32** H 4
Tubarão **76** G 4
Tubruq **51** K 2
Tubuai **47** F 4
Tubuai Islands **47** EF 4
Tucano **75** J 3
Tucavaca **74** E 4
Tucumcari **66** F 4
Tucuruí **73** HJ 4
Tufi **44** E 3
Tuguegarao **39** J 1
Tugur **33** P 5
Tuktoyaktuk **62** L 2
Tukzar **31** H 3
Tula **26** G 5
Tulancingo **68** C 4
Tulbagh **58** B 6
Tulcán **72** C 3

Tulcea **22** C 1
Tulchin **22** C 1
Tulsa **67** G 4
Tuluá **72** C 3
Tulun **32** H 5
Tulungagung **38** D 5
Tumaco **72** C 3
Tumanskiy **33** X 3
Tumany **33** T 3
Tumat **33** PQ 1
Tumbes **72** B 4
Tumd Youqi **34** F 2
Tumen **35** J 2
Tumeremo **73** F 2
Tump **31** G 5
Tümü **51** H 4
Tunas **75** G 5
Tunduru **59** F 2
Tunga **55** F 4
Tungsten **62** M 3
Tungus-Khaya **33** N 3
Tunguska, Nizhnyaya **32** F 3
Tunis **51** GH 1
Tunisia **51** GH 2
Tunja **72** D 2
Tununak **62** D 3
Tunxi **35** G 5
Tuŏroyri **16** A 1
Tuostakh **33** P 2
Tuotuo Heyan **34** B 4
Tupã **75** F 5
Tupelo **67** J 5
Tupiza **74** C 5
Tuquan **35** H 1
Tura **32** H 3
Turakh **32** M 1
Turana, Khrebet **33** O 5
Turanskaya Nizmennost
    30–31 FG 2
Turbo **72** C 2
Tureh **25** E 2
Tureia **47** F 4
Turfan Depression **34** A 2
Turgay **31** G 1
Turgayskaya Dolina
    27 M 5–6
Turgayskaya Stolovaya
    Strana **27** M 5
Türgen Uul **32** F 6
Türgovishte **22** C 2
Turgutlu **22** C 3
Turhal **23** E 2
Turin **21** E 2–3
Turkana, Lake **57** F 4
Turkestan **31** H 2
Turkey **23** DE 3
Türkiye **23** DE 3
Turkmenistan **30** F 3
Turks and Caicos Islands
    69 HJ 3
Turks Islands **69** H 3
Turku **19** H 3
Turnu Măgurele **22** BC 2
Turpan **34** A 2
Tursha **26** J 4
Turukhansk **27** R 2
Turukta **32** L 3
Tuscaloosa **67** J 5
Tuticorin **36** C 6
Tutonchany **32** F 3

Tutubu **56** E 6
Tutuila **46** D 3
Tuvalu **46** D 3
Ṭuwayq, Jabal **25** D 4
Tuxpan de Rodríguez Cano
    68 C 3
Tuxtla Gutiérrez **68** D 4
Tuz Gölü **23** D 3
Tüz Khurmátu **25** D 2
Tuzla **21** G 3
Tver **26** G 4
Tyan'-Shan' **31** JK 2
Tychy **17** G 4
Tygda **33** N 5
Tyler **67** G 5
Tynda **33** M 4
Tynset **18** F 3
Tyre **24** B 2
Tyrma **33** O 5
Tyrrhenian Sea **21** F 3–4
Tyubelyakh **33** Q 2
Tyukalinsk **27** O 4
Tyumen' **27** N 4
Tyungulyu **33** O 3
Tzaneen **58** DE 4

U

Ua Huka **47** F 3
Uatumá **73** G 4
Uauá **75** J 2
Uaupés **72** E 4
Ubá **75** H 5
Ubangi **56** B 4
Ubeda **20** C 4
Uberaba **75** G 4
Uberlândia **75** G 4
Ubolratna Dam **37** H 4
Ubombo **59** E 5
Ubon Ratchathani **37** HJ 4
Ubort' **19** J 5
Ucayali **72** D 5
Uch-Aral **27** Q 6
Uch Kuduk **31** G 2
Udachnaya **32** K 2
Udaipur **36** B 3
Udanna **33** Q 2
Uddevalla **19** F 4
Uddjaur **18** G 2
Udgir **36** C 4
Udine **21** F 2
Udipi **36** B 5
Udon Thani **37** H 4
Udskoye **33** O 5
Udzha **32** L 1
Ueda **35** L 3
Uele **56** C 4
Uelen **62** CD 2
Uel'kal' **62** AB 2
Uelzen **17** F 4
Uengan, Mys **27** N 1
Ufa **26** L 5
Ugalla **56** E 6
Ugalla River Game Reserve
    56 E 6
Uganda **56** E 4
Uglegorsk **33** Q 6
Ugoyan **33** N 4
Ugulan **33** T 3

Ugumun **32** L 2
Ugun **33** N 4
Uherské Hradiště **17** G 5
Uil **30** E 1
Uis Mine **58** AB 4
Uitenhage **58** D 6
Ujae **46** C 2
Ujarrás **68** F 6
Ujelang **46** B 2
Ujiji **56** D 6
Ujjain **36** C 3
Ujung Pandang **39** E 4–5
Uka **33** U 4
Ukelayat **33** W 3
Ukhta **26** K 3
Ukmergė **19** HJ 4
Ukraine **26** FG 6
Uktym **26** J 3
Ukwaa **56** E 3
Ulaanbaatar **32** J 6
Ulaga **33** O 2
Ulan Bator **32** J 6
Ulan-Ude **32** J 5
Ularunda **43** H 4
Uleåborg **18** HJ 3
Ulety **32** K 5
Ulhasnagar **36** B 4
Uliastay **32** G 6
Uliga **46** C 2
Ullapool **16** B 3
Ulovo **33** S 1
Ulsan **35** J 3
Ulster **16** B 4
Ulu **52** E 6
Uludağ **22** C 2–3
Uluru (Ayers Rock - Mount
    Olga) National Park **42** E 4
Ulutau, Gory **31** H 1
Ul'yanovsk **26** J 5
Uma **32** M 5
Uman' **22** D 1
Umanak **78**
Umari **39** J 4
Umba **18** K 2
Umboi **44** E 3
Umbria **21** F 3
Umeå **18** H 3
Umm Durmān **52** E 5
Umm Lajj **24** B 4
'Umm Qam'ul **25** G 4
Umm Ruwābah **52** E 6
Umm Urūmah **24** B 4
Umnak **62** D 5
Umtata **58** D 6
Umuarama **75** F 5
Umvuma **59** E 3
Unaí **75** G 4
Unalakleet **62** E 3
Unalaska **62** D 5
'Unayzah (Jordan) **24** B 3
'Unayzah (Saudi Arabia)
    24 D 4
Ungava Bay **65** O 4
Ungava, Peninsule d'
    65 MN 4
União do Vitória **76** F 4
Unimak **62** E 5
United Arab Emirates
    25 FG 5
United Kingdom **16** CD 3–4

United States **66–67**
Unity **63** Q 5
Universales, Montes **20** C 3
Unst **16** C 2
Uoyan **32** K 4
Upata **73** F 2
Upemba National Park
    56 D 6
Upernavik **78**
Upington **58** C 5
Upolu **46** D 3
Upper Red Lake **67** H 2
Uppland **19** G 3
Uppsala **19** G 4
Ur **53** H 2
Ur Suq ash Shuyükh
    25 DE 3
Ura-Tyube **31** H 3
Urak **33** Q 4
Ural **30** E 1
Ural Mountains **27** LM 2–4
Ural'sk **26** K 5
Urandangie **43** F 3
Urandi **75** H 3
Uranium City **63** Q 4
Uraricoera **73** F 3
Urbano Santos **75** H 1
Uren **26** J 4
Urewera National Park
    45 R 8
Urfa **23** E 3
Urfa Platosu **23** E 3
Urgench **30** FG 2
Uribia **72** D 1
Uromi **55** F 4
Ursus **17** H 4
Uruaçu **75** G 3
Uruapan **68** B 4
Urucará **73** G 4
Uruçuí **75** H 2
Uruguaiana **76** E 4
Uruguay **76** E 5
Uruguay **76** E 5
Urumchi **31** M 2
Ürümqi **31** M 2
Urup, Ostrov **33** S 6
Uryupinsk **26** H 5
Uşak **22** C 3
'Ushayrah **25** DE 4
Ushuaia **77** C 9
Üsküdar **22** C 2
Ussuriysk **35** K 2
Ust'-Bol'sheretsk **33** ST 5
Ust'-Chayka **32** J 3
Ust'-Ilimsk **32** H 4
Ust-Kada **32** H 5
Ust'-Kamchatsk **33** U 4
Ust'-Kamenogorsk **27** Q 6
Ust'-Karenga **32** L 5
Ust'-Karsk **32** L 5
Ust'-Khayryuzovo **33** T 4
Ust'-Kulom **26** K 3
Ust'-Kut **32** J 4
Ust-Labinsk **23** EF 1
Ust'-Nera **33** Q 3
Ust'-Olenëk **32** L 1
Ust'-Ozernoye **27** R 4
Ust'-Pit **32** H 4
Ust'-Port **27** Q 2
Ust'-Sugoy **33** S 3

Ust'-Tatta **33** O 3
Ust'-Tym **27** Q 4
Ust'-Ura **26** H 3
Ust'-Urgal **33** O 5
Ust'-Us **32** F 5
Ust'-Usa **26** L 2
Ust'-Uyskoye **27** M 5
Ust'-Vyyskaya **26** J 3
Ust'-Yuribey **27** N 2
Ustinov **26** K 4
Usu **31** L 2
Usulután **68** E 5
Usumacinta **68** D 4
Utah **66** D 4
Utah Lake **66** D 3
Utata **32** H 5
Utès **27** P 5
Utesiki **33** W 2
Uthumphon Phisai **37** H 5
Utiariti **74** E 3
Utica **67** M 3
Utirik **46** C 2
Utrera **20** B 4
Utsjoki **18** J 2
Utsunomiya **35** L 3
Uttar Pradesh **36** D 2
Uttyakh **33** O 2
Uuldza **32** K 6
Uusikaupunki **19** H 3
Uusimaa **19** H 3
Uvarovo **26** H 5
Uvinza **56** E 6
Uvs Nuur **32** F 5
Uxituba **73** G 4
Uyaly **31** G 2
Uyandi **33** Q 2
Uyega **33** Q 3
Uyuni **74** C 5
Uyuni, Salar de **74** C 5
Uzbekistan **31** G 2
Uzhgorod **22** B 1
Uzhur **27** R 4
Uzunköprü **22** C 2

V

Vaal **58** C 5
Vaasa [Vasa] **18** H 3
Vác **22** A 1
Vacaria **76** F 4
Vadodara **36** B 3
Vaduz **21** E 2
Vágar **16** A 1
Vaghena **45** G 3
Vairaatea **47** F 4
Vaitupu **46** C 3
Vakarevo **33** W 3
Val-d'Or **65** M 6
Valachia **22** BC 2
Valcheta **77** C 7
Valday **26** F 4
Valdepeñas **20** C 4
Valdés, Península **77** D 7
Valdez **62** H 3
Valdivia **77** B 6
Valdosta **67** K 5
Valença **75** J 3
Valença do Piauí **75** H 2
Valence **21** DE 3

Valencia (Spain) **20** CD 4
Valencia (Venezuela)
    72 E 1–2
Valencia, Golfo de **20** D 4
Valentine **66** F 3
Valera **72** D 2
Valga **19** J 4
Valjevo **22** B 2
Vall de Uxó **20** C 4
Valladolid (Mexico) **68** E 3
Valladolid (Spain) **20** C 3
Valle de la Pascua **72** E 2
Valle Grande **74** D 4
Valledupar **72** D 1
Vallenar **76** B 4
Valletta **21** F 4
Valleyview **63** O 4
Valparaíso **76** B 5
Vals, Tanjung **39** J 5
Vammala **18** H 3
Van **23** F 3
Van Diemen, Cape **42** D 1
Van Diemen Gulf **42** E 1
Van Gölü **23** F 3
Vanavara **32** H 3
Vancouver **63** N 6
Vancouver Island **63** M 6
Vanda **79**
Vanderbijlpark **58** D 5
Vanderhoof **63** N 5
Vanduzi **59** E 3
Vänern **19** F 4
Vangunu **45** G 3
Vanikoro Islands **45** J 4
Vankarem **62** B 2
Vannes **20** C 2
Vanoua Lava **45** J 4
Vanrhynsdorp **58** B 6
Vanua Levu **46** C 4
Vanuatu **45** J 5
Vanzhil'kynak **27** QR 3
Varangerfjorden **18** K 1–2
Varangerhalvöya **18** JK 1
Varaždin **21** G 2
Varberg **19** F 4
Vardö **18** K 1
Vardofjällen **18** FG 2
Varginha **75** GH 5
Varkaus **18** J 3
Värmland **19** F 4
Varna **22** C 2
Várnamo **19** F 4
Varsinais Suomi **19** H 3
Var'yegan **27** P 3
Vasa **18** G 3
Vashnel **27** N 3
Vasiss **27** O 4
Vassdalsegga **19** E 4
Västerås **19** G 4
Västerbotten **18** GH 3
Västergötland **19** F 4
Västervik **19** G 4
Vasto **21** F 3
Västra Granberget **18** H 2
Vasyugan **27** P 4
Vatnajökull **18** B 3
Vatoa **46** D 4
Vättern **19** F 4
Vatyna **33** W 3
Vaughn **66** E 5

Vaupés **72** D 3
Vava'u Group **46** D 4
Växjö **19** FG 4
Vaygach, Ostrov **27** L 1
Vayvida **32** F 3
Vazhgort **26** J 3
Veadeiros **75** G 3
Vefsna **18** F 2
Vega **18** F 2
Vegreville **63** P 5
Vejle **19** E 4
Velež **21** G 3
Vélez-Málaga **20** C 4
Velikiy Ustyug **26** J 3
Velikiye Luki **19** K 4
Veliko Türnovo **22** C 2
Vella Lavella **45** G 3
Vellore **36** C 5
Velsk **26** H 3
Vel't **26** K 2
Vemor'ye **33** Q 6
Venado Tuerto **76** D 5
Venda **59** E 4
Venezia **21** F 2
Venezuela **72–73** EF 2
Venezuela, Golfo de **72** D 1
Vengerovo **27** P 4
Venice **21** F 2
Venta **19** H 4
Ventersdorp **58** D 5
Ventoux, Mont **21** E 3
Ventspils **19** H 4
Ventura **66** C 5
Venustiano Carranza **68** D 4
Vera (Argentina) **76** D 4
Vera (Spain) **20** C 4
Veracruz **68** C 4
Veraval **36** B 3
Verbania **21** E 2
Verdalsöra **18** F 3
Verdun **21** E 2
Verkhneimbatskoye
    27 RS 3
Verkhneural'sk **27** L 5
Verkhnevilyuysk **32** M 3
Verkhneye Kuyto,Ozero
    18 K 3
Verkhnyaya Amga **33** N 4
Verkhnyaya Vol'dzha
    27 P 4
Verkhoyansk **33** O 2
Verkhoyansk Range **33** O 3
Verkhoyanskiy Khrebet
    33 N 2–3
Vermilion Bay **64** J 5
Vermont **67** M 3
Verona **21** F 2
Vérroia **22** B 2
Versailles **20** D 2
Vershina **27** M 3
Vershino-Shakhtaminskiye
    32 L 5
Vert, Cap **54** A 3
Vest-Agder **19** E 4
Vesterålen **18** FG 2
Vestfirðir **18** A 2
Vestfjorden **18** F 2
Vestmannaeyjar **18** A 3
Vestvågöy **18** F 2
Vesuvio **21** F 3

Vetlanda **19** G 4
Vetrenyy **33** R 3
Viacha **74** C 4
Vibo Valentia **21** G 4
Viborg **19** E 4
Vicecommodoro Marambio
    79
Vicenza **21** F 2
Vichada **72** E 3
Vichy **20** D 2
Vicksburg **67** H 5
Victoria (Australia) **43** G 6
Victoria (Canada) **63** N 6
Victoria (Chile) **77** B 6
Victoria (Hong Kong) **34** F 6
Victoria (Seychelles) **57** K 5
Victoria (TX, U.S.A.) **67** G 6
Victoria de Durango **68** B 3
Victoria de las Tunas **69** G 3
Victoria Falls **58** D 3
Victoria Island **63** PQ 1
Victoria, Lake **56** E 5
Victoria Land **79**
Victoria, Mount (Burma)
    37 F 3
Victoria, Mount (Papua New
    Guinea) **44** E 3
Victoria River **42** E 2
Victoria Strait **63** R 2
Victoria West **58** C 6
Vicuña Mackenna **76** D 5
Vidin **22** B 2
Vidisha **36** C 3
Vidsel **18** H 2
Viduša **21** G 3
Vidzemes Augstiene **19** J 4
Viedma **77** D 7
Viedma, Lago **77** B 8
Vieng Pou Kha **37** H 3
Vienna **21** G 2
Vienne **21** DE 2
Vientiane **37** H 4
Vierzon **20** D 2
Vietnam **37** J 5
Vigan **39** J 1
Vigevano **21** E 2
Vigo **20** B 3
Viiala **18** H 3
Vijayawada **36** CD 4
Vijosa **22** A 2
Vikna **18** F 3
Vila **45** J 5
Vila Conceição **73** F 3
Vila Nova de Gaia **20** B 3
Vila Velha (Amapá, Brazil)
    73 H 3
Vila Velha (Espírito Santo,
    Brazil) **75** HJ 5
Vilankulo **59** F 4
Vildız Dağları **22** C 2
Vilhena **74** D 3
Villa Abecia **74** C 5
Villa Bella **74** C 3
Villa Constitución **76** D 5
Villa Dolores **76** C 5
Villa Frontera **68** B 2
Villa Huidobro **76** D 5
Villa Ingavi **74** D 4
Villa María **76** D 5
Villa Mazán **76** C 4

Villa Montes **74** D 5
Villa Ocampo **68** AB 2
Villa Regina **77** C 6
Villa Unión **76** C 4
Villach **21** F 2
Villagarcia de Arosa **20** B 3
Villaguay **76** E 5
Villahermosa **68** D 4
Villalonga **77** D 6
Villanueva y Geltrú **20** D 3
Villarreal de los Infantes
　20 C 3–4
Villarrica (Chile) **77** B 6
Villarrica (Paraguay) **76** E 4
Villatoro, Puerto de **20** B 3
Villavicencio **72** D 3
Villazón **74** C 5
Villefranche **21** DE 2
Villena **20** C 4
Vilnius **19** J 5
Vilyuy **33** MN 3
Vilyuyskoye Plato **32** J 2
Vilyuyskoye
　Vodokhranilishche
　32 JK 3
Vilyuysk **32** M 3
Viña del Mar **76** B 5
Vindhya Range **36** C 3
Vinh **37** J 4
Vinh Giat **37** J 5
Vinh Linh **37** J 4
Vinh Loi **37** J 4
Vinkovci **21** G 2
Vinnitsa **26** E 6
Vinson Massif **79**
Virac **39** F 1
Virandozero **26** FG 3
Viranşehir **23** EF 3
Virden **63** R 6
Virgem da Lapa **75** H 4
Virgin Islands **69** K 4
Virginia (South Africa)
　58 D 5
Virginia (U.S.A.) **67** L 4
Virginia Beach **67** LM 4
Virginia Falls **63** N 3
Virrat **18** H 3
Virtsu **19** H 4
Visayan Sea **39** F 1
Visby **19** G 4
Viscount Melville Sound
　63 P 1
Vishakhapatnam **36** D 4
Vista Alegre **73** F 3
Vistula **17** G 4
Vitebsk **19** K 4
Viti Levu **46** C 4
Vitiaz Strait **44** E 3
Vitim **32** K 4
Vitim **32** K 4
Vitimskoye Ploskogor´ye
　32 K 5
Vitória (Espírito Santo,
　Brazil) **75** HJ 5
Vitória (Pará, Brazil) **73** H 4
Vitória da Conquista **75** H 3
Vittorio Veneto **21** F 2
Vivorata **77** E 6
Vizianagaram **36** D 4
Vladikavkaz **23** FG 2

Vladimir (Russia) **26** H 4
Vladimir (Russia) **35** L 2
Vladimir-Volynskiy **19** H 5
Vladimirovka **26** K 5
Vladivostok **35** K 2
Vlissingen **16** D 4
Vlorë **22** A 2
Vltava **17** F 4
Vogan **54** E 4
Voghera **21** E 2–3
Vohimena, Cap **59** GH 5
Voi **57** F 5
Voinjama **54** C 4
Vojnić **21** G 2
Volcán Citlaltépetl **68** C 4
Volcán Llullaillaco **74** C 5
Volcán Miravalles **68** EF 5
Volcán Misti **74** B 4
Volcán Ollagüe **74** C 5
Volcán Popocatéptl **68** C 4
Volcán Tajumulco **68** D 4
Volga **26** J 6
Volgodonsk **23** F 1
Volgograd **26** H 6
Volgogradskoye
　Vodokhranilishche **26** J 6
Volkhov **19** K 4
Volkhov **19** K 4
Volochayevka **33** O 6
Vologda **26** G 4
Volokon **32** J 4
Vólos **22** B 3
Vol´sk **26** J 5
Volta **54** E 4
Volta, Lake **54** DE 4
Volta Redonda **75** H 5
Volynskoye Polesye **19** J 5
Volzhsk **26** J 4
Volzhskiy **26** J 4
Vopnafjörður **18** BC 2
Vórioi Sporádhes **22** B 3
Vorkuta **27** MN 2
Vormsi **19** H 4
Voronezh **26** GH 5
Võrts Järv **19** J 4
Võru **19** J 4
Vosges **21** E 2
Vostochnaya Litsa **26** G 2
Vostochnyy Sayan **32** G 5
Vostok (Antarctica) **79**
Vostok (Kiribati) **47** E 3
Votkinsk **26** K 4
Voyampolka **33** T 4
Vozhega **26** H 3
Voznesensk **22** D 1
Vozvyshennost´ Karabil´
　31 G 3
Vran **21** G 3
Vranje **22** B 2
Vratsa **22** B 2
Vršac **22** B 1
Vryburg **58** CD 5
Vryheid **59** E 5
Vsetín **17** G 5
Vsevidof, Mount **62** D 5
Vsevolozhsk **19** K 3
Vukovar **21** G 2
Vyaltsevo **26** H 4

Vyatskiye Polyany **26** K 4
Vyazemskiy **33** OP 6
Vyaz´ma **26** F 4
Vyborg **18** J 3
Vychegda **26** J 3
Vyksa **26** H 4
Vyngapur **27** P 3
Vysotsk **19** J 3
Vytegra **26** G 3
V´yuny **27** Q 4

W

´´W´´, Parcs Nationaux, du
　54 E 3
Wabowden **63** S 5
Wabrah **25** E 4
Waco **67** G 5
Wad **31** H 5
Wad Madani **52** E 6
Waddān **51** J 3
Wādi al ´Arabah **24** B 3
Wādi al Bātin **25** DE 3
Wādī al Ghudāf **24** D 2
Wādi al Khurr **24** C 3
Wādi al ´Ubayyid **24** CD 2
Wādī at Ţubal **24** C 2
Wādī ath Tharthār **24** D 2
Wādi Ḩalfa´ **52** E 4
Wādī Ḩawrān **24** C 2
Wādi Qina **24** A 4
Wadley **67** K 5
Wafrah **25** E 3
Wagga Wagga **43** H 6
Wagin **42** B 5
Wah **31** J 4
Wahai **39** G 4
Wāḩāt al Khārijah **52** E 3–4
Waigeo, Pulau **39** H 4
Wajir **57** G 4
Wakayama **35** L 4
Wake **46** C 1
Wakkanai **35** M 1
Wałbrzych **17** G 4
Waldia **57** F 2
Walewale **54** D 3
Walgett **43** H 4–5
Walgreen Coast **79**
Wallaroo **43** F 5
Wallis **46** D 3
Wallis and Futuna **46** CD 3
Wallsend **43** J 5
Walnut Ridge **67** H 4
Walvis Bay **58** A 4
Wan Hsa-la **37** G 3
Wanaaring **43** G 4
Wanaka **44** P 9
Wandel Sea **78**
Wanganui **45** R 8
Wangka **37** G 4
Wangqing **35** J 2
Wanxian **34** E 4
Warangal **36** CD 4
Warburi **39** H 4
Warburton Mission **42** D 4
Waren **39** J 4
Warminster **16** C 4
Warner Peak **66** C 3
Warner Robins **67** K 5

Warragul **43** H 6
Warren **67** K 3
Warrenton **58** C 5
Warri **55** F 4
Warrnambool **43** G 6
Warrumbungle Range
　43 H 5
Warsaw **17** H 4
Warszawa → Warsaw
　17 H 4
Warta **17** G 4
Warwick **43** J 4
Wasatch Range **66** D 3–4
Washington (D.C., U.S.A.)
　67 L 4
Washington (U.S.A.)
　66 BC 2
Wasua **44** D 3
Wasum **45** E 3
Watampone **39** F 4
Waterberg **58** B 4
Waterbury **67** M 3
Waterford **16** B 4
Waterloo **67** H 3
Waterton Lakes National
　Park **63** OP 6
Watertown **67** L 3
Watheroo **42** B 5
Watrous (Canada) **63** Q 5
Watrous (NM, U.S.A.)
　66 F 4
Watsa **56** D 4
Watson Lake **62** M 3
Wau → Wàw **56** D 3
Wauchope **43** J 5
Wausau **67** J 3
Wave Hill **42** E 2
Waycross **67** K 5
Wayland **67** K 4
Weagamow Lake **64** J 5
Webbe Shibeli **57** G 3
Weddell Sea **79**
Weichang **35** G 2
Weiden **17** F 5
Weifang **35** G 3
Weimar **17** F 4
Weining **34** D 5
Weipa **43** G 1
Weirton **67** K 3
Wejherowo **17** G 4
Welkom **58** D 5
Wellesley Islands **43** F 2
Wellesley Islands, South
　43 F 2
Wellington **45** R 9
Wellington, Isla **77** AB 8
Wells (NV, U.S.A.) **66** C 3
Wels **21** F 2
Wendeng **35** H 3
Wenshan **34** D 6
Wentworth **43** G 5
Wenzhou **35** H 5
Wepener **58** D 5
Weser **17** E 4
Wesleyville **65** R 6
Wessel, Cape **43** F 1
West Antarctica **79**
West Bank **24** B 2

West Falkland **77** D 9
West Ice Shelf **79**
West Indies **69** H 3
West Memphis **67** H 4
West Palm Beach **67** L 6
West Plains **67** H 4
West Siberian Plain **27** OP 3
West Virginia **67** K 4
West Wind Drift **9**
West Wyalong **43** H 5
West Yellowstone **66** D 3
Western Australia
 42 BD 3–4
Western Ghats **36** BC 4–5
Western Sahara **50** C 4
Western Samoa **46** D 3
Westlock **63** P 5
Westmoreland **43** F 2
Westport **45** Q 9
Westralian Current **9**
Westree **65** L 6
Wetar, Pulau **39** G 5
Wetaskiwin **63** P 5
Wete **57** F 5
Wewak **44** D 2
Weyburn **63** R 6
Whale Cove **63** T 3
Whangarei **45** Q 8
Whealer Peak **66** E 4
Wheatland **66** F 3
Wheeler Peak **66** D 4
Wheeling **67** K 3
White Mountain Peak
 66 C 4
White Nile **52** E 6
White Pass **62** L 4
White River **64** L 6
White Russia **19** J 5
White Sea **26** HJ 2
Whitecourt **63** O 5
Whitehaven **16** C 4
Whitehorse **62** L 3
Whitewood **43** G 3
Whitmore Mountains **79**
Whitney, Mount **66** C 4
Wholdaia Lake **63** QR 3
Wichita **66** G 4
Wichita Falls **66** G 5
Wick **16** C 3
Wickenburg **66** D 5
Wien **21** G 2
Wiener Neustadt
 21 G 2
Wieprz **17** H 4
Wiesbaden **17** E 4
Wight, Isle of **16** C 4
Wilhelm, Mount **44** D 3
Wilhelmshaven **17** E 4
Wilkes-Barre **67** L 3
Wilkes Land **79**
Willcox **66** E 5
Willemstad **72** E 1
Willeroo **42** E 2
Williams **66** D 4
Williams Lake **63** N 5
Williamsport **67** L 3
Williston (South Africa)
 58 C 6
Williston (U.S.A.) **66** F 2
Williston Lake **63** N 4

Wilmington (DE, U.S.A.)
 67 L 4
Wilmington (N.C., U.S.A.)
 67 L 5
Wilowmore **58** C 6
Wilson **67** L 4
Wilson Bluff **42** D 5
Wilson, Mount **66** E 4
Wilson´s Promontory
 43 H 6
Windhoek **58** B 4
Windsor (MI, U.S.A.) **64** L 7
Windsor (Ontario, Can.)
 67 K 3
Windward Islands (French
 Polynesia) **47** F 4
Windward Islands (Lesser
 Antilles) **69** L 5
Winisk **64** K 4
Winisk River **64** K 5
Winneba **54** D 4
Winnemucca **66** C 3
Winnipeg **64** J 5
Winnipeg, Lake **63** S 5
Winona **67** H 3
Winslow (AZ, U.S.A.)
 66 D 4
Winslow (Kiribati) **46** D 3
Winston-Salem **67** K 4
Winterthur **21** E 2
Wisconsin **67** HJ 2
Wiseman **62** H 2
Wisła **17** G 4
Wismar **17** F 4
Wittenberg **17** F 4
Wittenberge **17** F 4
Witwatersrand **58** D 5
Włocławek **17** G 4
Wokam, Pulau **39** H 5
Woleai **46** A 2
Wolf, Volcán **72** B 6
Wollaston Lake **63** R 4
Wollaston Peninsula
 63 OP 2
Wollastone Lake **63** R 4
Wollongong **43** J 5
Wolstenholme, Cap **65** M 3
Wolverhampton **16** C 4
Wonga Wongué, Parc
 National de **55** F 6
Wonju **35** J 3
Wŏnsan **35** J 3
Wonthaggi **43** H 6
Wood Buffalo National Park
 63 OP 4
Wood River Lakes **62** F 4
Woodlark **45** F 3
Woods, Lake of the **64** H 6
Woodstock **43** G 2
Woodward **66** G 4
Woomera **43** F 5
Wooramel **42** A 4
Worcester (MA, U.S.A.)
 67 M 3
Worcester (South Africa)
 58 BC 6
Worcester (U.K.) **16** C 4
Worland **66** E 3
Wosi **39** G 4
Wotho **46** C 2

Wotje **46** C 2
Wrangel Island **78**
Wrangell **62** L 4
Wrangell-Saint Elias
 National Park and
 Preserve **62** J 3
Wrightson, Mount **66** D 5
Wrigley **63** N 3
Wrocław **17** G 4
Wuchuan **34** E 5
Wudaoliang **34** B 3
Wudu **34** D 4
Wugang **34** F 5
Wugong **34** E 4
Wuhai **34** E 3
Wuhan **34** F 4
Wuhu **35** G 4
Wüjang **36** D 1
Wukari **55** F 4
Wuliang Shan **34** D 6
Wun Rog **56** D 3
Wuppertal **17** E 4
Wurung **43** G 2
Würzburg **17** F 5
Wutunghliao **34** D 5
Wuvulu **44** D 2
Wuwei **34** D 3
Wuxi **35** H 4
Wuxing **35** H 4
Wuyiling **33** N 6
Wuyuan **34** E 2
Wuzhi Shan **34** E 7
Wuzhong **34** E 3
Wuzhou **34** F 4
Wynbring **42** E 5
Wyndham **42** D 2
Wyoming **66** E 3
Wyoming Peak **66** DE 3
Wyperfeld National Park
 43 G 6
Wysoczyzna Ciechanowska
 17 GH 4
Wyzyna Lubelska **17** H 4

X

Xai-Xai **59** E 5
Xainza **36** E 1
Xambioá **73** J 5
Xangongo **58** AB 3
Xánthi **22** C 2
Xanthos **22** C 3
Xapecó **76** F 4
Xapuri **74** C 3
Xayar **31** L 2
Xenia **67** K 4
Xiaguan **34** D 5
Xiamen **35** G 6
Xi´an **34** E 4
Xiangfan **34** F 4
Xiangshan **35** H 5
Xiangtan **34** F 5
Xiangyin **34** F 5
Xianju **35** H 5
Xianyang **34** E 4
Xiao Hinggan Ling **33** N 5–6
Xiao´ergou **33** M 6
Xiapu **35** H 5
Xichang **34** D 5

Xigazê **36** E 2
Xiliao He **35** H 2
Ximiao **34** D 2
Xin Barag Zuoqi **32** L 6
Xing Xian **34** F 3
Xingcheng **35** GH 2
Xingdi **34** A 2
Xingren **34** E 5
Xingtai **34** F 3
Xingu **73** H 4
Xingxingxia **34** C 2
Xingyi **34** D 5
Xining **34** D 3
Xinjiang Uygur Zizhiqu
 31 L 2
Xinjin (Liaining, China)
 35 H 3
Xinjin (Sichuan, China)
 34 D 4
Xinlitun **33** N 5
Xinxiang **34** F 3
Xinyang **34** F 4
Xinyi **35** G 4
Xinyuan **31** L 2
Xique-Xique **75** H 3
Xiushui **34** F 5
Xiuyan **35** H 2
Xiwu **34** C 4
Xixiang **34** E 4
Xizanq Zizhigu **36** DE 1
Xpuhil **68** E 4
Xuanhan **34** E 4
Xuanhua **34** F 2
Xuanwei **34** D 5
Xuchang **34** F 4
Xuguit Qi **32** M 6
Xümatang **34** C 4
Xuwen **34** F 6
Xuyong **34** DE 5
Xuzhou **35** G 4

Y

Ya Xian **34** E 7
Yablonovyy Khrebet
 32 JL 5
Yabrūd **24** B 2
Yacuiba **74** D 5
Yadgir **36** C 4
Yagoua **55** GH 3
Yagradagze Shan **34** C 3
Yakima **66** B 2
Yakmach **31** G 5
Yakoma **56** C 4
Yakrik **31** L 2
Yakumo **35** LM 2
Yakutat **62** K 4
Yakutsk **33** N 3
Yala (Sri Lanka) **36** D 6
Yala (Thailand) **37** H 6
Yalgoo **42** B 4
Yalnızçam Dağları **23** F 2
Yalong Jiang **34** D 5
Yalta **23** D 2
Yalutorovsk **27** N 4
Yamagata **35** LM 3
Yamal Peninsula **27** NO 1
Yamal, Poluostrov **27** NO 1
Yamantau, Gora **27** L 5

Yambio **56** D 4
Yambol **22** C 2
Yamburg **27** P 2
Yamdena, Pulau **39** H 5
Yamoussoukro **54** CD 4
Yamuna **36** D 2
Yana **33** P 1
Yan'an **34** E 3
Yanartaş Dağları **22** D 3
Yanbu' (Saudi Arabia)
   24 BC 4
Yanchang **34** EF 3
Yandrakinot **62** C 3
Yang Xian **34** E 4
Yangambi **56** CD 4
Yangjiang **34** F 6
Yangquan **34** F 3
Yangtze Kiang **34** F 4
Yangzhou **35** G 4
Yanhe **34** E 5
Yanhuqu **36** D 1
Yankton **66** G 3
Yano-Indigirskaya
   Nizmennost' **33** PR 1
Yanov Stan **27** Q 2
Yanqi Huizu Zizhixian
   31 LM 2
Yanshou **35** J 1
Yanskiy Zaliv **33** OP 1
Yantai **35** H 3
Yaoundé **55** G 5
Yapen, Pulau **39** J 4
Yapura **72** D 4
Yaqui, Rio **66** E 6
Yaraka **43** G 3
Yaransk **26** J 4
Yari **72** D 3
Yarlung Zangbo Jiang
   34 B 5
Yarmouth **65** O 7
Yaroslavl' **26** G 4
Yarram **43** H 6
Yarroto **27** O 2
Yartsevo **27** S 3
Yarumal **72** C 2
Yashkino **33** P 5
Yasnyy **33** N 5
Yaté-Village **45** J 6
Yathkyed Lake **63** S 3
Yatsushiro **35** JK 4
Yavi, Cerro **72** E 2
Yawng-hwe **37** G 3
Yazd **25** G 3
Yazd-e Khvāst **25** F 3
Yazdān **31** G 4
Yecheng **31** K 3
Yedoma **26** H 3
Yeeda River **42** C 2
Yefremov **26** G 5
Yegorlykskaya **23** F 1
Yei **56** E 4
Yekaterinburg **27** M 4
Yelabuga **26** K 4
Yelets **26** G 5
Yelizarovo **27** N 3
Yelizovo **33** T 5
Yellow Sea **35** H 4
Yellowhead Pass **63** O 5
Yellowknife **63** P 3
Yellowstone **66** EF 2

Yellowstone National Park
   66 D 3
Yelovka **33** U 4
Yelvertoft **43** F 3
Yemanzhelinsk **27** M 5
Yematan (China) **34** C 3
Yematan (China) **34** C 4
Yemen **53** GH 5
Yengisar **31** K 3
Yengo **55** H 5
Yengue **55** F 5
Yenice **23** E 3
Yenisey, Malyy **32** FG 5
Yenisey **27** R 2
Yeniseyskiy Kryazh
   32 F 3–4
Yepoko **27** OP 2
Yercha **33** R 2
Yerema **32** J 3
Yerevan **23** FG 2
Yergeni **23** F 1
Yermak **27** P 5
Yerofey-Pavlovich **33** M 5
Yeropol **33** V 2
Yertom **26** J 3
Yerupajá, Nevado **74** A 3
Yesil **27** N 5
Yeşilırmak **23** E 2
Yessentuki **23** F 2
Yetman **43** J 4
Yeu, Ile d' **20** C 2
Yevpatoriya **23** D 1
Yeya **23** E 1
Yeysk **23** E 1
Yi'an **33** N 6
Yibin **34** D 5
Yichang **34** F 4
Yichun **33** N 6
Yidu **34** F 4
Yıldız Dağı **23** E 2
Yilehuli Shan **33** M 5
Yiliang **34** D 6
Yinchuan **34** E 3
Yingde **34** F 6
Yingkou **35** H 2
Yining **31** L 2
Yirga Alem **57** F 3
Yitulihe **33** M 5
Yiyang **34** F 5
Ylikitka **18** J 2
Ylivieska **18** H 3
Yoboki **57** G 2
Yogyakarta **38** CD 5
Yokohama **35** LM 3
Yokosuka **35** LM 3–4
Yokote **35** M 3
Yola **55** G 4 a
Yolombo **56** C 5
Yonago **35** K 3
Yong deng **34** D 3
Yöngan **35** J 2
Yongchang **34** D 3
Yongren **34** D 5
Yonkers **67** M 3
Yonne **20** D 2
York (PA, U.S.A.) **67** L 4
York (U.K.) **16** C 4
York (Western Australia)
   42 B 5
York, Cape **43** G 1

Yorke Peninsula **43** F 5
Yorkton **63** R 5
Yosemite National Park
   66 C 4
Yoshkar Ola **26** J 4
Yōsu **35** J 4
Young **43** H 5
Youngstown **67** KL 3
Yozgat **23** D 3
Ytyk-Kel' **33** O 3
Yu Xian **34** F 3
Yuanping **34** F 3
Yucatán Peninsula **68** E 3–4
Yuci **34** F 3
Yudoma-Krestovskaya
   33 P 3
Yuexi **34** D 5
Yueyang **34** F 5
Yugorskiy Poluostrov
   27 M 2
Yugoslavia **14** A 2
Yukagirskoye Ploskogor'ye
   33 ST 2
Yukon **62** E 3
Yukon-Charley Rivers
   National Preserve
   62 J 2–3
Yukon Flats **62** H 2
Yukon Flats National
   Monument **62** HJ 2
Yukon Plateau **62** K 3
Yukon Territory **62** KL 3
Yulin (China) **34** F 6
Yulin (Shaanxi, China)
   34 E 3
Yuma **66** F 3
Yumari, Cerro **72** E 3
Yumen **34** C 3
Yumenzhen **34** C 2
Yunaska **62** C 5
Yunling Shan **34** C 5
Yunnan **34** D 6
Yunxiao **35** G 6
Yuriby **27** P 1
Yurimaguas **72** C 5
Yurty **33** U 4
Yushan (China) **35** G 5
Yushan (Taiwan) **35** H 6
Yuxi **34** D 6
Yuzhno-Sakhalinsk **33** Q 6
Yuzhnoye **33** Q 6
Yuzhnyy Bug **22** D 1
Yuzhnyy, Mys **33** T 4

Z

Zabarjad **24** B 5
Zabol **31** G 4
Zabrze **17** G 4
Zacapu **68** B 4
Zacatecas **68** B 3
Zadar **21** G 3
Zadetkale Kyun **37** G 5
Zadran **31** H 4
Za'faranah **24** A 3
Zag **50** D 3
Zāgheh-ye Bālā **25** E 2
Zaghwān **51** H 1
Zagreb **21** G 2

Zagros, Kuhhā ye
   25 EF 2–3
Zagros Mountains **25** F 3
Zahedan **31** G 5
Zahirah **25** G 5
Zahlah **24** B 2
Zahrān **53** G 5
Zaire **55** G 7
Zaire **56** CD 5
Zaire (Angola) **58** A 1
Zakamensk **32** H 5
Zakharov **33** O 3
Zākhū **24** D 1
Zákinthos **22** B 3
Zakouma, Parc National de
   55 H 3
Zalābiyah **24** C 2
Zalaegerszeg **22** A 1
Zalim **53** G 4
Zaliv Akademii **33** P 5
Zaliv Kara-Bogaz Gol **30** E 2
Zaliv Shelikhova **33** T 3–4
Zaliv Terpeniya **33** Q 6
Zallah **51** J 3
Zamakh **53** H 5
Zambeze **59** E 3
Zambezi **58** C 2
Zambia **58** D 2
Zamboanga **39** F 2
Zamora (Ecuador) **72** C 4
Zamora (Spain) **20** B 3
Zamość **17** H 4
Zanesville **67** K 4
Zanjān **25** E 1
Zanthus **42** C 5
Zanul'e **26** K 3
Zanzibar **57** F 6
Zanzibar Island **57** F 6
Zaouatallaz **51** G 4
Zaoyang **34** F 4
Zaozernyy **32** F 4
Zaozhuang **35** G 4
Zapadnaya Dvina **19** J 4
Zapadno-Sibirskaya
   Nizmennost' **27** NQ 3
Zapala **77** B 6
Zaporosh'ye **23** E 1
Zaragoza **20** C 3
Zarand (Iran) **25** F 2
Zarand (Iran) **25** G 3
Zaranj **31** G 4
Zárate **76** E 5
Zaraza **72** E 2
Zard Kūh **25** F 2
Zarechensk **18** K 2
Zarghun **31** H 4
Zaria **55** F 3
Zaruma **72** C 4
Zaskar Mountains **31** K 4
Zastron **58** D 3
Zatish'ye **33** T 2
Zatoka Gdańska **17** G 4
Zav'yalova, Ostrov **33** RS 4
Zawr, Ra's az **25** E 4
Zaysan, Ozero **27** Q 6
Zayü **34** C 5
Zduńska Wola **17** G 4
Zêkog **34** D 3
Zelenoborskiy **18** K 2
Zelenodol'sk **26** JK 4

Zelenokumsk **23** F 2
Zell am See **21** F 2
Žemaičiu Aukštuma **19** H 4
Žemaitiya **19** H 4
Zemgale **19** HJ 4
Zemio **56** D 3
Zenica **21** G 3
Zeya **33** N 5
Zêzere **20** B 4
Zhag'yab **34** C 4
Zhailma **27** M 5
Zhaksylyk **27** O 6
Zhanabas **31** H 1
Zhanabek **27** P 6
Zhangjiakou **34** FG 2
Zhangping **35** G 5
Zhangwu **35** H 2
Zhangye **34** CD 3
Zhangzhou **35** G 6
Zhangzi **34** F 3
Zhanjiang **34** F 6
Zhantekets **27** Q 6
Zhao'an **34** G 6
Zhaodong **35** J 1
Zhaojue **34** D 5
Zhaotong **34** D 5

Zhaoyuan **35** J 1
Zhaozhou **35** HJ 1
Zharkamys **30** F 1
Zharkova **27** R 4
Zharlykamys **27** P 6
Zharma **27** Q 6
Zharyk **27** O 6
Zhejiang **35** GH 5
Zhelaniya, Cape **78**
Zhel'dyadyr **31** H 1
Zhelezinka **27** P 5
Zheleznodorozhnyy **26** K 3
Zheleznogorsk **26** F 5
Zhenghe **35** G 5
Zhengzhou **34** F 4
Zhenjiang **35** GH 4
Zhenlai **35** H 1
Zhenning **34** E 5
Zhenxiong **34** D 5
Zhenyuan **34** E 5
Zhigalovo **32** J 5
Zhijiang **34** E 5
Zhitomir **19** J 5
Zhlatyr **27** P 5
Zhong Xian **34** E 4
Zhongba **36** D 2

Zhongning **34** E 3
Zhongwei **34** DE 3
Zhongxiang **34** F 4
Zhoukouzhen **34** FG 4
Zhovtnevoye **22** D 1
Zhuanghe **35** H 3
Zhupanovo **33** U 5
Zhurban **33** N 5
Zhushan **34** EF 4
Zhuzhou **34** F 5
Zielona Góra **17** G 4
Zigong **34** DE 5
Ziguinchor **54** A 3
Zihuatanejo **68** B 4
Zilair **27** L 5
Zile **23** E 2
Žilina **17** G 5
Zima **32** H 5
Zimba **58** D 3
Zimbabwe **58–59** DE 3
Zimbabwe **59** E 4
Zimi **54** B 4
Zimovniki **23** F 1
Zincirli **23** E 3
Zinder **55** F 3
Zlatoust **27** L 4

Zlatoustovsk **33** O 5
Znamenka **23** D 1
Znojmo **17** G 5
Zoigê **34** D 4
Zolotaya Gora **33** N 5
Zomba **59** F 3
Zonga **56** B 4
Zonguldak **23** D 2
Zorritos **72** B 4
Zrenjanin **22** B 1
Zufär **53** J 5
Zugdidi **23** F 2
Zugspitze **21** F 2
Zújar **20** B 4
Zunyi **34** E 5
Zurbāţiyah **25** D 2
Zürich **21** E 2
Zürich-See **21** E 2
Zurmat **31** H 4
Zuwārah **51** H 2
Zvolen **17** G 5
Zwickau **17** F 4
Žyrardów **17** H 4
Zyryanka **33** S 2
Zyryanovsk **27** Q 6

DATE DUE - DATE DE RETOUR

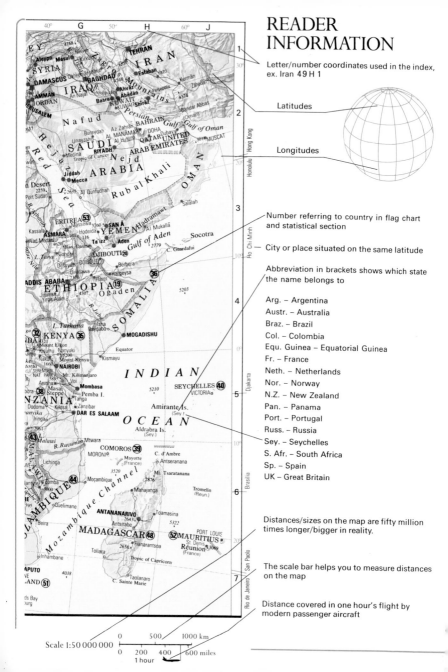

READER INFORMATION

Letter/number coordinates used in the index, ex. Iran 49 H 1

Latitudes

Longitudes

Number referring to country in flag chart and statistical section

— City or place situated on the same latitude

Abbreviation in brackets shows which state the name belongs to

Arg. – Argentina
Austr. – Australia
Braz. – Brazil
Col. – Colombia
Equ. Guinea – Equatorial Guinea
Fr. – France
Neth. – Netherlands
Nor. – Norway
N.Z. – New Zealand
Pan. – Panama
Port. – Portugal
Russ. – Russia
Sey. – Seychelles
S. Afr. – South Africa
Sp. – Spain
UK – Great Britain

Distances/sizes on the map are fifty million times longer/bigger in reality.

The scale bar helps you to measure distances on the map

Distance covered in one hour's flight by modern passenger aircraft

Scale 1:50 000 000

0 — 500 — 1000 km
0 — 200 — 400 — 600 miles
1 hour